Inflation
or
Depression

Inflation or Depression

The Continuing Crisis of the Canadian Economy

Cy Gonick

James Lorimer & Company, Publishers
Toronto 1975

ISBN 0-88862-079-9 paper
      0-88862-080-2 cloth

Cover Design: Robert MacDonald
Design: Lynn Campbell

James Lorimer & Company, Publishers
Egerton Ryerson Memorial Building
35 Britain Street
Toronto

Printed and bound in Canada

Canadian Shared Cataloguing in Publication Data

Gonick, Cy, 1936 -
    Inflation or depression: the continuing
crisis of the Canadian economy / Cy Gonick.

1. Canada — Economic conditions — 1945 -
2. Canada — Foreign economic relations — United
States. 3. United States — Foreign economic
relations — Canada. 4. Canada — Economic policy.
I. Title.

HC115.G64   330.971
ISBN: 0-88862-080-2; 0-88862-079-9(pbk.)

"A man who thinks that economics is only a matter for professors forgets that this is the science that has sent men to the barricades."

Robert L. Heilbroner

Foreword

This project began innocently enough. During the summer and autumn of 1974 I prepared a series of five articles for *Canadian Dimension* magazine on the state of the economy. It occurred to me that these articles could be gathered into a 75 to 100-page booklet, and with the encouragement of James Lorimer, I started working on this format as the snows first began to fall.

It seems that I had a much bigger project on my agenda — the book that I had been putting off writing these past ten years. Once freed from the limited scope of the original plan, the book took its own course and carried me into the diverse areas that now comprise the content of this work.

It has always been my belief that, to understand any aspect of the modern economy, one must adopt an approach that is both historical and multidisciplinary. I have found in my own work that a static approach which looks to discover some mythical equilibrium from which and towards which the economy is moving, and which confines the analysis within the narrow scope of conventional economics, is barren of insight. In my own way I have tried to make of economics an "evolutionary science," to borrow a term from Thorstein Veblen, and to bring to bear whatever tools and concepts were at my disposal regardless of their origin in the lexicon of modern-day social science.

One of the problems in writing this book was to find a way of integrating a great amount of material and giving it some coherence. I started out by talking about the workings of the modern corporation because, as someone once wrote, "to touch the corporation deeply is to touch much else." But to deal adequately with the current economic crisis I found that I could not avoid asking questions about our political system, the nature of trade unionism, ecology, the so-called population explosion, need creation, the class system, changing international alliances, the Canadian economy in relation to the world economy and particularly the U.S.A., and much, much else. No doubt my efforts to demonstrate how all these forces have come to affect the here and the now, and how they bear upon our future, are not entirely satisfactory. However, I feel that it is more valuable to attempt to say something about the "Big Questions" facing us than to say a great deal about the little questions which seem very remote and which too often amount to little more than an academic exercise of interest to no one except a handful of specialists.

My approach is decidedly eclectic. It will not satisfy those who are wedded to this dogma or that. At the same time I feel no need to apologize for the fact that it is also radical, in the original meaning of the term — that of seeking the root of a problem and exploring the consequences of that analysis regardless of where it leads. I can discover no easy solution to the current crisis, no simple formula that can lead us out of the dilemma of inflation or depression. For those who find themselves in agreement with my analysis I have added a chapter at the end of the book which I call "a sermon."

I make no claim for originality in this work. It is primarily a synthesis of a great many ideas I have come in contact with since I seriously began contemplating the whys and wherefores of the social system we call capitalism.

I owe an enormous intellectual debt to a number of writers both living and dead: to the founders of the *Monthly Review,* Paul Sweezy and Leo Huberman, who gave me my first introduction to political economy; to Erich Fromm, Bertrand Russell, G.D.H. Cole, C. Wright Mills, Maurice Dobb, Karl Polanyi, Simone de Beauvoir, Isaac Deutscher, Paul Baran, André Gorz, and Robert Heilbroner; to Karl Marx, Friedrich Engels, Thorstein Veblen, John Maynard Keynes; in my youth to writers like Upton Sinclair, G. B. Shaw, Sinclair Lewis, and Jack London; to the Root and Branch circle of my student days at Berkeley, California — Robert Scheer, David Horowitz, Maurice Zeitlin, Raymond Franklin, to name a few; and more recently, to people like Stanley Aronowitz, Eli Zeretsky, and the young men and women around the Union of Radical Political Economists. Among Canadian writers I have benefited from the works of John Porter, H. C. Pentland, Donald Creighton, Tom Naylor, C. B. Macpherson, Leo Johnson, the late Stephen Hymer, Melville Watkins, James Laxer, John Warnock,

Stuart Jamieson, Lorne Brown, and many others.

I am grateful to my students who suffered through my seminars over the years and helped me clarify my thinking; to Rubin Simkin with whom I have had continuous dialogue over the past eight years on these and other subjects; to the contributors and readers of *Canadian Dimension* magazine who have worked with me in developing an understanding of the political economy of Canada; to John Gallagher, John Richards, and Jim Harding, who have read parts of the manuscript of this book and with whom I have had fruitful discussions over the past few years.

To Irmie Wiebe, who is more than a typist and lent her considerable talents in shaking out ungrammatical sentences and correcting my poor spelling.

To Fay Gonick, my sharpest critic, who has endured much these past nine months and more, and who by example has educated me to the socialism of everyday life.

To my children, with whom I have much to make up — for as my five-year-old son said, when I promised to play with him more after the book was completed, "By then I will be too old."

May 1975

Contents

CONTENTS

I/The New Corporate Order

Governments the world over are floundering in their efforts to come to grips with what the French Prime Minister Giscard d'Estaing has called the "enduring crisis." Professional economists have been of little help. The reason is simple. The world they occupy bears little resemblance to the real world of corporate power. The modern corporation is the dominant institution today, much like the Church was in the Middle Ages. It is more than a business and it exercises more than economic power. The way we work, the way we consume, the way we relate in our communities and in our families, all come under its influence. There really is a monopoly capitalism, and it is increasingly pervasive, expansive, wasteful, and global in dimension.

That the theories and forecasts of economists are basically unsound is amply demonstrated by the fact they are mistrusted by decision-makers in government and business. Treating the consumer and the firm as isolated and independent entities rather than as elements of a political economy, they are unable to grasp the workings of the economy as a whole. The cause of inflation, we are told, is excess demand (too much money chasing too few goods), and/or cost-push (labour or business attempting to increase its share of the total income). These are not causes at all, but symptoms of the underlying forces that are working in society today.

The bulk of the research and investigation about the operations of the modern corporations has not come from leading scholars, but from muckraking journalists, environmental crusaders, a few junior professors, and bands of poorly-paid left-wing research groups.[1] They have uncovered scandalous data and numerous horror stories. But exposing abuses of this or that corporation can easily obscure the real issues if this exercise persuades people — as it frequently does — that all would be well if this or that industry were brought under firmer state control. The problem does not stem from how the oil industry or the automobile industry is run, but how monopoly capitalism is run. Unless an effort is made to order the data into some meaningful pattern which makes some sense of it, we tend to become overwhelmed and demoralized by it, or in helter-skelter fashion to join one unconnected crusade after another, or finally to work to replace the bad people that are in elected offices with more decent types.

The Bizarre World of Economic Theory

In 1848 John Stuart Mill insisted that "only through the principle of competition has political economy any pretension to the character of a science." In 1975, even in the face of its utter inability to explain the current economic crisis, the assumptions of the competitive economy remain the cornerstone of modern economic theory. In economics, as in other branches of theology, bad doctrine is apparently preferable to no doctrine at all.

In an article that explores the failure of the economics profession to forecast the events of the past two years, the insightful *Business Week* magazine has this to say:

> A forecast, essentially is the statement of a theory with specific values instead of abstractions. When the forecast goes seriously wrong, it suggests that something is wrong with the theory. And when all forecasts miss the mark, it suggests that the entire body of economic thinking — accumulated in the 200 years since Adam Smith laid the basis for modern theory with his *Inquiry into the Wealth of Nations* — is inadequate to describe and analyze the problems of our times.
>
> Somehow, today's economists must revise and extend this body of thinking so that it will apply to an inflation-prone world beset with shortages and far more unified economically than politically. The change could come dramatically, like the "Keynesian Revolution" of the late 1930s. Some economists are already looking for a modern Keynes whose sudden insight will generate a theory to explain what is happening today ... [2]

Such a body of theory already exists, but it has been assigned by the economics profession to the underground of academia. Marxist writers like Paul Sweezy and Harry Magdoff, editors of the periodical *Monthly Review,* who centre their analysis on the impact of the giant multinational corporations, have been kept on the fringe of academic life. [3] Their work and that of younger radicals around the Union of Radical Political Economists in the U.S.A., the *New Left Review* in England and, if I may say so, *Canadian Dimension*, is essentially unavailable to the majority of students who want to understand the real world around them. What they get instead is the fairy-tale world of Paul Samuelson's introductory textbook. As befits a branch-plant country, Canadian students have available to them a special version of Samuelson's textbook, adjusted for the Canadian reader in branch-plant style by Anthony Scott, a professor at the University of British Columbia.

Here one can still discover the marvellous delights of the competitive economy, of supply and demand, and marginal productivity, not to mention the old efficient-resource-allocation-through-profit-maximizing routine. The inter-relationships of corporate, political and economic power are dismissed as the preoccupation of propagandists or journalists rather than "scientific" economists. Thus we are advised on page 1020 of *Economics, Third Canadian Edition* that, contrary to the Marxist propagandists, the United States is not a permanent war economy. The U.S. and Canada could easily survive the day after the arms industry folded up simply by converting government spending on armaments to expenditures on various social needs. "There is but one possible flaw in the story," we are warned, but "it lies inside the realm of politics and not economics." And within the "political realm," mind you, the flaw does not lie with the power of the military-industrial-complex that would seem to have a vested interest in maintaining the armament industry. Being an unscientific, normative concept, this has no place in the 1,059 pages of this text. According to Samuelson-Scott, the flaw lies with an "economically illiterate electorate" that does not understand the wonders of the fiscal tools that have been developed "in the last thirty years."

One reason for the poverty of modern economic theory is the compartmentalization of the social sciences in a manner that excludes the examination of social forces vital to economic decision-making. Approaching the subject of economics as somehow separate from politics, psychology and sociology may make life easier for economists who dwell on their sophisticated mathematical models. It does little to help us understand the motions of the modern economy. Thus the tastes of consumers are treated as a given. The consumer is sovereign, "king" in fact. Samuelson-Scott devote a grand total of six lines to the subject of advertising as possibly having some influence over our lives. But if in fact demand is created by advertising and other manipulations, there can be

nothing efficient about allocating resources to meet that demand.*
Several chapters are given over to the subject of productivity but
nowhere will the reader find a single reference to the negative
impact on production of dull, boring, and fragmented jobs imposed
by a hierarchial, impersonal, and authoritarian organization of
work. The "firm" is treated as if it were not a part of the political
economy, even though the basic decisions of the corporation rest as
much on political considerations as they do on market considerations — on taxation, government regulations, subsidies, government contracts, foreign policy, or, in the case of multinational
corporations, on nationalization.

For a "science" that excludes all but economic variables from its
purview it will come as no surprise that the economy it deals with
has as much in common with reality as a game of parcheesi. Picture
thousands of clever university professors daily instructing hundreds of thousands of students across North America about the virtues of competition. It is like a daily ritual that requires students to
observe the elaborate construction of the competitive model and
then, as if at prayer meetings in which the congregation repeats
after the minister, to dutifully reconstruct the model at examination
time. Once outside of the classroom, the student leaves behind the
fantasy world of consumer sovereignty, where corporations have
no political power and where resources are allocated in an efficient
manner.

In the first 584 pages of the Samuelson-Scott *Third Canadian
Edition,* three pages are alloted to "the evil of monopoly" and "the
curse of bigness." Public ownership, corporations, and the multinational corporations are given one page each! The first two are not
mentioned again but the subject of foreign ownership appears once
again on page 848 as an appendix added for the Canadian reader.

---

* One economist who does not accept the limitations of conventional economic
theory is Kenneth Boulding. He has written: "One of the most peculiar illusions
of economists is the doctrine of what might be called the 'Immaculate Conception' of the indifference curves, that is, the doctrine that tastes are simply given
and we cannot inquire into the process by which they are formed. This doctrine
is literally 'for the birds,' whose tastes are largely created for them by their
genetic structures and can therefore be treated as a constant in the dynamics of
bird societies. In human society, however, the genetic component of tastes is very
small indeed. We start off with a liking for milk, warmth, and dryness and a dis-
like for being hungry, cold, and wet, and we have certain latent drives which may
guide the formation of later preferences in matters of sex, occupation, or politics,
but by far and away are learned again by means of mutation — selection process.
It was, incidentally, Veblen's principal, and largely unrecognized, contribution to
formal economic theory to point out that we cannot assume that tastes are given
in any dynamic theory, in the sense that in dynamics we cannot afford to neglect
the processes by which cultures are created and preferences are learned." *(Economics as a Science,* pp.118-9.)

In the 1,059 pages of the text, they devote sixty pages to analyzing imperfection and monopoly. To an outsider without a vested interest in this dogma, it is obvious that the notion of "imperfection" in the market is no longer valid if the imperfections are, in fact, the central characteristics of the system.

Another old favourite of liberal economics is the rubric of the "mixed economy." "Ours is a 'mixed economy' in which both public and private institutions exercise economic control," says Samuelson-Scott.[4] The mixed economy supposedly combines the efficiency of the free-market economy and the equity and balance of government regulation. True, government controls, welfare measures, and progressive taxation reduce incentives and diminish efficiency, but this is the price we pay for living in a democracy. And though "the age-old tendencies for the system to fluctuate will still be there, . . . no longer will the world let them snowball into vast depressions or into galloping inflations . . ." Governments now have the tools to win these battles if the people will only let them.[5] Government is pictured as some sort of benign neutral agency totally divorced from corporate political power, ready to step in at the call of people.

A more accurate version is that from the very beginning of Canadian history, from the days of the fur trade through the era of the railways and the resource and manufacturing industries, government and big business have forged a partnership to direct the pattern and character of the Canadian economy. The modern corporation ought to be viewed more as an administrator of political economic power, and less as a mere market phenomenon. Indeed, market forces are often more easily manipulated than other elements in the sociopolitical environment. Government, as learned scholars should know, provides business with tariffs that protect them from foreign competition; diplomatic instruments and, if necessary, armies to give them access to foreign markets; charters for railroads, airlines, and broadcasting systems; laws and the police to protect their property; an educational and vocational system to provide them with trained manpower; leases on public land; the public purse to provide them with research funds and subsidies; and special tax provisions to finance their investments.

Consumerism and Inflation

It is primarily in the realm of consumption that workers in capitalist societies seek satisfaction, status and individuality. To buy more satisfaction and status they need more income; to get more income they must demand more wages.* The super-consumer is not simply the creation of Madison Avenue; rather she/he is the other side of the coin to the alienated worker. Capitalism has created powerful instruments to fashion tastes and to manufacture wants. But the infinite consumer is already created by the work situation in which most of the labour force finds itself.

Work under capitalism (and state socialism of the Soviet variety)† is not organized with the purpose of helping individuals develop their mental and physical potential. Workers have very little say as to what they produce or how it is produced. Tasks are pre-set, repetitive, and often fatiguing. It is not the welfare of the factory worker that is being served when the capitalist decides to produce automobiles by routine and monotonous assembly line operations. Nor is it the needs of the secretary that are being considered when she (or he) is reduced to a subservient role of typing, filing, and stamp licking. The imperatives of capitalist production require that decision-making authority and control of the production process be concentrated at the top. Virtually all initiative regarding how the work is organized, for what ends, and with what technology, remains with the owners and managers. This places severe limits on the number of jobs that permit individuals to learn and to grow and to create. Work roles are arranged to maximize profits (or growth) and to centralize controls. Work is fragmented into a myriad of separate jobs and co-ordinated in hierarchical fashion with some workers being subjugated to the personal control of others and all workers being subjugated to the control of managers and capitalists. Individual initiative and autonomy in most jobs are constrained by a mass of regulations and operating procedures. Workers relate to one another not by inter-personal co-operation but through the foremen and supervisors who are

---

* Lest this be misunderstood, I am not contending that the demand for higher wages is simply a matter of achieving higher status. In the context of today's accepted standard of living, most families are indeed struggling to get by. It is the composition of that standard of living, and the social and economic forces that shape it, that I am trying to explore.

† While Soviet-style socialism has fundamentally altered the legal patterns of ownership of capital, this has not by itself fundamentally altered the patterns of control of production, which remains in the hands of a minority. In this respect, at least, the relations of production in the socialist U.S.S.R. resemble the relations of production in a capitalist enterprise.

imposed upon them. This kind of tyranny is so universal and pervasive that we tend to take it for granted and accept it as a necessity of modern life.*

Against this argument it is commonly alleged that bureaucratic organizations and hierarchical control are unavoidable aspects of industrial technology. However, recent research has discovered that bureaucratic organization was not chosen by capitalists only because of its efficiency. It was chosen as well, and perhaps primarily, as a device for preventing skilled workers from attaining an undue degree of control over the work flow.[6] The father of "scientific management," Frederick Winslow Taylor, could not have been more explicit:

> Now, in the best of the ordinary types of management, the managers recognize the fact that the 500 or 1,000 workmen, included in the twenty or thirty trades, who are under them, possess this mass of traditional knowledge, a large part of which is not in the possession of the management. The management, of course, includes foremen and superintendents, who themselves have been in most cases first-class workers at their trades. And yet these foremen and superintendents know, better than anyone else, that their own knowledge and personal skills fall far short of the combined knowledge and dexterity of all the workmen under them.[7]

Taylor asserted that employers must gain control over this knowledge: "All possible brain work should be removed from the shop and centred in the planning or laying-out department."[8] By insisting upon a rigid and total separation between mental and physical labour, Taylor's system deliberately aimed at robbing workers of any understanding of the work that they do. The secret of Taylor's "scientific management" lay in his conception of workers as nothing more than the agents of a series of motions which through observation and experiment could be timed and

---

* The phenomenon of the alienated worker was clearly illuminated 130 years ago: "What, then, constitutes the alienation of labour? First, the fact that labour is *external* to the worker, i.e., it does not belong to his essential being; that in his work, therefore, he does not affirm himself but denies himself, does not feel content but unhappy, does not develop freely his physical and mental energy but mortifies his body and ruins his mind. The worker therefore only feels himself outside his work, and in his work feels outside himself. He is at home when he is not working, and when he is working he is not at home. His labour is therefore not voluntary, but coerced; it is *forced labour*. It is therefore not the satisfaction of a need; it is merely a *means* to satisfy needs external to it. Its alien character emerges clearly in the fact that as soon as no physical or other compulsion exists, labour is shunned like the plague. External labour, labour in which man alienates himself, is a labour of self-sacrifice, of mortification." (Karl Marx, *The Economic and Philosophical Manuscripts.*)

regularized to produce maximum results. Work could then be reduced to an obedient and mechanical application of their strength and dexterity. While work becomes shredded and atomized and the worker is made dumb as regards the production process, his previous knowledge is distilled into engineering formulas that can be taught in universities and technical schools and handed back to workers in the form of orders.

Technology itself is not simply the industrial application of scientific knowledge. It reflects the particular use of that knowledge by those who control society's investment capital. The history of technology as it has come down to us represents the accumulation of past choices made by the employer class in its own interests. Surveying the literature in industrial social psychology, Victor Vroom has found that for tasks which are difficult, complex, or unusual, it is decentralized, not centralized organizational structures that are more efficient. Centralization is advantageous when tasks are simple and routinized.

Employers have tended to centralize control since the inception of the industrial revolution. Given this historical phenomenon, which rests more on questions of power than it does on efficiency, the most advantageous technologies will be those involving routinized, dull, and repetitive tasks.[9]

Technologies and organizations that could increase the breadth of worker control must be avoided even if they are efficient, for to that extent they remove some degree of control from the capitalist. Every known experiment that has allowed even moderate worker participation in decisions has resulted in increasing productivity. As an example, the Scanlon plan of "participatory management" which has been tried in ten U.S. plants resulted in average yearly increases in productivity of 23.1 per cent. In one company, 408 of 513 innovative ideas that emerged from the regular dialogue between workers, technicians, and planners were implemented because they led to real improvements. This plan gives workers unlimited authority to organize and improve the work process and working conditions and gives them a share in the proceeds of cost reduction.[10]

Such experiments in "job enrichment," which, it should be noted, transfer only a small area of control to workers, are rare. They occur in marginal areas and in isolated firms fighting for survival. When prosperity returns, these firms move swiftly to reintroduce normal patterns of control. The risk of an escalation of demands for greater and greater amounts of workers' control is too serious a threat to contemplate for very long. Efficiency is thus subordinated to the principle of managerial control.

In short, technology, contrary to conventional wisdom, is not a wholly independent variable that dictates one universal organization of work-roles. At least in part, technology is itself determined by the social structure in which it is established. It can be adapted to different social environments. When capitalist economic institutions are replaced by a system of direct worker and community control, technologies and work roles can develop that are tailored to workers' needs. The monumental experiment of the Chinese Cultural Revolution in decentralization and direct democracy suggests some of the historical possibilities. The people of China may not have the opportunity of voting every four years for an elite to rule over them, but they appear to have a great deal of control of their everyday lives in the work place and in the community.[11]

Nearly half of our life is engaged directly at work. It is potentially the single most fertile outlet for initiative, individuality, and creativity. This potentiality having been snatched from us, we turn to other outlets to realize these human goals. We may *want* good work and decent communities but we learn to *need* only more consumer goods. Because we cannot satisfy these goals in the work that we do, we look to the most available outlet, which is consumption. Consumption offers an escape from the oppression of work. The corporation does not simply sell consumer goods. It sells means of forgetting, means of distraction, "means of dreaming that one is human — because there is no chance of actually becoming such."[12] Or, as Erich Fromm has put it "under capitalism, man is transformed into a *homo consumens* who tries to compensate for this inner emptiness by continuous and ever-increasing consumption."[13]

The intensity of wage demands no doubt reflects, in part at least, the degree of oppression that exists in the work situation. It is part payment for "the time being lost, the life being wasted, the liberty being alienated." Of course, no wage can fully compensate for this loss and no amount of consumer goods can fully substitute for the sense of individual and collective creativity available from non-alienated work.

Indeed, there is much evidence to suggest that high wages paid in mass industry along with longer vacations, better washrooms, subsidized cafeterias, and other comforts, are less able to buy off worker discontent on the job than they once were. Hourly wages at General Motors were raised 25 per cent from 1965 to 1969. Yet the rate of absenteeism at GM has been steadily rising. It has reached the point where an average five per cent of GM's hourly workers are missing from work without explanation every day. On Fridays and Mondays the figure rises to ten per cent. The quit rate at Ford reached 18 per cent in 1969. Despite the high wages ($35 to $40 a day), many workers hate their jobs and won't stay. Managers report with astonishment that in some instances workers are so frustrated that they walk off the job in mid-shift and don't even come back to pick up their pay.[14] The effects of job hatred extend beyond absenteeism, high turnover, and lateness to continuous confrontation with foremen, shoddy work, deliberate sabotage, and increasing resort to alcohol and drugs. It seems that pay increases and improved amenities have less impact now in soothing worker discontent and inducing "good work habits" as most, if not all workers, now take these for granted as a matter of course.

Private possession is the mark of honour and distinction in a capitalist society. In the words of the iconoclast Thorstein Veblen, "The possession of wealth confers honour; it is an invidious distinction . . . It becomes indispensable to accumulate, to acquire property, in order to retain one's good name." If we produced only to provide for our physical comfort, then our needs could be satisfied with far less of our energy being devoted to economic activity. "But," says Veblen, "since the struggle is substantially a race for reputability on the basis of invidious comparison," no amount of production is sufficient. The significance of the "Jones effect" is that as new consumer items become incorporated into our standard of living as "necessities," they no longer assign status to their owners. New ones must be sought after if we are to retain our high standing. If the purpose of possession is to rank higher than others, then economic growth is essentially a zero sum game. The possessions proliferate but we feel no better off. Even when inflation is discounted, incomes double every 25 or 30 years in North America, and there is little sign that we are happier. On the contrary, all the signs point to a social life that continues to disintegrate and fragment. Few would disagree with Bessie Smith when she said, "I's been rich, and I's been poor and believe me rich is better." But the capitalist ethos takes Bessie one step further: "if rich is good, richer is better." Marx wrote, "accumulate, accumulate, that is the Moses and the prophets." In the era of monopoly capitalism he would have to amend this aphorism to read, "accumulate, accumulate, consume, consume . . ."

The capitalist engine thrives on growth, and the culture that it creates is a culture of competitive consumption. But economic growth itself gives the lie to the ethic of possessive individualism as the sole source of personal well-being. We cannot buy decent environment with more income. On the contrary, the environment deteriorates in the normal process of never-ending economic growth. Nor can we buy decent, democratic, and engaging communities, nor yet decent work activities. Nevertheless, just as continuous economic growth is a matter of survival for corporate enterprise, a continuously rising level of consumption and wages is the way the capitalist economy induces more work effort and attempts to buy social peace.

In a brilliant essay the American writer Barry Commoner demonstrates that the 126-per-cent rise in industrial production since the end of World War II has barely affected the degree to which individual needs for basic economic goods are being met. In his words:

> That statistical fiction, the "average American," now consumes, each year, about as many calories, protein, and other foods (although somewhat less of vitamins); uses about the same amount of clothes and cleaners; occupies about the same amount of newly constructed housing; requires about as much freight; and drinks about the same amount of beer (twenty-six gallons per capita!) as he did in 1946. However, his food is now grown on less land with much more fertilizer and pesticides than before; his clothes are more likely to be made of synthetic fibers than of cotton or wool; he launders with synthetic detergents rather than soap; he lives and works in buildings that depend more heavily on aluminum, concrete, and plastic than on steel and lumber; the goods he uses are increasingly shipped by truck rather than rail; he drinks beer out of nonreturnable bottles or cans rather than out of returnable bottles or at the tavern bar. He is more likely to live and work in air-conditioned surroundings than before. He also drives about twice as far as he did in 1946, in a heavier car, on synthetic rather than natural rubber tires, using more gasoline per mile, containing more tetraethyl lead, fed into an engine of increased horsepower and compression ratio.[15]

In short, what Commoner is arguing is that per capita "affluence," as it relates to food, clothing, shelter, and transportation, is little greater now than it was 30 years ago.* These basics come to us in different forms which are more profitable for manufacturers to produce but which offer us little more in the way of social value. In each of these cases what has altered is the technology of production rather than the output of social value. Businesses made the switch to the new technologies after World War II because they were more profitable than the old technologies: aluminum, plastics, and

---

* This is probably true, but Commoner clearly underestimates the quantitative importance to economic growth of new products like snowmobiles, tape recorders, air-conditioners, television sets, and a variety of other household and recreational products.

cement yielded higher profits than lumber and steel; truck freight yielded more profit than railroad freight; detergents yielded more profit than soap, etc., etc. In general, the more profitable technologies are the more polluting ones.* Indeed this is one of the main reasons why they are profitable. They substitute cheap energy for labour. The fouling of the air, land, or water, the disposal of waste materials, and the disappearance of non-renewable resources are costs that are seldom borne by the enterprises that produce them. They are passed on to consumers in the form of higher prices; passed back to workers in the form of shorter lives due to radiation, mercury, or DDT exposure; higher laundry bills due to soot; higher costs of recreation due to the pollution of nearby lakes; etc., etc. And they are passed on to future generations. They comprise a massive subsidization by society and by nature to private enterprise. It is their ability to escape paying these "external" costs that makes these new technologies so productive and profitable. They contribute both to the increased cost of living and the decreased quality of living and they are invisible components of wage demands.

One of the ways corporations offset higher wages is to pass them on to the consumer. Another way, which has the same ultimate effect, is to reduce the quality of the product. A recent issue of *Consumer Reports* discloses that of 90,000 colour television sets, 74 per cent required repairs of some sort even though most of them were less than three years old. Of 25 cameras purchased by *Consumer Union,* "one half of them were not operable or became inoperable after we got them." As quality deteriorates so does the ability to satisfy consumer needs from a given income. People are forced to buy more of the same products just to maintain their standard of living. And to buy more requires more income, which is translated into increased wage demands.

It is now widely recognized that profit-propelled growth ravages and destroys large portions of the natural environment. What is less well recognized is the effect this has on living standards. Needs formerly met by personal effort or simply by nature's abundance must now be purchased in the marketplace. Air, water, sunlight, and space used to be free goods. Now they have to be purchased. And the compulsory consumption of gases, chemicals, dusts, and other

---

* One of Commoner's favourite examples is the substitution of detergents for soap. For every shirt washed today the phosphate going down the drain to pollute surface waters is nearly twenty times more per shirt washed than in 1946 when soap, which is largely free of phosphates, began to be replaced by detergents. "The technological displacement of soap by detergents has caused a twenty-fold intensification of the impact of phosphate from cleaners on the environment — at no gain to the consumer. The displacement of soap by detergents has made us no cleaner than we were; but it has made the environment more foul." (p. 156)

pollutants costs untold millions of dollars in insurance, cleaning, and medical bills. Pollution adds dearly to the cost of living. Here again it is not so much rampant consumerism but simply the desire to maintain existing living standards that is the source of at least part of the demand for increased wages.

Another source of inflationary pressure comes from collective needs, both met and unmet. The proliferation of private consumer goods simultaneously creates new collective needs. The most glaring example is the massive public expenditures for highways required by the automobile. Failure of the market economy to provide steady employment for working people, and failure to provide any employment at all for large numbers, has resulted in a proliferation of welfare, income maintenance, and unemployment insurance programs. Failure to bring about even development in all regions of the country has produced a plethora of government incentive programs to attract industry into deprived areas. Shifting the function of job training from business to the school system, and the financing of industrial research from business to government, has forced these costly activities onto the public purse. As taxes rise to pay for these expenditures, disposable personal income declines, another pressure point for increased wage demands.

But unmet collective needs multiply even faster than those that are met, and these also have an inflationary import. Take for example such collective needs as public transit, public housing, recreation, and pollution control. Unmet through the public sector, these needs have to be purchased in the marketplace at far greater cost. Consumers have to spend hundreds of millions of dollars each year on air purifiers and moving their families to areas where the air is clear. If such needs were met through collective effort, the expenditures to satisfy them would be substantially less. But this would compete with corporate interest groups that are making sizable profits meeting these demands in the marketplace.

All of these are root sources of the inflationary process. They lie at the heart of corporate capitalism — in the alienating nature of capitalist production which forces individuals to achieve happiness and status through consumption rather than through the work that they do, in the deteriorating content of consumer goods, in the polluting of air, space, and water, in collective expenditures to support corporate expansion, and in unwillingness to meet needs collectively in ways which would hurt corporate expansion.[16]

The Age of Permanent Inflation

To be fully understood, inflation has to be viewed in its historical context. The present bout of inflation is of course not a new phenomenon. While it has approached hyper-proportions in recent months, it is important to recognize that it is part of an inflationary trend that has blanketed the capitalist world for the past three-quarters of a century.

During the competitive phase of industrial capitalism (eighteenth and nineteenth centuries), falling prices were the dominant trend. With many relatively small firms competing in an industry, capitalist firms were forced to fight each other by cutting prices. To increase its profits, a firm had to undersell its rivals by introducing more efficient technology and better machinery. Collusion being difficult or impossible, there was no other way of capturing larger markets. Wars and investment booms created waves of inflation, but these only punctuated long periods of declining prices.

This pattern changed dramatically around the turn of the twentieth century when concentration of capital gave control of markets to a few giant corporations in each industry. Price-cutting as a competitive weapon is ruled out in this age of oligopoly. It leads to price war and diminished profit margins.

Suppose that in an industry like automobiles where there are four major companies, one of them, Ford, decides to lower its price by ten per cent in order to attract customers away from the others. Can the other three companies allow their markets to be raided? Of course they can not. They will retaliate by lowering their prices — maybe even undercutting Ford. The net result of the exercise of open price competition is that all four companies will be in a worse position. No company gains on its rivals, and since all suffer from the uncertainties that price wars produce, price-cutting is unofficially banned except under rare circumstances. It is replaced by some form of price-leadership where price changes are initiated to benefit all companies together.

Sometimes rival companies may decide not to follow the price leader. In that case the price leader can rescind its initial price change. The point is that so long as all the large companies accept this pattern it is fairly easy for the group of them to feel their way towards a price that, all things considered, is in the best interests of all of them. It is easier in this situation for prices to be adjusted upward than downward. Any reduction in price might be regarded as an attempt on the part of one company to undercut the other. This would lead to a price war. Therefore, price cuts are undertaken only under the most unusual circumstances and even here they are initiated in a manner that attempts to preclude the possibility of a price war opening up. Large corporate enterprises do not always push their prices as high as possible, for they have vast reserves and unlike small business they can take a long view of profit maximization. What is more important about these firms is that they do not tend to drop their prices in a period of recession. To maintain their cash inflows they normally offset reductions in sales by raising prices. In the age of competition, by contrast, firms fought to retain their position by lowering their prices.

With the appearance of what is termed monopoly capitalism, long periods of declining prices gave way to long periods of rising prices — permanent inflation. Rising prices have been temporarily interrupted during times of major depressions, but over the past three-quarters of a century prices have steadily drifted upwards until by 1975 they are roughly five times what they were in 1900. The trend can be seen in the accompanying chart.

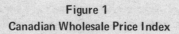

Figure 1
Canadian Wholesale Price Index

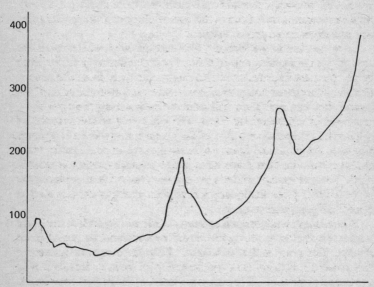

Corporate decisions about output, sales effort, investment, location, and prices are all aimed at ensuring a pre-determined profit-
target. The target range of large corporations is between 10 and 20
per cent return on capital after taxes.* When John M. Blair, the
former chief economist of the American Senate Subcommittee on
Anti-trust and Monopoly, examined the economic power of five
leading companies, he found that they met their desired profit
target goals almost perfectly whether the economy was prosperous
or in a recession:

> Over the 16-year period (1953-1968) the success of the 5 leaders
> in meeting their profit objective is little short of remarkable. As
> compared to its target return of 20 per cent, the weighted average
> of General Motors actual rate of return on net worth was 20.2
> per cent. As compared to its target of 8 per cent, U.S. Steel aver-
> aged 8.1 per cent. Of all firms, Alcan's profit rate experienced the
> widest year-to-year fluctuation, but its average of 9.5 per cent
> compared closely to its objective of 10.0 per cent. The company
> with the steadiest performance was Standard Oil of New Jersey,
> which matched its target of 12.0 per cent with an average perfor-
> mance of 12.6 per cent. The highest average return was recorded

---

* There are many variations of profit-targeting. Essentially it works as follows:
Whatever prices are decided on, times the volume which it is expected can be
sold at those prices, should yield a sales revenue minus the cost of producing the
output that gives a return on investment that has been set as a target. As an
example, suppose General Motors has decided that it must get a rate of return on
its investment of at least 20 per cent — after taxes. The price of a GM car is then
set to give GM this return once all costs are known. The cost of producing a car
depends on a number of things — labour costs, raw materials, depreciation of
equipment, advertising, distribution and transportation, executive salaries, etc.
But what is also crucial in the cost of producing a car is the extent to which the
production capacity is fully utilized, i.e. the volume of production. The greater
the volume produced, the lower the cost of producing each car. This is because a
lot of the costs are fixed and have to be paid regardless of the total volume —
costs like depreciation of equipment and buildings, property taxes, executive salaries, etc. The more cars produced, the lower these fixed costs per car.
Having established a standard sales volume, GM sets its prices to achieve a 20
per cent return based on the costs that result by operating at this standard sales
volume. GM figures that in its best year it can reach 80 per cent of its maximum
operating capacity. In an average year it expects to produce at 64 per cent of its
maximum operating capacity. It sets its prices so as to plan for a 20 per cent rate
of return after tax, on the assumption that its plants will operate through the year
for a total of only 200 days. Of course these prices will yield a bigger rate of return if the plants actually produce more than the 200 days. And this is quite common. GM often earns a profit of 30-35 per cent. By adopting a very conservative
standard sales volume, GM gives itself enormous flexibility. For example, it
could take a 3½-month strike and still get the 20 per cent return by operating for
the rest of the year at full capacity. (For other variations and a full discussion of
profit targeting see Neil Chamberlain, *The Firm.*)

by Du Pont, whose earnings for the entire period averaged 22.2 per cent as against its objective of 20.0 per cent.[17]

Profits of these giants were stable during a period which included two recessions and one boom, seemingly indifferent to shifts on wages, productivity, consumer demand and foreign competition. Prices were manipulated to compensate for these shifts. As long as these companies maintain their commanding position in the industries they occupy, their profits are rarely susceptible to the fluctuation in market forces. In 1954 and 1958, U.S. Steel's production dropped by more than 20 per cent, but they were able to maintain and even raise their profit margins in both these recessions by raising prices. While 30-40 per cent of the goods and services produced in North America are supplied under competitive conditions, the majority are produced by monopolies or shared monopolies. During boom times when general shortages appear, prices rise in all sectors. During recessions, prices usually fall in the competitive sectors but they continue to rise in the "administered" sector, giving an upward bias to the price level at all times.

Monopoly Capitalism: Centre and Periphery

It was the second technological revolution emerging in the last few decades of the nineteenth century in steel, hydroelectricity, oil, and chemicals that allowed for mass production and ushered in what has become known as the age of monopoly capitalism. Previous to these discoveries, firms were confined to local markets. Producing on a larger scale, they were bound to meet up with increasing costs, thereby being unable to compete with smaller producers. The new technology made possible the wave of mergers that swept the entire capitalist world around the turn of the century as the larger producers crushed the smaller ones, beginning a process of nationalizing local industry that is still going on today.

Modern technology greatly expands the scope of profit-making, but it has also transformed the nature of business enterprise. It requires much larger amounts of capital than in the past, and it involves a far greater degree of specialization of materials, equipment and manpower. More time, and therefore more capital, are needed to work up a new project and bring it into full operation. It is also more difficult and more expensive to alter products and equipment if errors are later discovered in marketing or product design. With hundreds of millions of dollars locked up in a product, decision-making is more complex and more risky. The firm can no longer afford to rely on free market forces to produce a price, a market and the required supplies that will guarantee a desired return on its investment. The only way to cope is to plan, but to plan effectively the corporation must be able to control its own destiny, as independent as possible of control by outside financial institutions. That means that its profits must be large enough to finance its future development and expansion. Such a profit goal is attainable only if the firm can first corner its markets and control its price. Prices that fluctuate from week to week or even from month to month are not conducive to planning. Absolute certainty is what is required. Short of obtaining a complete monopoly over the sales of its products, when a firm shares a monopoly position with two or three others, producing among them 50 per cent or more of the industry output, each one is in a dominant position.

Monopoly sharing among a few corporations is typical in most manufacturing industries: automobiles (General Motors, Ford, Chrysler); soap detergents (Proctor and Gamble, Colgate, Lever Brothers); cereals (Kellogg, General Foods, General Mills, Quaker Oats); electric light bulbs (General Electric, Westinghouse, Sylvania); cigarettes (Reynolds, American, Philip Morris); and of course many others. Four companies or fewer supply 55 per cent of the radio and TV sets produced in Canada; 85 per cent of the batteries; 80 per cent of refined petroleum; half of the sporting goods; 80 per cent of iron and steel; and 80 per cent of flour.[18]*

Business life in Canada is shared by about 170,000 corporations in addition to many thousands of farmers and individual business proprietors. Most of these are of little account in that their influence is not great even within their own industries, let alone in the economy at large. A relatively small number of giant corporations play a highly strategic role in the business life of Canada.

---

* The conventional measure of monopoly control is the level of industry concentration. Among industries where 4 or fewer enterprises supply at least 80 per cent of the output, the degree of monopoly control is considered "very high"; where 4 to 8 enterprises account for 80 per cent or more of the output, the degree of monopoly control is considered "high"; when it takes 50 or more enterprises to account for 80 per cent of industry output, the degree of concentration is considered so low that active price competition is assumed to exist. Almost two-fifths of all manufactured goods made in Canada are produced in 60 industries where there is a "high" or "very high" degree of monopoly control. Another fifth are produced in 42 industries displaying a "fairly high" degree of monopoly control, with 8 to 20 companies producing 80 per cent or more of industry output. On the other hand, highly competitive conditions prevail in 26 industries accounting for only a fifth of all manufactured products. (Department of Consumer and Corporate Affairs, *Concentration in the Manufacturing Industries of Canada*, p. 17.)

A comparison of the level of concentration in 40 comparable industries shows that the high degree of monopoly control that already prevailed in 1948 has increased slightly over time. Here are some examples:

In 1965 the 174 largest corporations had 50 per cent of total corporate assets. The largest 50 manufacturing enterprises, each with assets in excess of $100 million, operated 857 enterprises in 104 industries, accounted for 32 per cent of total manufacturing sales, 40 per cent of the assets, and 46 per cent of the profits. The 16 largest mining companies, each with assets in excess of $100 million, accounted for 44 per cent of the sales, 37 per cent of the assets, and 46 per cent of the profits. The 17 largest utilities accounted for 73 per cent of the assets, 52 per cent of the sales, and 64 per cent of the profits. The 7 largest retail distribution chains accounted for 17 per cent of the assets, 17 per cent of the sales, and 22 per cent of the profit.[19]

For the purpose of demonstrating the commanding position of the biggest businesses in the Canadian economy I have assembled a roster of companies whose only qualification is that they own a hundred million dollars of assets or sell a hundred million dollars worth of goods and services. There are over 250 companies that qualify as members of this roster. Some of these are subsidiaries of others: taking these into account, and ignoring for the moment the varying degrees of interlocking directorships that link others, the total number of separate companies reduces to about 200. How big are these companies within the Canadian economy? As a measure of their importance, suppose that they were to suddenly disappear from the ranks of the 170,000 business corporations. What would disappear with them?

To begin with, the country would come to a standstill. The CPR and the CNR, Air Canada, and Canadian Pacific Airlines would vanish along with most of the trucking capacity and pipelines (Trans Canada, Interprovincial, West Coast Transmission, Alberta Gas Trunk). The suppliers of gasoline, the makers of trucks and

---

No. of Largest Enterprises Accounting for 80% or more of Employment

	1948	1965
Flour Mills	22	3
Biscuit Manufacture	11	8
Sugar refineries	4	3
Distilleries	3	5
Breweries	9	3
Shoe Factories	110	65
Synthetic Textile Mills	11	11
Pulp and Paper Mills	23	19
Agricultural Implements	4	7
Cement Manufactures	1	4
Pharmaceuticals and Medicines	49	34
Median Values for 40 industries	13	11

(*Source: ibid.*, p. 45)

automobiles would cease to exist along with the makers of most of farm implements (Massey-Ferguson, International Harvester, John Deere). The bulk of our food-producing capacity — dairies, meat packers, bakeries, canned foods (Canada Packers, Ogilvie Flour Mills, Atlantic Suger Refineries, Westfair Foods, Maple Leaf Mills, General Foods, Swift Canadian, Burns Foods, Kraft Foods) — along with the system of food distribution and storage (Loblaw, Steinberg's, Canada Safeway, Dominion Stores, Federal Grain, United Grain). The cities would starve. The larger ones would also freeze and go into isolation and darkness. Gas, light, water, telephones would be cut off in the larger centres, and national radio and television would vanish. A national crisis in credit would follow the closing of all the chartered banks along with the largest finance, insurance, mortgage, and trust companies. The construction capacity in many of the large centres would be knocked out (Canada Cement, Campeau Corporation, Cadillac Developers, BACM, Trizek, etc.).

We would also have to do without the Steel Company of Canada, Aluminum Company of Canada, Dominion Foundries and Algoma Steel; the chemical output of CIL, Union Carbide, Dow Chemical, Proctor & Gamble, Lever Brothers, etc.; the electrical products of Canadian General Electric, Northern Electric, Westinghouse and RCA; the rubber products of Goodyear Tire, Firestone, Uniroyal and B. F. Goodrich; the textile products of Dupont, Celanese Canada and Dominion Textiles; the paper products of MacMillan Bloedel, Domtar, Consolidated-Bathurst, Crown Zellerbach and others; the metals of Inco, Noranda Mines, Cominco, Falconbridge, etc.

I need not press the point any further. The removal of 200 giant businesses would effectively destroy the economy. The list of 200 glosses over some important differences. It includes some companies that are large but declining; it excludes others, particularly in the mass media, that are vitally important. Power Corporation, which owns much of the print and broadcasting media in Quebec, is included. Others are not: F. P. Publications (Toronto *Globe and Mail,* Vancouver *Sun,* Winnipeg *Free Press,* etc.) the *Toronto Star,* the Irving Group, Maclean Hunter publications (*Macleans, Financial Post, Chatelaine,* and numerous trade journals), the Bassett-Eaton Group. Nevertheless, with all of its oversimplifications, the list makes a point of central importance: a tiny group of immense corporations has a stranglehold on the key financial, production, distribution, and ideological links of the economy.

This network of dominant corporations forms the centre of the modern business economy. Because of their large cash flow and excellent credit rating, these giants can raise the capital to finance labour-saving equipment, to develop new products and techniques, and to establish nationwide or worldwide marketing systems. In their hands lies the economic power to dominate the present and the economic capacity to shape the future.

At the periphery of the modern economy is the myriad of small businesses, most of which have only local or regional importance. Many periphery firms serve as satellites to the dominant corporations, supplying them with inputs or channelling their products to the final purchaser. In the automobile industry, for example, a host of firms sell parts to auto manufacturers, while franchise dealers serve as forward satellites. They often act as subcontractors for dominant corporations.

Another set of periphery firms comprise the competitive fringe for centre enterprises, serving regional markets or producing single line products. They typically surrender the power to make price decisions to the dominant corporation, but they may also be pioneers in developing new or improved products. A third periphery group fills in the cracks and crannies of the economy, usually in the repair, retailing, and service fields. Periphery firms are often labour-intensive, less productive enterprises, their management revolving around one or a few individuals who are also the owners. Their surivival prospects are precarious; they are perpetually short of cash, feel squeezed by government regulations, taxes, minimum wage laws, unions and threatened by the prospect of elimination at the hands of larger rivals.

Splitting the economy into two categories, centre and periphery, obviously compresses reality, but it is a useful conceptional device.[20] This model of the modern economy is peculiarly distorted in Canada, where, excepting the transportation, finance, and some merchandising fields, the centre economy is largely composed of U.S.-owned companies. It is a truncated centre. The technologically oriented growth industries are here typically organized as branch-plant assembly operations whose markets and research are circumscribed by the parent companies. The periphery, on the other hand, is fully occupied by Canadian business. The implications of this dichotomy, obviously essential to an understanding of the Canadian economy, are examined in subsequent chapters.

Bypassing the Market

Monopolies and monopoly sharing firms are able to maintain their high profit margins only by restricting the output of their product so as to keep their prices high. They can easily sell much more but only by lowering their prices, which would cut into their profits. A U.S. study concludes that the overall cost of monopoly and shared monopoly in terms of lost production is somewhere between $48 billion and $60 billion annually.[21] In Canada, lost output due to the same cause would be in the order of $4.5 to $6.0 billion dollars. The lost tax revenues alone from this wealth would go a long way towards ending poverty and pollution. The redistribution of income from monopoly profits that transfers income from consumers to shareholders is estimated at $23 billion annually in the U.S. and $2-3 billion in Canada. Monopolistic firms thus contribute to inequality, inflation and unemployment. Unemployment results since monopolies, as noted, significantly reduce output which in turn reduces the number of workers who would otherwise be producing. If such deliberate industrial sabotage accounted for only 20 per cent of all unemployed, this still translates into over 100,000 unemployed workers.

With investment in their products amounting to hundreds of millions of dollars, firms cannot afford to depend on the market to bring them sufficient consumers. Corporations must manufacture consumers as well as products. Advertising is thus a primary tool of corporation planning. With price competition banished, advertising, product design, and packaging are the main elements of competition among the giants. The advertising budget of Proctor & Gamble alone is twenty times as large as the budget of the U.S. Justice Department's Anti-trust Division, which must monitor a trillion-dollar economy. Even greater anomalies would be found in Canada and other countries.

Advertising is a kind of relentless propaganda on behalf of all the products that corporations supply. The free enterprise system dies if it does not expand, and expansion means selling new products as well as more and more of the old ones. People have to be made dissatisfied with what they have and to crave new things. They have to be made to feel inadequate. If that means terrorizing them about bad breath and under-arm perspiration or promising them remarkable new sexual powers, that's fair game — anything to get them buying again. As John Kenneth Galbraith has said so well:

> There is little that can be said about most economic goods. A toothbrush does little but clean teeth. Aspirin does little but dull pain. Alcohol is overwhelmingly important only as an intoxicant. An automobile can take one reliably to a destination and return him, and its further features are of small consequence as compared with the traffic encountered. There being so little to be

said, much must be invented. Social distinction must be associated with a house or automobile, sexual fulfilment with an automobile or shaving lotion, social acceptance with a hair oil or mouthwash, improved health with a cigarette or a purgative. We live surrounded by a systematic appeal to a dream world which all mature, scientific reality would reject.[22]

All of the incredible waste that goes with advertising and packaging — the extra brands, the effort that goes into trying to distinguish one product from the next when their physical content is all the same, the sales people, advertising copy writers, package designers, all of these resources that are used in sales promotion and that add quite substantially to many of the things we buy — is indispensable to the corporate economy. It appears as one of the social costs of maintaining this kind of economic system.*

Just as advertising encourages us to discard what we already have and replace it with new products, so does frequent style change. And built-in obsolescence, by deliberately increasing the rate at which products wear out, actually forces us to discard what we already have. Examples of this are numerous.[23] At one time the lamp bulb in a flashlight would outlast the life of the batteries. Obviously the makers of bulbs could sell a lot more bulbs and make a lot more money if they could shorten the life of the bulb to match the life of the battery. The General Electric Company actually received such a proposal from its sales division with the promise that it would increase its flashlight business by 60 per cent. This was about 35 years ago! It is probably impossible to estimate the extra profits G.E. has been able to make over the period since it adopted this proposal to deliberately degrade the quality of its product, but one can be certain that they are substantial.

One empirical investigation of the automobile industry took a 1949 model car and tried to find out how much of the cost of subsequent models could be explained by frequent style changes. They

---

* Advertising has been aptly described as "the institution of abundance." In a society of physical scarcity, the economic problem is one of production: "But in a society of abundance, the productive capacity can supply new kinds of goods faster than society in the mass learns to crave these goods or to regard them as necessities. If this new capacity is to be used, the imperative must fall upon consumption, and the society must be adjusted to a new set of drives and values in which consumption is paramount....Clearly it must be educated, and the only institution which we have for instilling new needs, for training people to act as consumers, for altering men's values and thus for hastening their adjustment to potential abundance, is advertising. That is why it seems to me valid to regard advertising as distinctively the institution of abundance." (David Potter, "The Institution of Abundance," in Finnigan and Gonick, *Making It: The Canadian Dream*, pp.226-7.)

did this by estimating the amount of money that would have been saved had cars with the 1949 model lengths, weights, horsepowers, transmissions, etc. been produced year after year. Whatever technological improvements had occurred in the meantime were still applied to the 1949 model. Only the length-weight-horsepower etc. is held constant. They discovered that without the frequent style changes the savings per car would be about $700, or about 25 per cent of the cost of the car. That was in 1960. By now the savings would be more like $1,500 per car. And this excludes the savings in higher repair costs and additional gas consumption. For example, gas mileage was 16.4 per gallon in 1949. It has fallen to 14-15 miles per gallon since. Had we stuck to the 1949 car with technological improvement, gas mileage would have increased from 16.4 to about 18 miles per gallon. This means that the average motorist is paying about $60-70 more for every 10,000 miles of driving than would be the case if the 1949 model had been continued.[24]

Engineers are trained to design. If they were asked to produce a car that lasts 10-15 years, they could do so. In fact they would prefer to do so because then they would be practising their skills. Now they are told to use their ingenuity and training to produce a car that will start falling apart in two years. But what would happen to sales and profits if the automobile industry produced cars that would last 10-15 years? Built-in obsolescence, designing products that are built to collapse, also seems to be a necessary cost of corporate capitalism.

Another way firms control their markets is to set up their own distributing systems. This has long been a common practice in the automobile and petroleum industries, but it is far more widespread than that, and it is spreading rapidly. About five years ago, for example, Silverwood Dairies purchased the Mac stores in Winnipeg to give itself a monopoly of the dairy sales in this chain. The trend is noticeable in every part of the retail sector.

Finally, to secure for itself a guaranteed flow of materials on acceptable terms, a giant firm must control the supply of raw materials and essential products that are important for its operation. The most potent way to do that is to become its own supplier, to do what is called "vertical integration." Most petroleum refineries produce their own oil, GM produces most of its parts, Safeway produces its own milk and bread as do many of the other chain stores, newspapers often use their own pulp and paper plants, and some steel companies supply their own iron ore.

These are devices by which the giant corporation attempts to supersede the market, or more precisely, to substitute its own controls for the traditional controls of the market. This process was duly noted by John Kenneth Galbraith in his book *The New Industrial State*. Nevertheless, Galbraith sees corporate planning as essentially healthy in that it allows for innovations, exploits efficiencies, and creates stability.

To be sure, it does create stability, but stability for *what* and for *whom?* And this question prompts another: with the competitive mechanism having been bypassed in the era of the giant corporation and corporate planning, what mechanism is there to protect the consumer from unchecked profiteering?

Galbraith, more than most economists, acknowledges the relevance of this kind of question. He attempted to answer it many years ago in his first book, *American Capitalism: The Concept of Countervailing Power*, in which he said that monopoly on one side of the market tends to beget counter-monopolies on the other side which hold the original monopoly in check — major tire companies forming to contervail the power of automobile companies in determining the price of tires, for example, or the chain stores forming to contervail the power of canning companies in determining the price of canned food. This theory satisfied most of the critics in the 1950s, but Galbraith himself soon appeared to realize that the process of vertical integration (and the ease with which the monopolists could, in the final analysis, pass off higher costs to the consumer after sharing profits between them) severely limited the applicability of countervailing power. Or as Edward Mason, former Dean of the Harvard Graduate School of Public Administration, has said:

> The "countervailers" have never been able to explain why countervailance does not lead to a sharing of monopoly profits at the expense of the rest of the economy[25]

In *The New Industrial State,* Galbraith made another try. The centre of power is not the owners but what Galbraith called the "technostructure" — a whole range of executives, sub-executives, scientists, technicians, and specialists which the new technology has spawned and placed at the centre of the controls. Their goal is no longer maximum profits (as in the case of the old-fashioned tycoon), but security and growth, which are of benefit to all of society. Thus the industrial technostructure merges with the bureaucracies of unions and government into a single interest group — hence the new industrial state — which has a wider concern than the mere profits of the corporation.

The trick here is that the technostructure is supposed to be the real power that chooses its goals independently of the property owners' urge to maximize profits. The whole thing is, of course, an illusion that stems from Galbraith's denial of the essential class character of corporate society. The unreality of this view has been exposed many times, but never better than in the famous court decision in which the Dodge Brothers won additional dividends from Henry Ford:

> . . . a business corporation is organized and carried on primarily for the profit of the stockholders. The powers of directors are to be employed for that end. The discretion of directors is to be exercised in the choice of means to attain that end and does not extend to a change in the end itself, to the reduction of profits or to the non-distribution of profits among the stockholders in order to devote them to other purposes.[26]

The Gospel of Social Responsibility

In the light of the recent spectacular rise of corporation profits, we are being swamped by another drumfire public relations campaign, the purpose of which is to justify these profits in terms of some concept of the public interest. Thus the gigantic profit of the petroleum industry is needed to explore for new sources of energy. Our very survival, we are warned, depends upon it. We are also advised that industry is the leader in the fight against pollution, and so on. As Earl Cheit, a University of California professor of Business Administration, has written, "the desire to justify power is a natural impulse, and its chronicles represent much of the political history of nations." But Cheit also adds, "it appears that businessmen are trying to fill an ideological gap between business and society . . . Thus managers must say that they are responsible because they are not."[27]

The business corporation is the leading institution of today, much like the Church was in medieval times. The power of the Church was legitimate because it emanated from a coherent body of accepted social thought, but the modern corporation cannot make a similar claim. And while some years ago people confronted with the facts of unbridled corporate power would shrug it off with "So what? The system works!" there is less sign of that today. That is why, in defence of their autonomy, corporation executives are seeking to blur the distinction between public and private interests. The new gospel of business stresses responsibility to shareholders, customers, employees, to the nation, to everyone.

Over a decade ago, the Canadian Marconi Company developed a formal statement of its primary responsibilities, representative of many similar codes:

PRIMARY RESPONSIBILITIES
of
CANADIAN MARCONI COMPANY:
1
TO THE SHAREHOLDERS
for successful results
2
TO OUR CUSTOMERS
for price, quality and service
3
TO OUR EMPLOYEES
for fair dealing and continuing opportunity
4
TO OUR INDUSTRY AS A WHOLE
for constructive and ethical action
5
TO CANADA
for economic and social advancement

In the late 1960s, a similar code of "good corporate citizenship" was distributed by the Liberal government under the tutelage of the late Robert Winters, emphasizing for the benefit of U.S. subsidiaries "responsibility to Canada." The business creeds of today put even greater stress on "social responsibility."

Earle McLaughlin, chairman and president of the Royal Bank, denies that he has any power:

> Power is something political. What we have is responsibility ... I don't believe that I have any power at all, though I do have a lot of responsibility ... Being a banker you can't exercise any power: all you can do is fulfill the responsibility you feel to your depositors, shareholders, staff and the public at large.[28]

Despite his denial of power, McLaughlin is one of the more powerful men in Canada. Besides being chairman and president of the Royal Bank of Canada, Canada's largest, he also sits on the board of directors of Power Corporation, Algoma Steel, Metropolitan Life, Genstar, Canadian Pacific, and the ultimate seat of corporate power in the world, General Motors Corporation of Detroit.

The latest fashion in corporate responsibility is "job satisfaction." According to Reginald Jones, chairman of General Electric, "the leading motivators of the new work force are achievement, recognition and the nature of the work. The new management has to set reasonable goals, and encourage and challenge the work force."

Whatever the current popularity of this or that dimension of corporate responsibility, the situation in terms of actual behaviour is as depicted by Edward Mason:

> Assume an economy composed of a few hundred large corporations, each enjoying substantial market power and all directed by managements with a "conscience." Each management wants to do the best it can for labor, customers, suppliers, and owners. How do prices get determined in such an economy? How are factors remunerated, and what relation is there between remuneration and performance? What is the mechanism, if any, that assures effective resource use, and how can corporate managements "do right" by labor, suppliers, customers, and owners while simultaneously serving the public interests? . . . I can find no reasoned answer in the managerial literature.[29]

The answer is that social planning of the kind that might be done by a few hundred sovereign corporations would produce nothing but chaos. In reality, of course, all corporate planning is designed within the context of long-term profit maximization. Greater public awareness of the social cost of private enterprise may complicate the calculations of managers to some degree, but all of their decisions still have to meet the ultimate test of profitability.

Neil Chamberlain, professor of economics at the Graduate School of Business at Columbia University, has provided us with what is perhaps the most sophisticated discussion of this theme.[30] Taking up the argument that the modern corporation narrowly confines the creative outlets of its employees — "the large corporation specializes the functions of its people and then coordinates them to achieve machine-like efficiency . . . the life of the mind of the individual is restricted in the firm to prescribed movements and routines" — Chamberlain quickly zeros in on the cause: "The life of the mind in the firm is hobbled and its vision is blinkered by the constraint to which the business institution is subject within the larger social system" — its profit-orientation. And he correctly points out that this argument has little to do with private ownership per se. As he says, "if our major corporations were wholly government-owned, but still applied only the profit-efficiency test to their operations, the result would be the same." Chamberlain argues in favour of the retention of private ownership of the giant corporation ("diffusion of discretion and power is a value not to be given up lightly") provided "we can free them from a test of efficiency more relevant to the past than to the present." He recommends a number of activities for which the corporation should take responsibility — low-cost housing, slum reclamation, recreational developments, education and training programmes — from which it would "not expect to reap any reward." Free from the constraints of profitability, the corporate mind would be liberated and invigorated in the pursuit of these social purposes.

Having provided this exciting view of a corporate utopia, Chamberlain is too much the realist to leave matters resting there. Corporations investing a portion of their capital in these non-rewarding projects would obviously earn lower rates of return. Their capital fund would diminish and they would have to resort more frequently to capital market to finance their growth. Some stockholders, who may not appreciate that their funds are being used to finance these non-profit activities, may pull their money out or even band together to turn out the incumbent management. Alternately, if the profit potential of such a firm is not fully realized, and this is reflected in a lower value of its shares, it exposes itself to a takeover assault by a company bent on realizing the profits implicit in its assets. To his credit, having recognized these complications to his scheme Chamberlain is ultimately unable to extricate himself from them. The reason is obvious enough, for they indicate the kind of economic chaos that would ensue should the goal of profit be tampered with on so vast a scale.

Profit: A Social Condition

The role of the individual functioning within the corporation is not unlike that of the hockey player. The temperament and behaviour of the hockey player off the ice does not matter in the least once he takes to the ice. There he must play according to the rules of the game, and that means helping his team score more goals than the opposition. He may like the game for itself or only be playing for the money. His motivation and personal character traits are beside the point. If he scores lots of goals for his team or is successful in stopping the other team from scoring he will advance up through the ranks to professional hockey. He will remain there so long as he is useful to his team. If he begins to slow down he rides the bench or he is sent back to the minors.

Similarly for Galbraith's technocrat. If he wishes to advance within the corporate hierarchy he must play according to the corporation's rule book. And, as numerous empirical studies have shown, the modern giant corporation is more, not less, profit oriented than its small scale predecessor. [31] As our corporation executive is useful to his "team" in improving its profits, he is slotted in more responsible and better rewarded posts. As he fails the test of performance, he is shipped back to the minors — very often the branch-plants. It is these rules of the game that ultimately determine his behaviour within the corporation, not the humanizing experience he may have enjoyed while a student at some liberal arts school.

Actually the much publicized separation of management and ownership in the U.S. economy has been grossly exaggerated, as recent literature has shown.[32] According to this view, which is similar to that of Galbraith, "The capitalist class has been transformed into the managerial class." It is a sort of capitalism without capitalists. Or as Galbraith himself puts it, "the decisive power in modern industrial society is exercised not by capital but by organization, not by the capitalist but by the industrial bureaucrat."[33]

Profit remains the single test by which managers survive in the face of competition from their peers and subordinates; it is still the way company divisions gain favours from corporate-level executive committees. While modern corporations can afford to take the long-run view of profits, which may include contributions to the arts, sports, and charities as part of their continuing campaign to improve their public image, profit has never been displaced as the criterion of success. That is why, even in the absence of an immediate ownership interest, managers have remained remarkably true to the interests of the major owners.[34]

There are very few instances where a significant and easily identified ownership group does not actively control large Canadian-owned corporations.[35] And most foreign companies are fully owned subsidiaries of parent corporations. John Porter states the situation in Canada very emphatically:

> The notion that directors are a kind of window dressing arranged by management follows from the theory of management control. Whether or not this situation applies to American industry . . . is not our concern here. It is doubtful, however, that it satisfactorily describes Canadian corporate power. It would be quite wrong to select a group of senior managers of Canadian corporations and describe them as an economic elite.[36]

Canadian corporations practise control with ownership of less than 50 per cent just as corporations do elsewhere. A case in point is the Argus empire headed up by E. P. Taylor. Argus holds a controlling interest in six major corporations with a minority of common shares:

B.C. Forest Products 6.6%
Dominion Stores 23.6%
Domtar 16.9%
Hollinger Mines 20.2%
Massey-Ferguson 15.6%
Standard Broadcasting 47.7%

Massey-Ferguson can serve as an illustration. With its investment of about $57 million, Argus is able to control a corporation with assets valued at over $1 billion. It is entitled to place six directors from its board on the 18-position board of Massey, one of whom is Massey's chief executive officer. In addition to the Argus holdings, the six Argus board members hold between them another $6 million of Massey-Ferguson shares.

While the ordinary shareholder is completely divorced from the operation of the property he has a share in and has been literally reduced to a clipper of coupons, this is simply not true for the few very large owners, who can have effective control over the key long-run decisions and generally want to exercise it. As Porter remarks:

> The aim of those who want to control a corporation is not to become managers, but to acquire seats on the ruling body of the corporation — that is on the board — and this goal is achieved by owning stock. Almost all takeovers of the recent period have involved changes in the board of directors and subsequent changes in management, and often a good deal of internal reorganization. [37]

Porter divides the dominant corporations and financial institutions into three groups: those in which there are large minority or majority holdings, the few in which there is a high degree of management control, and the American subsidiaries. In the second group, management, usually the president, recruits "outside" members of the board — mainly from a select group that are already directors of other large corporations. They may have knowledge which the president considers useful, or special contacts. This is one of the reasons why former cabinet ministers and former senior civil servants are often invited to sit on corporate boards. The boards of American subsidiaries always incude top management of the parent corporation, as well as one or two of the top management in Canada. Some also include high-ranking Canadian businessmen. Whether these Canadian-held directorships are honorific or whether they have been selected because of their special knowledge of Canadian conditions, they are essentially without power since the main policy decisions are made by the parent company.

Where top officers do not have control of a company by virtue of their stockholdings, they nevertheless do have large holdings that are significant for their own personal fortunes. Chairman F. C. Donner owns only .017 per cent of GM's outstanding stock, but it is worth $3,917,000, and Chairman Lynn A. Townsand owns 0.117 per cent of Chrysler, worth about $2,380,000. As a result of stock options plans which are prevalent in at least three-quarters of large non-financial corporations, top management is committed more strongly than ever to the corporations profit position, for without profit the options are largely worthless. Stock options aside, Robert J. Larmer found that the corporation's dollar profit and the rate of return on equity were the major determinants of the level of executive compensations. Compensation of executives, he concluded, has been "effectively harnessed to the stockholders' interest in profits."[38] Thus growth, sales, efficiency, and competitive position are not only inseparable managerial goals but also the determinants of high corporate profits — which in turn determine managerial incomes and status. Whatever the personal values and motivations of managers, they are driven to profit maximization because profits are the only unambiguous criterion of successful managerial performance and a necessity for corporate survival: "The separation of ownership and control shows that the 'profit motive' is not a *motive* at all . . .; it is not a psychological state but a social condition."[39]

Clusters of Corporate Power

Descriptions of the degree of business concentration in industry are illuminating for what they tell us about monopoly pricing and corporate planning. Yet they tell us more about the economic power wielded by big business than about its political power. To examine this we have to take a more macro view of the concentration of wealth and investigate the centres of economic power and their inter-relationship with the political realm.

It is generally conceded that in Canada the central institutions of capitalist control are the network of banks, trust companies, and insurance companies that accumulate the savings of ordinary citizens into vast pools of money which are made available to the industrial enterprises with which these financial agencies are connected. In 1974 their collective assets totalled $100 billion, and their profits were about $450 million.

In his study *The Canadian Corporate Elite,* Wallace Clement found that, between them, the resident directors of Canada's five largest banks account for one-quarter of the Canadian-held positions on the boards of directors of the 113 "dominant" corporations in Canada, that is, the largest nonfinancial corporations. He also found that the directors of the dominant banks hold over two-fifths of the directorships in the largest insurance companies. Just how important the banks are to the Canadian economy was revealed by a newly appointed director to the Royal Bank: "For a Canadian, becoming a bank director is the summit of one's business career. The banks are very powerful in the sense that no individual in Canada, in my mind, can do much without the support of the chartered banks." [40] Access to the banks and insurance companies is essential for Canadian businesses wishing to take advantage of new investment opportunities. The fact that banking and finance circles in general are so intermeshed with the established corporate elite is a major explanation for the exclusive nature of big business in Canada.

While this is not the place for a thorough study of corporate and political power in Canada,[41] a glance at the Power Corporation, probably the most influential corporate complex in Canada, is very revealing. The conglomerate is organized as a holding company with controlling interests as shown in the table.

Table I
Power Corporation's Empire

	% Control	Revenue	Profits $(1,000)	Assets
Canada Steamship Lines Ltd. (ships, grain elevators and shipbuilding)	88.2	242,767	23,907	360,684
Investors Group Mutual Fund	56.5	51,292	16,051	n.a.
Montreal Trust Co.	50.5	39,314	2,464	n.a.
Great West Life Assurance Co.	50.1	543,048	18,235	106,428
Consolidated-Bathurst Ltd. (pulp and paper)	38.1	689,009	47,712	n.a.
Dominion Glass (glass, plastic containers and gas)	96.0	111,441	3,730	99,091
Imperial Life Assurance Co.	51.2	130,653	3,737	654,244
Laurentide Financial Corp.	57.9	69,317	3,754	398,107
Argus Corp.	10.4	12,649	11,696	185,491
SMA	55.0	3,535	2,522	2,348

A fuller account of the power held by this company would have to include its two interlocking directorships with each of the Royal Bank and Imperial Bank of Commerce and its strong relations with the Bank of America, which has "introduced a new dimension to the financial group."[42] The Power Corporation and its chairman

34

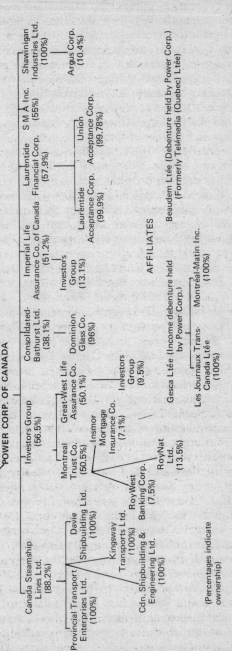

Figure 2
The Power Corporation Empire

and chief executive officer, Paul Desmarais, exercises extraordinary influence in Quebec by virtue of the fact that it owns much of the daily press (accounting for about 50 per cent of total French-language circulation) and many broadcasting stations in that province. It secured a great deal of influence in the province of Manitoba when it purchased Investors Syndicate, which in turn holds 50.1 per cent of the shares in Great-West Life, a company that has always played a leading political role in Manitoba.

That the Power Corporation conglomerate has strong ties with the federal and Quebec Liberal parties has prompted some questioning recently about the $10 million in federal grants received by the company between 1968 and 1972. Some of these connections include Paul E. Martin, son of Paul Martin, who is a vice-president of Consolidated-Bathurst, vice-president of Power Corporation, chairman of the executive committee and director of Dominion Glass and director of Canada Steamship Lines, Davie Shipbuilding and St. Maurice Capital Corporation; Claude C. Frenette, former president of the Quebec wing of the Liberal Party and now a vice-president of Power Corporation; Anthony Hampson, a former Power Corporation director and now chairman of the government-owned Canada Development Corporation; Jean-Luc Pepin, Minister of Industry, Trade and Commerce from 1968 to 1972 and defeated in a recent election, now a director of Power Corporation; Maurice Strong, former president of Power Corporation, now Undersecretary-General of the United Nations and a close friend of Anthony Hampson; Louis Desmarais, brother of Paul Desmarais, who is chairman of Power Corporation, himself a director of Power Corporation and president and chief executive officer of Canada Steamship Lines as well as being recently appointed to the deputy chairmanship of the Canada Development Corporation; Alfredo F. Campo, chairman and chief executive officer of Petrofina Canada and a director of Power Corporation as well as being a member of the General Council of Industry (Quebec) and a member of the National Advisory Committee on Petroleum (federal); J. Claude Hebert, a director of Power Corporation and member of the National Productivity Council (federal); Jean-Paul Gignac, brother of Jacques C. Gignac, Ambassador to Libya since 1970 and Chief of Cultural Affairs in Ottawa 1967-70, himself commissioner of Hydro-Quebec from 1961 to 1969 and now president of Sidbec (Quebec Crown Corporation) and a director of Power Corporation; Arthur Simard, chairman of Marine Industries as was his father Joseph before him, father-in-law to Premier Robert Bourassa of Quebec, and a director of Power Corporation.

Based on this evidence it might be possible to conclude that Power Corporation supports the Liberal Party. This would not be correct. Power Corporation has no special attraction to the Liberal Party *per se;* Power Corporation is attracted to power. Only because the Liberal Party has held political power during recent years in Quebec and Ottawa is there such an interchange between Power Corporation and the Liberals. Evidence that Power Corporation is attracted to power and not the Liberal Party comes from the fact that the Hon. John P. Robarts, Conservative Premier of Ontario from 1961 to 1971, also sits on the board of Power Corporation, in addition to the boards of Abitibi Paper, Bell Canada, Canadian Imperial Bank of Commerce and Metropolitan Life. Power transcends political affiliation. [43]

The Argus Corporation, originally built upon the foundation of E. P. Taylor's brewery empire, still represents an important nucleus of corporate power.* While Canadian Breweries (now Carling O'Keefe Ltd.) was sold to Rothmans of South Africa in 1969, Argus has retained controlling interest in Massey-Ferguson, Canada's largest multinational corporation, making farm machinery across the globe, and Dominion Stores Ltd., Canada's largest supermarket chain (4,000 stores). Through its controlling interest in Hollinger Mines Ltd. (iron ore) it has an indirect interest in the much larger Noranda Mines Ltd., one of the world's major mining organizations. Noranda, in turn holds a controlling interest in B.C. Forest Products Ltd., a significant proportion of which Argus controls. The Argus resources complex is rounded out by Domtar, whose products included pulp and paper, chemicals and building materials. Argus also controls one of Canada's most successful broadcasting operations through Standard Broadcasting Ltd., which controls some radio stations in Toronto and Montreal and has recently taken controlling ownership of the Bushnell empire.

These ownership links are illustrated in the accompanying chart and table. †

---

* The story of how Taylor built up his brewery empire is a classic tale of political intrigue and corporate infighting. It is described in detail in Frank and Libbie Park, *Anatomy of Big Business.*

† At the time of writing, Power Corporation has made a bid to take over controlling interest of Argus. Power already has 10.4 per cent of the shares in Argus. Its bid of $148.5 million has been initially rebuffed by the controlling shareholders of Argus. But Argus is in the hands of an aging group. John A. McDougald, president and chairman, is 67. He lives in Palm Beach, Florida. Major-General A.B. Matthews, executive vice-president, is 65. E.P. Taylor, who founded the company with McDougald, is 74 and resides in the Bahamas. Wallace McCutcheon and Eric Phillips, both prime movers in Argus, are now dead. It is broadly speculated that Argus Board members are interested in selling their interests but are waiting for a better price. Should a marriage between Argus and Power be consummated, it would constitute Canada's most powerful nucleus of corporate power by far. For one it would join their interests in forestry — Consolidated Bathurst, B.C.

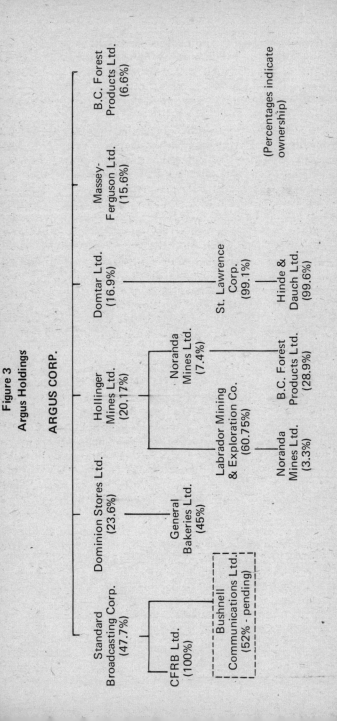

Figure 3
Argus Holdings

ARGUS CORP.

Standard Broadcasting Corp. (47.7%)

Dominion Stores Ltd. (23.6%)

Hollinger Mines Ltd. (20.17%)

Domtar Ltd. (16.9%)

Massey-Ferguson Ltd. (15.6%)

B.C. Forest Products Ltd. (6.6%)

CFRB Ltd. (100%)

Bushnell Communications Ltd. (52% - pending)

General Bakeries Ltd. (45%)

Labrador Mining & Exploration Co. (60.75%)

Noranda Mines Ltd. (7.4%)

Noranda Mines Ltd. (3.3%)

B.C. Forest Products Ltd. (28.9%)

St. Lawrence Corp. (99.1%)

Hinde & Dauch Ltd. (99.6%)

(Percentages indicate ownership)

Table 2
The Argus Empire

	% Control	Revenue	Profit ($1,000)	Assets
Standard Broadcasting Corp.	47.7	15,070	3,380	15,597
Bushnell Communications Ltd.	52.0	13,387	1,080	12,119
Dominion Stores	23.6	1,320,732	13,664	199,708
General Bakeries, Ltd.	45.0	43,115	453	13,950
Hollinger Mines Ltd.	20.17	27,860	7,130	n.a.
Noranda Mines Ltd.	7.4	1,151,900	154,870	1,707,296
Labrador Mining & Exploration Co.	60.75	19,570	10,100	n.a.
Domtar Ltd.	16.9	897,652	82,479	683,363
Massey Ferguson Ltd.	15.6	1,784,625	68,413	1,613,951
B.C. Forest Products	6.6	279,054	21,086	358,345

Historically, the most powerful economic and political centre in Canada has revolved around the CPR-Bank of Montreal complex. The CPR was chartered by the federal government to build a transcontinental railway that would make it possible to realize a design for a western empire. A western empire in Canada was the "national dream" of both Canadian and American capitalists. The crucial importance of the CPR is that it secured the west for the merchant capitalists of central Canada.

The CPR was as much a creation of the political elite as it was of a business elite. Indeed at the time of its construction and for decades before, the same men dominated both spheres. "Railroads are my politics," said Allan McNab, a leading political figure and the promoter of several large railroads.[44] John A. Macdonald risked his own career, the rule of the Conservative Party and much of the public treasury on the CPR. "My own position as a public man," he

---

Forest Products and Domtar. It would also join their interests in multi-media ownership. Power owns *La Presse,* Montreal's largest French-language daily. Argus owns one of Montreal's most prominent radio stations and is in the process of acquiring Bushnell Communications.

Even the *Financial Post* blanches at the degree of corporate concentration that would be represented by such a merger: "The investment interests of these firms are not acquired without purpose and their power of control will inevitably be exercised....It's hard to see at this juncture just what real benefit would accrue from a Power Corporation/Argus combination. And the increasing concentration of economic power that this country is experiencing as business holdings by corporations and governments intermesh must surely, at the very least, bring a degree of unease." *(Financial Post,* April 5, 1975.)

wrote to George Stephen, "is as intimately connected with the CPR as yours is, as a railway man." Stephen, a major financier of the railway, held a similar view: ". . . The Canadian Pacific Railway is in reality a partnership with the government. . . ."[45]

The government awarded the owners of the CPR $25 million in cash, $37.8 million worth of government-owned railway lines, 25 million acres of choice land and tens of millions of dollars of loans. In addition, the CPR secured 6,000 acres of land from the government of British Columbia which now constitute the central part of the city of Vancouver. By 1916 the company estimated its net proceeds from the sale of land at $68.25 million while valuing its unsold land a $119.25 million. These and other concessions such as a 20-year tax-free period on unsold land and a monopoly on western traffic do not begin to account for the total public subsidy given to the company. They exclude from account the value of the timber and minerals found on CPR land which became the basis for the CPR's forest and mining empires. To this day the CPR is a recipient of inordinate government subsidies, estimated at $230 million between 1967 and 1972.[46]

The power placed in the CPR's hands was enormous. It was the CPR that determined the pattern of development in the west and to large degree its pace of development. It chose the names, shapes, sizes, and locations of western towns from Brandon to Vancouver. In every instance the location and shape of western Canadian centres were determined solely on the basis of maximizing CPR profits on land. The southern route it selected through the prairies, contrary to the one the government had chosen, sent the railway through less favourable agricultural land and a more difficult passage through the mountains. This route, it has been suggested, slowed down prairie settlement for 15 to 20 years. The apparent explanation is that the original route, which already had settlers along it, and dozens of speculators with claims on nearby land, would not give the CPR the absolute control over land that it preferred.

The link between the Bank of Montreal and the CPR was there from the beginning. George Stephen was president of the Bank of Montreal until he moved over to the CPR in 1880. Donald Smith, another financier of the railway, became president of the Bank somewhat later. Donald Smith also linked the CPR to the Hudson's Bay Company, in which he had become the single largest shareholder. The Dominion government purchased the lands originally chartered to the HBC in 1670, for a sum of 300,000 pounds plus one-twentieth of the land in western Canada and the area around its trading posts. The best part of this land was turned over to the

CPR. Smith, with a substantial interest in both companies, was thus doubly rewarded. He died a baron and Canada's richest man.

The strong connection between the CPR and the Bank of Montreal still holds. There are five CP directors who are also directors of the Bank of Montreal, including bank chairman Arnold Hart and CP president Fred Burbidge (and six more, including CP's various subsidiaries). But there are also important linkages with other banks. CP chairman Ian Sinclair is one of four CP directors on the board of the Royal Bank of Canada, and Earle McLaughlin, chairman and president of the Royal Bank, sits as a director of CP. There are, as well, two Bank of Commerce directors on the CP board, while the Bank of Nova Soctia and the Toronto Dominion Bank are each represented by a single director. The banks are heavily represented on the board of CP because of their investments in the company. Others, like International Nickel, the Iron Ore Company of Canada, Du Pont, Eaton's, Stelco, Dominion Foundries, and Steel Ltd., are represented there primarily as major buyers of CP services.

In 1955 Canadian Pacific "was a railway company that happened to have a variety of other interests." In 1975 it is "a conglomerate that happens to run a railway" with total profits of $100 million a year.[47] Unlike Power Corporation, which acquired most of its holdings by taking over other companies, CP developed into a conglomerate mostly through the development of properties it already had. Some of these are listed below:

CP Air (airline) (100%)
CP Ships (shipping) (100%)
CP Transport (trucking and warehousing) (100%)
CP Express (trucking and warehousing) (100%)
Smith Transport (trucking and warehousing) (100%)
CP Rail (railway) (100%)
CP Telecommunications (telegraph and telex) (100%)
CP Hotels (hotels) (100%)
Marathon Realty (real estate and developing) (100%)
Cominco (metal mining, chemicals) (53%)
Pan Canadian Petroleum (oil and gas) (87%)
Pacific Logging (lumber and wood products) (100%)
CP Securities (credit agency) (100% subsidiary of CP Investments)
Trans Canada Pipeline (natural gas pipeline) (13%)

Through Pan Canadian Petroleum, Canadian Pacific is the largest private stockholder in Panarctic. The major shareholder is the federal government. Other private shareholders include Imperial Oil. Aside from its controlled companies, CP Investments has an

41

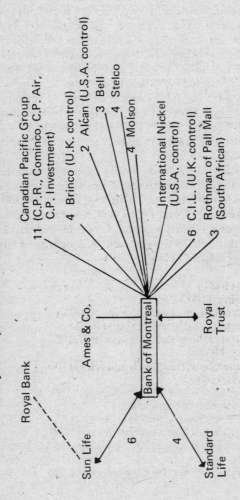

Figure 4

Major Companies Linked with the Bank of Montreal

Royal Bank

Ames & Co.

Sun Life

6

Standard Life

4

Bank of Montreal

Royal Trust

11 Canadian Pacific Group
    (C.P.R., Cominco, C.P. Air,
    C.P. Investment)

4 Brinco (U.K. control)

2 Alcan (U.S.A. control)

3 Bell

4 Stelco

4 Molson

International Nickel
(U.S.A. control)

6 C.I.L. (U.K. control)

3 Rothman of Pall Mall
   (South African)

1. The figures indicate the number of directors sitting both on the Bank's Board and on the board of the enterprise concerned (1969-70).
2. This is not an exhaustive list of industrial concerns.

investment portfollio of over $200 million including major share-holdings in MacMillan Bloedel, Husky Oil, Union Carbide Canada Ltd., Rio Algom Mines, The Investors Group, and many others.

Although the Bank of Montreal is no longer the most important bank in Canada in terms of its holdings, it remains one of the more influential because of its permanent and intense ties with extremely important industrial and financial corporations. As the accompanying chart shows, besides its eleven directors in common with the Canadian Pacific group there are four in common with Brinco, two with Alcan, three with Bell Telephone, four with Stelco, four with Molson's, six with CIL, and three with Rothmans. This is only a partial listing of the Bank of Montreal's interlocking directorships. A full listing would include Dominion Textile Co. Ltd., International Nickel, and many others. The Royal Trust was founded by the Bank of Montreal in 1892 and the Bank is still its largest share-holder with fourteen directors in common. The association with Sun Life and the important brokerage house Ames and Co. also goes back a long way. Between them the Bank of Montreal, Sun Life, Royal Trust, and Standard Life have assets of over $20 billion.

Power Corporation, Argus, and the CPR-Bank of Montreal complex are just three of several clusters of economic and political power. Wallace Clement[48] has identified 274 individuals who hold more than one directorship in Canada's top corporations. Together they account for 54 per cent of all the directorships held by Canadian residents in all the dominant corporations, 59 per cent of all insurance directorships, and 68 per cent of all the directorships in the five key chartered banks. This is indeed a select and powerful group of men. They move between the giant corporations, carrying with them a degree of knowledge about the corporate world much broader than any other group. Each of them makes decisions in a single year that determine the allocation of hundreds of millions of dollars and that affect the lives of millions of people. Three-fifths of these men were born at or near the top of the class system. They inherited their position from their fathers, or married into it, or their fathers already owned substantial businesses. For those born into middle-class families, which accounts for all but a few of the rest, the climb to the top is a long one. It is a testing period within which they compete against others of their class and prove to those at the top that they are worthy. Spending most of adult life climbing to the top, a few of them will break into elite positions.

According to the established view, "the system of property and family . . . have broken down," resulting in a "breakup of 'family capitalism' which has been the social cement of the bourgeois class

system."⁴⁹ There has been no radical separation between property
and family in Canada, and perhaps less in the U.S.A. than is usually imagined. Long lists of examples of prominent family firms
could be provided.⁵⁰ C. L. Burton became president of Simpson's in
1929, succeeded by his eldest son Edgar with his youngest son Allan
holding a vice-presidency in the company. The fifth generation of
Molsons are still in control of the Molson empire, which now
extends far beyond brewing. Five Eatons have been president of
Eaton's since Timothy Eaton first opened a store in Toronto in
1867. Two sons of John David Eaton still run the company. W.
Galen Weston became chief executive officer of Loblaw Companies at the age of 30, after sitting for three years on the board of
George Weston Ltd., Loblaw's parent company founded by his
father. Carl A. Pollock is a director of the Royal Bank and
chairman of Electrohome Ltd., a firm established by his grandfa-
ther in 1907. His brother John is president of the company. There
are five Bronfmans associated with Distillers Corporation-
Seagram and Cemp Investments. A recent newspaper announcement gives some insight into the running of the Seagram empire
and to the transfer of family fortunes from one generation to
another.

> Cemp Investments Ltd. provides a partial glimpse into the for-
> tune that has been built from profits in huge, world-wide Dis-
> tillers Corp-Seagrams Ltd., Controlled by the Bronfman family
> of Montreal. Distillers' sales run to over $1.5 billion a year.
> Cemp is owned by four trusts established by the late Samuel
> Bronfman — creator of the world's largest distilling organiza-
> tion — for his four children and his grandchildren. The name is
> taken from the first name of Bronfman's four children: Charles,
> Edgar, Minda and Phyllis. Charles runs the Canadian opera-
> tions of the Distillers Corp-Seagrams; Edgar, based in New
> York, is president of the big firm; Minda is married to a French
> baron; and Phyllis is a Chicago architect.⁵¹

It is still possible to name the propertied ruling class in Canada.
To a large degree they are descendants of our original merchant-
finance class or the children of founding families of more recent
vintage. This is becoming less and less the case in the U.S.A. Few
Americans could name the presidents of the leading U.S. corporations — Exxon, General Motors, Du Pont, General Electric, et al.
One of the prime features of corporate capitalism is that the holders
of power are far more anonymous than they were in earlier eras.
They wield power by virtue of their occupying key offices in giant
enterprises and their influence lasts only so long as they sit
at particular desks. In many cases it is difficult to distinguish an

officeholder from his predecessor. The Rockefellers seem to be more a throwback to J. P. Morgan and William Randolph Hearst than akin to the civil service types who run many of the world's largest corporations. It is precisely the pervasive control of American corporations that accounts for the still infantile state of Canadian corporate development and the more lasting relationship here between family, property, and power.

Beyond the Board Room

"At the upper levels of power in Canada," writes Wallace Clement, "there is a society very much different from the rest of Canada's society . . . [It] is a set of people who become involved at the executive level in a range of philanthropic and cultural activities ranging from the Boy Scouts to the boards of Canada's major universities." In a chapter aptly titled "The Private World of Powerful People", Clement says that "from private schools to private clubs they lead a life quite apart from, although very much affecting, the existence of the vast majority of Canadians. Through a series of elite forums and political connections, they make decisions well beyond those confined to the dominant corporations where they gain their power."[52]

Some of the elements of this private world are well known and need not delay us for long. The private schools like Upper Canada College and Trinity College School have long served as a training ground for the elite of Canada. Attending dad's school, as Clement remarks, "is just another form of inheritance which preserves the continuity of the elite."[53] The thousands of dollars it costs to send their children to these private schools pays off many times over in the life-long contacts that are made there, and more generally in the "social capital" they accumulate during these formative years. The national clubs like the Toronto Club, Mount Royal Club, and the Winnipeg Club which serve as the preserves of the upper-class male are meeting places and social circles where the business elite nourish old friendships and talk over deals.

The boards of charitable organizations, symphony orchestras, art galleries, hospitals, universities, and several other public and cultural institutions are almost the exclusive preserves of the corporate elite. In part the role they play is honorific and a mark of their leadership position in society. But there is also an element of decision-making. What is deemed worthy of support and what is not is often a decision that they are in a position to make. That certainly is the case of the large foundations, many of which, like the Garfield

Weston, Donner, Molson, Beaverbrook, R. J. McLaughlin, Eaton, and Bronfman foundations hold over $700 million in assets.[54] Through them, the corporate elite is able to determine what type of "good works" will be supported. The foundations are legal devices which not only keep family fortunes intact but also perpetuate the influence of their origination long after they are dead.

More directly related to the organization of corporate power are the several trade and professional associations like the Canadian Metal Mining Association, the Canadian Petroleum Association, the Pulp and Paper Association, the Canadian Bar Association, and the Canadian Institute of Chartered Accountants. These associations act as pressure groups representing the economic interest of their members and creating a climate of opinion within their respective industries and professions. Like the more ubiquitous Canadian Manufacturers' Association and Chamber of Commerce, they are an extension of corporate power and a social network that serves to create business and professional solidarity and homogeneity. The Canadian Bankers' Association, for example, with its staff of 30 employees and an executive director, provides a regular channel of communication with the government. The executive council of the Association meets with the governor of the Bank of Canada and senior officials of the Finance Department at its quarterly annual meetings. This is but one example of the direct channels the corporate elite has open to the federal government. It is usually well represented on government royal commissions and tends to dominate the boards of federal agencies like the National Productivity Council and the Economic Council of Canada.

Important to the on-going influence of and communication among the corporate elite are what Clement calls the "elite forum" — these meeting places "are not public forums but forums for Canada's elite." They provide avenues of contact, channels of communication, and sometimes essential information for the corporate elite. They also serve to shape corporate opinion. One such forum is the Canadian-American Committee, an association of Canadian and U.S. business leaders and to a lesser degree leaders of "international" unions. In a clear understatement, Wallace Sterling, a member of the U.S. component, is reported to have made the claim that "the members have not been without rather acute influence on their respective governments."[55] One of the major on-going projects of the Canadian component has been a number of academic publications that attempt to lay the theoretical and empirical justification for free trade between Canada and the U.S. and a continental energy policy. One such series, authored by some of Canada's leading professional economists, was recently published by the

University of Toronto Press, lending added prestige to this project. The Committee's full-time staff sends dozens of articles pleading the case for continentalism to popular magazines and newspapers throughout North America. Some of the Canadian members of the Committee include W. O. Twaits, chairman of Imperial Oil, Paul Desmarais, chairman of Power Corporation, Paul Leman, president of Alcan, and John Clyne, chairman of MacMillan Bloedel.

The Conference Board of Canada, a branch of the U.S.-based Conference Board, plays a similar role. It is currently headed by Arthur J. R. Smith, a former chairman of the Economic Council of Canada. Another elite forum is the 41-member Advisory Council to Industry, Trade and Commerce, a body set up by Jean-Luc Pepin when he was minister of the federal department. Its purpose is to "examine and keep under review the policies, programs and services of the department, advise on the adequacy and recommend improvements on new activities."

The most recently established forum, set up by an initial federal government grant of $1 million with promises to match an expected $10 million endowment, is the Institute for Public Policy Research, "Canada's first independent think-tank." Head of the Institute is Ronald Ritchie, formerly a vice-president of Imperial Oil, who emphasizes that the Institute will be accountable "to a board of directors who will be self-replacing as are the boards of most voluntary institutions in our society." In this instance the board includes John Clyne, chairman of MacMillan Bloedel and a director of Canadian Pacific Ltd.; John Robarts, former Premier of Ontario and presently a director of Power Corporation, Metropolitan Life, Canadian Imperial Bank of Commerce, Bell Canada, and Abitibi Paper; and a few other corporate luminaries. The first edition of its publication *Canadian Public Policy* reflects their business interests. The contributions of Ronald Ritchie and three academic economists provide a blatant, though not overly successful, defence of the oil and resources industries. The journal provides still another proposal for continental free trade. And there is expatriate Scott Gordon championing the gradualism and marginalism of economic theory and congratulating his fellow economists for staying away from what he calls "The Big Question."

There are still other types of ad hoc forums, such as the 80 "top Canadian business executives" who went on a "remarkable mission" to Washington in February, 1973 to meet with top ranking U.S. politicians and civil servants.[56] A month later the Hudson Institute was invited to hold a private workshop for leading corporation and government figures:

Herman Kahn and his Hudson Institute set up shop here Sunday for a three-day conference that will see some impressive brain-power focused on "The Corporate Environment, 1975-1985." But the participants will be keeping most of their superthoughts to themselves. The conference is the 11th to be held as part of the institute's three-year corporate environment study sponsored by about 60 corporations. Since two federal government departments and 10 Canadian corporations are among the sponsors much of the three-day meeting will focus on Canadian problems. The meetings are closed and "off the record," the institute says. Canadian participants include Bell Canada, Hydro-Quebec, MacMillan Bloedel, Power Corp., John Labatt, Ltd., and the Royal Bank of Canada. The federal government departments are Industry, Trade and Commerce and the Minister of State for Science and Technology.[57]

Frequency of interaction both within the corporate world and outside it among men from common social backgrounds who personify ruling class continuity leads to a consensus about the social system and the place of corporate enterprise within it. In particular, as John Porter stresses, "the fact that the corporate elite hold important positions behind the corporate world means that they are in a position to make their ideology pervade the entire society until it becomes identified with the common good."[58]

Liberal Democracy: The Final Defence

In view of the growing evidence that a narrow corporate elite holds a preponderance of influence within the "private" world, defenders of liberal democracy ultimately pin their faith on the impartiality of an elected government that in their view exists to represent the "public interest" or more precisely to mediate and resolve the antagonisms that inevitably arise between different social groupings. This interpretation of the role of the state is supported by the convictions of political office-holders themselves, who ardently claim that they stand above the battle of civil society, that they are concerned to serve the nation as a whole, rather than any one class. That they are utterly and sincerely persuaded of the nobility of their task, free from class-bias, need not be doubted. But we may well question the validity of their claim.

What is missing from this understanding of reality is consideration of the historical context within which liberal democracy arose. "Responsible" government came into being in England in the seventeenth century, in the U.S.A. and France in the eighteenth century, and in Canada and elsewhere in the nineteenth century. It came by way of revolutionary action by the rising capitalist classes who required for their full development the kind of laws, subsidies, tax structure, tariffs, regulations, and military support that were thought necessary to make the market system efficient and profitable. If government was to be responsive to their needs, government authority must be placed in the hands of men who were made subject to periodic elections involving a choice of parties and candidates. The electorate need not be a democratic one. In fact, it was deemed essential that the franchise be restricted to men of substance. Democracy, which originally meant rule by the common people, was feared and rejected by men of wealth and learning. What was wanted was an electorate that consisted of property-owners, so that the government would be responsible to their choices. As the Canadian author and political theorist C. B. Macpherson has said: "The liberal democracies that we know were liberal first and democratic later."[59]

Democracy came as a late addition to capitalism and the liberal state, and in most cases it required decades of agitation and struggle as wage-workers and women used the new freedom of association and speech to demand the vote. By the time it was won, industrial capitalism was by and large an accomplished fact and broadly accepted. The rise of welfare and government intervention to blunt the accompanying dislocations is generally held to be the result of the democratization of the franchise. But public regulation and provision of social services would have had to come anyway from the sheer need of government to allay working-class discontent that threatened the stability of the state. It was Bismarck, no great democrat, who pioneered the welfare state in the 1880s with just this in mind. As Macpherson writes, "What the addition of democracy to the liberal state did was simply to provide constitutional channels for popular pressure, pressures to which governments would have had to yield anyway, merely to maintain public order and avoid revolution."[60] It was Joseph Chamberlain who, in 1885, spoke of this ransom that would have to be paid precisely for the purpose of maintaining the rights of property. In insisting that this ransom be paid, governments render capitalists a major service, though they are seldom prepared to acknowledge it.*

Besides the provisions of social welfare, the state must, within

---

* The architect of Canada's welfare state legislation was William Lyon Mackenzie King, who had written in his *Industry and Humanity* (1918) that the provision of social benefits and the involvement of moderate trade unions in the management of industry would guarantee a social harmony between the classes, moderating

the limits imposed by the prevailing economic system, assume responsibility for many functions and services which are beyond the scope and capacity of individual capitalists, even giant corporations. These include establishing a favourable fiscal and monetary climate for economic growth; underwriting private risks at public expense through a wide variety of incentive programs, grants, subsidies, tariffs, accelerated depreciation allowances, etc.; state financing and ownership of public utilities, railroads, airports, and highways to assure low cost or free services to facilitate growth; an immigration policy to provide both skilled and unskilled labour; a public land policy that leases land on favourable terms for mining, forest, and recreation development; sanitation, hospitals, medical care, educational facilities, unemployment insurance, and manpower services which absorb the social costs of private enterprise production; financing all basic research and most commercial research to develop new products and techniques of production.*

As the state undertakes these various functions, what the French author Jean Meynard calls "the bias of the system" ensures that

---

the demands of the working class and inducing a sense of "responsibility" among its leaders. King visited Germany in 1937 and was duly impressed by the corporatist character of German fascism. After his meeting with Hitler, King noted in his diary (June 29, 1937): "Like Henderson, The British Ambassador, I feel more and more how far-reaching in the interests of the working classes, are the reforms being worked out in Germany, and how completely they are on the right lines. They are truly establishing an industrial commonwealth, and other nations would be wise to evolve rapidly on similar lines . . . . Of all that I have seen on this trip abroad, I have been more impressed and more heartened by what seems to be working itself out in Germany in these particulars than in almost anything else." (I am indebted to Leo Panitch for acquainting me with this quote.)

These sentiments do not make the Liberal leader a fascist by any means. However they give us an insight into the motives behind the establishment of the welfare state in Canada, which in fact was closely modelled on Britain's famous Beveridge Report. They also tell us something of the considerations that lay behind Canada's labour laws, which were framed by King early in the century, as well as post-World-War-II amendments. What is notable about them is the extent to which the terms of collective bargaining and unionization in Canada are defined, restricted and in general thoroughly integrated in the legal and penal systems — far more than is the case for many other countries.

* Canada's evolution from colony to nation to dependency has produced a peculiar pattern of economic development in which the objective function of the state has been to foster a satellite economy that is an extension of a larger metropolitan economic system. The sheer dominance of foreign capital over the economy has removed much of the substance of political sovereignty to external decision-making centres. To a large degree, the policies of the Canadian state are adjustments, reactions or supplements to policies set elsewhere. As I elaborate in Part II, the dominance of foreign capital has also fragmented political power in Canada by strengthening the authority of the provinces and weakening the authority of the federal government.

these interests will, in the final analysis, benefit from state involvement. Because of the corporate ownership of the means of production, Meynard writes,

> . . . all the measures taken by the state to develop and improve the national economy always end up by being of the greatest benefit to those who control the levers of command of the production-distribution sector: when the state cuts tunnels, builds roads, opens up highways or reclaims swamps, it is first of all the owners of the neighbouring lands who reap the rewards. . . . The concept of the "bias of the system" makes it also possible to understand that the measures taken to remedy the derelictions, shortcomings and abuses of capitalism result ultimately, where successful, in the consolidation of the regime. It matters little in this respect that these measures should have been undertaken by men sympathetic or hostile to capitalist interests.[61]

Capitalism has always been governed by men who believe in its virtues or by men who can see no other alternative and therefore seek to modify its worst features.* A basic consensus on the necessity of capitalism does not preclude genuine differences on how it can be managed. Thus there can be and there always have been real distinctions between parties and leaders around the question of the proper degree of state intervention in economic and social life, some wanting more of it and some wanting less. Appearances and rhetoric aside, however, the quarrel revolves around differing conceptions of the best way to manage the same social and economic system, not about radically different social systems. Modern liberalism, social democracy, and conservatism are variations on the same theme.

---

* A striking feature of the Canadian state has been the close tie-up between the so-called political elite and the economic elite. To take just one early example, the board of directors of the old Grand Trunk Railway reads like a list of the Fathers of Confederation. A study of the industrial elite at the turn of the century reveals that no less than one-third held political office at some time in their careers. (See T. W. Acheson, "The Changing Social Origins of the Canadian Industrial Elite 1880-1910," in B. Porter and R. Cuff, *Enterprise and National Development.*) This pattern repeats itself through the era of Mackenzie King (advisor to the Rockefellers), C. D. Howe, Louis St. Laurent, and the Pearson-Trudeau cabinets of Robert Winters, Mitchell Sharp, James Richardson, et al.

No less striking has been the strong links between the upper echelons of the state bureaucracy and the economic elite. This tie-in took a qualitative leap during the reign of C. D. Howe as Minister of Defence during World War II. Howe brought in a large number of top business executives to manage publicly owned enterprises during the war and to set up various regulatory agencies. The pattern has continued to this time. As John Porter, the noted sociologist, has observed: "It was not surprising that a close relationship should develop and career lines became confused between the corporate world and the public service in and around departments which through planning, regulations and defence contracts, came into close contact with industry." *(Vertical Mosaic,* p. 431.)

Viewing capitalist enterprise and the profit system as desirable, or at least necessary, it is easy to see why elected representatives should act to enhance the prosperity and stability of businesses without in any way seeing this as favouring any particular class or group. For, as Miliband has written:

> If the national interest is in fact inextricably bound up with the fortunes of capitalist enterprise, apparent partiality towards it is not really partiality at all. On the contrary, in serving the interests of business and in helping capitalist enterprise to thrive, governments are really fulfilling their exalted role as guardians of the good of all. From this standpoint, the much-derided phrase "What is good for General Motors is good for America" is only defective in that it tends to identify the interests of one particular enterprise with the national interest. But if General Motors is taken to stand for the world of capitalist enterprise as a whole, the slogan is one to which governments in capitalist countries do subscribe, often explicitly. And they do so because they accept the notion that the economic rationality of the capitalist system is synonymous with rationality itself, and that it provides the best possible set of human arrangements in a necessarily imperfect world.[62]

The various incentive programs sponsored by Canadian governments to induce corporations to locate in poorer regions is one illustration of how this general outlook gets translated into practice. DREE is a classic case of the state using corporate enterprise as instrumentalities of government policy. The stated purpose of this and similar programs is to reduce regional inequality, a commendable goal. It is not at all clear that they have succeeded in achieving this goal, but many wealthy corporations have been enriched along the way.

The identity between corporate prosperity and the common good has been brought to light in spectacular fashion during the recent economic crisis, in which all manner of governments, ranging from the Republican administration of the U.S.A. to the Labour Party of Great Britain, have been bailing out large enterprises who are on the verge of bankruptcy. According to *Business Week*, "a visitor from Mars might see little difference between the government and the ailing corporations it is propping up."[63] As the same article points out, "the huge U.S. corporations have become such important centres of jobs and incomes that it does not let any of them shut down or go out of business. It is compelled, therefore, to shape national policy in terms of protecting the great corporations instead of letting the economy make deflationary adjustments." In the days of competition, when there were several hundred producers of automobiles and most every other commodity, the market was allowed to penalize bad judgment and the system emerged stronger then ever as poorly managed enterprises were weeded out. But with the high degree of industrial concentration today, each producer is so important that its collapse would be an economic disaster. *Business Week* concludes that "the willingness of the government to shelter a big corporation from the pain of retrenchment takes the flexibility out of the system. A game in which there are no losers puts no premium on good management or good economic policy. This is one of the reasons the U.S. has developed a chronic inflationary bias."

That some of these companies may be nationalized is indeed possible. But such action under these circumstances cannot be interpreted as a threat to the capitalist system. The classic example is that of our own CNR. Afraid of the implications of bankruptcy for its international credit position and the effect it would have on the Bank of Commerce at home, the government invented another form of what Donald Creighton has called "the railway dole," namely nationalization. Neither Mackenzie and Mann, the two promoters of the railway, nor the Bank of Commerce, who helped finance it, suffered. The two promoters made a fortune from the project in spite of its failure and the Bank of Commerce, which is well represented on the board of the CNR, is still the recipient of government payments.

The growing interdependence of the modern economy has placed a premium on the stable flow of goods and services. We are witnesses to a new attack upon the validity of free collective bargaining and the right to strike in "essential industries." Direct government intervention in disputes between employers and workers is nothing new. It has always tended to occur when antagonism between them endangers the stability of the system, and strikes that endanger the stability of the system are what the current fuss is all about. When the state does intervene, whether by the use of outright violence, coercive back-to-work legislation, or more moderate kinds of mediation, the result almost invariably supports the employer. And this is so regardless of the official reasons invoked to justify the action: law and order, protection of the public interest, national interest, or whatever. The fact that the means of production is in private hands must mean that the ownership class is the ultimate beneficiary of state action to keep the production of goods and services flowing. Similarly, it is precisely when wages begin to encroach upon profits that governments bring to bear the famous fiscal and monetary levers to cool the economy off by causing mass unemployment.* There is nothing neutral about these tools of

---

* Precisely this principle was being illustrated during the heights of the debate over

modern economic management. The public reasons offered to justify these policies may include the health of the economy, the defence of the currency and so on, but this does not alter the fact that they act to weaken the collective bargaining position of labour.

I am not arguing here for a mechanical Marxism that insists that the state always and everywhere serves the interests of "the ruling class." (An even cruder view is that the state merely acts on the instructions of the ruling business circles.) For one thing, there are occasional cleavages within "the ruling class" whereby the interests of one segment conflict with the interests of others. To accomplish the task of managing the affairs of the nation in the best interest of the business class as a whole, the state must have a certain degree of independence from its various components so that it can adjudicate among their different needs. For another, there are circumstances in which other classes or groups can force the state to make concessions to their interests. This has been the main contribution of working-class movements, which have been able to wrest some major improvements in social conditions and, in particular, far greater security for working people and the elderly. There are, of course, limits to these achievements, but as the society grows richer it can better afford to expand its provisions of welfare. These measures have more often than not been forced down the throats of business, which sees in them the sinister signs of "creeping socialism." But once the dust has settled and the immediate battle is over it soon becomes evident that the expansion of the state sector is in no way an anti-capitalist plot and, in fact, is required to preserve the main institutions of the business system from self-destruction.[64]
* It is true, of course, that big business feels anything but unchallenged by the myriad of regulations and controls with which governments intervene into formerly untrammeled operations of the private sector. But this is more a reflection of its ideological blinkers than a sober view of the over-all reality.

In the final analysis, the purpose of the state within capitalist society must be to protect private property, meaning the corporate ownership of the means of production. Private property, as capital,

---

voluntary wage restraint in the spring of 1975 when Finance Minister John Turner noted that the wage and salary share of GNP was approaching 55 per cent, after having fallen to a low of 53.1 per cent in the first half of 1974. It was this gain in labour's share of the total income and the accompanying decline in the share of profits that prompted Turner to warn labour leaders that unless they accepted voluntary wage restraints, he would, in effect, force down wages by instituting a policy of severe fiscal restraint which would slow the economy down and create additional unemployment. *(Winnipeg Free Press,* May 10, 1975.)

* This is not to gloss over the inflationary bias of the mammoth growth of the state sector in recent years, a theme that I examine in subsequent chapters.

is not a thing. It is first and foremost a social relationship between people — between those who own the means of production and therefore dispose of the labour of others and those who own only their labour. Consequently, it is also a power relationship. It is the right to reap private benefit from the control over the means of production and, control over the labour power that operates it, and to utilize the marketplace for personal enrichment.

The element of power and privilege that is embodied in the institution of private property is invariably passed over in silence in favour of its purely functional aspects. Land, Labour and Capital are ordinarily treated as nothing more than "factors of production" which are co-ordinated by impersonal market forces. As Samuelson-Scott explain it, "where a democracy does not like the For Whom pattern that results from *laissez-faire* it puts in tax changes, education and other expenditures, fiats and subsidies to change the pattern. This helps some incomes, some property and hurts others."[65] According to this view there are few if any constraints placed upon the distribution of income by a productive apparatus that is based on private property. If "society" is willing to "distort incentives" and "lessen efficiency" in order to realize "notions of equity and greater equality of opportunity" it can do so through the political system.

This view of reality assumes that land, labour and capital are simply functional parts of a production mechanism whose rewards can be altered at will outside the marketplace. The view that I am proposing asserts that these are categories of social existence and a social relationship that necessarily bring with them vast differences in life chances which can only be tampered with at the margin. In sum, capitalism (more precisely, the particular relationship that land, labour, and capital take in a capitalistic society) as a functional system results in a structure of wealth and income that is a system of privilege. It is a structure in which the top one per cent of all Canadian income earners own between them about 50 per cent of all corporate wealth, and the top two per cent of all income recipients enjoy incomes that are roughly eight to ten times larger than the average received within the nation as a whole.

Such concentration of wealth and disparities of income can be found in greater or lesser measure in most other societies in history. What marks off capitalism from these other societies is that these inequalities are mainly a function of the economic system rather than being derived mainly from war, plunder, and coercion. Relationships of power and privilege are in full view in a slave society or a feudal society. In the slave society, labour itself is the property of masters, and therefore everything that is produced is also their property. In feudal societies, serfs are required to give their lords several months of compulsory and unremunerated labour as well as a portion of their crops. Capitalism liberates people from this kind of direct subordination. In its place is the free wage contract. Workers sell their labour power for a wage agreed upon by employers. Why this remains a power relation is that workers' labour power is useless unless it is combined with tools, machinery, and raw materials. As these become concentrated in the hands of relatively few, the bargaining position of the ownership class is much the stronger.

If all individuals owned their own capital, none would be compelled to sell his or her labour power to someone else. Hence inequality of capital ownership is fundamental to the capitalist mode of production. As Milton Friedman has written, the principle of income distribution under capitalism is "to each according to what he and the instruments he owns produces."[66] The amount of income each individual receives depends on the labour-power and the capital he owns and the values that are placed on these in the market. The amount of capital a person owns depends on how much he inherits from his family and how much he accumulates himself. Capital is accumulated by individuals who save part of their incomes and invest it in the purchase of new capital. The amount of income a person can save depends on how much income he receives compared to his consumption requirements. The higher one's over-all income, the greater is the surplus that is available for investment in more capital assets. Large owners of capital are clearly at an advantage because they receive sizable incomes from their capital possessions. Inequalities are thus likely to increase over time. This process is further reinforced by virtue of the fact that parents with high incomes can use some of their money to invest in longer and better education for their children, thus adding to their earning power in the labour market.*

While the dynamics of income distribution is far more complicated than can be shown here,[67] it is possible to conclude at least this

---

* Samuelson-Scott attempted a neat distinction between profit and wealth: "Much of the hostility towards profit is really hostility toward the extremes of inequality in the distribution of money income that comes from unequal factor ownership; this attitude to wealth should be kept distinct from hostility toward profit created by imperfections of the competitive process." (pp. 746-7) Here again the authors insist on regarding capital (wealth) as a function, with profit as its reward. They exhort us to blame the extremes of inequalities on the imperfections of competition as if (a) these imperfections did not arise from the normal functioning of the system, (b) the receipt of large profits did not result in further inequalities of "factor ownership" which results in further "inequalities in the distribution of money income," and (c) such inequalities in either "factor ownership" and in "money income" could be simply reformed away.

much, that capital is a highly valuable possession that its owners will do their utmost to protect. These underlying factors that set the distribution of income and privileges in motion are so basic that they go largely unnoticed. What we observe are the public battles over minimum wage, taxes, welfare, and collective bargaining. The more fundamental forces of the supply and demand of privately-owned factors of production are so totally embedded in the social structure that we tend to forget that they are even there. Moreover, privilege and power is much less visible under capitalism than under other systems because it is limited mainly to advantages that derive from the economic structure of society. However one-sidedly it is administered, the same civil and criminal law and the same duties in war and peace apply to all individuals — in contrast to the differing system of law and duties that apply to the privileged and unprivileged in other societies.

The productive energies released by capitalism, which have created so much wealth and have permitted our living standards to rise to such unprecedented levels, further blind us to the basic inequality of the relationship. Indeed, the wealth of modern capitalism could not have been created without this inequality — for under capitalism it is the reinvestment of the surplus incomes of the rich that has built the productive capacity that helps produce society's wealth. Now that it has created the full infrastructure of an industrial society, it has completed its historic mission and can have no further justification. As this realization begins to take hold and others stake their claim to a larger share of that wealth, the state is forced to intervene more persistently, even violently, if need be, to preserve the *status quo.*

Liberal democracies take for granted that the fundamental issues bearing upon the nature and distribution of power have been settled. They are generally codified in written constitutions and as such are not subject to public debate, let alone changes through the parliamentary system. These are the foundations upon which the political economy operates, and are therefore not susceptible to democratic change. Democratic elections cannot, by themselves, settle anything of vital importance, by which I mean issues of political and economic life and death. At best they result in adjustments within the *status quo.** Liberal democracy serves to institutionalize class conflict and guide it along peaceful paths. But when the electoral system, even with its manipulative devices to stave off the opposition, fails to defend the system, the capitalist class does not fail to move with force to secure it. The raw power of the state flashed momentarily into view during the month of Common

---

* I discuss this point at length in the final chapter of this book.

Front actions in Quebec and more permanently in Guatemala, Greece, and Chile when all pretence of democracy was abandoned as the elected governments of Arbenz, Papandreou, and Allende were summarily overthrown and the *status quo ante* was re-established by military regimes.

In the words of political theorist Hans J. Morgenthau:

> Insofar as the popular challenge to the status quo is feeble, the democratic procedures are irrelevant to the fundamental issues that agitate society. Insofar as that challenge is perceived as a genuine threat by the ruling elite, the democratic procedures will be shunted aside if it appears to be necessary for the defence of the status quo. Thus the lack of consensus on the fundamentals of power in society renders government with the consent of the governed, that is democracy, either irrelevant or obsolete. The opposition turns its back on democracy because democracy withholds the chance to get what it wants. The powers that be dispense with democratic procedures because they fear to lose what they have.[68]

Morgenthau insists that the really important decisions are made neither by the people at large nor by the official government "but by the private governments where effective power rests. . . ." While Morgenthau may go too far in downgrading the role of the state in co-ordinating and ultimately protecting the economic and social status quo, he is unquestionably right when he argues that men and women throughout the world have been disappointed in their expectation that their well-being would be advanced through the democratic republic. The conclusions he draws from the existence of this vacuum of faith in the prevailing order are far-reaching:

> No civilized government that is not founded on such a faith and rational expectation can endure in the long run. This vacuum will either be filled by a new faith carried by new social forces that will create new political institutions and procedures commensurate with the new tasks; or the forces of the status quo threatened with disintegration will use their vast material powers to try to reintegrate society through totalitarian manipulation of the citizens' minds and the terror of physical compulsion. The former alternative permits us at least the hope of preservation and renewal of the spirit of democracy.[69]

It is my conviction also that we have urgent new tasks before us; that the present political-economic system is incapable of undertaking these tasks; that in attempting to preserve the existing arrangements, it will increasingly be forced to resort to authoritarian measures; and that we must organize ourselves to resist such attacks while preparing the way for "new political institutions and procedures commensurate with the new tasks."

II/The Political Economy of Canada

To understand the economy of a country you must place it within the larger economic system of which it is a part. Capitalism is a global economic system with one or a few metropolitan centres. These can shift about from century to century, as has in fact occurred — from Holland to Spain, France, England, Germany, Japan, and the U.S.A. In chain-like fashion, capitalism extends from the metropoles to their satellites. Any economic analysis must start by locating a country within this chain. No capitalist country is autonomous. It is linked to other parts of a single economic system. In particular, the economic advancement of one country is not unrelated to the economic impoverishment of other countries. Overdevelopment and underdevelopment are the opposite sides of the same coin.

The concept can also be applied within countries. The underdevelopment of some regions is usually linked with the overdevelopment of other regions. "Probably the most interesting way to write the history of Canada," writes Mel Watkins, "is to write the history of Ontario: look up the chain and you see New York — at least if you sit in Toronto that is what you see. Then look down the chain and you see the Atlantic provinces, the Prairie provinces (and further down, the Caribbean and Brazil)." The overdevelopment of Ontario is the other side of the coin to the underdevelopment of rural, northern and fishing communities in Canada's Prairie, Atlantic and Northern regions.

The underdevelopment of hinterlands and the overdevelopment of metropolitan centres is a universal feature of capitalist economic development. Examples of the former include: the Maritimes, Quebec, and the Prairies in Canada; the South and the Appalachians in the United States; Flanders in Belgium; the south and the east of the Low Countries; the centre and the southwest of France, Ireland, and Great Britain; southern Italy; Bavaria, and large parts of the centre, north, and east of Germany.

The existence of regions of stagnation has played an important role in the economic history of capitalist countries. As is well known, growth under capitalism occurs sporadically rather than evenly, in spurts rather than in a gradual climb. A sudden spasm of growth requires a surplus labour force which can be mobilized at reasonable wages. Depressed regions furnish a reserve army of labour that is mobile and available at relatively low wages. But they also serve as an important market for the products of rich regions. Primary producing regions buy more from industrial regions than they sell to them. A process is set in motion whereby the resources and wealth of the poor, underdeveloped regions are drained off and transferred to the overdeveloped region.

In Canada the flow has been from the provinces to Ontario, and from Ontario to the United States. The provinces are hinterlands of Toronto. They house the local branches and serve their own hinterlands. Toronto is the national depot that collects both money and talent from the provinces and ships them out to the American metropolis.

Tom Naylor, a Canadian economic historian, distinguishes four stages of empire.[1] Those built on the multinational corporation are the highest stage of imperialism. *Mercantile empires* are based on looting and piracy and also on the extraction of primary staples from colonial lands, with mercantile companies regulated by the imperial governments. *Lassez faire empires* are based on the free exchange of staples and finished products. In both cases, profits are appropriated through market exchanges that are tilted in favour of the metropolitan economy.

Empires that are built on portfolio investments extract their wealth from interest payments on loans. These three stages of empire are built on the slender frame of the family firm, which did not have the administrative structure to move enterprises between countries. The best it could do was to move commodities and loan capital.

It was the rise of the national corporation that opened up new possibilities of transferring production and marketing organizations abroad. These *direct investment empires* are founded on the take-over of the actual production process abroad. Unlike portfolio investment empires, which are self-liquidating as the loans are paid back, direct investment grows on its own volition, as a portion of the profits generated by subsidiaries are reinvested in the hinter-land regions.

The multinational corporation, the instrument of the new imperialism, is on a collision course with the nation-state. The two are not compatible. The sales of multinationals typically exceed the total production of most countries. Backed up by the metropolian government, they have more power than many of the nation-states they deal with. They can usually shift and adjust within their global operations so as to avoid the restrictions placed upon them by host governments. They can render ineffective their fiscal, monetary, and commercial policies.

This has been the Canadian dilemma for some years. Foreign direct investment and international trade are the transmission belts by which American inflation and American recession are imported into this country. The two economies are so intertwined that the government of Canada has lost the capacity to direct the economic affairs of the nation. This capacity has been further weakened by the balkanization of the Canadian economy into identifiable sub-regions that directly serve the American metropolis without the necessary mediation of the federal government. The overwhelming presence of the multinational corporation has tended to fragment Canada economically and politically.

Multinational corporations integrate one industry vertically over many countries. The alternative to this kind of global corpo-rate planning is to integrate horizontally many industries within one country by means of a national plan, and to develop non- cor-porate linkages between countries for the flow of goods, services, and information. Technology can serve either system equally well. The trend is towards the first alternative, but as somebody once observed, countries like France and Great Britain existed long before the multinational corporation and it would be unwise to assume that they will not survive them.

The Multinationals Emerge

The structure of business enterprise has its own history which affects the entire character of the political economy of capitalism. It began with the small family firm in which the proprietor performed the function of financier, entrepreneur, and supervisor of produc-tion and distribution. Under the impact of the new technology of mass production, the family firm gave way, in the modern sector of the economy, to the national corporation. Its chief characteristic was its elaborate and specialized administrative structure, which could better utilize the physical and social sciences and co-ordinate mass production and distribution in geographically dispersed plants and sales outlets. It is precisely here, in the field of business administration, that U.S. capitalism took the lead over Europe, Canada and rival nations elsewhere.

It was a short step from here to the multiproduct national enterprise which required further sophistication in management techniques. By now U.S. corporations had the centralized administrative brain-power which could allow them to organize production and sales on a global scale.

In the graphic terms of the late Stephen Hymer:

> The Marshalian [i.e. family] capitalist ruled his factory from an office in the second floor. At the turn of the century, the president of a large national corporation was lodged in a higher building, say on the seventh floor, with wider perspectives and greater power. In the giant corporation of today, managers rule from the top of skyscrapers; on a clear day, they can almost see the world.[2]

This organizational revolution is a necessary condition for the phenomenon known as the multinational corporation. But it is not a sufficient condition. What further compels businesses to go multinational is the condition of expansion that prevails under monopoly capitalism. Continuous expansion is, of course, the *sine qua non* of capitalist production. As the annual report of one major corporation makes clear,

> the only real security for this company or any other company is through healthy, continuous and vigorous growth. A company is like a human being. When it stops growing, when it can't replenish itself through growth, then it starts to deteriorate. . . . There is no security where there is no opportunity for growth and development and continuous improvement.[3]

In the case of the small competitive firm, it is presumed that the company can sell all that it can produce at the prevailing price. It cannot influence its price, but it can raise its profits by cutting costs and introducing improved technology. This is the path that expansion takes. Those who follow this path prosper and grow, while those who falter fall by the wayside.

As the small competitive firm expands in size and begins to produce a sizable proportion of industry output, its path of expansion changes in a significant way. Each of a few large firms must now take into account the effect of changes in its output on the market price. A firm that supplies 30 per cent of the industry output, for example, cannot expect that it can increase its production and sales by, say, 10 per cent without having to lower its price. It can still raise its profits by reducing cost but it cannot increase its output faster than the increase of the market demand unless it is willing to lower its prices. In order to expand, the monopolistic firm is therefore driven to seek new markets and to manufacture new products beyond its traditional field of operations. This compulsion to diversify geographically and industrially is the greater the more profits the monopolistic firm disposes over and wishes to capitalize. Thus the need to become a conglomerate and/or a multinational corporation — producing a variety of unrelated products and/or in a variety of national markets.

Pressures emanating from the need to find new investment outlets for surplus funds are not the only explanation for foreign investment. Capital will move to low-wage areas where it can better exploit labour and secure other cost advantages. Tariffs imposed by foreign governments may make it more profitable to set up branch-plants than to export. And once one leading corporation sets up operations in a foreign country, rivals in the same industry are quick to follow suit to secure for themselves a significant share of the local market.

The era of the multinational corporation represents a dramatic increase in the concentration of private economic power — more precisely of American private power. While 200 of the largest multinational corporations in the world are American-based, only 20 or 30 operate out of other countries. It has been conjectured that approximately 300 multinational corporations alone will control one-third of the output of the non-communist world by 1987, comprising more than half of the world's goods and services.[4] Already the multinationals account for one-fifth of the non-Communist world's GNP. And since the multinationals are not responsible for the wide range of social health and educational and military services that are the responsibility of national governments, their one-fifth is really a far more decisive sector of economic activity.

While it is true that European investment in the U.S.A. is about the same as U.S. investment in Europe, the form of that investment is fundamentally different. Seventy per cent of European investment is in U.S. stocks and bonds, while 80 per cent of U.S. investment in Europe is direct investment through American-owned affiliates. General Motors makes decisions that affect wages, employment, prices, and investment in Great Britain, whereas a British stock-holder in General Motors makes no decisions at all.

Multinational corporations control 60 per cent of Canadian manufacturing and 65 per cent of mining and smelting output. U.S.

investment represents only 4 per cent of the total investment in Western Europe but the influence of U.S.-based multinational corporations is underestimated by such aggregate figures, for their activity tends to be concentrated in the most vital economic sectors. American corporations control over 30 per cent of Europe's automobile industry, 50 per cent of Germany's and Belgium's oil industry, 90 per cent of the French computer industry.

The totality of U.S. foreign assets abroad has increased from $31.5 billion in 1950 to $170 billion in 1970. The largest single factor in this growth has been the rise of investment of U.S.-based multinational companies. Even the U.S. secretary of State conceded that:

> U.S. foreign investors have been hyperbolically characterized as the "world's third greatest power." Tensions are greatest when U.S. controlled MNC's take over established industries and concentrate in the advanced sectors of the economy. Developing countries, too, worry about the large size of MNC's in relation to their own economies.[5]

It is self-evident that organizing production, marketing and finance on a global scale must confer significant advantages to firms. These are distinguished by David Rutenberg, an employee, aptly enough, of the Carnegie-Mellon University.[6] "Production planning in a multinational company poses the opportunity to build plants so that the total world-wide production and transportation costs are minimized." As these plants are often located in "unstable nations," vulnerability to nationalization is reduced by disposing subproducts over several independent nations. "Liquid assets may be moved between pairs of subsidiaries as dividends, inter-subsidiary loans, managerial fees and royalties, and manipulated transfer process." Similarly it is in a position of being able to shift its locations to minimize its global tax bill in ways not available to national companies. Also, "the multinational company has potential access to all capital markets in the world. To the extent that the company can move money between nations, it can stand aloof from the monetary policy of individual nations and raise capital from the cheapest sources anywhere." Finally, in marketing, "a multinational company has an advantage over a collection of national companies in being able to use national markets as test markets for other nations."

While this is a good list which I would not quarrel with, it is by no means the whole story. What it leaves out of account is the enormous power of the multinationals which dwarfs that of the governments they deal with. A recent U.N. survey held that "the general conclusion that many multinational corporations are bigger than a large number of entire national economies remains valid. Thus, the value added by each of the top ten multinational corporations in 1971 was in excess of $3 billion or greater than the gross national product of over 80 countries."[7] What gives them the advantages Rutenberg cites in playing one country off against another to obtain the most favourable conditions is their power to withhold investments or access to markets from economies that are smaller than their own operations. The arrangements that these companies make with nation-states are not called treaties, but in terms of their significance for international affairs they are on a par with agreements between nations. And while the power of the multinational corporation is great, "it is impossible to overestimate the extent to which the efforts and opportunities for American firms abroad depend upon the vast presence and influence and prestige that America holds in the world, . . . [and] the extent to which they benefit from our commitments, tangible and intangible, to furnish economic assistance to those in need and to defend the frontiers of freedom. . . . In fact if we were to contemplate abandoning those frontiers and withholding our assistance . . . I wonder not whether the opportunities for private American enterprise would wither — I wonder only how long it would take."[8] This essential point made by Henry Fowler, as U.S. Secretary of the Treasury, is further explained:

> Let no one forget the crucial importance to the multinational corporation of a United States government that commands world respect for its economic and military progress as well as for its commitment to the highest human ideals — a United States government whose political, diplomatic and military strength is fully commensurate with its role as a leader of the free world . . . for let us understand that the United States government has consistently sought, and will continue to seek to expand and extend the role of the multinational corporation as an essential instrument of strong and healthy economic progress through the Free World.[9]

The multinational corporation is thus a mechanism for the penetration of the U.S.A. into the economic life of other nations, largely determining their investment, wage, price and marketing patterns. As one author has said, "There really is another U.S.A. out there."[10]

The reason why the multinationals are so enthusiastically supported by the diplomatic and military arsenals of the American state is not difficult to discover. They are, to be sure, an "essential instrument of strong and healthy economic progress through the

Free World" (that is, the capitalist world). But more particularly, foreign direct investments are very profitable for American capitalism. According to the U.N. study, the gap between money invested in the Third World and that taken out has been increasing substantially. By 1970 almost 4 billion more dollars were taken out of the underdeveloped countries as income on previous investment than were being put back into them in the form of new investments.[11] That $4 billion made an important contribution to the troubled U.S. balance of payments, and it was twice as large as all the foreign aid offered by the U.S.A.

Foreign investment is important to more than a handful of U.S. companies. Virtually every leading American corporation is multinational. The same corporations that dominate the U.S. economy dominate the world economy. Among the top 250 world industrials listed by *Fortune,* all of which are multinational, 150 are based in the United States.*

Top 250 World Industrials by Nation, 1971

United States	150	Australia	2
Japan	21	Belgium	2
Germany	20	Netherlands	2
Britain	19	Neth.-Britain	2
France	14	Brazil	1
Italy	4	Luxembourg	1
Switzerland	4	Mexico	1
Sweden	3	Britain-Italy	1
Canada	3	TOTAL	250

The U.N. survey found that a corporation like the Heinz Company receives about half of its profits from the direct returns on its foreign operations. U.S. Steel gets 62 per cent of its profits from its foreign operations, Exxon over 50 per cent, Ford and Chrysler 24 per cent each, and foreign profits are even the key to General Motors, providing a fifth of its total profits.[12] The importance of profits earned abroad cannot be mechanistically measured in terms of their relationship to the American gross national product, but rather in terms of what they represent to these and other corporations that control the American economy.[13]

Direct earnings from abroad do not indicate the full extent to which multinational corporations benefit from their foreign operations. Most of the exports by U.S. companies are conducted through their foreign subsidiaries, which are often required to pay

---

* It is interesting to note that the largest "Canadian" industrial, Alcan, is controlled from the United States. The fourth largest "Canadian" industrial, Inco, is also U.S.-controlled.

abnormally high prices for these products. *Business Week* magazine explains the point:

> The goal in the multinational corporation is the greatest good for the whole unit, even if the interests of a single part of the unit must suffer. One large manufacturer, for example, penalizes some of its overseas subsidiaries for the good of the total corporation by forcing them to pay more than necessary for parts they import from the parent and from other subsidiaries.[14]

A manufacturing subsidiary could lose money and still make a net contribution to the parent company's income — by the profit on purchases of raw material, parts, and finished products from the parent, by payment of royalties and fees from management, marketing, and research services. Hearings before the U.S. Senate Committee on Ways and Means in 1961 demonstrated that the major purpose of mány subsidiaries is not to make a large profit themselves, but to contribute to the profit maximization of the parent firm by providing an automatic export market for equipment, materials and parts.

The case of Proctor & Gamble is typical. During the 10-year period of 1951-61, its capital outflow from the U.S. was $11 million. Its income from subsidiaries over the same period was $290 million. The bulk of this income came in the form of sales of raw materials and equipment and new products to the subsidiaries ($243 million); only $47 million was received in the form of dividends. And, as the Chairman of Proctor & Gamble, Neil McElroy, pointed out, net export of capital from the U.S. comprised only a small portion of the investment of the foreign branch-plants. The subsidiaries reinvested out of profits and borrowed from local financial institutions $67 million. This is over six times the contribution made by capital exported by the parent company.

An executive of the Joy Manufacturing Company explained for the Committee how direct investment abroad increases parent company exports:

> The surprising volume of exports to our foreign subsidiaries results first from the sale, from parent factories, of critical components of machines made abroad and, second from Joy International's constant pressure on each subsidiary to import new Joy products brought out by the parent company.
>
> I must emphasize that without these foreign subsidiaries operating as they do, our exports would be only a fraction of what we see here.[15]

It may not appear clear why a practice which reduces the profits of subsidiaries can nevertheless contribute more-than-compensatory increases of profits to the parent company. It might be explained in this way. Most giant manufacturing corporations earn no profits at all over much of their output. Before they earn any profits, they must produce beyond a certain level of output, usually referred to as "the break-even point." This is because of the large overhead capital which yields high per-unit costs for low levels of output. For example, a study of U.S. Steel Co. showed that the break-even point is 40 per cent of capacity. At 100 per cent of productive capacity the rate of profit is 13 per cent. But it is the last 15 per cent of the corporation's output that accounts for 35 per cent of its profits. Since exports by the typical giant American corporation account for anywhere between 5 per cent and 20 per cent of its total output, these can be of crucial importance for the overall profitability of the corporation. Exports to foreign subsidiaries thus account for a disproportionate share of the profits of parent corporations. Any resulting increased production costs to subsidiaries and correspondingly reduced subsidiary-profits are a small price to pay for the major contribution subsidiaries make as markets for output which could only be absorbed by the U.S. domestic market through lowering prices.

The Age of the Multinationals

The name "multinational" is a cause for some confusion. It suggests the transcendence of ugly national rivalries and the possibility of a new development towards one-worldism. This has been suggested in so many words by its proponents. The former Under-Secretary of the State, George Ball, for example, in addressing the U.S. Chambers of Commerce has stated: "The multinational corporation is ahead of, and in conflict with existing political organizations represented by the nation state."[16] As Ball and others see it, the multinational corporation is a unifying force throughout the world, the catalyst of a global government.

The one sense in which this phenomenon is multinational is that it operates in a number of nations. In all other respects it is a national corporation. With two known exceptions, Royal Dutch Shell and Unilever, ownership and control are located in one nation. Strategic functions of the global enterprise are centralized in the home headquarters: long-range investment planning, finance, including how the profits of subsidiaries are to be utilized, and research and development. Production and marketing are decentralized on a regional basis. The late Stephen Hymer wrote about the social and political implications of this kind of international specialization.

One would expect to find the highest offices of the multinational corporations concentrated in the world's major cities — New York, Paris, Bonn, Tokyo. These, along with Moscow and perhaps Peking, will be the major centres of high-level strategic planning. Lesser cities throughout the world will deal with the day-to-day operations of specific local problems. These in turn will be arranged in a hierarchical fashion: the larger and more important ones will contain regional corporate headquarters, while the smaller ones will be confined to lower level activities. Since business is usually the core of the city, geographical specialization will come to reflect the hierarchy of corporate decision-making and the occupational distribution of labor in a city or region will depend upon its function in the international economic system. The "best" and most highly paid administrators, doctors, lawyers, scientists, educators, government officials, actors, servants and hairdressers, will tend to concentrate in or near the major centres.[17]

Through the kind of global unity spawned by the multinational corporation, which Hymer called the New Imperial System, income, status, authority and consumption patterns radiate out from the centres in a declining fashion and hinterland regions are denied independence and equality. And while attaching the local economies to the metropolitan centres, the multinational corporations open up new social divisions within these dependencies. The upper and middle strata, which may comprise one-quarter of their populations and receive 60 per cent or more of the total income, provide the multinationals with their labour force and their markets. The integration of this indigenous ruling class and foreign investors represents a formidable alliance against the remaining three-quarters of the population which in turn is the source of an unlimited supply of cheap labour for services and manual work.

Osvaldo Sunkel, a U.N. economist, describes the multinational corporation as "a kind of 'fifth column'" transferring the loyalty of a significant part of the national bourgeoisie away from their own country to the parent company, for it is within the multinational corporation that they have been trained to rise, not within the nation-state: ". . . this process . . . prevents the formation of a national entrepreneurial class . . . and even creates privileged and underprivileged sectors within the working class, adding another serious difficulty to the creation of a strong labour movement."[18] The social and economic divisions that accompany the penetration of local economies by the multinational corporation is not confined to the Third World. The same forces can be seen to be operating in Canada with its truncated economy, weak industrial entrepreneurship, and divided trade union movement.

One-third of U.S. direct foreign investment is in the underdeveloped countries. Much of the new investment is no longer concentrated on plantations and mines. It has been spreading to manufacturing and services. In Central America, fully 30 per cent of total manufacturing output is produced by foreign subsidiaries.[19] These investments and others in the Third World would not have been possible without the system of bank credits and military and economic aid sponsored by the American state as well as its vast network of advisors, military bases, CIA-arranged coups, and, ultimately, the threat of military intervention. One of the reasons why a country like Canada is so highly valued by the Americans is that ours is one of the few stable and friendly countries with extensive undeveloped resources as well as a growing market. As such, no expensive support system to guarantee easy access is required. The American state has been satisfied that the Canadian state is capable and can be trusted to protect U.S. property here.

In the world as it is constituted today, there can be no supranational state. Capitalism has always had a flag. In its earliest stages the rising merchant bourgeoisie allied itself with the monarchy against the feudal nobility. In return for helping them finance their campaign against feudal lords and rival kingdoms, the monarchs rewarded the merchants with monopoly charters that excluded foreign merchants from domestic soil, and they lent them their armies to secure access to foreign markets. As capitalism developed within these national frameworks, the power of an increasingly industrial bourgeoisie grew to the point where they were able to reduce the monarchs to figureheads or eliminate them entirely and take control of the state apparatus to match their control over the economy. The relationship between capitalism and the state has not basically changed since then. In the final analysis, the state remains both the shield and the sword of capitalism.

There are, of course, severe conflicts within the new global system — the national rivalry between major capitalist countries, as some of these begin to challenge the leadership of the U.S.A.; the threat posed by the frustrated middle classes and excluded groups in the underdeveloped countries; more generally, the inevitable collision between the multinational corporation and the foreign countries within which they operate. The "internationalism" espoused by America is understood in many countries as simply an expression of American nationalism with the multinational corporations as its key instrument.

The most fundamental requirement of the MNCs is freedom to do business whenever and wherever they choose, unrestricted by governmental authorities, freedom to move capital, materials, technology, and technicians without regard for national boundaries. "But nations cannot grant these sweeping freedoms without denying their essence as nations, i.e., as collectivities with pretensions to sovereignty, which mean simply the right to run their own affairs without interference from those outside the nation."[20] As Canadians are finding out, the effectiveness of government policy instruments such as monetary and fiscal policy, taxation, wage, and income policy diminish when important segments of the economy are foreign-owned. Multinational corporations, because of their size and flexibility, can usually escape the regulations of any one nation. The integration of the world economy through the multinational corporation has even placed limits on the effectiveness of U.S. government policies.

In an essay that is remarkably prophetic, the late Stephen Hymer asked:

> If national power is eroded, who is to perform the government's functions? For example, if nation-states, because of the openness of their economy, cannot control the level of aggregate economic activity through traditional monetary and fiscal policy instruments, multinational agencies will need to be developed to maintain full employment and price stability. Yet such organizations do not exist at present, nor can they be built quickly. Either one must argue that the Keynesian problem (along with a host of other problems) has somehow been solved by the creation of the multinational corporation or else one must agree that it is not feasible to have international business integration via direct foreign investment proceeding at a much faster rate than political integration. Yet, this seems to be precisely what is happening.[21]

The Keynesian problem of unemployment and inflation has not been solved. The integration of the world economy has eroded the ability of the nation-state to control aggregate economic activity. Multinational public planning agencies have not developed. Here is a hint of the explanation of the economic crisis of today.

Staples and Empire

Canadian economic history may be understood in terms of its evolution through the four stages of empire elucidated by Naylor, the first three as a colony under the French and British and the last stage as a dependency of the U.S.A.

It is the pattern of empire that defines the particular character of the economic development of hinterland areas. Changes in the organization of the hinterland do not occur independently but are rather a consequence of changes in the pattern of empire. Naylor outlines this relationship:

> From the structure of the metropole, its dominant class, its stage of development and the structure of capital, and its external requirements, we can deduce the character of the imperial linkage. From the form of the imperial linkage follows the political economy of the hinterland and the degree and pattern of development. From the political economy of the hinterland the nature, horizons and policy of its dominant class can be deduced. The dominant class is directly dependent on the metropole; other classes, in contrast, are defined by their productive relationships with the dominant class and thus are related only indirectly to the metropolitan class structure.[22]

Our economic history can also be divided into separate periods, each one depending on the export of a particular kind of resource product. The first period, lasting for over a hundred years until the early 1800s, was the era of the fur and fish trade. The second, lasting until well into the nineteenth century, was the era of timber and lumbering. The third, from the turn of the century until the early 1920s, was characterized by the wheat boom. The fourth was based on pulp and paper. The fifth, beginning in the 1950s and continuing to the present day, is the era of petroleum and metal mining, including iron ore, nickel, aluminum and the like. General economic prosperity in each period depends on the export of these key resources and their related products. These staple products are the basis of economic expansion; all other economic activity is derivative. In each case the growth of external demand was the key. Hinterlands are, by definition, suppliers of raw materials to more advanced industrial nations. The nature of the particular staple product had much to do with the definition and the content of the imperial relationship.[23]

In the first phase of empire which arose in the era of commercial capitalism under the old mercantile system, the relationship between metropole and hinterland was a colonial one governed by a set of regulations enacted into law that ensured that the colony would remain a supplier of raw materials and a market base of the metropole. When fur, fish, and timber were the main staple products, Canada was a hinterland of the French and subsequently the British colonial systems. Metropolitan merchants, financiers and trading houses were the key imperial agents. During the wheat and lumber period of the 1850s and the prairie wheat boom half a century later, foreign investment, tied to trade and railways, was largely loaned by British financial houses to Canadian companies who developed some degree of autonomy. With the rapid depletion of U.S. resources, Canada was converted into an American continental hinterland supplying first lumber, then pulp and paper and minerals, to feed her industrial mills. Branch-plant manufacturing operations to supply the Canadian consumer market and that of the British Empire were a parallel development. The key imperial agent became the multinational corporation, and foreign investment now gave economic control to giant American companies. In this last stage, imperial subservience is no longer the result of colonial control but of economic dependence.

Canada's business class has been dominated historically by finance and merchant capitalists who have made their profits on the export of staple products and the import of manufactured goods. Their "horizons and policies" were set by the possibilities that emerged during the four stages of development within an imperial system. For well over a century the economic foundation of Canada rested on fur. The fur trade nurtured the first indigenous class of capitalists around the North West Company and the Hudson's Bay Company. It ceased to be the centre of economic activity in Canada when the fur country south of the Great Lakes was transferred to the U.S.A. (1783) and secured by them finally in the War of 1812. The fur merchants of Montreal switched their capital into the entrepôt trade, banking, and timber. They also made fortunes speculating on land given to them by the Crown and purchased from the seigneuries. They turned their sights to capturing the trade between the American midwest and Britain. Their vehicle was the St. Lawrence River. But the St. Lawrence lost out to an American waterway system; New York was triumphant over Montreal. New York capital, which built the Erie Canal and a railway network, dwarfed the amount of capital that Montreal merchants could raise from their British backers and from Crown subsidies and grants. The abolition of the Corn Laws in 1846 ended the preferential treatment for Canadian grain in the British market and together with the folding of the square timber trade, doomed whatever chance Montreal had of dislodging New York as the entrepôt centre between the new world and the old.

During the 1830s, democratic movements arose to challenge the rule of the merchant class. They brought together the grievances of farmers, French Canadians, and the emerging industrial bourgeoisie, who were more interested in developing local markets than long distance trade. Their demand for liberal democracy, couched in terms of "responsible government," ended in civil war in 1837 but the rebellion was easily defeated. The dismantling of the British mercantile system soon led to the granting of responsible government by the British. These developments led many of the merchants to abandon their fervent loyalty to Britain and seek an alternative imperial power with which they could be linked. The annexation manifesto of 1849 was a foretaste of things to come.

Unable to capture the intercontinental trade, seemingly abandoned by Great Britain, sectionally split, with agricultural settlements in Upper Canada reaching the limit of good land, and without the resources and the imagination to open up the Canadian West, the merchants began their campaign to attach the Canadian economy to the developing metropolis of the U.S.A. The Reciprocity Treaty which lasted from 1854 and 1864 opened up the American market for Canadian raw materials and the Canadian market for U.S.-manufactured products. It was an arrangement which, in one form or another, would survive until today. Maritime fish merchants were quick to shift to the U.S. market and, in much of what is now Ontario, there was an assault of major proportions on Canadian forests to supply lumber to the expanding cities of the mid-western United States.

North American integration was temporarily disrupted by the American Civil War. The hostility of Washington towards Britain and its colonies led to American cancellation of the agreement upon its expiry. Once again rejected by an imperial power, the Canadian merchant and finance classes grasped what seemed like the only available alternative — launching their own empire by consolidating and unifying the British colonies of North America and expanding to the west.* They employed the conventional mercantile instruments: political unity through confederation, economic unity through tariffs, and a national transportation system.

---

* Confederation was conceived as an instrument of empire by more than one participant in the Confederation debates. George Brown, in particular, defined the urgency of occupying the northwest as a race with the Americans. The northwest could become the hinterland of a grand Canadian empire, but if the Canadians did not take up the task quickly, it would fall to the American empire: "The non-occupation of the North West Territory is a blot upon our character for enterprise. We are content to play the drone while others are working. We settle down quietly within the petty limits of a province while a great empire is offered to our ambition. If Canada acquires this territory it will rise in a few years from a position of a small and weak province to be the greatest colony any country has possessed. . . . The wealth of 400,000 square miles of territory will flow through our waters and be gathered by our merchants, manufacturers and agriculturalists. Our sons will occupy the chief places of this vast territory, we will form its institutions, supply its rulers, teach its schools, fill its stores, run its mills, navigate its streams. . . . If we allow the North West to slip from our grasp and to pass into the possession of the U.S., if all the rest of the continent outside of Canada and the Atlantic provinces acknowledges the sway of the republic, we should be unable to contend with her. Our ultimate absorption would be a foregone conclusion."

By World War I, when this "national policy" had reached its height, the logic of its design had become clear. The British North America Act was a creature of an imperial system which accorded great power and fiscal authority to a central government and little power and few sources of finance to lower levels of government. With all instruments of control concentrated in the federal government, which was the government of the dominant merchant and finance capitalists, policies to strengthen their position and financial support from British banking houses were assured. It got them what they wanted: a transcontinental railway to link the potential wheat lands of the Canadian west to Montreal, the promotion of immigration to cultivate the lands and a system of tariffs to force farmers and workers to purchase their manufactured goods from Central Canada.

The American Design

Confederation and the national policy was a blow to American expansionists who had their own continental policy. The dominant influence in American foreign policy in this period and through the 1880s was exercised by the Secretary of State, William Henry Seward. Seward was one of the key architects of the rising American Empire. He based his vision on "a political law — and when I say political law, I mean a higher law, a law of Providence — that empire has, for the last 3,000 years ... made its way constantly westward, and that it must continue to move westward until the tides of the renewed and of the decaying civilizations of the world meet on the shores of the Pacific Ocean."[24]

Seward had in mind an integrated empire including Latin America and Canada as part of the continental base. During the presidential election campaign of 1860, he had this to say about Canada:

> I can stand here and look far off into the Northwest and see the Russian, as he busily occupies himself in establishing seaports and towns and fortifications as outposts of the Empire of St. Petersburg, and I can say, "Go in, build your outposts to the Arctic Ocean. They will yet become the outposts of my country to extend the civilization of the United States in the Northwest." So I look upon Prince Rupert's Land and Canada, and see how an ingenious people are occupied with bridging rivers and making railroads and telegraphs, to develop, organize, create and preserve the great British provinces of the north, by the Great Lakes, the St. Lawrence and around the shores of Hudson's Bay, and I am able to say, "It is very well you are building excellent states to be hereafter admitted to the American Union."[25]

Seward's most notable achievement was the acquisition of Alaska from the Russians in 1867. He hoped to achieve two things by the purchase of this immense territory, an area twice the size of Texas: the first was to sandwich in British Columbia, thus coaxing her annexation; the second was to provide a northern bridge between America and Asia to complement the southern bridge from California. "The nation thus situated," gloated Seward, "must command the empire of the seas, which alone is a real empire."

In British Columbia, the inhabitants did feel a much closer bond to their American counterparts on the Pacific coast than to the distant government in central Canada. And on the Prairies, an annexation movement was supported by local residents who heard they would lose title to their land, and by recent arrivals from the United States. Their agitation found support in Minnesota, whose legislature passed a resolution in 1858 in favour of annexing the Red River District. A decade later, the American Senate passed a resolution introduced by Senator Ramsay of Minnesota, which called for the Committee on Foreign Relations to investigate the desirability of a treaty between the U.S. and Canada which would provide for the annexation of all territories in North America west of the 90th meridian. The construction of the Northern Pacific was regarded by the American Congress as an instrument for the economic conquest and eventual occupation of this area. In 1868 and 1869, an American Senate Committee urged its early completion, arguing as follows:

> The opening by us of a Northern Pacific Railroad seals the destiny of the British possessions west of the 91st meridian. They will become so strongly Americanized in interest and feelings that they will in effect be saved from the new Dominion and the question of this annexation will be but a question of time.

The administration of Ulysses S. Grant took office in 1869. Grant stands with Teddy Roosevelt as perhaps the most aggressive president of the United States throughout the century. However, he was often restrained by the more subtle Hamilton Fish, his Secretary of State. Lafebre writes that "The Grant Administration did not debate the desirability of annexing Canada; most Americans wanted it." For example, Horace Greely of the New York *Herald Tribune* declared that though "our country has already an ample area for the next century at least . . .[Canada] would always be a welcome addition." And Senator Justin Morrill, who argued furiously against the U.S. having foreign entanglements of any kind, also made an exception of Canada. He was one of those who had argued against renewing the reciprocity agreement because it would lead to annexation. "Marriage," he said, "seldom follows seduction."

Americans were only divided on the means by which Canada was to be taken. There were some who did recommend force. President Grant, for one, demanded that Britain compensate the U.S. for the damages done to the U.S. fleet and merchant marine by the British ship *Alabama* by handing Canada over to him. He advocated that the U.S. settle the matter by marching across the border and taking Canada by force. Fish, on the other hand, was an advocate of diplomacy. Others favoured reciprocity as a first step.

Continental integration in the form of reciprocity was offered to the Canadian electorate whenever the success of the National Policy appeared to be in doubt. In spite of the heavy burden placed upon the population by the dominant business class, reciprocity was rejected by the electorate in 1891, 1911, and 1921. The National Policy had succeeded in preventing the political absorption of Canada by the United States. The same cannot be said about economic absorption. However, economic absorption would not come about by way of reciprocal trade agreements, but rather by way of foreign investment. The era of the multinationals in Canada had begun.

Industrial Versus Finance Capital

The dominant business class in Canada remained the merchant-financiers whose interest lay in guaranteeing to themselves a monopoly of the carrying trade and financial system in the new Dominion. While Canadian-owned manufacturing did grow under the National Policy, its more important consequence was the establishment of branch-plant U.S. companies in Canada. The locus of ownership of industry was of no import to the merchant-financiers. They held branch-plants as being of equal value as Canadian-owned industry. What mattered is that they brought more production, supplying more goods to be shipped and sold through the mediation of their various enterprises. Canada's place in the British Empire stood them in good stead during this period of the National Policy. A Canadian location for American business was promoted as a way not only to gain access to the Canadian market but also to the preferential system of the British Empire.

The main motivation behind the protective tariff was not so much to protect existing industry but to expand the economy and block the outflow of population by inducing foreign capitalists to set up shop in Canada. Debating the issue in the House of Commons in 1878, John A. Macdonald argued:

> We have no manufacturers here. We have no work-people; and work-people have gone off to the United States. These Canadian artisans are adding to the strength, to the power, and to the wealth of a foreign nation instead of adding to ours. If these men cannot find an opportunity in their own country to develop the skills and genius with which God has gifted them, they will go to a country where their abilities can be employed. If Canada had a judicious system of taxes [i.e. tariffs] they would be toiling and doing well in their own country.

At first most Canadian industrialists oposed higher tariffs. With some exceptions, they were convinced that the existing tariffs offered them sufficient protection from foreign competition. Their main concern was to *lower* the tariff on imported materials so that they would reduce their costs. Their position was to change as increasing numbers of them, former advocates of freer trade, now became staunch defenders of increased protectionism. What occurred to change their opinion was a major change in their real circumstances. The period from 1895 to World War I witnessed the first giant merger movement (to some extent a slopping over the border of the American mergers). The stock of the resulting new corporations was greatly watered, with the promoters extracting fabulous profits from their new ventures.* With these huge water-logged mergers the tariff became essential as a means of raising prices in Canada to levels which allowed these companies to squeeze out earnings that were commensurate with their bloated capitalization. The Canadian Manufacturers' Association was by now a consistent advocate of higher tariffs, and the Liberal Party subsequently came to abandon its efforts to dismantle protectionism and renew a free trade arrangement with the U.S.A. By World War I, protectionism was no longer a vital issue in Canadian politics, having been accepted by industry as well as by merchant-financiers and by Liberals as well as by Tories.

The policies adopted by both government and the dominant business class were designed to promote the interests of Canadian merchant capital. The interests of industrial capital were secondary. The needs of the two are sharply distinct:

---

* For example, of the nineteen largest firms that merged in 1908-10, the total issued stock was $165 million compared to the $65 million which represented the combined capital of the component companies. (*Monetary Times*, September 24, 1910.) This data is taken from Tom Naylor's forthcoming study *The History of Canadian Business 1867-1914*, which provides a thorough elaboration of this and subsequent topics.

Industrial capital needs cheap raw materials, easy credit conditions, and low transport costs; merchant capital relies on regional scarcities of raw materials and goods to obtain high prices extracted through credit costs, transportation rates, and merchandise mark-up. Merchant capital, typified by a low ratio of fixed to circulatory capital, also needs rapid turnover, and cannot undertake long-term risky investment. It is, therefore, oriented towards abetting the quick extraction of staple output, rather than industrial processing.[26]

This meant following a freight rate policy that discriminated in the form of long distance staple trade as opposed to building up local traffic; plundering the Maritimes and rural Ontario of their savings by channelling them to the booming west, meanwhile imposing exorbitant interest charges on loans to farmers; and exporting vast amounts of savings to the U.S.A., the Caribbean, and South America.

Even before Confederation, Montreal financiers moved Canadian capital to New York in quantities far in excess of what they invested in Canadian industry, creating a north-south flow of funds at the expense of Canadian development. During the American civil war, Canadian banks largely replaced eastern American banks in financing the movement of western crops. To a discomforting degree, Canada ended up "borrowing" back its own money in the form of direct investment by U.S. firms as these began setting up their branch plants. While financial capital moved from Canada to the American money markets, industrial capital moved back to Canada.

William Van Horne, one of the architects of the CPR, is alleged to have said that "patriotic sentiments have never in the history of the world stood against the pocketbook." This was at least true in his own case. After the CPR project was completed, Van Horne shifted his sights to South American and the Caribbean. On Cuban land seized by American military authorities and given over to his syndicate, he constructed a steam railway and an electric tramway. These projects were designed to open up sugar lands, and in short order Van Horne also had a sugar refinery in operation. Seeing opportunities for a quick profit, other Canadian capitalists also invested substantial sums on the island. A group of Toronto capitalists established a colony that they called "New Toronto" which they advertised as "Cuba's largest Canadian Colony."

Along with Donald Smith (Lord Strathcona), James Ross and G. Drummond, head of Canada's sugar cartel, Van Horne was involved in a company to build and operate Trinidad's telephone system, electrical power station, and tramways. In partnership with the president of the United Fruit Company, he established a railway system in Guatemala. And with the builders of the CNR, Mackenzie and Mann, he founded Mexican Light and Power Co. It was Mackenzie and Mann, along with a group of Canadian financiers, who established a huge utility complex in Brazil that became known as Brazilian Traction, Light and Power. In 1913 alone, Mackenzie and Mann were given a subsidy of $15.6 million which was, in the word of the *Grain Growers' Guide* (June 25, 1913):

> Thirty-one times greater than the entire grant to agricultural development, and they may spend it in buying coffee plantations in Brazil, wheat land in Argentina or on a picnic to the Fiji islands.

As Lenin was to say a few years later, "the bourgeoisie will compete to sell the rope to hang themselves."

With private capital channelled into trade, real estate, and investment abroad, the funding of domestic industry fell largely to government. And with the federal and provincial governments concentrating their capital in cash subsidies to railway companies and to the primary iron and steel industry that was associated with railroad construction, it was the municipal governments that assumed responsibility for attracting manufacturers. What emerged was a bonus craze with municipalities desperately competing with each other to induce manufacturing firms to locate their shops inside their city limits. They offered potential companies tax-free holidays and sold debentures at home and abroad and used tax receipts to raise capital for the cash grants. The net result of this absurd arrangement was that municipality after municipality found itself with enormous fixed debts which placed it on the brink of perpetual bankruptcy. Many industries were clogged with new entrants, far more than were necessary to supply the available markets. The company bankruptcy rate during the bonus craze period rose to dizzy heights, culminating in the wave of mergers. Needless to say, many of the beneficiaries of the bonus system and the subsequent mergers were wealthy foreign firms.

It is not surprising, then, that industrial pursuits were left to newly arrived immigrants from the U.S. and the U.K. and ultimately to well-capitalized American corporations. In a study of industrial elites in the period of the 1880s, T.W. Acheson found three distinct groups. The largest consisted of individuals of British, American, and German backgrounds, "scions of industrial or commercial families in their native lands" who imported their skills and capital to Canada to take advantage of the growing opportunities. The smallest was a group whose wealth dates back to the old commercial and mercantile families. The third group, of Canadian farm or small business origins, "succeeded over a life-time in achieving a significant degree of vertical mobility." Ranking Canadian wealth in the year 1892, the *Canadian Journal of Commerce* gave first place to the transportation entrepreneurs whose personal resources frequently exceeded several million of dollars. A second group of millionaires were all "merchant princes" — wholesalers and shippers. (By 1907 the T. Eaton Co. was the third largest employer in Canada, behind the federal government and the CPR.) By contrast, the personal fortunes of the typical industrialist of the period amounted to between $100,000 and $300,000.[27]

It was not industrialists who dominated economic and political life, but the likes of Donald Smith of the CPR-Bank-of-Montreal-Hudson's-Bay-Company and member of Parliament; and Sir Hugh Allan of steamships, banking, insurance, railway, and telegraph fame. They set the policy for the country within which the emerging industrialists had to manoeuvre. Not many native-born industrialists, except those associated with financial interests, could survive. A good example is the Steel Company of Canada (Stelco). Being spin-off creatures of the railway boom, all the early producers of steel were dependent on the mercantile-railway tycoons. William Kilbourn, who has written a history of this company, tells how Toronto banker George Gooderham came to the rescue of the company during its early days when it had run into financial difficulties. The board of directors of Stelco included men such as:

> William Molson, president of Molson's Bank and of the Champlain Railway Company, director of the Grand Trunk, Governor of McGill University, and scion of the brewing family which was so successful at breeding generations of able sons. And there was Peter Randolph, of the sugar refinery and many other commercial interests, a member of one of those Transatlantic Montreal families which still maintained their social roots and business ties on both sides of the water. The company's board would include in the future several distinguished and influential senators. Among its future presidents, besides Molson and Redpath themselves, would be the shipping magnate Andrew Alland, and Sir Edward Clouston of the Bank of Montreal, the accepted financial oracle of his day. These were men of substance whose advice was based on experience in many fields. They could talk on equal terms with Cabinet ministers. And they would bring back valuable intelligence and tangible support from their friends in the City of London on their regular visits to the world's financial capital.[28]

The list also includes Senator Cox of Canada Life; Sir Edmund Walker of the Canadian Bank of Commerce; Sir Edmond Osler, president of the Dominion Bank; and W. D. Mathews, a director of the CPR and vice-president of the Dominion Bank. What this list illustrates is that in this, one of Canada's foremost enterprises, the men that came to control it were not industrialists at all but financiers and merchants who saw in it another important link with the railways, the key to all of their fortunes.

American Capital in Control

Historical statistics on foreign investment can be misleading unless they are disaggregated. Through all of the nineteenth century, Great Britain was clearly dominant but most of its investment took the form of self-liquidating capital loans to railways and the government. In 1913 the U.K. had over three times as much foreign investment in Canada as had the U.S.A. But total U.S. investment was beginning to catch up, and what is more important, in equity (direct) investment, she was already ahead. In the fourteen years from 1900, American investment increased more than five times in value and doubled again between 1914 and 1918. By now, branch-plants had begun to take on real significance. There were 450 such operations in Canada in 1913, including such companies as Imperial Oil, International Nickel, Westinghouse, Gillette, American Tobacco, and Singer Sewing Machine. The sudden proliferation of American branch-plants reflected the growing strength of the.U.S. economy and in particular the new phenomenon of the multinational corporation. Canadian tariff policy and the booming wheat economy caused one company after another to set up assembly-line operations in Canada to take advantage of the growing market. The increasing importance of the motor car saw U.S. giants like General Motors and Ford extend their operations into Canada. In 1918, R. S. MacLaughlin sold his Oshawa automobile industry to GM.

With ample supplies of British portfolio capital available, the influx of U.S. direct investment cannot be explained by a simple shortage of capital. But neither can it be explained by a shortage of entrepreneurial talent, for, as Naylor insists, "'entrepreneurship' can be either industrial or mercantile, and Canada, much to its misfortune, had no lack of the latter throughout its history .... The real problem was the stultification of indigenous industrial capital by the continued dominance of merchant capital in alliance with British finance capital," together with the technological and organizational strength of American capitalism.[29] A generation gap had opened up between Canadian and American industry. Stimulated by a rapidly growing population and burgeoning domestic markets, the American enterprise was passing through its family firm stage and graduating to the stage of the giant corporation. In

Canada the family firm remained typical except in those industries which had developed mass domestic markets such as cotton textiles, primary iron and steel, farm implements and food processing and resource industries which were oriented to the export market. Canadian merchant capital supported the development of these industries but elsewhere the field was largely left to the Americans. Until a mass market was built up American companies were satisfied to limit their Canadian operations to sales organizations or licensing arrangements with Canadian firms. Direct investment and branch-plants followed, induced by the tariff and patent legislation and supported ultimately by a growing domestic and British Empire market.

The large-scale liquidation of British investment during and after World War I and the continued expansion of American investment ended British economic supremacy in Canada. The British went into decline after World War I, never to fully recover. British stagnation after the war and the decline of Canadian wheat markets in Europe struck a blow at the east-west system of the National Policy. American capital and American capitalism were now clearly in control. The U.S.A. accounted for 53 per cent of foreign investment by 1926 compared to 21.5 per cent in 1913. The 1920s saw the rise of new staple industries that basically altered Canadian development and created a permanent north-south trading nexus. Hydroelectricity, pulp and paper and new mineral industries increased in importance. Provincial governments, strangled by the narrow fiscal base awarded to them by the BNA, found a new autonomy in the tax revenues from the resource industries which had been placed under their jurisdiction. They began to replace the federal government as the level of government closest to business.

The Great Depression finalized the end of the British empire, for Canada's National Policy collapsed with the collapse of the market for Canadian wheat. In 1935, on Remembrance Day, the recently-elected government of Mackenzie King signed a reciprocal trade agreement with Washington. In 1940 the same Mackenzie King motored down to Odgensburg, New York, to meet with Franklin Roosevelt. There, without prior consultation with his cabinet or the House of Commons, he signed a permanent military alliance with the United States, establishing the permanent War Defence Board. This marked the political passage of Canada into the American empire.[30]

On the other hand, the stimulus to the economy brought about by World War II together with the withdrawal of U.K. investment, the slight rise in U.S. investment, and the general reduction of imported manufactured goods allowed for a truly Canadian program of industrialization and a new fling at national capitalism. Manufacturing, particularly in the areas of chemicals, electronics, and tool-making, began to blossom. The output of steel increased by 120 per cent and aluminum by 500 per cent between 1939 and 1942.[31] Some areas of war-related production were established on the basis of newly founded Crown Corporations. In those areas where firms already existed, new products and new plants were supported by various government measures: construction by the government of plants and capital equipment which would be operated by private industry, subsidies to private industry, and a fast write-off of new capital equipment. In total, the government invested $790 million in war-related industrial expansion — $450 million in crown-owned plants operated by private companies, $160 million in direct aid to private enterprises, and $180 million in crown plants operated by the government.[32] By war's end, with international trade and investment patterns re-established, state controls removed, and most of the new Crown Corporations dismantled and the assets sold to private enterprises for a nominal price, the Canadian economy fell once again into the American ambit.

Beginning in the 1850s, continental trade patterns were firmly established and from the 1900s intermittently capital and resource integration were also on the American agenda. Yet foreign investment had increased only slightly during the 1930s and not at all during the war years. The gigantic war effort was internally financed. In fact, Canada was a net exporter of capital. Foreign control over the economy dropped off in the case of mining and smelting and rose only slowly in manufacturing. But beginning in the 1950s the Canadian economy regressed permanently into a state of dependency. U.S. control of Canadian manufactures rose from 34 per cent in 1948 to 46 per cent in 1963; in mining and smelting it rose even more from 37 per cent to 52 per cent. New American capital flooded into Canada, and together with the reinvestment of subsidiary profits it accounted for the remarkable accumulation of foreign-owned capital assets in the post-war period. As late as 1950, half a century after active U.S. investment had begun, total U.S. direct investment amounted to only $4 billion. Over the next 15 years $11 billion was added to American holdings.[33]

The period saw a striking shift in the nature of Canada's exports, with pulp and paper capturing 34 per cent of the export market by 1954, non-ferrous metals 17 per cent, and agricultural products declining to 9 per cent. Oil was struck in Alberta in 1947 and in the following ten years the production of crude petroleum increased from 8 billion to 220 billion cubic feet. The giant Ungava iron ore mine was opened and the St. Lawrence Seaway was constructed to carry the iron ore to U.S. steel mills. The St. Lawrence, once the link with the U.K., was now serving to integrate the continental economies.

As elaborated upon earlier, with increased foreign ownership came industrial stagnation. Between 1964 and 1969 Canada boasted the highest level of foreign ownership among 14 countries belonging to the Organization for Economic Cooperation and Development; at the same time its unemployment rate was second only to that of Ireland. And in terms of investement in research and development, the key to industrial growth, Canada was surpassed by all but four of the poorest OECD countries. The response to the problems inherent in foreign ownership — the draining of Canadian savings to cover interest and dividend payments to the U.S.A., and a perpetual unemployment crisis due to a distorted industrial structure — has been to attract even more foreign capital. Returning to the tradition of the bonus craze, all levels of governments have established a myriad of aid programs, tax concessions, and cash gifts to induce foreign companies to locate in their jurisdictions.

More than any other single individual, it was C.D. Howe, Liberal minister of Trade and Commerce and Defence Production, who ushered in the new era of continental resource integration. Possibly the most dramatic event illustrating his role was the Trans-Canada pipeline he engineered in 1956. Guided by the Alberta and federal governments, the privately-owned Trans-Canada Pipe Lines Company was formed to transmit natural gas from the west to central Canada and the U.S. markets. For funding the company requested a $275 million bond issue from the government of Canada. Despite strong opposition, Howe pushed the legislation through the House. Historian Donald Creighton describes Howe's central role:

> The close integration of Canada into a North-American economy dominated by the United States was, to a large extent, a development of the two decades in which he [C.D. Howe] had watched over Canada's economic progress; and Canada's new continental orientation was in effect a gigantic amplification of his own continental outlook.[34]

Our first mass export of oil was born of California's energy shortage at the time of the Korean War. The U.S. Petroleum Administration for Defence decided in 1951 that California needed a new source of oil, the American west's traditional oil shortage having been aggravated by the war. Canada was chosen to be the supplier, not on the grounds of the economics of the project, but from considerations of political and military security. The framework for this first exercise in continental planning was set out in the New Hyde Park Agreement of October 1950, a precursor of the NORAD agreement seven years later. The agreement declared, among other things, that the two governments agree "to co-operate in all respects practical ... to the end that the economic efforts of the two countries be co-ordinated for the common defense, and that the production and resources of the two countries be used for the best combined results ...."

Barely a half century had passed since John A. Macdonald had refused a bid to build a portion of the CPR on American soil, but there was no opposition to building part of the oil pipeline through the U.S., nor was there opposition to the U.S. companies who owned the reserves of the west and proposed to sell the oil to the U.S.

American Politics in Control

It was around the time of the natural gas pipeline fiasco that the decision was taken to enter into a continental air defence program with the U.S.A. A delegation of Canadian officials proceeded to Washington in March 1957 to assure the Eisenhower administration that the plan would be implemented but that it had to be suspended temporarily to avoid it becoming an issue in the forthcoming general election. When the Diefenbaker government was presented with the decision he bowed to pressures from the military which, according to General Guy Faulkner, then Chairman of the Chief-of-Staff Committee, had "stampeded the incoming government with the NORAD agreement."[35] NORAD marked a dramatic change in the structure of Canada's military forces as it effectively placed them under U.S. authorities.

The NORAD agreement was actually an extension of the policy that came into force with the "New Hyde Park Agreement" and the Distant Early Warning (DEW) Line. Besides forging a continental energy deal, the effect of the 1950 agreement was to develop standardization of weapons and equipment with the United States. The construction of the DEW Line, beginning in 1957, had the effect of transferring political sovereignty over part of the Arctic to the U.S.A. This became something of a political issue when the Liberal M.P. for Mackenzie River, Mervyn Hardie, objected to the fact that when he wanted to visit his constituents at the stations he had to obtain a permit from the American head office in New Jersey.[36] In a widely read article, *Maclean's* editor Ralph Allen argued that the DEW Line agreement "is the charter under which a tenth of Canada may very well become the world's most northerly banana republic. For a sum of money that has been officially estimated at four hundred million dollars we have at least temporarily traded off our whole northern frontier. In law we still own this northern frontier. In fact we do not."[37] It was criticisms such as this that caused John Diefenbaker to secure control of the DEW Line stations in 1959.

But that same year, Diefenbaker signed the far more strategic Defence Production Sharing Agreement which opened up the area of defence sub-contracting to Canadian industry. From 1959 through 1967, the U.S. government procured $1.8 billion worth of contracts and sub-contracts in Canada. In various years this amounted to an impressive 26 per cent to 68 per cent of Canada's inedible end-product exports to the U.S.[38] The agreement stimulated Canadian manufacturing and eased the balance of payments problem. It also further integrated the economy with the United States, stimulated the American takeover of firms manufacturing arms, caused Canadian-produced arms to be shipped to Vietnam[39] and absorbed a substantial portion of government subsidies for research and development.

While Canadian arms and components are not vital to American needs, this is not the case with Canada's supply of strategic war materials. Professor Gideon Rosenbluth of the University of British Columbia estimated that in 1962, before the intensification of the U.S. war effort in Vietnam, the U.S. military demand accounted for 14 per cent of Canadian production in metal mining and smelting and electrical apparatus, 10 per cent of coal mining, petroleum and natural gas and 7 per cent of the output in primary iron and steel and non-ferrous metal products.[40] In an article written in 1966, I had noted that "between 1962 and 1965 Canadian exports of iron ore rose from $178 million to $285 million; exports of aluminum from $55 million in 1961 to $156 million in 1965; nickel from $151 million in 1961 to $202 million in 1965; sheet and strip metal from $9 million in 1961 to $42 million in 1965. These increases are not normal. They are to a large degree, directly related to the war in Vietnam."[41]

The integration of Canadian defence beginning with World War II and intensifying during the Cold War and Vietnam eras is a strategic component in the absorption of the Canadian political economy. It rests on the assumption that in world affairs Canada's interests are basically the same as those of the United States. This is indeed the liberal interpretation of Canadian reality. One of our foremost liberal historians, Edgar W. McInnis, has written that "Canadian interests must be virtually identical with American interests as the United States conceives them." And John W. Holmes, Director General of the prestigious Canadian Institute of International Affairs, goes even further: "Knowing on which side of the Cold War our own interests lie, we are not disposed to press our independence farther than would be allowed. We can tell our neighbour when we think he is wrong, but we know that in the end we will, in our own interest, side with our neighbour right or wrong."[42] Similar views have been expressed by the late Lester Pearson and Prime Minister Trudeau. As late as 1958, for example, Pearson urged that "western democratic governments have no aggressive or imperialistic designs. This is as true of the most powerful, the United States of America, as it is of say Uruguay or Iceland. "Indeed", he added in an astounding flight of fantasy, "Americans . . . are perhaps the least imperialistically minded people that ever achieved great power in the world. . . . They are homebodies, and their 'westerns' give them an adequate if vicarious sense of adventure." Canada's role, as devised by Pearson, was to assist the United States to achieve its goals, which were by definition the same as Canada's. This reads like a sick joke after Vietnam, but in the late 1940s and 1950s many Canadians believed it.

This liberal view of world reality led to our complicit International Control Commission function in Vietnam. In his celebrated 1965 Temple University speech, Pearson ventured the tentative suggestion "that a suspension of air strikes against North Vietnam *at the right time* [Pearson's italics] might provide the Hanoi authorities with an opportunity, if they wish to take it, to inject some flexibility into their policy." This was no denunciation of America's role in Vietnam, for in the same speech Pearson was quick to point out that in his view American "motives were honourable; neither mean nor imperialistic." But as we know, President Johnson blew his top and summoned the Canadian Prime Minister the next day for a Texas-style chewing out at Camp David. This was to be the last time that a Canadian government spokesman would summon up the courage to comment independently on American foreign policy.

The Canada-U.S. auto pact, the mammoth James Bay Project which converts Quebec into a permanent supplier of power to New York State, and the Mackenzie Valley pipeline projects are the creations of the 1960s and seventies, designed, as were the earlier agreements, to fashion a North American continental political economy. But as the 1970s approached, the signs were already present that the American empire had passed its zenith. Coming out of the Vietnam War, as rivalry with the Europeans and Japanese deepened in the late sixties, and facing chronic balance of payment problems, the United States has been forced to turn her attention to the economic rationalization of the empire. This means the beginning of a new economic era for Canada.

Foreign Investment and Canadian Independence: Theory and Practice

There are four essential components of any imperial relationship: the economic instruments of the metropolis and the economic intermediaries of the hinterland; the political instrument of the metropolis and the political intermediaries of the hinterland.

Contemporary Canadian governments continue in their traditional roles of providing the economic infrastructures upon which business can construct profitable enterprises. The building of the St. Lawrence Seaway, the James Bay Hydroelectric project, northern roads and air strips, and the financing and subsidization of oil and national gas pipelines are all variations on the theme of the CPR. While Canadian governments occasionally play the role of state entrepreneur, their more common role has been like that of a financial holding company that provides the social overhead capital that even large enterprises cannot profitably finance themselves.*

The state has always had a large presence in the economic affairs of Canada. Various interpretations have been put forward to explain this phenomenon — a remnant or fragment of British tory paternalism; a defensive expansion designed to forestall, counteract, or restrain the more aggressive economy of the United States; a substitute for a weak capitalist class. There is some element of truth to all these theories.[44] Another cogent explanation for the extensive use that has been made of the state to develop the country lies in the mercantile origins of the Canadian ruling class. The primary role of the state has been that of facilitating the production and transport of staple products. Merchant capitalism has never been averse to using the instruments of the state to maintain its monopoly position in trade and finance. The philosophy of mercantilism gave formal recognition to the essential partnership

---

C. D. Howe, for example, argued in favour of government ownership of air travel on the grounds that private enterprise could not afford to finance it but would benefit from it very substantially. On this point, see Lloyd Masolf, "The Boundaries of Public Enterprise" in K. J. Rea and J. T. MacLeod (eds.), *Business and Government in Canada*, p. 173.

between business and the state and the political economy of
Canada in its origins and to this day remains an extension of classical mercantilism.

That much public expenditure today goes to support the projects
of foreign-owned corporations is simply a reflection of the fact that
they are the dominant force in Canadian economic life. The willingness of Canadian governments to support the economic activities of multinationals reduces the burden that is commonly
assumed by the metropolitan government in its less stable and less
affluent hinterland regions.

It is important to distinguish between two segments within
Canada's own capitalist class. There is an independent segment,
largely the descendants of merchant-finance capital. Until recently
this segment has never been threatened by the U.S. multinational
corporation, and in fact enjoys a favourable position in serving the
industrial development stimulated by U.S. investment. It still has a
robust existence. Its members are commonly found on the boards
of U.S. subsidiary companies and a handful of them even sit on the
parent boards of multinational corporations based in the U.S. Several of them operate branch-plants in the U.S.A. They have created
their own sub-imperial system, with Canadian banks and insurance
companies being dominant in several of the Caribbean nations and
Canadian railway and utility companies having significant holdings in the Caribbean and Central America.

There is also a dependent segment composed of leading Canadian executives who have been relegated to the position of managing branch-plants for foreign masters. They are the hired managers, not the ultimate controllers, of the corporations they serve.
They make day-to-day decisions but the key decisions which affect
the future — on profit allocation, technology, trade —are beyond
their jurisdiction. Their ranks are swelled regularly as independent
industrialists, unable to maintain their autonomy, are forced to sell
out their interests to the multinationals.

The independent core of finance capitalists remains a highly
influential and powerful group who have a hand in most of what
goes on in Canada. Yet their role is overwhelmingly shaped by the
forces of continentalism that they and their antecedents helped to
create. The dominant economic force in Canada is clearly the
American-based multinational corporation. Canada is a hinterland
or more precisely a series of sub-regions that serve the American
metropolis. As in all imperial relationships, it is the metropolis that
determines the pattern and directions of the economies of its hinterland.

It is still being argued that U.S. direct investment comes to

Canada because capital is scarce in this country. The statistics indicate otherwise. In addition to the net outflow of funds from subsidiaries to their parent companies, which in the form of dividends, management fees and royalties runs to around $2 billion a year, there is the fact that most of the foreign capital for expansion is obtained within Canada. Foreign-controlled firms spent $43.9 billion in capital expansion between 1946 and 1967 of which only $9.7 billion, 22 per cent, came from foreign sources. In the period 1960 - 1967, foreign sources contributed only 19 per cent. In the words of McGill economist Kari Levitt:

> The brutal fact is that the acquisition of control by U.S. companies over the commodity-producing sectors of the Canadian economy has largely been financed from corporation savings derived from the sale of Canadian resources, extracted and processed by Canadian labour, or from the sale of branch-plant manufacturing businesses to Canadian consumers at tariff-protected prices.[45]*

Contrary to current mythology, Canadian savings are not low, nor is the Canadian investor averse to taking risks. Canadians save a higher proportion of their disposable incomes than do Americans and they are more inclined to invest their savings in equity stock.[46] It is available stock that is in short supply, a result of the fact that significant branches of the Canadian economy are closed to Canadian investors. Wholly-owned subsidiaries do not offer their shares to Canadians. Investors, eager to participate in dynamic industries and their glamour stocks, must invest in the parent companies (whose shares are often listed in Canadian markets) since few, if any Canadian stocks of these industries are available. IBM is one U.S. corporation with a wholly-owned Canadian subsidiary. At the end of 1966, Canadian mutual funds held about $60 million in IBM stock, more than their holdings of any single Canadian stock. Canadians who want to invest in General Motors can do so only by buying shares in the parent U.S. corporation.

The point is not to decry the financial policies of U.S. corporations in limiting opportunities for Canadian investors, for a more

---

* 70 to 75 per cent of the funds of foreign subsidiaries come from returned earnings and depreciation reserves, a further 10 to 15 per cent from Canadian banks and other intermediaries, and less than 20 per cent in the form of new funds from the United States. In addition, a good deal of Canadian capital, particularly that held by financial institutions, is invested outside of Canada. This phenomenon has important results. In 1960 Canadian financial institutions held only 10 per cent of their stock portfolios in foreign equities; the proportion rose to 24 per cent by 1966. Pension funds have also tended to place their portfolio investment in foreign institutions, amounting to $600 million between 1962 and 1969 while during the same period mutual funds invested $1 billion aboard. (Government of Canada, *Foreign Direct Investment in Canada,* p. 81.)

liberal policy would bring few benefits to the general community. It is rather to demonstrate that the already dominant American position in the Canadian economy limits still further opportunities for Canadian participation and control of the country's economic development, while it induces greater Canadian investment in the economy of the metropolis.

On the matter of entrepreneurship, Kari Levitt reminds us that the entrepreneurship does not bear any simple relationship to high levels of income, or to high levels of education.[47] Canada has far higher per-capita income than that which prevails in Britain, Germany, and the U.S. at the peak of their "take-off," and a far higher level of per-capita income than contemporary Japan. What this indicates is that the branch-plant economy is not the product of low incomes and lack of industrial entrepreneurship, but rather the reverse; the continuing absence of industrial entrepreneurship is the product of the branch-plant economy. Foreign economic domination by itself precludes innovation. It establishes the social conditions for the replication of existing technological patterns.

In *Economics, Third Canadian Edition,* authors Samuelson and Scott present a three-stage debtor-creditor theory that purports to explain how a nation evolves within the international economy to finally achieve a state of economic independence.[48] First, as a young debtor nation, it imports foreign capital to finance the formative years of industrial growth emerging when commodity imports exceed exports. In the second stage, the trade relationship is reversed, but payment of dividends and interest on past debt keeps the current account of the balance of payments, more or less, balanced. The capital account also balances with new foreign investment, just cancelling out new borrowing. In the third stage the nation moves into a creditor position. Its exports may still exceed its imports, as it supplies the additional purchasing power to importing countries through its own foreign investment. Or it could be financed by gold inflows. But ultimately, in the mature creditor stage, it buys more than it sells, the deficit being made up by dividends and interest received from past foreign investment.

This model seems to fit the historical experience of both the U.K. and the U.S. Samuelson-Scott express some doubt that it fits Canada as well, but they let the matter drop with no further discussion. According to the model, Canada should be advancing to stage three. The truth of the matter is that Canada has yet to advance through stage two. Our present circumstance is that exports normally exceed imports, but there is such a large outflow of dividends and interest — payments on past foreign investment — that the current account is continuously imbalanced. The deficit has to be offset by still more capital imports from abroad, and the debt keeps rising as the new capital imports add still greater burdens to future balance of payments. Evidently we are caught in a vicious circle, trapped forever, it seems, between stage one and stage two. Economic independence is as distant as ever.

Why has Canada been unable to move through the three stages? Primarily because of the nature of the foreign investment that has been attracted to this country. During the formative years of American industrialization, the U.S. borrowed large amounts of capital from abroad. Foreign investment took the specific form of loan capital (indirect) rather than equity capital (direct). As the economy grew, the loans were paid back and the economy became financially independent. Stage two was complete.

During the formative years of Canadian industrialization, we too received large amounts of capital from abroad. Some of it, that part which was imported from the U.K., was also loan capital. But a growing proportion was equity capital which has a special quality: as the economy grows, it grows too. It is self-generating rather than self-liquidating. When foreign investment takes the form of loan capital, the "foreign sector" of the economy recedes as the economy grows. Loans are redeemed leaving no trace of foreign ownership. When foreign investment takes the form of equity capital, the "foreign sector" expands as the economy expands. It may well expand faster than the general economy, since it is usually concentrated in the most dynamic and most profitable branches of economic activity. Unlike loan capital, equity capital is not distant, passive, and self-liquidating. It is, on the contrary, present, active, and self-perpetuating, and it has no termination.

Prior to World War I, Canada was unquestionably short of capital. The wealth generated in the country was not sufficient to finance the capital-intensive infrastructure of the railways, the wheat loans, and the early industrialization. Net capital imports reached a peak of $12 per person during the five years of 1909-13. In the 27 years spanning the Depression and World War II, there was very little increase in the value of foreign assets in Canada, and between 1946 and 1950 there was a net export of capital averaging $8 per head.[49] But during the boom of the fifties net capital imports were averaging $12 per head, and even during the stagnation of the late fifties and early sixties foreign investment continued to rise though it was clearly not required. Hugh Aitkin gives a perceptive analysis of the peculiar impact of direct investment:

> Direct investments typically involve the extension into Canada of organizations based in other countries; these organizations establish themselves in Canada for purposes of their own and

bring with them their own business practices, their own methods of production, their own skilled personnel, and very often their own market outlets. If all Canadian borrowings from other countries were to cease tomorrow, these direct investment organizations would continue to exist and function. Many of them, indeed, would continue to expand, financing their growth from retained earnings. And the corporate linkages which integrate them — and the sectors of the Canadian economy that they control — with organizations in other countries would still survive.[50]

Some economists go so far as to argue that foreign investment contributes to our national independence.[51] By stimulating economic growth, foreign investment, it is alleged, generates new wealth and savings which establish the basis for an ever-increasing degree of independence. That is the theory. In practice, while the expensive infra-structure required by our geography has long been put in place and largely paid for and while our level of per-capita income is among the highest in the world, the degree of dependence and the degree of control by metropolitan corporations steadily increases. The key to this common error lies in treating direct investments as capital inflows similar to portfolio borrowings. As Kari Levitt has remarked, "dependence is addictive and the dynamics of dependence are cumulative."[52]

Since all U.S. subsidiaries and branch-plants operate in monopoly-sharing market structures with high barriers to entry for new firms, the very considerable growth of Canadian industrial output has been accomplished largely through the internal growth of the American affiliates. Unlike the era of relatively small-scale enterprise, new products and new techniques are usually introduced by existing rather than new firms, and unexploited mineral deposits and timberlands are usually developed by existing mining and pulp and paper companies. In short, given the early settlement of U.S. affiliates in the Canadian market and given the nature of the market structures that developed, American enterprise in Canada has grown in size and importance along with the growth of the Canadian economy.

Economic Fragmentation, Political Disintegration

One of the most disturbing effects of Canada's piecemeal absorption into the American imperial system is the growing balkanization of the country that it helps to produce. John A. Macdonald's National Policy, which created an east-west flow of trade and investment, was designed by the dominant class of financiers and mercantile tycoons and administered by a strong central government. The pecuniary interests of the ruling class coincided at this time with a keen sense of nationalism. Nationalism no longer serves the purposes of this class. As George Grant has said, "Capitalism is, after all, a way of life based on the principle that the most important activity is profit-making. That activity has led the wealthy in the direction of continentalism."[53]

While it would be a gross exaggeration to say that the north-south traffic in capital and trade has totally obliterated the east-west basis of a national economy, it is clearly the case that Canadian regions are becoming increasingly appendixed to the American market. The Canadian economy is best described as a collection of specialized regional sub-economies, each closely linked to nearby areas of the United States. Lumber, pulp and paper account for over half of B.C.'s exports to the United States; crude oil, gas and byproducts make up about 60 per cent of the exports to the U.S. from the prairie region; the automotive industry provides 55 per cent of Ontario's exports; pulp and paper account for 42 per cent of Atlantic region exports to the U.S.A. and 24 per cent of Quebec's exports. Looking at it from the U.S. point of view, American imports of many commodities are drawn overwhelmingly from a single province: 90 per cent of motor vehicles and parts from southern Ontario; 89 per cent of oil, natural gas, and byproducts from Alberta; 75 per cent of lumber from B.C.; and 73 per cent of aluminum from Quebec; virtually all of its potash imports from Saskatchewan, to give a few examples.

Traditionally, Canadian manufacturing, including that of American branch-plants, has been oriented to domestic markets and secondarily to Commonwealth markets. This pattern was abruptly changed when the federal government signed the Defence Production Sharing Agreement in 1959 and the Canada-U.S. Autopact in 1965. These agreements fundamentally altered Ontario's historical role as the supplier of industrialized products to the rest of Canada. Prior to the Autopact, Ontario's factories produced most of the motor vehicles used in Canada. Today, 70 per

cent of Ontario's output is exported to the U.S., while the western
Canadian market is largely supplied from the U.S.A. As Garth
Stevenson has written,

> Today Ontario is economically integrated with the United
> States to a greater degree than any other Canadian region. Its
> traditional role as the supplier of industrial goods to the Cana-
> dian hinterland matters less to the Ontario economic elite than
> its new role as part of the American industrial economy.
> Ontario's economic health depends less on discussions made in
> Ottawa about freight rates and the tariff than on decisions made
> in Washington about defence contracts and the Autopact.[54]

On emerging from World War II, the Canadian federal system
was dominated by the central government. The expectation of
another depression, the experience and expertise developed in the
conduct of the war years by both federal politicians and federal
bureaucrats, and the predisposition of most Canadians, at least
those outside of Quebec, to look to Ottawa rather than the provinces for leadership — all worked strongly in favour of the central
government. "The story of Canadian federalism since the late
1950s," writes Donald Smiley, "is the story of the steady attrition of
the powers of the central government."[55] The main force was the
increasing economic integration with the U.S.A. "The new pattern
of north-south trade and investment based on resource development and branch-plant manufacturing, does not require a strong
central government. The central government is left to manage the
old infrastructure of communications and commerical institutions
carried over from the previous era."[56]

But there were other forces, too. The Liberal party, so long in
office, had become arrogant in power and insensitive to regional
needs, particularly of the Prairies and the Maritime provinces. And
Ottawa's paralysis in the face of the stagnation of the late fifties cost
the central government its legitimacy as the dominant political
force in Canada. Political action to encourage economic development shifted to the provinces and even to local governments.
Without a national plan for economic growth, they sought to hitch
their economies onto the American growth wagon. The absence of
a national economic plan and the consequent scramble for investment by the provinces and municipalities could only strengthen the
bargaining position of the multinational corporations.

With the development of the new staples, the provincial governments gained the fiscal independence that had been denied them by
Confederation. As the source of timber rights, mining leases, and
exploration permits, they gained power and status while the federal
government had limited means to intervene in these vast sectors of

economic life. Nevertheless, the expensive infrastructure of roads, hydroelectric power, and other services that are required to support the expansion of resource-based industries leads the provinces to borrow money abroad, seek out still more taxable investments and demand that Ottawa surrender even more "tax room" to them. Meanwhile, with their new-found resource taxes and royalties, provincial authorities can try to bribe secondary manufacturing industries to locate within their jurisdictions.*

The growing specialization of the provinces, each with its distinctive interests, has made it all the more difficult for the federal government to get a consensus on national policies. Ontario is primarily concerned with safeguarding the Autopact and securing supplies of cheap fuel from Alberta; Alberta is demanding unrestricted right to develop its petroleum and natural gas; Alberta and Saskatchewan are concerned with maximizing their petroleum royalties and tax revenues while some of the other provinces are starved of public revenues; Nova Scotia is demanding unrestricted off-shore mineral rights, and so on. While the small provinces still have an interest in a strong central government, depending on federal equalization payments and the Wheat Board, Ontario, Alberta and B.C. together with Quebec have come to regard the federal government as increasingly irrelevant. They have led the assault on Ottawa over the past 15 years, forcing successive federal governments to relinquish a large share of their tax revenues and controls. Many of the provincial governments now send trade missions abroad, demand to be consulted about taxation, external trade, monetary and fiscal policy, and any regulations of foreign investments.

In the words of R. T. Naylor:

Concentrations of [foreign] direct investment tend to fragment national markets and balkanize the state structure. . . . The advance of industrialism is normally an integrating social force

---

* It seems doubtful that such schemes will succeed in redistributing secondary manufacturing more evenly around the country. U.S control of manufacturing activity in Canada casts an economic shadow over the country in the sense that the location of U.S. subsidiaries is largely determined on the basis of proximity to American centres. By the early 1900s southwestern Ontario had already become an extension of the U.S. manufacturing belt. Of the 1,618 U.S.-controlled subsidiaries in Canada, 1,132 are in the Toronto Southwest Ontario region. While Canadian manufacturers also cluster in this region, they do not do so to the same extent. Forty-five per cent of American-controlled employment is within 100 miles of Toronto compared to 31 per cent of Canadian-controlled employment, and 83 per cent of the American-controlled employment is within 400 miles of Toronto, compared with 70 per cent of Canadian-controlled employment. (D. Michael Rae, *Dimensions of Canadian Regionalism*, p. 28.)

producing nationalism; it is clear that second-hand industrialism is a disintegrating social force producing Pearsonian "internationalism."[57]

The former Under-secretary of State, George Ball, once said that multinational corporations cannot prosper within the confines of the nation state. Fortunately for the multinational corporations, the central government of Canada is gradually disintegrating. It has lost its main purpose to the American metropolis and it has given over some of its main functions to the provinces. This functional fragmentation, in turn, serves to further strengthen the north-south pull, for the provinces are inherently parochial and fully absorbed in achieving maximum economic growth within their own boundaries. The scramble for local industry easily overrides any concern for the preservation of Canadian economic independence.

The shift of the location of governmental control can be seen in the dramatic change in the fiscal balance between Ottawa and the provinces between 1955 and 1965. In 1955, federal expenditures on goods and services were 8.5 per cent of the GNP while provincial and local expenditures were 6 per cent. In 1965 the corresponding proportions were 5.1 per cent and 7.9 per cent. Health, education, and social welfare, all within provincial jurisdiction, were expanding rapidly while federal responsibilities like defence were declining. Federal taxes were 74.3 per cent of total levies paid by Canadians in 1955, while provincial and municipal taxes were 25.7 per cent. The corresponding proportions in 1965 were 60.9 per cent and 39.1 per cent. As well, federal transfer payments to the provinces increased from $440 million to $1,570 million. In 1962 the provinces were allowed to levy their own taxes on personal and corporate incomes. In 1965 the Canada Pension Plan was established, giving the provinces access to a new source of capital funds.

The expected accumulation by the provinces of over $20 billion of royalties and other levies from oil and gas in the five-year period 1975-80 threatened to destroy whatever balance remained in the structure of Confederation. The provinces are the rightful collectors of these royalties according to Section 109 of the BNA Act. Yet the federal government felt it had to take measures to block them. By removing the right of companies to deduct provincial royalties from their incomes for tax purposes, the provinces were put in a position of either cutting back on the royalties or seeing the resource industries drift away. It did not take the western provinces long to cut their share of the royalties and call for a hike in oil prices to aid the companies. This was the first time in well over a decade that the federal government moved vigorously to defend its own integrity. But the cumulative encroachment of the provinces over the 1960s has nevertheless taken its toll in reducing Ottawa's capacity to effectively control either employment or inflation.

With over a third of the goods produced in Canada being exported to U.S. markets, and with even a greater proportion of the goods consumed in Canada being imported from the United States, Canada has, in any event, never been able to prosper in the face of a depression in the U.S. economy; and has never been able to stabilize its prices in the face of American inflation. Trade ties and U.S. ownership of Canadian industry are the main links which integrate the two nations within one continental economy. They complement and reinforce each other.

There is a temptation to debate the primacy of trade ties or foreign ownership in the continentalizing of the Canadian economy. But the distinction is futile, for trade and foreign ownership are ineluctably tied together. Data compiled for 266 of the larger foreign-owned companies in 1964 and 1965 indicate that these firms alone account for about one-third of both Canadian exports and imports. If all subsidiaries and foreign affiliates were included, the proportion would be even greater. A study comparing the import propensities of non-resident-owned firms and resident-owned firms has shown that foreign-owned firms are more import-oriented, less inclined to use local suppliers.[58] About two-thirds of subsidiary exports go the U.S. and about three-quarters of subsidiary imports come from the U.S., and much of the trade is intra-company. These statistics demonstrate that the setting up of American branch-plants and subsidiaries in Canada greatly strengthens trade ties between the two countries. Trade and direct investment are the transmission belts of American inflation and depression into Canada.

The Socialist Alternative to the Multinational Corporation

During the heady decades of U.S. expansion, the American connection was understandably celebrated. Canada's "Special Status" with the largest and most buoyant market in the world stood us in good stead. With our growth attached to hers, we were able to prosper within the American system. Then came August 15, 1971, the date when American capitalism reached its postwar watershed. On that day President Nixon outlined a series of measures that signalled the collapse of the Pax Americana and an official recognition of the decline of American power. Reeling from balance of payments problems and with traumatic resource shortages just around the corner, government officials began the major task of reassessing U.S. worldwide commitments and priorities. It soon became clear that "Special Status" for Canada no longer served her interests. While access to Canadian resources was now more crucial than ever, retrenchment of the manufacturing activities of U.S. subsidiaries seemed also to be required.

With the American economy in decline, "Special Status" does not seem so attractive from Canada's point of view either. Locked into a continental economy, Canada seems destined to join the U.S.A. in its long descent. Whether Canadian political rulers can extricate us from this unhappy position seems problematical at best in view of the strong regional and national economic ties that already exist. Only a fundamental re-arrangement of the economy can wrench us out of the American system.

It is not technology that imposes the metropolis-hinterland chain. It is rather the imperial relationship that determines how technology is used. Empires existed long before the development of the new technology. The new technology has permitted a different kind of imperial system to develop. It implies a greater degree of interdependence, but not necessarily one based on a hierarchical structure that prevents the growth of many independent centres of decision-making. As Stephen Hymer has noted, this suggests the possibility of an alternative system of organization, namely national planning:

> Multinational corporations are private institutions which orga-
> nize one or a few industries across many countries. Its polar
> opposite (the anti-multinational corporation, perhaps) is a
> public institution which organizes many industries across one
> region. This would permit the centralization of capital, i.e., the
> co-ordination of many enterprises by one decision-making
> center, but would substitute regionalization for internationaliza-
> tion. The span of control would be confined to the boundaries of
> a single polity and society and not spread over many countries.
> The advantage of the multinational corporation is its global per-
> spective. The advantage of national planning is its ability to
> remove the waste of oligopolistic anarchy, i.e., meaningless
> product differentiation and an imbalance between different
> industries within a geographical area. It concentrates all levels of
> decision-making in one locale, and can thus provide each region
> with a full complement of skills and occupations. This opens up
> new possibilities for local development by making possible the
> social and political control of economic decision-making. Multi-
> national corporations, in contrast, weaken political contact
> because they span many countries and can escape national regu-
> lation.[59]

Empires have come and gone. The new imperialism is not without its own internal contradictions. The centre is troubled. Excluded groups revolt. The globalism of corporate operations has caused the power of American unions to slip away. In the process, the marriage between the big-labour and big-business bureaucracies is beginning to disintegrate. Even the conservative AFL-CIO is showing an awareness that by shifting their shops around the world the multinationals are moving outside the traditional control of American workers. In a report submitted to the United States Senate, the AFL-CIO said that "what may be a rational decision for a U.S.-based multinational company may be harmful to the American economy."[60] The labour unions are, of course, merely the most organized of the disenfranchised. Nationalistic rivalry between the major capitalist countries also looms as a major divisive factor. And the example posed by the centrally-planned economies may prove significant in the foreseeable future. Finally the popular revolt in the underdeveloped world could be decisive. The victory of the Vietnamese revolutionary forces and the seizing of control over the strategic oil industry in the Middle East point to some of the weak links in the new imperial system.

III / The Crisis of the Seventies

With the economy teeter-tottering between a seemingly uncontrollable inflation and severe unemployment, the heavy world of economics, the "dismal science," has invaded all of our lives. Most of us had become complacent in the fifties and sixties, and understandably so. We had experienced a quarter of a century of continuous prosperity with promises and assurances from corporations and government leaders and from professional economists of more to come. There were still some nasty problems to be sure — regional disparities, some pockets of poverty, occasional unemployment, and a Third World of underdeveloped nations struggling to take off into a sustained industrial development. But the power of technology tied to the engine of modern captialism had overtaken the limits of the past and would, in time, resolve the problems of the present too. Besides, governments had discovered new techniques of "fine-tuning" the economy to remove the violent ups and downs of earlier times. We had entered the age of the managed economy. Continuous growth was the answer to all of our problems. With the great corporations providing for all of our private wants, balanced by governments providing for our social needs, there would be plenty for all. There could be arguments about how much government and how much free enterprise, but this debate took place within a consensus that accepted the prevailing economic and political institutions.

That consensus has now been broken. With the sudden appearance of material shortages, of skyrocketing prices, of a wave of corporate bankruptcies, plant closures, and heavy unemployment occurring simultaneously throughout the capitalist world, and with government leaders at a loss to know how to bring order out of this chaos, complacency has been replaced by confusion, anxiety, anger and growing social tensions. Cries of "corporate rip-off," of government corruption and ineptitude, have become part of our daily diet.

The current crisis cannot be measured by a single indicator. Its severity is revealed by a combination of developments that have evolved over the past decade and that reinforce each other today.

Take, for example, unemployment. Official rates of unemployment, while the highest in 35 years, provide only a partial count of the jobless. The U.S. government records more than 8 million as unemployed. There are at least another 5 million overlooked workers who have given up looking for jobs or who have been forced to accept part-time employment. Added together, the offical and "unofficial" unemployed constitute nearly 15 per cent of the American labour force. The Canadian government records more than 800,000 on the unemployment rolls, but to these should be added several hundred thousand jobless or part-time workers that have been defined out of the labour force. Western Europe and Japan count about 5 million workers among the unemployed. Towards the end of 1974, inflation approached 25 per cent in Italy and Japan, 20 per cent in the United Kingdom, 15 per cent in France and 12 per cent in Canada and the U.S.A. (See the accompanying chart).

Unemployment and inflation have combined to erode workers' purchasing power. The average American working family can buy less with its weekly earnings than it could in 1964. Adjusted for inflation, workers' incomes have declined as rapidly over the past 18 months as they did at the beginning of the Great Depression. Average weekly earnings of Canadian workers, adjusted for inflation, were lower at the end of 1974 than they were in 1972. Declining consumer demand and rising prices have caused industrial production to decline in nearly every capitalist country — a 14 per cent drop from November 1973 to March 1975 in the U.S.A. and over a 6 per cent drop from March 1974 to March 1975 in Canada. To maintain spending and maintain payments on accumulated debts, both corporations and families have been forced to borrow in ever larger amounts, with the result that the credit structure gets shakier and shakier. By 1974 American banks had lent a higher percentage of total deposits than before the Great Depression.

For the first time in the post-war period the recession, or mini-depression as it is now called, is synchronized throughout the capitalist world. The volume of world trade has virtually stood still through 1973 and 1974, accelerating the drop in income almost

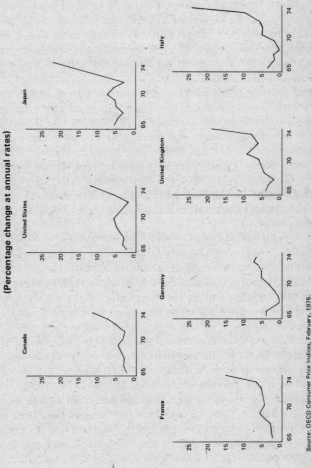

Figure 5
Year-to-Year Change in Consumer Prices
Seven Major Countries
(Percentage change at annual rates)

Source: OECD Consumer Price Indices, February, 1975.

everywhere. It should come as no surprise that economic stability of this order breeds political instability. There have been major changes of administration during the past three years in the United States, Japan, and 14 of the 16 capitalist countries in Western Europe. Only Spain, waiting for General Franco to die, and Austria have escaped the trend.

There is a new credibility gap, but more serious is a crisis of legitimacy. Capitalism, as we know it, has endured because it has been able to "deliver the goods." It was saved from collapse in the thirties by the stimulus of war. Without a handy war around the corner we have entered a period of perpetual crisis oscillating between massive inflation and massive recession. The fine-tuning has failed. The classic remedy for inflation was depression, but that remedy is no longer available. No government is prepared to risk a repeat of the Great Depression. The very success of the system in providing 25 years of relative prosperity has made a return to mass impoverishment an impossible remedy even to consider. Our leaders have taught us too well that economic failure is not a natural phenomenon that we must suffer but a political failure that we need not accept. The continued stability and steady growth of the centrally planned economies is an example that confirms this lesson.

The uncertainties, indebtedness, and distortions arising from inflation, first in the late sixties, and now in the mid-seventies, produced their own recessions. But fearing the consequences of a full-fledged depression that alone could cure the inflation, government leaders in North America and Europe acted swiftly to abort the recessions by injecting new monies into their economies. The result of their actions could only and can only set the stage for a new round of accelerated inflation.

This is a unique crisis in the history of post-World War II capitalist development, unique because it is a crisis that is continuous and international. It has already led to a breakdown of the unity of the capitalist world so carefully constructed at the end of World War II, with each country or bloc now trying to export its crisis to rival nations. The present path leads nowhere but to chaos. It seems most unlikely that we can travel it much longer. Henry Kissinger, at least, understands this; witness his desperate efforts to establish a unified capitalist bloc against the OPEC Nations.

As ever, the two actors on the capitalist stage are labour and capital. The crisis will end only with an assault on one or the other. An assault on labour means wage control, a repression of living standards, forced speed-ups and stretch-outs, a ban on strikes in "essential" industries, and other measures which add up to a "friendly fascism." An assault on capital means an end to the reign of the giant corporations and some form of a socialist planned society. We are already beginning to see the signs of this battle shaping up — in Great Britain, France, Italy, and also here in North America. In one fashion or another we will all be forced to take up sides as the century stretches to its limit.

A Pattern Emerges

Since the end of World War II, there have been very few years in which unemployment has dropped below three per cent — the rate of unemployment which is usually considered to represent full employment; and there have been few years where prices have failed to rise by less than two per cent a year. We have had, on the one hand, permanent pools of unemployed workers — usually young blue collar and service workers — and on the other hand permanent inflation. What is unique about the seventies is the simultaneous appearance of heavy doses of both — in a word, slumpflation.

The consumer price index has risen almost one-and-a-half times since 1947. While every year has seen some price increase, most of the inflation has been concentrated in two distinct periods. In the period 1947 to 1952, prices jumped by almost 40 per cent — an average increase of 7.3 per cent a year. In the period 1965 to 1974, prices jumped by over 50 per cent — an average increase of about 5 per cent a year. A broad pattern emerges that has important ramifications for the present crisis:

— The years following the war were years of rapidly rising prices and low rates of unemployment. At its worst, inflation reached levels of over 12 per cent in 1948 and 11 per cent in 1951, while unemployment never rose beyond 4 per cent.

— There followed a long period of relative stagnation when unemployment hit rates of 7 per cent or worse between 1957 and 1961 and prices were remarkably stable, rising 3.7 per cent in the exceptional year of 1956 but averaging less than 2 per cent a year for the 12-year period, 1953-1964.

— The third period has seen both rapidly rising prices and continuously high rates of unemployment. While the rate of unemployment has only twice fallen below 4 per cent, price increases have invariably exceeded 3 per cent a year, increasing dramatically most recently to levels of 10 per cent a year and higher.

The pattern is depicted in the chart and is summarized in the table below:

Figure 6
Percentage Change in Consumer Prices

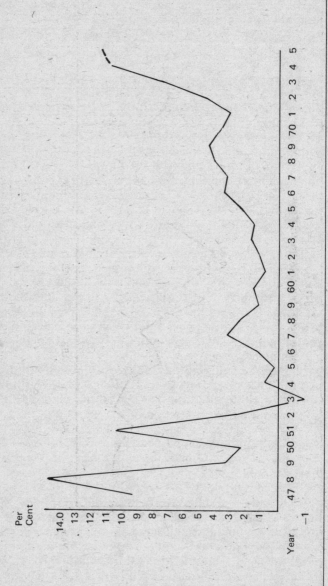
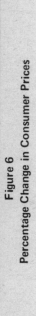

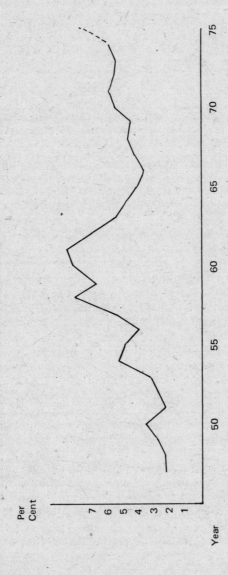

Figure 7
Percentage Unemployment Rate

Table 3

	Period I *1946-1952*	*Period II* *1953-1964*	*Period III* *1965-1974*
Rate of unemployment annual average	2.8%	5.6%	5.1%
Rate of inflation annual average	7.3%	1.5%	5.0%

Expansion

The characteristics of the early post-war boom period are well known. Productive capacity was overwhelmed by demand pressure emanating both from within the domestic economy and outside of it. There was a large pent-up demand for consumer goods and new capital goods. Households had to forego new purchases of consumer durables during the Great Depression for lack of incomes, and again during World War II because of shortages and rationing. Businesses were in the same straits. As the country emerged from the war, both households and businesses had to replace the equipment and appliances that had been long worn-out, and purchase the new things that were being made available by new technology. Moreover, they had the resources to do it because of the large incomes that had been stored up during the war in the form of savings bonds. The population boom — resulting from a catching-up of postponed marriages, younger marriages, larger families, and high immigration — and the widespread population movement from rural to urban areas — all placed new demands on housing, schools, hospitals and roads which could only be answered by expanded private and public construction.

There were also vigorous external demands on the economy, and because of the state of Europe's wartime economy, international competition provided few restraints. Just as the economy began to falter ever so slightly in 1949, it was recharged by the Korean war. Canadian military outlays rose from $500 million to $1,800 million between 1950 and 1952, and over the same period investment spending rose by close to 40 per cent. Another round of heavy demands for Canadian exports, fostered by the war and by business and consumer speculation to gather inventories in the expectation of new price increases, added to inflationary pressures, causing prices to rise by more than 11 per cent in 1951, almost as much as it had in 1948.

Even before the outbreak of the Korean war, the ideology of anti-communism had replaced anti-fascism as the raison d'être of permanent war preparations in the U.S.A. Besides equipping large American occupation forces in Europe and Asia, the U.S. government began to stockpile all types of weapons and material. Permanent war industries became a major instrument to forestall post-war depression. Being a major supplier of war material and, with the Defence Sharing Agreement, a minor supplier of weapons, the Canadian economy became an extension of the U.S. military-industrial complex and prospered from the connection.

The dominant thinking in the final few months of World War II was that the economy would sink back into a depression. It was widely recognized that it was the war that had brought the country out of the Great Depression. In the absence of the stimulating effects of the war, the likelihood was a return to economic stagnation. This belief — shared by economists, government officials, and political leaders — proved to be entirely unjustified by actual events. They failed to take account of the massive forces of economic expansion that would soon take hold. Nevertheless, government policy was initially predicated on the belief that the major problem facing Canada was the maintenance of full employment and rising incomes. It was entirely unprepared to deal with what emerged as the real problem during these years — inflation. In fact, government policy seriously added to inflationary pressures.

In the first two post-war budgets, Finance Minister J. L. Illsley cut taxes by 25 per cent and interest rates on money were kept low. This was simply mistaken judgment on his part. He was budgeting for an expected depression. This expansionary policy was followed again in 1947 by Finance Minister Douglas Abbott, who engineered another round of tax cuts (between 1945 and 1947 personal income taxes were reduced by more than half) and still again in 1948 and 1949. The large government surpluses recorded in this period occurred in spite of, not because of government policy. It was the buoyancy of the economy, bringing in unexpectedly large tax revenues, that produced the surpluses, even with the tax cuts. Had governments practised a policy appropriate to the raging inflation that was then going on, they would have raised taxes and restrained the supply of money and incurred much larger surpluses.

The misguided but well-intentioned Keynesian policy of Illsley was a momentary aberration. Actually, the "new economics" of John Maynard Keynes had not yet dented government circles. Illsley's successor, Abbott was more a disciple of Gladstone than a convert to Keynes. It was his conviction that the war-time tax structure was unacceptable to Canadian capitalists. His first priority was to bring taxes down to their pre-war level, whatever the consequences this might have on the economy. For Abbott and his cohort, C. D. Howe, the large surpluses were a sign that taxes could be pared down and, to the accolade of Bay Street, they did so freely. It was only in the face of the budgetary requirements of the Korean War that taxes were finally raised and the money supply restrained. When the economy turned down in the spring of 1953, Abbott explained that he could not make any appreciable tax cuts because there was not much of a surplus margin in the government budget.

Stagnation

By the mid-1950s the expansionary forces of the post-war world had lost their momentum, in both Canada and the U.S.A. The Gross Domestic Product crawled along at an average rate of increase of 3.6 per cent between 1953 and 1963, compared to 5.1 per cent in the earlier period. Along with the U.S.A. and the United Kingdom, Canada had the lowest growth performance of any industrial country. What prolonged the stagnation was a remarkable upsurge of investment spending in 1955 and 1956, which was based on the unfounded expectation that the earlier expansion would continue at about the same pace. The new productive capacity that came on stream a few years later saddled the economy with an excess of capacity which could only put a damper on new investment spending. Further capital expansion would have to wait until output would finally rise to a level that would fully utilize the existing stock.

While consumption spending is fairly steady, changing roughly in proportion to national income, investment spending is the volatile and undependable sector of the capitalist economy. It is necessarily speculative. When a firm invests in new plant and equipment it estimates, in isolation from its rivals, the prospect of its future growth and profits. Whether or not it actually earns the expected rate of return depends on what happens to future prices and costs, whether or not its newly purchased equipment is rendered obsolete by technological changes, how much rival firms also expand, the tastes of consumers, the discovery of new sources of supply, and changing foreign markets and tariff conditions. In short, investment in a capitalist economy, with its lack of comprehensive co-ordination, is really a leap of faith. New research methods can lessen the risks, but only partially. Sometimes the guesses are wrong. In their impatience to grab as much as possible of the rising profits for themselves, businesses inevitably over-invest and over-produce. Production is then cut back, workers are laid off, and future investment plans are shelved.

Talk of absolute surpluses of foodstuffs or housing seems callous when there is massive malnutrition and overcrowding among millions of people. So too, talk of excess capacity when there is widespread unemployment. And yet from the viewpoint of making profits a crisis of overproduction is what occurs. For should businesses attempt to utilize their "excess" productive capacity, they could sell all of their output only by cutting prices and taking smaller profits. This is one of the eternal contradictions of the capitalist system.

Output, prices and employment are byproducts in capitalist economies. Capitalism is based on production for *profit,* not for employment or needs. Businesses count their earnings, not the jobs they create or the needs that they satisfy. The source of these earnings is the surplus value workers produce over and above the wages they receive. Over-investment has a second shattering consequence for corporations, for during a boom the supply of labour becomes exhausted and workers, taking advantage of their scarcity, demand and receive wage increases that cut into profits. Businesses must restore competition in the labour market in order to ease labour scarcity and undercut labour strength. This is the classic function of economic depressions. By cutting down on investment spending and production, and creating unemployment, businesses are able to reproduce a labour reserve. As the competition for jobs returns, worker power is trimmed and wage demands decline. In short, periodic business downturns are indispensable for a return to profitability, for they restore the conditions for renewed expansion.*

It is important to bear in mind that Canada, due to its peculiar industrial structure, is particularly prone to violent fluctuations in investment spending. As a resources satellite to the U.S.A., its investment booms mirror the demand for resources by U.S. industry. Because of the economies of scale in the resources industries, investment occurs in clusters. To increase productive capacity marginally in the resources industries is not efficient. If expansion is to occur, there are economies to be gained by large additions to capacity. And this usually requires accompanying large public expenditures in such fields as transporation and power. Capacity is therefore built up much beyond current demand, resulting in years of under-utilization and producing a consequent drag on future investment spending. This is illustrated for the period at hand in the following table.

---

* The dynamics of depression are further elaborated upon in Part IV.

Table 4
Approximate Percentage Increase
in Capacity in Two-Year Period
1957 and 1958

Commodity	% Increase
Newsprint	15
Wood pulp	15
Aluminum	16
Nickel	9
Copper	15
Asbestos	13
Iron Ore	26
Petroleum Crude	60
Petroleum Refined	22
Cement	25
Iron and Steel	15
Electric Power	25

Source: Wm. C. Hood, "The Demand for Labour", in Proceedings of the Special Committee of the Senate on Manpower and Employment No. 2.

While the post-World War II-Korean-War boom had already petered out, business investment was surging forward, accompanied by large public projects such as the St. Lawrence Seaway constructed to ship iron ore from Labrador to the U.S.A. It would take six years before output began to reach levels that justified these heavy expenditures. The years in between were years of stagnation and severe unemployment.

The Canadian economy was dragged down by two other forces operating at this time. The first relates to the massive inflow of foreign investment through the fifties, starting with the capital boom in 1955 but continuing on during the years of heavy unemployment and large excess capacity. This anomaly sparked the famous "Coyne Affair." James Coyne, Governor of the Bank of Canada until 1961, was appalled, as well he might have been, by the government's failure to deal with this tidal wave of foreign capital. While John Diefenbaker, as Prime Minister, was allowing his government to build up substantial deficits so as not to further dampen the already depressed economy, Coyne as Governor of the Bank of Canada was concerned that Canadians ought to live "within their means," which for him meant foregoing their reliance on foreign capital. His way of achieving this end, a restrictive monetary policy, produced effects that were exactly the opposite of what he intended. He believed that a tight money policy that kept interest rates high would attract sufficient domestic savings so as to make foreign borrowing unneccessary. Instead, it not only depressed the economy but also attracted large amounts of loan capital from the U.S. Moreover, the large capital inflow caused the value of the Canadian dollar to soar to $1.10 of the U.S. dollar. Such a high exchange rate was totally out of line with Canada's comparative productivity and costs. For most manufacturing industries, Canada's costs were in the range of 10 per cent to 25 per cent higher (productivity lower) than that of the U.S. The exchange value of the Canadian dollar should reflect this gap. The effect of the high exchange rate was to raise Canadian prices in international markets and lower the prices of imported goods in Canada. This could only make it more difficult for Canadian producers to export, and it encouraged a flood of imported goods to the detriment of both Canadian production and employment. Moreover, the capital that flowed in from the U.S. in no way added to Canadian investment. It was entirely unneeded at the time because of the already existing over-capacity. What it did was to displace Canadian savings from the limited investment opportunities still available. Hence the level of economic activity in Canada had to fall still further to reduce Canadian savings to accommodate the available investment opportunities left over after foreign money had taken its share. Had the government halted the inflow of capital in this period, it would not only have been spared the burden of unnecessary indebtedness that result from such inflows, but it would have been able to operate nearer to full employment. The exchange rate would have been more realistic, allowing for greater exports and fewer imports, and there would have been greater investment opportunities for domestic savings. Because this action was not taken, the deficit in the balance of payments reached crisis proportions until it was eventually solved by a sudden devaluation of the Canadian dollar enforced in the last months of the Diefenbaker regime.

The other economic force depressing the Canadian economy was the so-called terms of international trade — the prices of the goods we export relative to the prices of the goods we import. International trade is overwhelmingly important to the Canadian economy. We export about 50 per cent of the goods we produce and we import about 50 per cent of the goods we consume. During the 1950s, for the first time in this century, growth in world trade outpaced growth in world production due to an increase in international specialization and growing international interdependence. It was during this period that Canada (and the U.S.) began to lose their previous share of world trade to Europe and Japan. As a producer mainly of raw materials and semi-processed goods, Canada was especially penalized along with the underdeveloped nations which likewise export staple products and import manufactured products. This is because the international terms of trade were turning in favour of the nations that specialize in finished products, and turning against nations that specialize in raw materials. Resources seemed to be in abundance while the supplies of manufactured goods were kept down by the operation of monopolistic forces bent on maintaining a high and stable level of prices. The result is illustrated in the following table, which shows the ratio of export prices to import prices in certain countries.

Table 5
Ratio of Export Prices to Import Prices, 1953-63

	1953	1963
Germany	100	120
U.S.A.	100	112
Canada	100	92
Argentina	100	83

Source: Economic Council of Canada first Annual Review, 1964.

What this table shows is that for countries in Latin America, Asia, Africa, and for Canada as well, a larger volume of (raw material) exports was required in 1963 than in 1953 to finance a given volume of imports (manufactured goods). The U.S.A. and the European economies could export a smaller value of manufactured goods to purchase a given volume of raw material imports. Such trends hurt the underdeveloped nations in the fifties and sixties, and it is these trends which many of them are trying to reverse in the seventies since the relative scarcities of raw materials and manufactured products began to reverse themselves.

The large deficits incurred in the Diefenbaker years were not planned for. In Herbert Hoover fashion, Diefenbaker's Finance Minister, Donald Fleming, was forever proclaiming a return to prosperity. Fleming's "next year country" routine meant that fiscal tools would never be put to active use. The large deficits that occurred were not due to deliberate policies such as reducing tax rates or expanding government spending. They occurred because the tax revenues collected from a stagnating economy were never large enough to cover the vast expenditures that by the late 1950s were a normal part of government operations. Nevertheless, these "passive" deficits had a definitely stabilizing effect on the economy. Had Fleming reverted to pure Gladstonian economics, he would not have tolerated these deficits; he would have raised the rate of taxation and cut government spending until he had achieved a balanced budget. This would, of course, have deflated the economy still further. By the late 1950s, Canadian governments were at least "passive Keynesians" and this allowed for a significant, if less than a maximum degree of economic stabilization. For as the size of the government sector of the economy grows, the magnitude of the deficits that appear in times of unemployment — and that are allowed to remain because governments dare not raise taxes or cut back on expenditures — automatically increases also, and these exert a stabilizing effect on the economy. Tax deductions from workers' pay cheques increase at a slower rate than usual, or even decline owing to slowdowns or declines in total payrolls. These resulting deficits, further enhanced by unemployment insurance and welfare programs, are the so-called automatic stabilizers that bolster incomes in the face of economic downturns. They operate without deliberate government intervention, being built into modern state-capitalism.

While it is easy to demonstrate government short-sightedness and to condemn the economic illiteracy of politicians, the underlying economic forces were beyond the power of government to overcome, committed as it was to upholding the prevailing social and economic order. It was the lack of co-ordination in decision-making and, ultimately, the profit system that restrained the economy well below its potential. The lost income over the 1956-65 period was in excess of $20 billion or about $1,000 per person! The cost in human terms was colossal: on any one day during these years an average of 300,000-400,000 workers were without jobs. And as is widely acknowledged these official statistics seriously understate the number of unemployed.

Recovery - Inflation - (Planned) Recession: The New Dialectic

Full recovery from the stagnation of the fifties set in as the Liberal government under Lester Pearson took over the reins in Ottawa. It was not that the Pearson Liberals were any better managers of the economy than the Diefenbaker Tories. The recovery had little to do with Liberal policy. It had to do with events mainly external to the Canadian economy, beginning with the lower exchange rates forced down in the dying moments of the Diefenbaker years. Massive crop failures in the Soviet Union and China sparked a recovery in Canadian agriculture, which had been in the doldrums through much of the fifties. Crop failures were nothing new in a country like China. But whereas in former years such a failure would have resulted in mass starvation, the Red Chinese government had launched a social and economic revolution such that by 1961 it could afford to purchase large volumes of food to feed her people. The prairie farmer, it turned out, would be a major beneficiary of Mao's China!

The third external event was the new fiscal measures designed by John F. Kennedy to jolt the U.S. out of its equally dismal economic performance. It was Lyndon Johnson who was to implement Kennedy's major tax cuts. This turn in policy caused an upsurge in the U.S. economy and a consequent rise in demand for Canadian exports. Largely in response to these external forces, the Canadian economy moved ahead rapidly in the early sixties.* Nor was there much sign of inflation. With its large supply of unemployed workers and substantial amounts of unused capacity, the economy could easily respond to the increased demand. Few bottlenecks had yet appeared, and there was still little strain in the economy's capacity to produce.

Indeed, Canada's experience was not unique. In its *Third Annual Review,* the Economic Council of Canada noted euphorically that "the industrially advanced world, as a whole, had been passing through an extended period of unprecedented prosperity. The trends of output, productivity and living standards have been, without exception, tilting up far more steeply than could have been anticipated from historical experience." [1] Canada's real output grew by almost a third between 1960 and 1965, while the unemployment rate fell by almost 50 per cent from 7.1 per cent to 3.9 per cent and prices were rising by less than 2 per cent a year.

It was actually the fourth external force, appearing in 1965, that began the inflationary surge that is still with us today. This was the Americanization of the Vietnam war. U.S. military outlays rose by 59 per cent between 1964 and 1969 while investment in plant and equipment was rising by a similar extent. The boom conditions brought (to the U.S.A.) by the war were bound to have major repercussions in Canada. Indeed, the value of Canada's merchandise exports almost doubled between 1964 and 1969, most of the increase being a response to U.S. requirements. By now the slack in certain parts of the economy had been all but eliminated and new capacity would have to be added if Canada was to be able to answer the call on her resources.

The cumulative effect of these diverse trends was bound to result

---

* To be fair, the Pearson government also introduced new fiscal measures including accelerated depreciation allowances for businesses and reduced corporate taxes.

in a new burst of investment, the first since the mid-1950s. But while the ultimate effect of capital investment is an enlarged productive capacity capable of accommodating a larger demand for goods, the immediate effect is to add to the inflationary pressures just beginning to emerge. The sudden explosion of investment in new plant and equipments created shortages of materials and of certain kinds of labour, resulting in major cost increases which were soon to work their way through the economy. While the investment boom began in 1963, it reached its peak in 1965 and 1966, when business investment accounted for 16 per cent of GNP. Vast expansions also occurred in housing, schools, universities, roads, hospitals and the like. By 1966, total investment absorbed one dollar in every four dollars of income, a phenomenal proportion. Much of the investment was financed by the super-profits being earned in this period. For while unit labour costs were dropping, profits per unit of output were rising by about a third between 1960 and 1964.

While there were still about 300,000 workers out of jobs, around 4 per cent of the labour force, and many parts of the economy still had available capacity, there was a serious shortage of food, and severe bottlenecks had appeared in certain key industries. Dramatic price rises occurred in these areas in 1965, and they soon spread throughout the economy until the inflation became widespread. This pattern of a "partial inflation," beginning in certain areas and spreading from these points to engulf the entire economy, had already been observed in the late 1950s after the brief but substantial inflation of 1956.

What it means is that in the monopoly stage of capitalism inflation is possible without there being a general excess of demand. It is enough that demand should push on supply in a few important areas of the economy, permitting giant corporations in these industries to raise prices and reap higher profits. Unless prices fall elsewhere, the average level of prices increases. But the process does not end there, for the increased demand for labour, materials, and equipment in the dynamic industries raises the prices of their inputs and they spread to other industries in the form of higher costs. To compensate for the higher costs, capitalists then raise their prices and the inflation becomes general. All affected, including trade unions, naturally try to protect themselves by raising the prices of their goods or services. The process becomes self-perpetuating and does not easily subside even after demand eases up in the sectors where the inflation started. Only a severe recession or a prolonged stagnation which produces massive unemployment and excess capacity can grind it to a halt. [2]

This theory accounts very well for the inflation spread that began in 1965 — in the U.S.A. as well as in Canada. A steep recession would have corrected the imbalances that were surfacing. But the war effort called for a policy of expansion, not a policy of contraction. Moreover, because of the political opposition to the war, the government of Lyndon Johnson felt that it would be unwise to finance the war by raising taxes. To avoid fanning anti-war sentiment, the government ran large deficits which added further to inflationary pressures. But as the inflation spread and the supply of unemployed labour was reduced, wages and salaries caught up to and began to outpace price increases. Between 1960 and 1964 Canadian wages and salaries rose by 43 per cent while profits increased by 63 per cent. But between 1966 and 1970 wages and salaries rose by 46 per cent while profits were only rising by 15 per cent. Profits actually fell between 1969 and 1970. The same trend was observable in the U.S.A., and other capitalist countries.

In classic response, corporations launched a production speedup campaign which in turn caused workers to strike more frequently. By 1970, work-time lost through strikes had risen to three-and-one-half times its 1963 level. The notorious wildcat strike at Lordstown, Ohio, where General Motors had increased the speed of the assembly line from 60 cars per hour to 100, dramatized this resistance.

Stuart Jamieson, in his *Times of Trouble: Labour Unrest and Industrial Conflict*, a study commissioned by the Woods Task Force on Labour Relations, observes that the only periods in Canadian history that match the degree of industrial conflict beginning in 1965-66 were 1919-20 and 1946-47. This was the time of the three-week strike of mail carriers and postal workers, one of the largest illegal strikes, the largest involving government employees, and one of the few to occur on a nation-wide scale. The strike focussed public attention on the issue of collective bargaining rights for the federal civil service and helped lead to the passing of new legislation in this field.

The year 1966 brought rank-and-file pressure on trade union leaders probably unequalled in Canadian labour history since the western revolt against the old Trades and Labour Congress leadership of 1918-20. Nearly 16,000 Inco employees began a spontaneous wildcat strike in July that lasted for three weeks and required the presence of three hundred provincial police. The final agreement made Inco workers the highest paid group in the United Steel Workers of America. This was followed by a wildcat strike at Stelco's Hamilton plant that involved 12,500 production workers and 3,500 non-union office workers. The extent of their frustration was revealed by the amount of property damage done and the violence which led to major battles with the police and dozens of arrests.*

This was also the time of the strikes around the construction sites at Expo '67; of the longshoremen in Montreal, and other Quebec ports, that ultimately saw 500 police patrolling the waterfront; of the thirty per cent wage increase given to St. Lawrence Seaway workers over two years; of the strike of 110,000 CNR and CPR employees, only the second time in Canadian history that workers of both railways would walk off simultaneously. Jamieson correctly points out that such periods of industrial unrest are not simply related to conditions of full employment but are more likely during such times and particularly so in countries like Canada with consistently unstable economies. Workers in highly volatile economies find it more necessary than most to "go for broke" while conditions are favourable. †

Business executives were openly complaining that too much control had passed from management to labour, that their profits were being squeezed by wage demands that had become "excessive." Nixon and Trudeau knew the remedy. They slammed on the fiscal and monetary brakes. The recession of 1969-70 followed. President Nixon ordered a 75 per cent reduction in new contracts for federal government construction, and in January 1970 he ordered a $5 billion reduction in defence spending. Prime Minister Trudeau followed suit. In a dramatic and well-remembered television speech he assured his viewing audience that he would take the necessary steps to stop the inflation and if that meant creating 6 per cent unemployment, his government would not back off from doing so. In fact he did readjust his fiscal policy, cutting back on government spending and piling up a huge surplus of over a billion dollars in 1969. And this had the immediate impact he planned for. It forced the economy into a recession at a cost of $2 billion of lost output and an additional 170,000 unemployed workers.

Messrs. Nixon and Trudeau deliberately planned this recession to bring a halt to a rate of inflation that was already considered dangerous. The "fight against inflation" was almost a code name for the fight to keep down wage increases and to protect profit margins.

But neither Nixon nor Trudeau would see the battle through. While unemployment mounted to levels approaching 7 per cent of

---

* Jamieson quotes a local newspaper account on the extent to which union leaders had lost control of the situation: "Wildcat strikers defied and mobbed their union leaders, shoved police aside and closed off all access to the company's plant and offices. The strike appeared to be well organized, but neither the union nor the company could identify those behind it." (p. 433)

† Similar signs of industrial conflict were also manifest in Europe during this period, as I illustrate in Part VII.

the labour force, inflation hung on, as yet barely affected by the contraction they both carried out. And Nixon was afraid to campaign for President with millions out of work. Early in 1971 they revised their course and resumed an expansionary monetary and fiscal policy that facilitated the rapid recovery and massive inflation that was just around the corner. Almost immediately, prices began to climb, and labour contract settlements, some as high as 15 per cent, chilled corporate spines. Most important, profits in Canada and the U.S.A. fell in 1970-71 to their lowest share of national income since World War II. Nixon now substituted a policy of wages and prices control in place of recession as a means to bolster profits, while Trudeau established the totally ineffective prices and income review board headed up by John Young. Some bankers, like the Bank of Montreal's G. Arnold Hart, warned Trudeau of the dangers of a loss of nerve:

> The longer inflation continues, the more difficult it will become to avoid massive increases in unemployment while bringing price increases into line. If we were to change course now and relax prematurely or too much, not only would the sacrifices that have already been made be in vain, but also the credibility of official intentions would once again be called into question. [3]

Hart and the other financial tycoons who were giving similar advice were right. In the context of monopoly capitalism the only way inflation can be checked is by creating a prolonged recession — by locking the levers of monetary and fiscal policy in a contraction position. But politicians like Nixon and Trudeau were not yet prepared to follow this advice —not because of concern for the unemployed, but for reasons suggested by the Organization for Economic Cooperation and Development in its 1970 report on *Inflation, The Present Problem:*

> People's reaction to going bankrupt or being thrown out of a job may have been different in the 1930s when it could be thought that this was the result of a natural disaster. But today, a serious recession would be clearly recognized to be the result of a deliberate policy being followed by the government. The experience of those few countries which, at one time or another during the 1960s, fell short of their potential growth rates for some period of time, suggests that the undercurrents of social and political discontent thus generated may eventually have rather violent economic repercussions in the form of wage explosions which are difficult to foresee or control. [4]

A prolonged recession that removed 10 per cent to 12 per cent or more of all workers from their jobs would likely create a degree of social and political discontent, particularly among the young, the blacks, and the Quebecois, that could only be contained by a state repression of the kind that we saw in the black ghettos of the U.S.A. and in Quebec during the FLQ fiasco.

More particularly, American capitalists were facing a liquidity crisis that was being aggravated by Nixon's brief fling at anti-inflationary measures. The long upswing of the 1960s promoted a wild scramble for profits among the giant corporations. What this involved was not only an upsurge of capital investment but a huge boom of unprecedented proportions. A whole series of new multi-billion-dollar conglomerates arose, mostly spawned out of armament profits. The older corporate giants, not to be outdone, stepped up their pace of acquisitions and diversified into wholly unrelated fields. The drive for growth leads to putting every available cent into expansion. Reserves of cash for a rainy day were allowed to fall to dangerously low levels.

The standard measure of liquidity is the ratio of cash and government securities to current liabilities, that is, payments due within a year. A "liquidity ratio" of 50 per cent is regarded as ample. In 1945 the liquidity ratio was 93 per cent; by 1955 it had fallen to a healthy level of 48 per cent; it then fell dramatically from 36 per cent in 1960 to 19 per cent in 1969. For many individual corporations like the Penn Central, the country's largest railroad, and the LTV Corporation, a multibillion-dollar conglomerate thrown together by Texas promoter James Ling, current liabilities exceeded current assets. In short, they were technically insolvent. So long as the volume of business continued to expand, few took notice of the situation. But the moment business stopped increasing and a downturn set in, a crisis in payments became intolerable. By now the *New York Times* financial commentators were saying: "put bluntly, responsible analysts are beginning to ask whether there is a danger of a 'liquidity crisis', perhaps even approaching the magnitude of those that periodically sent business through the wringer in the latter part of the 19th century."

In the lead article of the August 1970 issue of *Fortune* magazine, Gilbert Burck launched into a familiar celebration of the profit system, but warned that the anti-inflation drive had gone too far in the light of the liquidity squeeze:

Profits are the driving force in the complex interplay of capital supply, interest rates, liquidity, employment and securities prices. When profits are ample . . . both long and short-term capital tends to be plentiful. . . . Anticipating still better business, corporations enlarge their operations and hire more people . . .

but when earnings begin to decline . . . this whole elegant process reverses itself. It is such a reversal, exacerbated by the governments' anti-inflation policies, that bedevils business today.

Burck, along with the commentators, advised the government to cut corporation taxes. "Anyway you look at it, the country's enormous capital needs will have to be raised at the relative expense of consumption." This was the traditional call of business leaders and commentators — this time stated with unusual bluntness — for a policy which would allow business to climb out of its crisis on the backs of the working class. Nixon accepted this advice when he ended his anti-inflation drive and instituted price and wage control. While price controls were selective and only partially enforced, wages were ruthlessly restrained, resulting in a substantial recoupment of profits. [5]

In addition to the liquidity crisis at home, America's dominant position in the world economy was in jeopardy. Politically, the experience in Vietnam demonstrated her inability to effectively police the world. Economically the shift, in the balance of U.S. international trade brought the new reality into stark relief. From 1960 through to 1965, U.S. power was reflected in large trade surpluses averaging $5.8 billion annually. The trade surplus began to disappear in 1966, and in 1971 it turned into a deficit. The challenge from Europe and Japan, which had been on the horizon since the late fifties, had finally arrived, hastened no doubt by the economic problems created in the U.S. by the Vietnam war. The official American response to the challenge was Nixon's declaration in 1971 of the New Economic Policy and the devaluation of the dollar. It was a policy of aggressive retreat that would have an important bearing on the economic developments in the 1970s.*

Dependence Takes Its Toll

This review of the penultimate phase of the current inflationary binge permits a further examination of some of the operative limitations on Ottawa's ability to exercise economic controls.

In *Economics, Third Canadian Edition,* Samuelson-Scott devote 200 pages to "the Keynesian analysis." They find room for one-half a page to explore the possibility that "the open economy" may place certain limitations on the ability of the government to control the "international flow of unemployment" and inflation. As a political scientist pointed out, "the Keynesian analysis did not take

---

* This subject is given fuller treatment in Part V.

into account the constraints imposed on national governments from developments outside their borders, or in the case of federations, from states or provinces with important and autonomous powers."[6] By the 1960s, most Canadians recognized that their country had been reduced to a northern frontier region within the North American economy, a sub-American economy fully subject to the vicissitudes of the U.S.A. and the economic policies shaped in Washington, and essentially uncontrollable by their elected representatives.

More than that, government officials in Ottawa were acting as tireless workers for a continental economy — beginning with William Lyon Mackenzie King and C. D. Howe; continuing with Lester Pearson and Walter Gordon; and the current coterie of P. E. Trudeau, Jean Luc Pepin, John Turner, and Donald Macdonald. The close ties between the two economies and the persistent efforts of Ottawa officials to maintain them became noticeable in the mid-1960's. It was only later on that we learned of the immediate costs imposed by this policy.

In July 1963, the U.S.A., faced with a growing balance of payments problem, introduced an "interest equalization tax" designed to reduce foreign borrowings in the U.S. by increasing the cost to foreigners of raising funds in the U.S. capital market. This was a fine opportunity for Canada to cut down on the unnecessarily large inflows of new U.S. capital coming into the country, and it was handed to Ottawa on a silver platter. Yet the new Minister of Finance, Walter Gordon, his rhetoric to the contrary notwithstanding, sent his officials running to Washington to plead for an exemption from this legislation. Like his predecessors, Gordon was acting on the fallacious belief that Canada needed uninhibited access to U.S. capital to achieve an adequate rate of growth. An exemption was granted — for a price: Gordon agreed not to permit Canada's foreign exchange reserves to rise above the then existing level. This restriction satisfied Washington's double concern that a large-scale exodus of American capital to Canada might otherwise occur and that Canada would build up a large trade surplus at the expense of U.S. manufacturers.

In December of 1965, Ottawa mandarins again made the trek to Washington to gain exemption from a new set of controls. The U.S. Treasury had given instructions to 900 multinational corporations to take steps to expand their exports, increase the remittance of dividends and other payments from abroad, increase their borrowing in other countries, and repatriate short-term assets held abroad. As Eric Kierans observed at the time, this was "a tightening of the American grip on our economy that threatens the attainment of our economic objectives and are an infringement of our political sovereignty."[7]

The price for a partial exemption from these controls was an agreement to lower the reserve ceiling. Agreement to these restrictions proved fatal in 1965 and 1966, years of rapid inflation. The Bank of Canada wished to pursue a tight money policy to discourage spending. But a tighter monetary policy in Canada than the U.S. would have increased Canada's interest rates relative to those of the U.S.A., and attracted additional U.S. investment dollars to Canada, thus increasing this country's foreign exchange reserves in violation of the reserve ceiling. The Bank of Canada not only failed to restrict the supply of money, it expanded it by almost 55 per cent compared with less than a 20 per cent increase in real output, thus helping to fuel the inflation. The effect of the agreement entered into by Walter Gordon neutralized Canada's monetary policy at a time when it was needed to combat this, the first sign of long-term inflationary pressures. In January 1966, Mr. Earle McLaughlin, chairman and president of the Royal Bank of Canada, remarked that "under the new arrangements, our own monetary authorities appear to be attached to a string, or a system of 'guidelines' the business end of which is held in Washington."[8]

Two years later, the U.S. balance of payments crisis having worsened, the directives were made mandatory. They resulted in a considerable outflow of funds from Canada. It seemed as if the Canadian dollar was in trouble and the resulting panic in Ottawa led to "the usual emergency dispatch of the finance minister to Washington to plead Canada's special status as America's most dependable satellite."[9] The crisis apparently ended with a frantic telephone call from Mitchell Sharp to Henry Fowler, U.S. Secretary of the Treasury, pleading with him to tell the American parent companies to instruct their Canadian subsidiaries to moderate the outflow of funds. As Mel Watkins has written of this incident, "Ottawa found it could communicate with Canadian incorporated firms only through Washington."[10]

This time, in return for an exemption, Canada agreed to convert one billion dollars of her exchange reserves into U.S. securities. Half of Canada's exchange reserves could now be called on only with the approval of the U.S. Secretary of the Treasury. The final remnant of monetary independence was liquidated. The only available weapon to fight off the inflation was a cut-back in government spending. As Levitt correctly concludes: "Evidently, Canadian monetary and fiscal policies have both been harnessed to serve the U.S. Treasuries in their efforts to close the U.S. balance of payments gap and protect the value of their dollar. This is indeed the classical position of a colonial economy."[11] It was only in 1969 that the reserve ceilings were finally lifted when both countries launched their anti-inflation drive.

Another Round

Political rulers and corporate czars heaved a sigh of relief as the turbulent 1960s finally came to an end. The new Metternich, Henry Kissinger, had arrived to "settle" the Vietnam war. The ghetto uprisings had passed. The leaders of the Black Panthers were in jail, in exile, or in hiding. [12] The American New Left was in disarray. The upheavals in France (1968) and in Italy (1969) had passed. China and Cuba, the betes noires of the early sixties, were now too preoccupied with their own revolutions to foment new ones abroad. The world was once again safe for capitalism and the multinational corporations. Only madmen and Marxists — in official circles they are thought to be one and the same — were predicting that a new economic crisis was just around the corner.

Yet, the inflationary explosion of the seventies is only the unfinished business of the sixties. Commentators who view the current crisis as a series of unfortunate coincidental accidents that mysteriously emerged are profoundly mistaken. The elements: the food and energy crisis, the shortages in industrial capacity and industrial materials — and the consequences: widespread hunger and mass starvation in the Third World, a decline in living standards and the growth of labour militancy in the capitalist world, political instability, a rise in corporate bankruptcy, balance of payment crises — are clear enough. What is apparently not clear, or at least not admitted, is that both the elements and the consequences of the current crises are inseparably connected to the political economy of modern capitalism. While this is easily said, it is not easily shown. Much of what follows in this and subsequent chapters is an attempt to demonstrate this proposition.

The recession designed and executed by Nixon-Trudeau was aborted before it could make a serious impact on inflation. This was the perfect expression of the political cycle in which the ruling elite, fearing the political consequences of a long drawn-out recession, frees the fiscal-monetary restraints — before the recession has been allowed to draw down on the productive capacity of the economy and before it has broken the back of trade union militancy. Having applied the medicine of recession, the patient was put on the recovery table before the medicine was allowed to work its way through the system, or in other words, before the patient was cured. It should come as no surprise that the patient quickly suffered a relapse.

In the short-run, the policies designed to push the economy out of recession were effective. Wage-price controls served their intended purpose of boosting profits; devaluation of the dollar led to a surge in exports; and a huge government deficit fuelled the whole process. But these actions, at best, only postponed the day of reckoning and, in fact, they soon had the U.S.A. (and Canada) rushing headlong into the new crisis.

This would be the briefest expansion in recent history. The boom-to-bust cycle has averaged about 40 months on the upswing and 10 months on the downswing since World War II. The recent boom which began in 1971 reached its peak midway through 1973 in the U.S. and 12 months later in Canada. In some respects, today's economy closely resembles the pre-World-War-II boom-and-bust cycles, when the average expansion phase lasted a mere 24 months while contraction lasted 20 months.

Unlike the economic recovery of the early 1960s, the recovery of the early seventies did not have the large pools of unemployed workers to draw upon nor the large excess capacity. Strains soon developed that brought on inflationary pressures many months before the food shortage and the "energy crisis". As illustrated in the accompanying chart, when Canadian businesses entered the new expansion phase, the economy was already being operated at 87 per cent of productive capacity. In the early sixties the economy was only being operated at 78 per cent of its capacity. Businesses were therefore bound to move up to the zone of peak operations much sooner.

A significant feature of the 1970s is the growing integration of the capitalist world — a result of the lowering of tariff barriers, the free flow of investment capital across national boundaries, and the preponderant role of multinational corporations, including banks and finance houses. In the early years after World War II and through the fifties and early sixties each economy had its own business cycle. Slack times in North America were often matched by vigorous growth in Europe and Japan. Now the booms and the slowdowns of all capitalist countries coincide. The upswing of the North American economy in 1972 and 1973 was accompanied by booms in Europe and Japan. World trade in 1973 expanded by 37 per cent over 1972. With factories everywhere going all-out, demand for materials overtook supply. Shortages of materials, wood products, and some agricultural products, which had been predicted for some time in the 1990s, materialized in 1973 and 1974.

Figure 8

Rate of capacity utilization: Non-farm goods producing industries

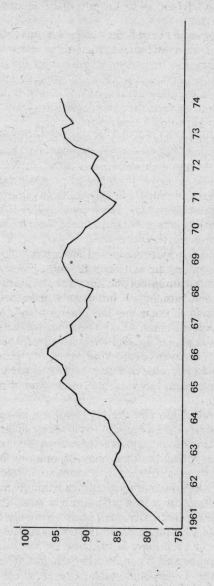

Source: Research Department, Bank of Canada.

In the light of the boom in commodity prices, pressures to maintain full employment, and the need to accommodate the large inflow of American dollars while maintaining fixed exchange rates, all countries allowed their supply of money to grow at a rate that far exceeded the growth of real output.

Table 6
Growth in Output, prices and the Supply of Money, 1967-1973

	Money	Output	Prices
	(average annual % change)		
Japan	19.3	10.9	5.4
Britain	14.3	2.8	7.3
France	14.2	6.0	5.7
Germany	13.6	5.4	5.3

The boom in world trade, while straining productive capacity in all countries, was bound to have a particularly strong impact on Canada and the United States. There are two reasons for this: Between April 1971 and May 1973, Nixon's forced devaluations of the American (and Canadian) dollar had raised the value of the German mark 32 per cent compared to the U.S. and the Canadian dollar; the yen rose by 36 per cent and the franc by 25 per cent. These sharp changes in exchange rates drastically lowered the prices of American and Canadian products abroad. Canadian and American producers were besieged with orders from all over the world. The value of U.S. exports soared by 50 per cent between winter 1971 and spring 1973; while the value of Canadian exports rose by 40 per cent between spring 1972 and spring 1973. American and Canadian suppliers were soon caught short of productive capacity.

When the mini-recession of 1969-70 hit, both had already been plagued with excess capacity due to over-building in the mid-sixties. Investment spending stagnated since that time. With little growth in new plant capacity, operating rates in Canada moved up to 95 per cent early in 1973. For the stock of capital to have grown by the same rate as output in 1973, the value of net investment would have had to grow by over 35 per cent. Nothing like this occurred. The resulting shortages of plant capacity, along with shortages of raw materials, soon caused a rise in costs which suppliers were quick to pass on to their buyers. In the U.S.A., the overall rate of capacity utilization was only 83 per cent, seemingly allowing for substantial room for growth. But there was a real capacity shortage in a number of key industries — so much so that some analysts called it the worst shortage situation since the 1920s.

Two other factors greatly aggravated the shortage situation in the U.S. One was the new environmental standards imposed by U.S. government agencies. The other was the price controls. Expenditures on environmental controls absorbed 11 per cent of investment spending in 1973 (compared to only 4 per cent in 1969). A dollar spent on equipment today creates only 70 cents of added production capacity compared to 1969. The rest pays for anti-pollution and safety devices. Price controls, particularly on resource products which are most easily policed, also cut into profit margins. Many American capitalists decided to hold off future expansion to coerce the government into lifting price and environmental controls.

There is an important lesson here to those in Canada who call for temporary legislated price freezes or price roll-backs and legislation to force improved environmental control. They forget that the motivating factor under capitalism is profits, and that capitalists do not have to produce and will not produce if they cannot receive their targeted profits. Attempts to control inflation by price controls predictably cause capitalists to go on strike. Ultimately this means less expansion in productive capacity and a greater strain on the economy. The medicine of price control can serve to worsen the disease of inflation.

Lurking behind the world-wide inflation was the boom in primary commodities whose prices increased 2 1/2-fold between 1971 and 1974. Every major commodity group experienced this price acceleration: grains, beverages, oils and oil seeds, fibres, metals, and fuels. The main impetus was shortages, rising demand, monopoly controls exercised by the OPEC countries, and in particular the instability of the world monetary system. The decline in the value of the dollar made investment in commodities a profitable hedge against future depreciation. A large supply of Euro-dollars and "oil" and multinational corporation dollars spilled over from the gold market into commodities. While speculation may have been a short-term factor, growing world demand, stimulated by a 10 per cent rise in industrial output in the capitalist world, led to under-supply and rising prices that would take three to five years to overcome.*

Survival of the Fittest

"To the extent that there is a crisis in the Debt economy," writes *Business Week* magazine, "only the biggest and fittest will survive."[13] Corporate strategies in this Darwinian world are not

---

* The food and energy crises are dealt with in detail in Part VI.

without interest, particularly to the non-survivors. And some of them are not lacking in irony.

When I was a graduate student at the University of California in the twilight years of the Cold War, one of the favourite targets of western economists in their relentless campaign against central planning was the alleged distortions that are produced in the Soviet economy by the persistent shortages of parts and materials. Soviet managers, we were told, are forced to send their most talented personnel snooping around the countryside looking for spare parts and materials. As often as not, these scarce commodities have to be pirated away from other enterprises by the use of bribes. The men who perform this task have a special name, *tolkachi* or "pushers," a perennial joke of our sophisticated Soviet-watchers. As well, Soviet managers are forced to hoard material and to set up small backroom machine shops because there is no certainty that the required parts and materials will be delivered in time for them to fulfill the targeted output. The distortions and alleged inefficiencies that result are blamed on the centralized nature of Soviet planning and the absence of a price mechanism or profit system which would allow all requirements to be handled through a market.

But faced with a similar situation of shortages, the managers of U.S. and Canadian corporations are responding in precisely the same way as their Soviet counterparts. The Sun Oil Co., to assure itself of equipment that it fears will not be forthcoming through the market, is considering producing its own pumps, motors, valves, and the like. The research department at Kaiser Aluminum, which formerly had spent most of its time on marketing, now spends 75 per cent of its time studying supply. A home-furnishings manufacturer has appointed a "materials manager to be the traffic cop, so to speak." A Gillette executive admits that "I might be willing to buy three years in advance to make sure I had what I need next year." Another common tactic is to order more than is needed from a number of sources to ensure an adequate supply. E. Patrick McGuire, senior research specialist for the famous Conference Board, tells the story of a company product manager who was recently offered a new Mercedes by one of his customers if he could increase the customer's allocation. Another marketing manager in the same company received an engraved card from one of his customers seeking preferred treatment. The card read: "Your Swiss Account No. is . . . ." McGuire claims that as shortages and inflation persist, these practices will become widespread and they are "bound to have a big impact on the role of the salesman." The appearance of the *tolkachi* in North America is a sign of the breakdown of the market system. In the competition for scarce resources, the survivors turn out to be the companies that can offer the biggest bribes and who are big enough to manufacture their own parts and machinery.[14]

In the chaos of material shortages, zooming prices, and liquidity squeezes, the corporate world has been in a shambles. Many large businesses are at the point of insolvency. Others are swimming in profits. The securities market is open to only the largest corporations, and even among them only to the ones with the healthiest balance sheets. All other companies are obliged to depend on the banking system for funds, but the banks too, hard-put to attract savings and equity capital, are scrutinizing their loans very carefully. The depression in the stock market opens the door for the winners to acquire the losers at bargain-basement prices. Outside the mysterious world of the giant corporation, we are only allowed glimpses of one of the most thorough shakedowns in recent history.

One such instance is the case of "our own" International Nickel Company. Inco made more than $300 million in profits after taxes in 1974. It also got another $200 million in extra cash because of the accelerated depreciation allowances, depletion, exaggerated exploration and development expenses, and the like that the federal and provincial governments allow it. Inco could, of course, distribute the extra $500 million to its shareholders or even to its workers, or it could return it to its consumers in the form of reduced prices. But such behaviour is totally outside the parameters of corporate capitalism. Some of it is no doubt being used to expand Inco's productive capacity in Canada, Indonesia, and Guatemala. But there is a limit on the expansion that can be justified at any moment. With the large surplus at its disposal, Inco is shopping around to acquire new corporate entities. Its major acquisition to date is a very large American battery-manufacturing company called the Philadelphia Main Line, purchased for a price of $230 million. Another mining company, Noranda, also swimming in profits, invested $63 million in other companies in 1974 while at the same time increasing its working capital by another $61 million. Its main acquisition is a controlling interest in a pulp and paper complex, the Fraser Company. And Abitibi Paper Co. paid $125 million to take over controlling interest of Price Co. The two pulp and paper giants combined account for 35 per cent of the total newsprint production in Canada. None of these investments will add anything to the economy's capacity or employment opportunities. It does permit Noranda's chief, Alfred Powis, to take his place in the high council of the Canadian Pulp and Paper Association, as he has already done in the Mining Association of Canada. It allows Inco to go conglomerate, extending its field of control outside the mining industry. And it consolidates Abitibi's position as the number two producer in the forestry industry. As in all crisis situations, some capitalists are scrambling to survive; others are scrambling to invest their surplus cash. The net effect of this shakedown is to intensify the grip of fewer and fewer giant corporations over the global economy.

Among some of the U.S. corporate giants, the wreckage is so complete that only government intervention will save them. Strapped for funds, some American power corporations have announced stretchouts and abandonment of new construction. Excess demand and poorly kept equipment have made brownouts a fairly frequent occurrence in the industrial belts. New York's Consolidated Edison Company has asked the New York State Power Authority to take over some of its new nuclear plants. Other companies are asking for government guaranteed or tax-exempt debt. The poorly regulated American transportation industry is in even more trouble. There are, according to *Business Week,* too many airplanes, trucks, containerships and railroad companies. Pan Am, with a monthly deficit of $10 million, is technically bankrupt. It currently owes $400 million to various institutional lenders, at least some of whom may be dragged under with Pan Am. Excluded from the securities market and with steadily declining operating incomes, most railroads cannot afford to buy new rails, ties, bridges, yards, cars, and locomotives to handle their loads at safe speeds. Penn Central, which has lost over $1.2 billion since it filed for bankruptcy in 1970, would require $3.2 billion over an eight-year period just to catch up in maintenance. A quasi-government corporation has been set up to finance the rehabilitation of seven bankrupt roads in the northwestern United States. *Business Week* notes that the cost of rehabilitation is so great that "Congress might nationalize the bankrupts and be done with it. That would be one way to get back on the right side of the power curve," *Business Week* admits, but "it would also create a precedent that could be extremely dangerous to private enterprise."[15]

Not that bailing out private capital really solves anything. Warding off financial panic now helps lay the groundwork for a bigger one sometime in the future. As long as "prosperity" is maintained by inflation, ever-increasing pyramiding of corporate debt is unavoidable, pushing governments deeper and deeper into the swamp of corporate bankruptcy, without their being able to find a way out.

We have historical precedents for a government bail-out operation. The most comprehensive experience occurred in pre-World-War-II Italy. When the Great Depression struck Italy, practically the whole economy faced imminent bankruptcy. Mussolini's government rose to the occasion and by the mid-1930s a state agency, the Institute for Industrial Reconstruction (IRI) owned the three largest commercial banks and the largest iron and steel, shipping, public utilities and broadcasting companies. Far from being an expression of socialism, these "nationalizations" were merely a new face for capitalism. According to the leading authority on the subject:

> From a mere device used to rescue the banking system, it was transformed into an instrument for furtherance of the industrial policy of the Fascist state. . . . IRI slowly proceeded to invest in the industrial areas that were being developed by the Fascist policies of self sufficiency . . . as well as to expand the capacity of those industries that were specifically devoted to war production.[16]

Adjusting to Inflation the Corporate Way

When the Parisians demanded bread, Marie Antoinette answered, "Let them eat cake." Then, as now, the dominant elite resorts to substitution as the classic economic response to shortages. To keep a handle on costs, businesses are now madly substituting less expensive materials for more expensive ones. More often than not, this has meant substituting highly pollutant synthetic materials for natural ones: candy makers are rushing work on cocoa substitutes; jam and jelly packers are substituting synthetics for fruits; the rise in metal prices has given a special boost to plastics. As the ecologists have warned, these synthetics use up much more energy and non-renewable resources and create much more pollution than natural material. But these ecological costs never appear on the balance sheets of business. They are a subsidy from nature. As is so often the case, what appears as a cost-saving solution to private enterprise ends up being a burden to the rest of society.

The automobile industry has also discovered an interesting solution to its problem. For years it has scorned the smaller cars because they contained less profit. A 1971 article in *Fortune* magazine informs us that a standard sedan selling for $3,000 yielded a profit of $200-$300. When the price falls by a third, to $2,000, the profit drops by half. Henry Ford II had a saying: "minicars make mini-profits." Because the demand for cars has shifted dramatically to the smaller models in view of the high price of gasoline, the auto-makers can no longer ignore the tide. But with their good old American ingenuity they have devised a way to make money from the smaller models — by making optional equipment standard and building only the costlier version of cars advertised as small and economical. Optional equipment returns up to 40 per cent to manu-facturers as profits. A Ford executive explained the precedure to Business Week: You make more money on a Pinto runabout (loaded with options) than on a basic Pinto. So you'll find that basic Pinto is nailed to the dealer's showroom floor. If you want to play in the Pinto game, you drive a runabout."[17]

If the consumer, the weak producer, and nature are the losers in the struggle for survival, what can we say about the worker? The worker is the other victim of the corporation in its scramble to cut costs and maintain profits. Stepped-up emphasis on increasing pro-ductivity and replacing labour with equipment is a long-standing practice of capitalists as the wage-bill mounts. Many of the lay-offs announced in the automobile industry and elsewhere are "inde-finite," a euphemistic term that really means that the workers are being permanently displaced. Nor are the permanent lay-offs being confined to the traditionally vulnerable blue-collar worker. While other corporate operations such as payroll and accounting have been well computerized by now, automation is just coming to gen-eral office operators. "The timing could not be better," according to *Business Week*. "Business has been fighting a losing battle against the rising cost of office labour." It is the "incredibly shrinking com-puter" that is the key to the widespread use of automation in the office and the small manufacturing plant. The price of a mini-com-puter that can be plugged into almost any machine will soon be less than $100.00. More than 100,000 of them are already installed in the U.S. Canadian businesses are not far behind.[18]

The elimination of jobs usually places an increased burden on the remaining work force in the plant or office. It is expected to pro-duce as much or more than the previous large work force. In the words of Jack Rasmus, a trade union organizer:

Speed-ups, stretch-out, and related measures become more common, as does management reliance on time-and-motion stu-dies and other so-called scientific job-evaluation techniques designed to force more productivity out of workers. . . . This will mean an increase in safety and health hazards associated with physical and emotional stress. Cost-cutting will also lead to widespread cut-backs in maintenance crews and fewer preventa-tive maintenance shut downs, thus increasing safety hazards on the job as well.

Even more dangerous, Rasmus says, is that management will become even more rigid in its opposition to investing in and maintaining the necessary, but expensive, ventilation systems required to protect workers from highly dangerous and often cancer-producing dusts, gases and chemicals.[19]

The spread of worker militancy, while no doubt directly related to the drop in living standards, is also spurred on by the deterioration in the quality of the work environment. Management pressure to cut costs and raise productivity raises serious issues on the shop floor as regards job safety and health, job classifications and rates, work assignments and schedules, job transfers, promotions, and demotions. As these pressures are resisted, frequent confrontations occur over discipline, discharge, suspensions, firings, discrimination, and the like. In some instances these confrontations have led to work stoppages, slowdowns, and wildcat strikes. In large part, it is management's attempts to speed up, stretch out, and cut back on health, safety, and environmental standards, that explain the growing bitterness and the new militancy that is being displayed in strikes that are ostensibly only about wages.

Financing the Investment Boom

Shortages ultimately led to a new boom in investment spending in Canada. Investment in new plant and equipment rose by 18 per cent in 1973 and by another 20 per cent in 1974, compared to only 6 per cent in 1972. While new investment spread throughout the economy, the biggest expansion of facilities was in industries where price pressures have been the greatest — steel, paper, petroleum products, chemicals, and transportation equipment. Underlying the investment boom are the huge energy projects underway in James Bay, the Alberta tar sands, and Northern Manitoba, and on the Atlantic coast.

An investment boom produces the conditions for continued, if not accelerated inflation. It will be a few years before the additional production capacity is sufficient to meet existing and future demands for many materials. In the meantime, shortages of skilled labour and shortages of steel and paper, chemicals, and plastics will push up prices throughout the economy, creating a continued squeeze on living standards. Only a generalized, deep and sustained depression can break the inflation.

The economic strains in fulfilling these investment plans can be illustrated by the demands of the Syncrude tar sands project. This project alone requires prompt delivery of 3,000 skilled tradesmen,

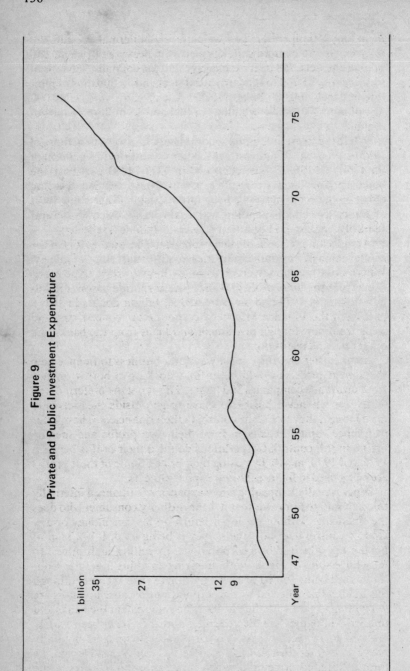

Figure 9

Private and Public Investment Expenditure

including 750 pipefitters and welders, 300 boilermakers, and 400 electricians; 61 compressors, 69 pieces of heavy equipment, 250 pressure vessels, 768 heat exchangers, 150 tons of nails, 350 tons of welding rod, 15,700 tons of structural steel and 12,500 tons of reinforcing steel, 500,000 bolts, 110,000 feet of conveyors, 1,749,000 feet of piping, 10 million gallons of fuel and 15 million pounds of cement!

While the latest investment boom is not quite so lusty as those of 1957 or 1966 (in 1957, investment spending absorbed 26 per cent of the GNP; in 1966, 25 per cent, and in 1973-74, 23 per cent), the build-up of productive capacity is bound to have a similar dragging effect on the economy as we head into recession. Thus a few years of ferocious capital-spending will again be followed by several years of stagnation. The pattern of feast-to-famine is repeated.

An investment boom of such proportions, located as it is in the capital-intensive resource industries, requires vast sums of money. Where does the money come from? A large part of these funds come from the huge profits taken by the corporate barons (15 billion dollars in 1973 and an estimated 21 billion dollars in 1974), part from the Finance Minister's corporate tax concessions, and some from new foreign investment and loans from the banks and other financial institutions.

In an earlier era, the typical way for a business to finance new investment projects would be to float stock or to borrow money from insurance companies and banks. This is not the preferred way today, for whenever businesses have to go outside themselves to raise money, they lose some control to their financiers. They prefer to finance capital expansion from their own profits and thereby maintain full control. Corporations doubled their profits between 1972 and 1974, mostly by raising their prices. Some of these profits are being used to finance the new capital projects.

What is really happening when expansion is financed internally through inflated prices is that it is the ordinary consumer who does the financing, without getting a return on his/her money or any kind of control over how the money is being used. It is a kind of hidden tax which allows corporations, by setting high prices, to raise huge sums of money without giving anything in return. Consumers are being forced to save a portion of their incomes through this hidden tax collected by the corporations because investors are not willing to part with their dollars. To some extent the banks and finance companies are also sources, and they have been widely resorted to in recent years. Yet corporation managers naturally prefer to extract their savings cost-free — from consumers in the form of inflated prices and, when they can, from workers in the form of deflated wages.

One billion of the 4-billion-dollar increase in 1973 corporate profits come from John Turner's tax concessions. These concessions, came out of the debacle surrounding the recommendations of the Carter Royal Commission and (former Finance Minister) Edgar Benson's minor gestures outlined in his White Paper. Out of the furor raised by the business establishment, all progressive measures were removed save one — a tax on capital gains — but only at half the normal rates. It was then that the corporations really swung their weight. They wailed about over-taxation of the wealthy "which makes this country strong," claiming also that they were being forced to operate at a disadvantage compared to companies located elsewhere in the world. "John Turner's reply came in May of 1972," wrote Nick Fillmore of *The Fourth Estate:*

> And his reply was clear, as befits his membership in Canada's corporate elite. The rate of tax on corporate profits was cut down from 49 per cent to 40 per cent, the largest business tax cut in 25 years. But this wasn't enough. Turner also allowed for corporations to write off the capital costs of manufacturing machinery and equipment in two years.[20]

The Canadian system of depreciation is already considered pretty generous by international standards, permitting corporations to depreciate their equipment in five to ten years when the average useful life of that equipment is more like 25 years. Turner's beneficence, renewed in his 1974 budget, this time without a "terminal date," allows them to write off their new manufacturing equipment in only two years. Where previously a manufacturing company purchasing a machine worth $100,000 could reduce its taxable profits in the first year by $20,000, Turner lets them reduce taxable profits by $50,000, a saving for the company of $30,000.

Besides renewing the two-year write-off for manufacturers, Turner's 1974 budget also exempts manufacturers from his much heralded increase in corporate taxes. Not only were manufacturers exempted but just about every important sector of business — resource companies, investment companies, and "small businesses." Small businesses get a special break from Mr. Turner. They will pay tax at a rate of 25 per cent instead of the normal rate of 50 per cent on the first $100,000 of net income instead of the first $50,000.

Why is This Crisis Different from the Others?

Inflation in the closing months of 1974 and in 1975 is no longer simply the classic case of too much money chasing too few goods. That description applies to the first round of inflation generated by the great budget deficits in the second half of the 1960s and the large outflow of American dollars that were absorbed by Europe. It also covers the runaway inflation of 1972, 1973, and early 1974, fuelled as well by enormous deficits and the shortages of materials, food, fuel and metals. Now, aside from food, most of the shortages are easing. But the inflation process is running on its own momentum as labour attempts to make up for past losses and wholesalers and retailers attempt to pass on their increased costs of manufactured goods. This so-called "cost-push" inflation is likely to continue stubbornly, if somewhat more moderately, even as the economy goes into a deep recession, what is now being called a mini-depression. Since it is no longer generated by excess demand and shortages, it will not be broken by a temporary drop in demand. Only an old-fashioned depression, lasting a few years, reducing output by 10 per cent or more a year and creating an unemployment rate of 10 to 15 per cent would eventually bring down the inflation rate to "normal" levels — by crushing organized labour and shrinking markets so drastically that sellers would have to move their goods at a loss. This sort of squeeze-play is out of the question.

If the inflation will not cure itself easily, neither will the mini-depression. In his monumental study, *Measuring Business Cycles,* the late Wesley Clair Mitchell claimed that every economic down-turn sows the seed of recovery. For all post-war recessions this has been the case. The process works like this. When profits and income fall and unemployment rises, taxes go down and unemployment insurance and welfare payments go up. Disposable income is thereby maintained, stimulating consumption spending despite the recession. Moreover, consumers cut their savings rate too in an effort to maintain their living standards in the face of falling incomes. Business sales thus begin to pick up even while income is still declining. Similarly, businesses cut down on their inventories by selling them off and not replacing them. As stocks are liquidated the way is prepared for an eventual rise in new orders to manufac-turers. Declining interest rates, which are characteristic of normal recessions as business and consumer loans drop off, help to stimu-late investment and consumption. These "automatic stabilizers," with a little help from the monetary and fiscal authorities, bolster consumer and business spending and the economy soon snaps back.

It remains the case that every business downturn brings about its own recovery, but this time the automatic rebound model does not apply so easily. There is first of all the extreme depression in the stock market and the hesitancy of most corporations to invest new funds in capital equipment. As Arthur M. Okun, former Chairman of the U.S. Council of Economic Advisors, has remarked, "if there is any law in economics that still holds water, it is that businessmen don't invest in plants and equipment for a market that isn't there." With industrial output falling by 10 per cent in the first quarter of 1975 and profits down even more and with plant capacity in use only 65 per cent of potential, capital spending plans were in a state of suspension. The drop in industrial production registered little immediate effect on inventories because sales were dropping off almost as fast as industry could cut back on output. Because of inflation and fears of unemployment, consumer savings actually rose in the fourth quarter of 1974. Short-term interest rates did come down but long-term rates — which are more important for housing and business investment — remained high because inflationary expectations had not evaporated and because of the absence of alternative sources for investment capital.

Inflation not only played havoc with the normal responses to recession in the private sector, it also unstabilized the automatic stabilizers. Inflated incomes and inflated profits sent taxes soaring. While output was falling and unemployment rising, the tax system was causing a drain on consumer and corporate revenues, compounding the recession rather than automatically countering it. By January 1975, a consensus had formed that only a massive cut in the rate of taxation could reverse the recession.

This is the first generalized recession experienced by the international capitalist economy since World War II. It is the most serious recession in the post-war period, precisely because it is generalized. The lack of synchronization of the business cycle in the last 20 years reduced the breadth of recession. When one country experienced a decline in its internal market it could compensate by expanding exports to countries that continued to prosper. This time virtually no capitalist country has escaped the crisis.

In the past, each country has faced its own recession by expanding exports abroad and increasing credit at home. But with inflation accelerating in all countries, these solutions were unavailable. That is why all governments had to apply an anti-inflationary policy simultaneously. Hence all find themselves in the midst of recession. This synchronization is reflected in the dramatic falling-off of international trade. World trade grew 13 per cent in 1972 and 15 per cent in 1973, but only 5 per cent in 1974 and a projected 2 per cent in 1975 — "rates that will expose and exacerbate conflicts between nations," according to the assessment of *Business Week* magazine.[21]

Table 7

	% change in industrial production in the fourth quarter of 1974	Average unemployment in the fourth quarter of 1974*	
		No. (million)	% of labour force
Japan	-2.6	.75	1.5
U.S.A.	-2.5	7.00	8.0
Britain	-1.5	.70	3.0
West Germany	-1.5	1.00	4.2
Italy	-1.2	1.00	6.0
France	-1.0	1.00	3.3
Canada	-0.5	.70	6.1

*all figures rounded

The threat of worldwide recession was spelled out officially in the OECD's July 1974 report. In 1973, the OECD reported, its member nations experienced the strongest economic upswing the industrialized world had ever seen. In the first half of 1973 real growth was running at an annual rate of about 8 per cent of the seven major "bellwether" countries — Britain, Canada, France, Italy, West Germany, and the United States. Twelve months later, the economic activity of the nations was actually shrinking. "The OECD area has just gone through the most exceptional deceleration of growth ever experienced," the report said. For the first time in the post-war period, three of these countries were experiencing simultaneous slowdowns. And the slowdowns were accompanied by a rise in consumer prices that averaged 13 per cent in the area.

The rapid rise of consumer prices, unmatched by equivalent increases in wages and social benefits, cut down purchasing power and led to a drop in consumer spending, especially in the U.S., U.K., and West Germany. High mortgage rates collapsed the housing market in a number of countries. On the supply side, shortages in productive capacity, particularly in the U.S.A. and Canada, and shortages in industrial materials, whether real or artificial, caused further slowdowns. A sharp rise in inventory stocks caused many businesses to cut their purchases, leading to a further drop in the general level of business activity. Worldwide recession was helped by government measures designed to bring inflation under control. "Monetary policy has converged internationally in recent months towards a more general position of restraint, with record or near-record market rates of interest prevailing in most countries," according to the report. The rise of corporate, government, and consumer debt, both a cause and an effect of the inflation, has put upward pressures on interest rates which were reinforced by the authorities when they reduced the growth of the money supply. While this policy had little noticeable effect on inflation, it discouraged both business and consumer spending. Housing and automobiles, in particular, experienced dramatic declines throughout the capitalist world. Most countries, and particularly those plagued by unmanageable oil bills, moved to slow down their economies by phasing down government expenditures.

But they are all caught in a common dilemma: they know that the only effective way to halt the inflation is to support the worldwide major depression by a policy of severe and sustained contraction; on the other hand they fear the consequences of widespread unemployment and corporate bankruptcy. The following subheads appeared in a special October 1974 supplement of *Business Week* magazine: "No Right Answer" and "A Choice of Disasters." By a "choice of disasters" the editors of this staid business journal meant that either the credit bubble will burst, as it has so many times in the past, most recently in the 1930s, or the government will ease its monetary and credit policies and thereby feed the inflation.

Many governments seem to have adopted the strategy of restraining their own economies while pressuring Washington to expand the American economy, their largest external market. In an interview released August 24, West German Chancellor Helmut Schmidt took the extraordinary step of publicly warning the U.S. government that if it continued to pursue recessionary politicies, the U.S. could pull the rest of the capitalist world down with her. "There is a danger," he told James Reston of the *New York Times,* "that if the United States goes deflationary . . . this will inevitably spread to the world markets. It will mean that we can sell less."

Ford did not oblige. Production bottlenecks had forced the discontinuation of wage-price guidelines. With business desperate to regain liquidity, profit margins had to be enlarged. But 1974 promised to be a period of intense collective bargaining with the contracts of millions of Americans expiring. Backed by free marketeers Alan Greenspan and William Simon, Ford decided to restore some serious competition in the labour market. The Administration moved quickly. Government spending was cut sharply in the middle of 1973. The monetary screws were tightened soon after. These policies were sustained throughout 1974 to produce a major decline.

The watchwords during these months were fighting inflation and saving energy. Ford called for a national campaign to exorcize inflation by wearing buttons labelled "WIN" (whip inflation now): "I call on each of you to become inflation fighters. Draw up lists of ten ways to save money and fuel. Exchange your family's list with your neighbours and send me a copy." Ford's prescription for inflation brought out a counter-button: "BATH" — Back Again to Hoover. Ford's collection of slogans, his pep talks, incantations, and voluntarism, were indeed a fair imitation of Herbert Hoover. But public appearances aside, the President did make a choice — to beat back inflation by breaking the strength of labour. This was another planned recession, though a year was to pass before Ford gave it official recognition.

Even before the massive layoffs in the automobile industry were fully underway in the winter months of 1974, 6 million American workers were unemployed, about 6½ per cent of the labour force, up from 5 per cent as recently as April 1974. Among blacks and other minority groups the unemployment rate was 12 per cent. Unemployment figures in Canada and the U.S., as I have already noted, systematically understate the degree of forced idleness. They do not count people who can only find part-time jobs, people who have been searching in vain for so long that they have dropped out of the labour market altogether, and people who are too discouraged about the prospects even to start looking. Even so, by the spring of 1975, the number of American workers officially unemployed stood at 8 million, about 9 per cent of the labour force, the highest level in 33 years. Among blue-collar workers it reached double-digit proportions. In the highly industrialized districts of Michigan, Ohio, and southern California, one out of every five or six workers were cut off from their jobs; one out of every five teenagers were without work, and, for black youths, more than one out of every three!

From the business perspective, the strategy is working. Real wages of American workers have fallen sharply and the incidence of strike action is down. But there is a risk that significant numbers of Americans will be pushed toward some kind of political rebellion. As even *Business Week* magazine warned, "Further increases in unemployment would not only mean lost production, income and profits, but would heighten social tensions and might set the stage again for riots in the cities."[22] It seems that growing numbers are recognizing the recession's political roots, with job marches on Washington having begun and likely spreading.

There is a second risk, which relates to the fact that the American economy is teetering closer to the brink of a major depression than Ford and his free marketers realized. What makes the economy so vulnerable to a depression now is the state of indebtedness of so many large corporations and the consumers at large. Even a relatively mild slump that reduced sales and incomes would cause liquidity-short business and consumers to default in their debts. Should a major bank or corporation fall prey to liquidity problems, its collapse would drop dozens of others down with it. In 1955, U.S. companies were in debt to the tune of 21 cents for each dollar of equity they had; by the summer of 1974 the debt had soared to nearly 44 cents for each dollar of equity. Several large corporations have already suspended dividend payments for lack of cash, and a number have been forced to go to the government for an injection of funds. The banks aren't much better off. Five years ago, U.S. commercial banks had 65 cents loaned out for every dollar they had in deposit; in 1974 they had nearly 77 cents in outstanding loans for every dollar in the till. Government officials were sufficiently concerned to take precautionary measures as monetary authorities of ten western nations pledged to bail out any international bank in danger of collapse.

As *Business Week* magazine has written in its special issue "The Debt Economy":

> One way or another, U.S. business and those that it borrows from have become extraordinarily vulnerable. Frightened investors show no willingness at all to buy common stock. There is worrisome uncertainty about the ability of many corporations to keep servicing their long term debt. . . . If inability to meet internal obligations is seldom the last nail in a corporate coffin, the burden of excessive debt is often what drags it down toward a premature grave. In the case of Pan Am, the airline analyst suggests, the rising cost of fuel "came and speeded up a pack of troubles" that was coming anyway because of Pan Am's overwhelming debt. They got themselves such a high level of fixed costs that with any deterioration, either on the expense side or the revenue side, they just had to have serious trouble.[23]

Consumers are in an analogous position to business. Take a worker who buys a house with a $35,000 mortgage at 12 per cent. He is relying on a steady rise in his pay cheque to handle the payments. If his wage were to rise from $10,000 to $16,000 in five years, as expected, the fixed debt becomes progressively easier to handle. But if he were laid off or his income frozen or raised only minimally, even if prices also fell, his mortgage debt would remain the same. It would now claim a much higher proportion of his income.

His total payments might now exceed the value of the house, should it fall in price. Under the circumstances, if he has any choice in the matter, it becomes profitable to default.

President Ford found himself in the same dilemma in 1975 as Nixon did five years earlier: fight and sustain a war against inflation at the cost of massive unemployment and widespread corporate bankruptcy, or fight off the impending depression at the cost of reviving galloping inflation. The only difference is that because of the extraordinary expansion of debt and the widespread inflationary expectations, the cost of doing either has increased. Ford's anti-recession budget called for a deficit of $86.6 billion in 1975-76. The American Congress upped it by several billion dollars more. Even so, this deficit, the deepest in U.S. peacetime history, is only expected to reduce unemployment a mere half of one percentage point. And as *Business Week* magazine warns, the "high and volatile inflation which has persisted for a decade, raises serious questions as to whether fiscal stimulus can result in anything but an early resurge of inflation . . ."[24] This danger was freely admitted by U.S. Treasury Secretary William E. Simon in an interview with *Business Week:*

> Normally, in a period of recession, when other demands fall away to such a large degree, the government has ample room to borrow without putting tremendous pressure on the marketplace. But this time we have a different set of circumstances. We have had a sustained rate of inflation, illusory profits, an illiquidity problem, an inability of our corporations to finance in the equity market, a debt-equity ratio that is completely out of kilter, so corporations are going to require financing at a very high level, just to maintain present activity. This suggests we may be in for a period of congestion.
>
> If the government demand for short-term money continues — and it will — some companies may be forced out of the market, and there could be some bankruptcies among those pushed out as the government encroaches in the market. We have forced people out, into higher cost sources of money.[25]

With the U.S. Treasury seeking $70 billion in the capital markets, more money then was raised by all borrowers, public and private in 1974, interest rates will be driven up threatening private borrowers. Thus the stimulating impact of the record deficit is limited while the inflationary impact could be substantial.

Policy makers assume that no country can go the route in eliminating either inflation or unemployment. Their aim is to establish a new stable equilibrium featuring permanently higher levels of both. Whether the North American economy can be stabilized with rates of unemployment varying from 5 per cent to 10 per cent and rates of inflation varying from 7 per cent to 13 per cent is highly questionable.

While all predictions are subject to grave error due to unforeseen circumstances, the most likely scenario is that the anti-recession policies now being followed by all governments will cause an upturn in the international economy sometime in late 1975 or early 1976. Since there is a time gap between the moment when the money supply expands and the moment this reflects itself in higher prices, inflation could moderate in 1975. A new inflationary wave should get underway sometime in 1976-77. However, the projected recoveries are so tepid that average yearly unemployment will still be rising in 1976 for countries like Italy and the U.K. and will be declining only marginally in Canada, Japan, the U.S., and France. As the pattern repeats itself, this would be followed by a new and deeper recession as governments will once again be forced to restrain the growth of the economy.

Slumpflation could be interrupted by war, a wave of bank failures that governments are unable to forestall, or a serious and systematic program of wage-price controls. The likelihood of the first two occurring is slight, but price-wage controls may very well be on the agenda.

Limits of Liberalism

When Finance Minister John Turner presented his June 24, 1975 budget, among his first words were:

> We are now faced with a dilemma. If we follow more expansionary policies at this time we run the risk of making inflation worse. If, on the other hand, we follow contradictory policies, we risk worsening unemployment.

With 700,000 Canadians unemployed and the inflation rate improving but still running better than 10 per cent, the situation facing Canada's Liberal government could not have been better expressed. In broad outline, Turner's dilemma is the same as that confronting the cabinets of other governments. The capitalist world is teeter-tottering between massive inflation and massive unemployment. The resting point between is one of slumpflation. Due to the peculiar policies of the Liberal government, however, there is a uniquely Canadian kink to this common dilemma.

While most other leaders of the capitalist world were desperately deflating their economies, Pierre Trudeau's Liberals chose to turn their back on the inflationary problem through the critical months of 1974. Viewing the inflation as an international phenomenon, their claim was that the government of Canada could do nothing effective to control it. Besides easing up slightly on the supply of money, they went no further than moderating the impact of inflation by a variety of devices forced upon them by their NDP rump in the 29th Parliament: pensions were raised and indexed to the cost of living, income taxes indexed as well, subsidies paid to keep down the price of milk; baby bonuses raised, and a two-price system established for oil and wheat to isolate Canadians somewhat from the ravages of the international food and energy crises. Fiscal policy became more restrictive, although probably unintentionally, as the federal government ran up a surplus of $685 million in 1974 compared to a surplus of $43 million in 1973.

John Turner's 1974 budget delivered a few crumbs to the average Canadian in the form of a small break in income taxes. Its real thrust was to put large sums of money into the hands of investors to encourage them to increase Canada's productive capacity.* Turner's theory: let the U.S. and other countries fight inflation with

---

* The 1975 budget was essentially a continuation of the mildly expansionary budget of 1974. The actual deficit in 1974 was $1.56 billion. The planned-for deficit in 1975 was $5 billion. The stated aim of the 1974 budget was to protect the poor, and those most vulnerable to the "ravages of inflation." Actually it did nothing of the sort. While families receiving under $2,000 received a tax benefit of $30.00, families receiving between $2,000 and $2,999 a tax benefit of $80.00, and families receiving $3,000-$3,999 a tax benefit of $120.00, families in the lowest income category benefited to the extent of 1.4 per cent to 2.2 per cent of their income, while the highest income families benefited to the extent of 3.6 per cent of their incomes, a clearly regressive measure. (See W. Irwin Gillespie, *An Analysis of Recent Federal Budgetary Policy in Canada*, Carleton University Papers.)

While the 1975 budget offered little change in the structure of income taxes, it continued in this regressive pattern. The tax on gasoline added about $100.00 a year for every motorist. The increased price of natural gas and heating added about $65.00 to the heating bills of households. Employees' contributions to the Unemployment Insurance Commission rose by about $25.00 to $35.00 a year under the revised financing formula in which the federal government abandoned the 4 per cent unemployment rate beyond which it formerly contributed to the UIC. Ceilings placed on federal contributions to health care services will undoubtedly force provincial governments to raise their taxes in order to finance health needs.

While socking it to Canadian workers, the 1975 budget offered still more benefits to the business community, including a new 5 per cent tax credit on new investments, a new 25 per cent tax reduction from income earned in petroleum and mineral resource production and a cut in the corporation resources tax from 50 per cent to 46 per cent. As well, the 15 per cent withholding tax on corporate bond interest to holders outside Canada was removed, making it easier for larger corporations to borrow in New York.

their restrictive policies while Canada goes on prospering. It was a feasible policy because, being self-sufficient in oil, Canada did not face the balance of payments problems of other countries. But it was a short-sighted policy fraught with contradictions which were bound to surface.

The chickens came home to roost mid-way through 1975 as the rest of the capitalist world was beginning to emerge from the recession and prepare for recovery. By sustaining economic growth even after prices had accelerated to the double-digit level, Ottawa did not subject the country to the economic "discipline" that comes with declining economic activity. Inefficient businesses were allowed to prosper. Continual growth strengthened labour's bargaining position. The mildness of the recession here (by comparison to that in other countries) meant that Canada was operating at closer to full capacity than was the case in other countries. Canada was thus bound to run into capacity shortages sooner than elsewhere as economic recovery set in.

By introducing two-price systems for oil and natural gas, the government was able to delay the rise in domestic fuel prices temporarily. There was no reason to believe that the oil companies would accept the resulting lower returns indefinitely. As they threatened to reduce their investments, the government had the choice of replacing them with publicly-owned enterprises or abandoning the two-price system. It was bound to choose the latter option. The country faced a rise in fuel costs that would add at least two percentage points to the consumer price index at a time when consumers in Europe and Japan and to a lesser extent the U.S.A. already absorbed the increased price in fuel.

In sum, while other governments accepted the need to engineer sharp declines in economic activity and have been at least partially successful in dampening internal inflationary pressures, our government chose to ride with the inflationary waves and now faces the consequence of a raging inflation, a raging recession and continuously worsening trade balances. Faced with these conditions, partly of his own making, the Liberal Finance Minister had three options: adopt a very restrictive fiscal and monetary policy that would deliberately reduce the level of production and employment; impose direct controls over wages and incomes; or with these as bargaining weapons, persuade Canadian workers to accept voluntary wage restraints. These are the kinds of choices that will arise again and again in Ottawa and other capitals as the crisis develops in the years ahead.

Having failed in his efforts to pressure Canadian workers to accept voluntary restraints, Turner also failed to persuade the Liberal cabinet to implement a program of legislated controls, and he dismissed as politically suicidal a severe deflationary budget. Complete paralysis was avoided when the government committed itself to setting an example in the field of wage settlements with federal civil servants. With corporations complaining that high settlements in the public sector have set the pace for industry, "a tighter fist at the Treasury Board will provide the main thrust of his support for fellow employers in the private sector," according to the *Financial Post's* post mortem on the 1975 budget. But he also injected new restrictions in the Unemployment Insurance Act to "create a greater incentive to remain at work or to search more actively for a job."

In his budget address Turner conceded that labour's share of the national output had fallen significantly in the earlier stages of inflation, "but the balance has since been fully restored" and he warned once again that efforts to raise labour's share of the national output would not be tolerated. In his words, these efforts are expressed in "wage and salary demands [that] appear to bear little relationship to economic reality." According to the Liberal view of "economic reality" any attempt by labour to raise its share of the national output is simply outside the rules of the game. Should the combination of government measures and continuing high levels of unemployment be insufficient to tame wage demands, legislated controls could and probably will be introduced.

The Liberals chose to sit out this inflationary round of the inflation-recession dialectic. A recession came anyway, largely imported from the United States. As a consequence the inflation problem was aggravated. The capitalist economy has its own laws of development, which governments can attempt to influence, for better or for worse, but cannot undo or ignore, as our Liberal government came to discover.

The Anatomy of Unemployment

A pool of 586,000 unemployed Canadian workers had been created by the end of 1972. The slow growth of investment during the five previous years generated fewer new jobs than were required to absorb the growing labour force. Although employment increased significantly in 1973 and the first quarter of 1974, the increase was still not large enough to provide jobs for this pool of the unemployed. The hardest hit group was in the 14-24 age category, which has also been the one increasing the most rapidly. From 1966 to 1971, additional jobs were created for only 67 per cent of the new 14-24 age group in the labour force and the rapid growth in 1973 affected them the least. In 1973 and 1974 the unemployment rate for young workers was 10 per cent, with single young males experiencing a staggering unemployment rate of 12.5 per cent. The recession does not spread evenly across the country. It is barely felt in the wheat and oil belt; in the Atlantic provinces, unemployment was in the range of 13 per cent; Quebec, 10 per cent; B.C., 9 per cent; and Ontario 7-8 per cent. The actual number of unemployed greatly exceeds the official total. Most of the native people are not counted in among the labour force. Unemployed workers who give up looking for jobs as the recession deepens are not counted. But what is also often overlooked in interpreting unemployment statistics is that a 7 per cent annual rate of unemployment means that the average percentage of unemployed workers *at any one time* during a year may be 7 per cent, representing, say, 700,000 workers. A far greater proportion of the labour force will have lost jobs *at some point* over the year.

For example, if the average annual unemployment rate is 7 per cent and the average period of unemployment is 8 weeks, then assuming each person is only unemployed once during the year, 46 per cent of all workers, totalling over 3½ million people, will have lost their jobs during the year, as well as 15 to 20 per cent of their potential wages. In the Atlantic Provinces and Quebec, which have perennially higher rates of unemployment extending over longer periods, the impact is more severe. A 12 per cent annual unemployment rate in the Atlantic Provinces with an average duration of 13 weeks means that 48 per cent of the work force could have lost their jobs at some point during the year, along with about 25 per cent of their potential earning power. Of course, these figures tend to overstate the number of people affected. They assume that each person is unemployed only once during the year. If half the persons affected lost jobs twice during the year and half once only, a third of the labour force would be affected, still a formidable number.

Economists have traditionally employed two divergent theories to explain post-war unemployment. Keynesians view the labour market as a long queue. If the economy is expanding rapidly enough then eventually almost everyone in the line will be absorbed. Unemployment arises because of the failure of governments to practice expansionary policies. The structuralists, on the other hand, view much of the unemployment being caused by technological displacement, shifting patterns of industrial production, foreign competition, and similar changes that disrupt the matching of jobs and workers in the labour market. Both of these explanations assume that unemployment is involuntary. Individuals actively seek jobs and are unable to find them for reasons not of their own making. Their remedies differ. The structuralists argue for programs to correct inbalances through improved information, retraining and relocation — an approach that has been embodied in the various manpower programs created in the 1960s. The Keynesians favour increasing the level of economic activity through more aggressive monetary and fiscal policies.

A third explanation has been recently offered that disputes the involuntary character of unemployment. It holds that the official level of unemployment exaggerates the degree of real unemployment. According to this view, a substantial number of unemployed, particularly the young, have a casual attitude towards work. Their unemployment reflects neither Keynesian shortages nor structural skill imbalances, but rather a more critical attitude towards jobs that are unattractive because of low pay or other undesirable characteristics. Many young workers choose an in-and-out pattern, combined with unemployment compensation, rather than accepting this kind of work on a steady basis. Prime Minister Trudeau appears to be a convert to this theory. In his opinion the lingering high rate of unemployment in the early 1970s was caused by the choosiness of young people, a change in the work ethic. From here it is a short step to argue that responsibility for such unemployment rests with the individual, not with society. The decision of young workers to refuse jobs becomes the root cause of much of the unemployment, not the inadequate level of economic activity or ineffective manpower policies. If this is the case, then efforts to reduce unemployment to a three or four per cent level are misguided. The best that governments can do to eliminate this source of unemployment is to tighten up the administration of unemployment insurance and welfare programs. Campaigns to this end have in fact been pursued by governments throughout Canada in the last few years.

The spread of mass unemployment to all age groups and occupations affected by the current recession does not settle the question. The incidence of unemployment is not distributed evenly throughout the labour force. Contrary to the Keynesians, employers do not draw workers from a single labour market. There is instead a dual labour market, a "primary" and a "secondary" labour sector — somewhat analogous to the centre and peripheral dual organization of business. In the primary labour market, jobs typically come with high wages and salaries, good working conditions, job security, and chances for advancement. In the secondary labour market, jobs usually offer low wages, unstable employment, poor working conditions, exhausting work, and little opportunity for advancement. Although the secondary labour market is the camping ground for some people, like teenagers and women, who may be only temporary residents there, it also involves a large number of persons who are permanently trapped. Their mobility is restricted to moving with great rapidity in and out of jobs within the secondary labour market. Their other possibilities lie with unemployment insurance and welfare, which pay nearly as well and, in the case of welfare, sometimes more.

All jobs in the secondary labour market have a high turnover rate. Some are not organized to provide continuous employment. Others, like mining, menial jobs in hospitals, factories and restaurants, and low-skill jobs in offices, are fairly stable, but these kinds of jobs do not attract a stable work force. There is much coming into and going from these jobs and there is always an excess supply of these workers. "Labourers" is a statistical category that includes one element of the secondary labour market. In 1972, 16.7 per cent of "labourers" were officially unemployed. By contrast, "craftsmen, production process and related workers," which includes blue collar primary workers, had an unemployment rate of "only" 7.6 per cent. These "dirty" workers, as they have been called, constitute a significant and irreducible minority of manual workers. I have estimated that they number about 2 million out of our 8 million work force.* Highly developed capitalist societies like our own need a mass of outcasts or "marginal" people that can be burdened with the kinds of work the rest of the population considers too degrading to be acceptable. In Canada these marginal elements are the native people, Quebecois, women, teenagers, and recent immigrants.

It is argued by the "voluntarists" that such casual labourers, particularly young workers, are interested only in short-term employment which interferes minimally with school or leisure-time activities. These jobs in the secondary sector, with their greater tolerance of lateness, absenteeism, and high turnover, are particularly suited to such workers, and it is this combination of casual work attachment and irregular jobs that is used to explain the high incidence of youth unemployment. Yet virtually all young people decide eventually to settle into permanent jobs. The timing of such decisions is surely affected by the availability of preferable jobs. More to the point, many young people who are not saddled by the

---

* They break down as follows: 700,000 in service occupations, 680,000 in clerical and other white collar occupations, 450,000 in factories or on construction, 200,000 in farm labour, and 90,000 in mining, logging and fishing.

Depression mentality *are* more "choosy" about the work that they do. They view most work in the primary labour market as stifling their creative abilities. That is why many choose casual work in the secondary market. They have not lost "the work ethic," but they have come to expect more from their jobs than a regular pay-cheque. It is quite true that neither Keynesian economics nor man-power programs will reach many of them. Their job expectations can be realized only by a restructuring of the organization and con-tent of work, and this lies beyond the boundaries of liberal reforms.

Immigrant people have always tended to cluster in certain occu-pations, the lowliest ranking being given the "dirtiest" jobs. In 1931, when 18 per cent of the Canadian labour force worked at unskilled occupations, 30 per cent of Canadians of East-European origin clustered in these jobs along with 44 per cent of Italian origin, 28 per cent of Asian-Canadians, 21 per cent of French Cana-dians and 63 per cent of the native Indian labour force. This ordering has persisted over time. In 1961, for example, when 10 per cent of the labour force worked at these low level jobs, Italians (22 per cent), French Canadians (13 per cent), Asians (23 per cent) and native Indians (45 per cent) were still over-represented. A minority of immigrants find their way into more stable and higher skilled jobs before they end their job careers. Their sons and daughters and, more likely yet, their grandsons and granddaughters will have a better chance of beginning their job careers in the primary labour market. In the meantime, as Montreal journalist Sheila Anopoulos discovered, "while they dream of 'tomorrow' they man the dingy textile and clothing factories, they clean toilets and glittering down-town high-rises, wash dishes in grimy restaurant kitchens, pull switches and operate machinery in fuming plastic and chemical factories, abattoirs and machine shops."[26]

As the history of Canadian immigration shows, there will always be new waves of immigrants to take the place of previous genera-tions of immigrants. In the mid-1800s it was the Irish peasants who constructed the canals and early railroads; in the late 1800s, the Chinese coolies laid the rail lines for the CPR and worked the mines of British Columbia;* at the turn of the century, the Ukrain-ians and Poles built the cities and cleared and worked the land. Today it is the Greeks, Italians, and Portuguese from Southern Europe, West Indians from the Caribbean, Filipinos and other

---

* Indentured Chinese labour was Lord Elgin's final gift to Canada, for upon leav-ing Canada Elgin went to China as special emissary of the British government. By force of arms he imposed upon the Emperor a stipulation in the treaty whereby Britain would extract supplies of Chinese labour for its colonies. (*Royal Commission on Chinese Labour*, 1885.)

Asians, who take their place alongside of native Indians, French Canadians, migrant Maritimers, and a large contingent of exiled prairie farmers at the bottom of the labour heap.*

Women constitute the other major element in the pool of "dirty" workers. While women accounted for one-half of the increases in the labour forces from 1963 to 1973, most of them were still confined to traditional "women's work" in clerical and sales occupations.† Even in these occupations their wages were half or less of what their male counterparts received.

A number of historical forces interact to create the separation between the two markets. The importance of skills acquired through on-the-job training gives employers an incentive to retain their most stable workers, but to do so is expensive. It involves offering various fringe benefits — pensions, relatively safe working conditions, decent cafeterias, longer vacations with pay, and other amenities that are needed to attract and hold reliable employees. These inducements are costly, and employers naturally try to confine these extra expenses to the narrowest range of jobs they can get away with and to isolate other jobs where productivity does not depend as much as on job tenure and training. As well, seniority provisions demanded by unions, along with limitations placed on lay-offs, grievance procedures that limit arbitrary discharges, termination pay — all of which make jobs in the primary labour market more attractive — have encouraged employers to do as much work as they can outside the primary market, by designing their enterprises with internal secondary job shops or subcontracting some of the work out to smaller non-unionized businesses.

In manufacturing, some assembling, material handling, and most packaging are separated out; some machine tool companies have foundry and labouring divisions. Workers for woodyards operated by pulp and paper companies are usually drawn from the secondary labour market pool. Even on construction sites, there is a small crew of highly-paid, well organized workers manipulating levers and buttons and a somewhat larger crew of low-paid, unorganized workers bending their backs with picks and shovels. Not all of the "dirty" jobs are low-paying and non-unionized.

---

* In recent years, with the co-operation of the Department of Manpower and Immigration, employers have been bringing in several thousand "guest workers" on limited contracts to do stoop labour during the harvest season. Both government and employers look upon this as a more efficient system of guaranteeing a labour force for "dirty" jobs. Labour turnover among "guest workers" is virtually nil. They are a captive labour force that can draw on none of the rights and social services available to Canadians.

† By 1973, 73 per cent of clerical jobs, 58 per cent of service jobs, and 40 per cent of sales jobs were held by women.

Underground miners, for example, earn a relatively high wage. Yet the turnover rate among miners is particularly high because of the exhausting and dangerous nature of the work and poor working and living conditions. In Thompson, Manitoba, the average stay of miners is 17 days, not much less than when Inco first opened up the town ten years ago.

Because of their relatively high fixed investment in primary workers, employers use elaborate screening devices to select a stable and reliable primary work force. But since turnover is high and the right to fire is virtually unrestricted, pre-employment screening devices among secondary workers is unnecessary. Employers seem to hire their "dirty" workers from an undifferentiated labour pool of people who are seen as characteristically unstable and unreliable. Thus certain groups, particularly women, teenagers and native people, are stereotyped as unreliable and screened out of primary jobs and deposited in the secondary job market. Investigators of the dual labour market insist that most adult workers who begin their work histories in the secondary labour market will never get access to the primary jobs. Primary employers, primary workers, and secondary employers all have a vested interest in preserving the prevailing arrangement:

> The separation between primary and secondary work is so firmly rooted, in other words, the expectations of secondary workers and primary employers are so firmly entrenched, and the standard operating procedures for channeling workers among the two markets have such great utility to both primary and secondary employers that an opening of primary employment to secondary workers would entail too much disruption in the normal procedures of the establishment, the cost of which would be enormous.[27]

During periods of sustained full employment, primary employers are forced to recruit from among previously rejected or excluded sources of labour, and to enlarge their training and upgrading programs. This is in fact what occurred during World War II. However, temporary periods of full employment allow employers to resort to other techniques such as subcontracting and the use of temporary workers. This has been the experience since the end of World War II, with employers being unwilling to draw on the secondary labour pool to fill jobs that are preserved for the primary labour market, even when primary workers are unavailable. Thus the coincidence of high skill vacancies and high unemployment.

It is in periods of general unemployment, when the labour market is loose and employers can pick and choose among primary workers, that the separation of the two labour markets is most extreme. Primary workers are the first hired and the last fired. Because of their investment in them and the skills they have acquired through training and experience, employers are reluctant to lay them off even in slack times. To a degree they have become fixed costs that do not vary with sales unless sales drop off drastically. "Dirty" workers, on the other hand, are the last hired and the first fired. They are an entirely variable cost. At the first sign of a recession, they are laid off. That is why, even in a general recession when unemployment deepens, it is among the "dirty" workers that unemployment is severest.

They are double victims of the inflation-recession dialectic, in a weak position to protect themselves from an attack on their living standards from either source. Located in low-productivity, low-wage, and unorganized industries, their living standards fall furthest as inflation takes hold. Representing a minimal investment on the part of their employer and in chronic excess supply, they are most easily displaced in times of recession. Because they are scattered throughout the economy rather than being concentrated in large factories, they have little opportunity for contact with others like themselves or with primary workers. Because they work at unstable jobs in thousands of small shops and construction sites, most trade unions are unwilling to invest the energy and money to organize them.

The existence of a super-exploited sub-proletarian stratum that does the dirty work in our economy and is available to move from one giant construction project to another suits the interest of both employers and the capitalist state. It also seems to suit the short-term interests of primary workers. All of these groups would have to make colossal adjustments if the "dirty" work were to be shared and "dirty" workers, as such, eliminated and fully integrated into the primary labour force. Yet this appears to be the only solution to their intolerable condition. Individual solutions like special training programs for the "disadvantaged" can only help a tiny minority out of the secondary labour and welfare markets. On the other hand, sustained full employment, perhaps with a reduced work week, is an essential prerequisite. Another is persistently raising the legal minimum wage and broadening the coverage of minimum wage legislation to incorporate all workers. By substantially raising the minimum wage, employers would be forced to rationalize jobs in the secondary labour market, to eliminate some of them through greater mechanization, and in general to be more concerned about labour turnover and training.*

---

* The sharp distinction that is drawn between the primary and secondary labour

Lest I have overdrawn the economic strength of primary workers, I hasten to add that they seem strong only by comparison to "dirty" workers. Even the most powerful trade unions have failed to protect the purchasing power of their members through most of the inflation spiral and in North America, at least, they have been paralysed in the face of plant closures and mass layoffs. In the final analysis, primary and secondary workers face the same class enemy. They are separated and isolated from each other because employers and sometimes trade unions find this arrangement profitable. Their continued separation only assists in their mutual exploitation.

Detroit's Dream — Our Nightmare

More than any other commodity, the automobile has become the symbol of affluence in North America. It is also the bellwether industry that best reflects the health of the economy. Its current crisis has reached traumatic proportions. Leonard Woodcock, president of the United Automobile Workers, was right when he said that the American economy may be in a recession but the automobile industry is in a deep depression with no sign of recovery on the horizon. With its huge backlog of unsold cars, the stock would last for three or four months even if all plants were shut down. By the end of January 1975, 300,000 hourly workers, 40 per cent of the industry's blue-collar work force, were laid off, with at least half of that figure considered permanent. The ripple effect in related industries reached about 750,000 additional workers before the end of 1975. Because the auto industry accounts for 15 to 20 per cent of the GNP of the U.S., the drop in auto sales transmits waves to other industries such as glass, textiles, and plastics. 65 per cent of lead production, 60 per cent of synthetic rubber, 48 per cent of iron, 21 per cent of steel, and 35 per cent of zinc depend on the automotive market. Harvard's Otto Eckstein, a leading American forecaster,

---

market obviously compresses reality. This reflects the weakness of all economic models, which must of necessity gloss over important details. Yet the dual labour market is a useful way of analyzing the structure of work. There are, in effect, 8 million job slots in the Canadian economy. The kind of work that each slot requires — along with the kind of education, training, skills, and attitudes required — is determined by the way employers organize the work function. Workers must adjust themselves to this organization. Each must find a place among the available slots. It is commonplace to group these slots into blue collar, white collar, and service and professional categories. These distinctions may still serve a useful purpose, but in many respects, factory operators, clerks, railway and maintenance employees, and others work under similar conditions today. Grouping these slots into dual markets, primary and secondary, however simplifying this may be, affords some important insights.

says 'that auto sales will not recover their 1973 level until nearly 1980.

Profits in the industry plunged drastically in 1974 — GM's by 60 per cent, Chrysler's by 90 per cent and Ford's by 50 per cent. Auto workers are partly protected by Supplementary Unemployment Benefits which compel the auto companies to add cash payments to a worker's regular unemployment insurance compensation. Laid-off workers receive the equivalent to 95 per cent of their normal take-home pay. But the plan ceases to function after one year of unemployment. In any event, the fund ran out by June. Unlike the autoworkers, the automobile executives have built up a lot of fat over the years from the excess profits earned over the years. In 1973, GM's world-wide profits, after taxes, amounted to $2.4 billion, an average of $3,000 extracted from each GM worker around the world. If GM were satisfied to accept a rate of 13 per cent, the average after-tax return in manufacturing, it could have reduced the wholesale price of each of its trucks and cars by $300. Henry Ford II, setting an example to his employees, announced that he had voluntarily slashed his salary because of the company's poor sales. The reduction dropped his pay by just over one per cent, to a modest annual figure of $865,000. It is true that his income from dividends is reduced even more. As the largest shareholder in the company, he personally netted a large share of its $900 million profits in 1973. Somehow, Ford and the rest of the industry's executive branch will manage to sit out the recession in relative comfort.

The immediate crisis in the automobile industry can be explained by the structure of the industry and the greed and ineptitude of its owners. For two years the automakers dismissed signs of consumer resistance to their higher pricing policies. Business as usual was the rule for the 1975 models: protect profit margins by raising prices ($500 on top of a similar increase in 1974) and maintain full production schedules. Finally, the huge inventory of 1.7 million cars could be reduced either by price-cutting or by massive production cutbacks. In spite of dealer pressure, the industry stood firm on its pricing policies and ordered production cutbacks of a magnitude seen only in the Great Depression. This is the behaviour that is common to oligopolistic industry structures. It was only in January that the companies finally introduced a temporary rebate system on some of their most over-stocked models.

Not surprisingly, the United Automobile Workers of America, junior partner to the Big Three, has joined the industry on a crusade for government handouts. It has also joined the industry in an advertising campaign to urge consumers to buy more cars, and it has joined lobbies with the industry to urge Congress to declare a moratorium on new government requirements for safety and pollution standards. From its micro viewpoint, the UAW is acting perfectly rationally. In accordance with the laws of the capitalist jungle, each of us learns to protect himself or herself against others and, if need be, against society. We pick and choose as allies the people who can best help us defend ourselves. In a hostile environment of generalized unemployment, without a national plan that incorporates our social priorities and without agencies that can easily transfer unemployed resources to areas of real need, we are left to fend for ourselves as best we can in the here and now. We choose short-run solutions to solve immediate problems though these can lead to long-term disasters, because in the jungle there is only today. The proliferation of energy-wasting and pollution-creating automobiles is a rational solution to the UAW because it has no macro-view. Collaborating with industry to promote the sale of more unneeded automobiles and to support sagging business profits, rather than collaborating with other trade unions to promote a balanced economy that meets the real needs of people including decent transportation, is the logical outcome of a trade union movement that resorts to business solutions to solve what are ultimately political problems.

The immediate crisis in the auto industry masks a deeper, worldwide crisis in the industry. The rapid expansion of automobile production during the 1950s and sixties was probably coming to an end even without the assistance of the recession. The life-cycle of all products in capitalist economics takes on an S-shape. The automobile has reached the second upper turn of the "S", and the market will be saturated long beyond any upturn in the economy. Given the present distribution of income, practically all households who want to buy a car, and are able to do so, already own one. Aside from young buyers in the market and two-car families, current production serves an almost exclusively replacement function. And in view of the high costs of repairs, insurance, and gas, fewer families are able to afford two cars. This situation could be changed if there were a large increase in the incomes of the lowest-paid workers, or if the prices of automobiles were sharply reduced. Neither is likely to occur in the foreseeable future. It is unlikely that Canada has reached this degree of market saturation, so that considerable expansion is still possible here, but the continental integration of the industry means that the Canadian industry will derive little benefit from our more favourable position.

Sales of North American vehicles reached record levels in Canada in 1974 — 1,057,244. This was only 1.5 per cent over 1973, but in sharp contrast to the 23 per cent decline of sales in the U.S.A.

However, the spread of the American slump showed itself in the last three months of the year. In December the drop in sales was 14 per cent, compared to December of the previous year. By the end of January 1975, 7,150 Canadian workers were laid off and the number of jobs affected in both the automobile manufacturing and parts industries numbered 16,400 by mid-March — 20 per cent of the work force normally employed in the industry. With the Canadian auto industry consuming 70 per cent of the natural rubber produced in Canada, 19 per cent of the steel production and 11 per cent of the nickel, to take a few examples, the spin-off effects of a decline in the auto industry are staggering. It is apparent that the 1965 Autopact is now being used to shift jobs from Canada to the U.S. In 1974, Canada's auto trade deficit with the U.S. amounted to over a billion dollars, substantially more than what existed before the Autopact came into effect. Estimates suggest that it could go as high as $1,500 million in 1975.

The Canada-U.S. Autopact was ten years old as of January 16, 1975. Signed at Lyndon Johnson's Texas ranch, the pact was initiated by the government of Lester Pearson to reduce Canada's trade gap with the U.S.A. The deficit in automobiles stood at $711 million in 1965, accounting for most of Canada's trade deficit with the U.S.A. It was not a deal that the U.S. really wanted, but American officials feared that, without it, Canada might take more drastic action such as taking over the U.S. auto plants and developing a purely Canadian auto industry. The pact was a form of freer trade between the two countries, creating a single continental auto market. With various safeguards it was an arrangement that sought a bigger share of the North American market for the Canadian branch-plants and, with the resulting efficiencies, savings for Canadian consumers in the form of prices similar to the ones being paid for by American consumers.

In the pact's early stages, many of these objectives were met. There was a surge of investment in the late sixties, with new factories going up in Windsor, Oshawa, Oakville, and St. Catharines. With 70 per cent of Canadian production being exported to the U.S.A., Canada's share of the North American market expanded faster than the growth of sales in Canada. The $711 million deficit in 1965 turned into a $200 million surplus by 1972 — a turnaround of about $1 billion. The Canada-U.S. factory price gap narrowed to 6.5 per cent in 1974, compared to 16 per cent in 1965. Not surprisingly, U.S. officials were not happy with these results. Neither was the international headquarters of the UAW. It was contended that the pact was a transitional step to unrestricted free trade without the safeguards. Efforts to end the pact or remove the safeguards have been resisted by the Canadian government, but in the meantime growth in the industry and marked shifts in the industry strategy have meant that the provisions of the pact have all but lapsed. In particular, the shift of auto parts manufacturing to the lower-wage underdeveloped countries has created problems not only for Canadian workers but also for European and American workers.

The Autopact made the Canadian industry an adjunct of the U.S. industry. The mechanics of Canada's subordinate position works as follows. Ever since 1966, Canada has enjoyed a surplus with the U.S. in trade of motor vehicles. What creates an over-all deficit is the imbalance in trade of automotive parts. Between 1965 and 1969 the over-all deficit was gradually reduced so that in 1970 Canada enjoyed a small surplus. The new over-all deficit position is explained by a return to a deficit in the trade of automobile parts. In the first nine months of 1974, for example, the Canadian surplus in vehicles was $570 million but the deficit in parts and engines was close to $1,270 million. What makes the Canadian position vulnerable is that the decisions as to where parts are to be purchased are made in the U.S.A. The Canadian auto industry is 97 per cent U.S.-controlled and the Canadian parts industry is 80 per cent U.S.-controlled. In spite of the safeguards in the Autopact there is not much that the Canadian government can do to influence these decisions. It is part of the price we pay for being a branch-plant economy. It is rumoured about that since 1972 the U.S. government has been leaning on Detroit to convert what was then a U.S. deficit, thereby shifting the deficit to Canada and shifting Canadian jobs to the U.S. W. S. Campbell, a Canadian parts manufacturer (Consumers Glass Co.) sees the end of the Canadian industry in sight:

> We may well be seeing the beginning of the end of much of the automotive parts industry in Canada. If it is more attractive for U.S. companies to manufacture in the U.S. than Canada, or, if it is more attractive for companies to start operations in countries such as Brazil and Mexico, surely these are the initial steps to closing or paring down of Canadian production.
>
> It is apparent that in the long term, the auto pact will indirectly cause the decline of the industry in Canada to the point where it represents little more than assembly lines for imported or integrated parts.[28]

Investment in the Canadian auto industry has been steadily diminishing since the early days of the Autopact. Between 1965 and 1967, capital expenditures in the industry totalled $554 million. Between 1968 and 1971, it fell to $440 million, and between 1971 and 1973 it dropped a further 25 per cent to $331 million — or 40 per cent below the first three years of the agreement. In 1970 Canada's share of the North American capital expenditure peaked at 13 per cent. In 1973 it had declined to 5 per cent of the total. Job expansion has also been disappointing. In the past ten years the number of jobs in vehicle assembly rose by only 3,000 and in the parts industry by 14,000. The 1974 trade deficit alone transfers 10,000 jobs from Canada to the U.S.A. Worst of all is that, with the integration of the industry on a continent-wide basis, jobs in research design, and engineering have largely disappeared and have been replaced by jobs on the assembly-line — the industrial equivalent to hewing wood and drawing water.

Canadians have been building cars for over 70 years. The industry reached it peak in 1929 when Canada out-produced all the great nations in Europe. By 1960 our industry was producing only a fifth of the cars being produced in most European nations. The reason is clear: we are the only industrialized country in the world with a market as large as ours that does not design and build its own cars.

Within the terms of the pact, the Canadian auto industry is being used as a surplus production capacity. When times are good, production will take place here. When the American market turns sour, production in Canada is cut back. The automobile industry is the key sector in southern Ontario, the nation's industrial heartland. Before the Autopact, it was also a key link between the various regions of the country. Today most of its production is geared to the U.S. market, ensuring that whenever the U.S. industry falls apart, the Canadian industry must fall apart too. As a recent report says:

> The Autopact is the ideal pressure point for maintaining U.S. control of the Canadian economy. This is so because the importance of the pact is so much greater for Canada than for the U.S. Its cancellation would deny Canada access to 70 per cent of its present market and would cut off the flow of parts. . . .[29]

The threat of cancelling the Autopact has already been used to bring pressure on Canada to come to terms on other issues such as oil. The U.S. is not interested in purchasing automobile products from Canada. Her own industry could easily supply all the cars that are sold in the North American market. What the U.S. wants from Canada is our resources and access to our markets. It was naive to believe that the Autopact could alter these priorities.

The UAW once challenged the auto industry to "open its books." While the union didn't succeed, the point is pertinent today. The industry is in a long-term slump that is partly explained by the product that it produces and the prices that it demands. It has come under attack for its inefficient use of high-cost energy, its damaging effect on the environment, its harm to the urban landscape and the mind-numbing working conditions of its assembly lines. These are some of the social costs that automobile companies have been passing on to others for decades. The Canadian economy and automobile workers in particular pay a heavy penalty to maintain this industry. Opening the books is a solid first step towards public accountability and to worker control over production, pricing, and product planning.* Ultimately, the solution to the provision of decent transportation is public ownership and co-ordination of the entire transportation industry. Transportation is too important today to be left in the hands of the financiers and accountants who run the industry from Detroit.

Are We Heading Toward a Repeat of the Great Depression?

Analogies with the Great Depression of 1929 are commonplace today. So far as the stock market is concerned, the disintegration of Wall Street has been of a comparable magnitude to that of the Great Crash. In some respects it has been a greater crash. The current market plunge is already in its sixth year. This is the longest decline of the century. In 1929 it was only about three years from the top of the market to its bottom. In the 1929-32 crash the market dropped by 89 per cent in value. That record still holds, but the gap is rapidly closing. The market is currently 70 per cent below its 1968 level and still sliding. From the autumn of 1929 to the summer of 1932, New York Stock Exchange stocks lost $74 billion in paper value. This record has been easily broken. The aggregate value of securities fell by more than $170 billion in 1973 alone, and by another $250 billion in the first nine months of 1974. Of course, the dollar value of stock market investments is ten times what it was in 1929. That this collapse of stock prices has not had the dramatic impact of 1929 is due to the securities laws of the New Deal era, which reduced the extent to which investors could speculate with borrowed money. Nevertheless, the massive loss of value on the stock market is a chief cause of the liquidity squeeze. The nine-month loss of $250 billion in the first three-quarters of 1974 is alone ten times the loss due to the rise in the price of imported oil into the U.S. This is the impetus behind efforts that are being made to coax money back into the market to reverse the decline.

* Short-term demands for a shorter work-week are surely in order as a means of spreading jobs.

If the parallels to 1929 are eerily striking, there are some important differences. One of them is that bank deposits are government-insured. A second is that farmers are prospering and likely to continue doing so, unlike the situation before 1929. A third is that governments today are not prepared to allow banks and other major companies to go bankrupt by the score. A fourth is the network of government income-support programs — welfare payments, unemployment insurance, old age pensions — which didn't exist to nearly the same degree in the 1920s and thirties. These would maintain consumption spending in a manner that could not occur in the thirties. A fifth is that government today is accustomed to large deficit financing and would surely make use of all fiscal levers to avoid catastrophic levels of unemployment which are today politically unacceptable. It is the sixth difference, however, which causes a problem. The pre-Depression era was plagued by over-production and falling prices and wages. Today we have double-digit inflation, a liquidity crisis, and some lingering shortages. The Keynesian prescription could have been fully applied in the thirties without any fear of inflation. That is not the case now. An expansionary policy capable of achieving a swift reversal from a depression would soon refuel the inflation that stubbornly persists.

This is the dilemma faced by the leaders of the capitalist world. As even *Newsweek* magazine admits (without, it should be added, an understanding of the root of the problem): "While plain citizens could once hope that some combination of economic wizardry would pull them through, that no longer holds true — and the result is a pervasive feeling of helplessness both at home and abroad."[30] *Newsweek* adds that economists have lost faith in their own conventional wisdom. Nobel-prize-winning Harvard economist Wassily Leontief is quoted as saying, "The longstanding claim of economists that they know how to control inflation is an empty pretense." He could have added that in an environment of persistent inflation, the economists' even more confident claim that they know how to control unemployment is an qually empty pretense. Leontief predicts that the United States will eventually be forced into some form of economic planning if no solution is found to the convergence of inflation and recession. His Harvard colleague Otto Eckstein similarly predicts that "we either work our way out of this mess in 1975, or we are in real trouble. If (conventional) policy does not meet the challenge next year, we'll have to examine how to change the economic system."[31]

Of course it's not as easy at that. The likelihood is that the downturn will again be aborted by government intervention before it has been allowed to cure the inflation, and that a new round of even greater inflation will soon force the government to apply the brakes again, causing an even greater recession a few years hence. The utter incapacity of orthodox economic tools to deliver minimally acceptable solutions is what gives credibility to the likes of Leontief, Eckstein, John Kenneth Galbraith, and others who are calling for some form of price and wage controls and planning.

State Planning: Capitalist Style

In an article written for the *New York Times*, Galbraith argues that the reason why the Nixon controls failed is that they were "irresponsibly administered by men who opposed the policy." The lesson he draws is that "controls must be administered by people who believe in them" and that they "must be for as long as we have big corporations, strong unions and reasonably satisfactory employment." In his concluding sally, Galbraith warns that "something has to give to end inflation, and it cannot be the incomes of the poor. So the spending of the affluent and the profits of the corporations are what must be squeezed. Complaints from these quarters must be heard with the utmost compassion and then largely ignored."[32]

This is the kind of stuff that we have come to expect from the iconoclastic Professor Galbraith. Yet for all its wit and forthrightness it bears the same crucial weakness as all of his other works. It leaves the giant corporations in place as the key units of social life. They exist and grow because they have political power. The capitalist state, as Galbraith refuses to acknowledge, is not a neutral agent that can be allied against corporate enterprise. Each endorses the same definition of reality. Economic controls and planning are not hard to imagine, but to imagine that they will be used in capitalist America to attack corporate profits is to have a false sense of class interests. If corporations are judged a menace as Galbraith now implies, then they must have their power taken away from them and different ways of organizing economic activity must be created.

Galbraith has one cogent argument in his article. In answer to a question posed to himself "Isn't inflation a world-wide blight?" he answers:

> Don't buy this excuse either. The Communist countries have stable prices and hard money . . . and they put to shame, in this regard, what pre-Kissinger statesmen called the free world. More important, the United States is decisive for the control of inflation in other countries. If we do, given our position in the world trading community, others can. If we don't they can't. Other countries can have more inflation than we do but, given

the effect of our prices on their imports, not much less. Canada is the case in which to reflect.[33]

Free marketeers still blanch at the thought of state planning. For them any incursion of the state into the life of the economy smacks of "creeping socialism." But many unregenerate capitalists, who know better, have become advocates of some form of planning. Unlike Galbraith, it is not the squeezing of profits that they have in mind but rather its opposite. The background to their thinking was provided by *Business Week:*

> It is inevitable that the U.S. economy will grow more slowly than it has. . . . Some people will obviously have to do with less. . . . Indeed, cities and states, the home mortgage market and small business and the consumer, will all get less than they want because the basic health of the U.S. is based on the basic health of its corporations and banks. . . . Yet it will be a hard pill for many Americans to swallow — the idea of doing with less so that big business can have more. It will be particularly hard to swallow because it is quite obvious that if big business and big banks are the most visible victims of the Debt Economy, they are also in large measure the cause of it . . . Nothing that this nation, or any other nation, has done in modern history compares in difficulty with the selling jobs that must be done to make people accept the new reality.[34]

From this perspective, state planning may become the mechanism by which the corporations will get the rest of Americans to swallow the pill of material sacrifice. As Kenneth Arrow, a hard-headed Nobel-prize-winning economist, has speculated, "if the economic stakes in planning were ever high enough, business interests would try to use planning to maintain the status quo. They would attempt to corrupt the system for their own advantage."[35]

In May 1975 U.S. senators Hubert Humphrey (Democrat) and Jacob Javits (Republican) introduced a bill that would establish an economic planning board. The legislation is backed by a private group that includes Professor Leontief, Leonard Woodcock of the United Auto Workers, and Robert V. Roosa of Brown Brothers, a leading financial corporation. Public discussion is also being focused around the resurrection of the New Deal's Reconstruction Finance Corporation. Among its advocates are Henry Ford II and Felix G. Rohatyn, an international banker. According to their revised version:

> The RFC should . . . become a permanent part of our economic establishment, not just as a last-ditch creditor but as a vibrant instrument of both rescue as well as stimulus. It need not, and should not, be a permanent investor in any one particular

enterprise. It should only remain as an investor, either as a part-owner or creditor, until such time as it can, in the public interest, divest itself of the enterprise in which it invests and this investment is eligible for normal market channels or until the markets are capable of performing their function. The RFC therefore should, in effect, become a revolving fund — hopefully a profitable one — which steps in where no alternatives are available and which steps out when the public interest has been served and normal market forces can again operate.[36]

The promotors of a revised RFC are advocating that through the instrumentality of the state the capitalist class should create a new permanent institution which would use public moneys, first to provide liquidity to shaky corporations by providing them with equity capital, and second to provide corporations with the wherewithal to undertake large projects needed for the sustained growth of the economy but insufficiently profitable to attract private investors. If by chance some of these projects turn out to be profitable, they would be turned over to private hands. As *Forbes Magazine,* a business journal, characterized the proposal: "Socialize the losses and keep the profits private."

Whatever the prospects for the RFC, permanent wage and price controls would have to be supplemented by some form of planning. Planning could entail rationing, centrally controlled allocation of credit, key raw materials, and capital exports and measures to eliminate strikes in key industries. Government would of necessity be directly involved in determining the distribution of income among workers and also the share of output that is allocated to consumption as against investments. In short, permanent controls over wages and prices bring the question of income distribution into the political arena. Though they may have some effect in dampening the current economic crisis, they could create a new kind of crisis, overtly political in nature.

IV/Keynes and His Consequences

The economic crisis of the 1970s, the worst since the Great Depression, is the product of five forces that have combined and reinforced each other: the rebelliousness of a new generation of workers, the growing monopolization of industry, the cumulative impact of three decades of Keynesian debt economics, the increasing integration of the world economy, and the defensive moves of the United States in the early disintegration of its empire.

Intolerability of the conditions of work has become a new factor in the constellation of forces that has led to an economic breakdown. Many workers are beginning to feel that no matter what their pay, it cannot compensate for the time and freedom sacrificed to an employer, public or private, who dictates the entire nature and conditions of work. Wage claims are simply the most immediate form of protest against the social subordination of the worker, against non-recognition in the factory, the office and in society. Large wage claims, work-to-rule, acts of sabotage, and an increased readiness to strike — even among previously passive categories of workers — are expressions of revolt against despotic work conditions, of insubordination, of a demand for recognition. In part it reflects the disparity between the level of education required of an increasing number of workers and the underemployment of their abilities in monotonous and fragmented tasks.

The concentration of control over wealth, markets, and supplies produces a permanent upward bias in the direction of prices. During periods of rapid growth, monopoly-sharing corporations repress the rate of increase in supply to hold up prices. When demand falls off, inflation is much less likely to slow down because monopoly sharing corporations respond to slack demand by raising prices to protect their revenues.

A second effect is equally important. The size of the modern corporation complicates the traditional cleansing effects of economic recessions in at least two ways. It can afford to keep its inefficient operations afloat for a longer time. The absence of a severe and prolonged recession for nearly 30 years has allowed the giants to accumulate much excess baggage. Only a sharp and sustained decline would force them to eliminate inefficient divisions. Several of the giants deserve to disappear altogether, having consistently failed the ultimate test of profitability. But whereas governments can easily afford to allow peripheral businesses to sink, this is not the case of businesses which are important centres of production and jobs. Instead of allowing the economy to eliminate these failures as a necessary part of a deflationary adjustment, governments feel obliged to protect them.

In the same vein, governments through most of the last 30 years have been applying some variation or another of Keynes' prescription to avoid another major depression. While the rest of the economic profession was hopelessly baffled by the Great Depression of the 1930s, Lord Keynes showed that severe unemployment is a natural state of affairs in a mature capitalist economy — unless goverments deliberately and persistently intervene to counter this tendency. While Keynes was no Marxist, he came by a different route to the same pessimistic conclusions. But where Marx's antidote was socialism, Keynes thought he had a remedy that would rescue capitalism from this revolting prospect. What all ruling circles learned from the Great Depression is that they must never again risk the danger of massive unemployment of the white, male, urban labour force. What they learned from Keynes was that active government intervention could stave off the dreaded depression.

This is the upshot of the Keynesian revolution Ultimately it turns out to be a counsel of inflation. From a tonic drug, stimulating production and reducing unemployment at the first sign of recession, it turns into its opposite — a toxic drug that accelerates inflation, produces a money and credit crisis and, perhaps, hyperinflation. The patient, the capitalist economy, becomes so addicted to the drug that the dose must be ever increased. If the drug is withdrawn there is a justified fear that the patient might die. The problem is that the patient may just as probably die of an overdose.

The effect of persistent government efforts to avoid serious declines — by pumping increasing amounts of money into the economy and permitting the public deficit to balloon in size — has also been to destroy or seriously weaken the cleansing function that severe recessions typically provide. During periods of rapid growth business firms become flabby, labour unions become militant, and the entire economy ensconced in financial debt, much of it speculative. However painful the remedy, depressions perform the necessary task of eliminating weak firms, breaking the back of labour militancy, and destroying bad debt. The Keynesian prescription may have solved the problem of the depression, but no substitute has been discovered to perform its essential cleansing functions. As a consequence the inevitable distortions that accompany long periods of economic prosperity are not eliminated. The economy theory of John Maynard Keynes is clearly one of the victims of the present shambles of world capitalism.

The increasingly unstable international economy* is clearly related to the erosion of American domination of world business. American corporations emerged from World War II as unchallenged leaders of world capitalism. The dollar cemented trade relations and helped stabilize the world economy. Three developments combined subsequently to weaken international stability. First, with the West European and Japanese economies fully recovered from the effects of World War II and unencumbered with huge military budgets while at the same time benefiting from American military adventures, their corporations began to challenge U.S. producers in international markets. Second, the American empire became increasingly expensive to police. Successful interventions in Greece, Iran, Guatemala, Lebanon, the Dominican Republic, and Chile were interspersed with losses in China and Cuba. But the recent defeat in Vietnam, the fall of Cambodia, the revolution in Portugal, and the Arab challenge all dramatize the decline of American power. Third, the multinationalization of corporations to some extent frees the giant enterprises from the effects of government economic policies. With global networks, they can shift their plants and their investments to avoid tax increases or government controls.

These sources of international stability have contributed to the economic crisis in a number of ways. Trade rivalry from Western Europe and Japan has hurt the American balance of payments. Even more so, the costs of the Vietnam war. Ultimately the U.S.A. was forced to launch an all-out trade war against her western allies, and to arrange a detente with the U.S.S.R. and China to get access to their markets. The growth of the multinationals has helped bring business cycles into a single world-wide cycle. Charles Kindleberger, professor of economics at the Massachusetts Institute of

---

* This is the subject of Part V of this volume. Only a brief outline is presented here.

Technology, has written that "for the world economy to be stabilized there has to be a stabilizer." The U.S.A. occupied that role from World War II to the end of the 1960s and benefited from it. The world economy is anything but stable today, and however mightily Henry Kissinger has tried to have it otherwise, the U.S.A. seems no longer in a position to bring order to it.

Keynesian Economics: An Introduction[1]

When employment and national income increased, Keynes noticed, total consumption spending also increased, but not by so much as income. "Hence employers would make a loss if the whole of the increased employment were to be devoted to satisfying the increased demand for immediate consumption. Thus, to justify any given amount of employment there must be an amount of current investment sufficient to absorb the excess of total output over what the community chooses to consume . . ."[2]

A portion of all income received at any time is saved — not immediately turned back into the economy. If a given level of economic activity is to be sustained, these savings will have to be attracted back into the income stream by businesses who will invest the savings in capital expansion. Only then will the total expenditures in the economy, on both consumer goods and capital goods, provide the business sector with sufficient revenue to cover its cost of production — including wages, salaries, and profits to itself. If business revenues (derived from the *demand* (for their goods) are less than their costs (including profits) required to *supply* these goods, they will cut down on production and employment and the level of economic activity will thereby decline.

Providing there are profitable investment opportunities there may be sufficient investment spending to fully offset the volume of savings and attract these savings back into the income stream. Should sufficient profitable investment opportunities be lacking, capitalists will refuse to risk their capital. They will hoard it and, in effect, go on an "investment strike," thus forcing the economy to a contraction.

While a newly developing capitalist economy is perennially short of investment capital, the problem of stagnation arises in a mature capitalist economy which generates and regenerates massive amounts of savings out of its much bigger income and which already has a large stock of capital equipment. As basic industries and transportation systems come into being, the production apparatus gradually becomes large enough to supply most of the expansion and replacement demand from both the consumption and the capital sectors of the economy. The natural over-all tendency is therefore towards what Keynes called a "quasi-stationary community" where change "would result only from change in technique, taste, population and institutions." As population and basic tastes change only slowly, the burden of absorbing growing amounts of savings falls upon technological and institutional change. Leaving institutional change aside for the moment, unless the existing stock of capital equipment is continuously outmoded by recurrent waves of technological breakthroughs, capitalism necessarily stagnates.

Technology is, of course, always in a state of flux, but most technological change is of a minor nature. Occasionally a radically new technological breakthrough occurs — like the railways in the nineteenth century, the automobile in the early twentieth century, and the electronic and chemical revolution of World War II, and these open up vast new investment opportunities which can absorb the surplus. During such periods, the economy will boom. Any contractions that occur are of short duration. The periods between such episodic technolgical revolutions are periods of economic drought, where contractions are long and severe and upswings are partial, never bringing the economy to full employment.

In short, the richer a capitalist society becomes the more it is faced with a critical problem of surplus absorption. What happens to an economy which generates surplus that cannot be utilized is vividly recorded in the annals of the 1930s.

The monopolization of the economy intensified the problems by raising the level of savings through monopoly profits* and by retarding the introduction of innovations, thereby reducing the available investment opportunities.[3] Moreover, because of the expanding labour force and ever-increasing labour productivity, the level of output and income required to fully employ the labour force is forever growing. Hence the liberating promise of automation is converted into a boundless menace.

The significance of the achievement of this mature stage of development is that society need no longer devote its energies to building up its industrial infrastructure. The long hours of work for the many and the concentration of capital among the few, which are requirements in the build-up phase, no longer serve a social function as there is no further need for a large net surplus. As a

---

* Gross profits constitute the source of most savings.

result of the previous accumulation of capital, a decent living standard for all and more time for leisure, culture, politics, and education are fully available with existing resources within the present generation. A redirection of energies from the struggle for existence to the realization of a truly human culture is a practical historical possibility. It is the class structure of capitalist society that forecloses this possibility, for the capital surplus which society no longer needs is also the income of the capital-owning class, the economic foundation of its existence. Capitalism is unable to make a rational adjustment to the onset of abundance because the end product of capitalist economic organization is not the fulfilment of human need but the expansion of private capital.*

Contrary to some opinion at the time, Keynes' prescriptions were anything but anti-capitalist: rather they were designed to give a second life to capitalism. He rejected, for example, boosting consumption spending by raising wages, for this would impinge further on profits. He also rejected reducing working time as a solution to unemployment. Further, he saw no "reason to suppose that the existing system seriously misemploys the factors of production"; the system had failed only in "determining the *volume* not the *direction* of actual employment."[4] By insisting that only the volume, not the direction, of production should be subject to government planning, Keynes indicated that he was not concerned with altering class relationships but only with removing their dangerous economic consequences. Centralized control of the amount of economic activity was the only way to overcome capitalist inertia. Since it is only during a boom that capitalism comes near to providing full employment, the "right remedy for the trade cycle," in Keynes' view, is to be found in "abolishing slumps and thus keeping us permanently in a quasi-boom."[5]

The economic model advanced by Keynes, while it illuminated the problem of surplus absorption, gives us a short-run analysis that understates the problem. It seeks to discover the amount of investment that is necessary to absorb the savings out of the current level of income so as to establish full employment of the labour force. It avoids the long-term dynamics of investment spending. Other economists, most notably Evsey Domar and Roy Harrod, have noted

---

* This subject is, I realize, far more complex than these few sentences suggest. It opens vast areas — such as what is human need, how are needs determined; how are human beings motivated; why are we compulsive workers and compulsive consumers? Do these questions perhaps transcend capitalism? Some of these questions are dealt with in different parts of this book, though nowhere are they treated fully. For an interesting discussion of them, readers are referred to R. Simkin, *Essays on Consumption, Income Distribution and Growth*, Agassiz Centre, University of Manitoba, 1975.

that investment also adds to the stock of productive capital. Income must grow to utilize the larger capital stock so as to justify its existence. Harrod, Domar, and others have determined the equilibrium growth rate of the economy, that is, the rate which will generate the appropriate amount of demand to utilize the growing capacity of the economy. This larger income, in turn, generates a still higher level of savings which must again be offset by an equal amount of investment, which again increases the productive capacity of the economy, and so on *ad infinitum*.

The crucial implication of this dynamic model is that continuing growth is the *sine qua non* of an efficiently functioning capitalist economy. The difficulties of maintaining a smooth running system are compounded when consideration is given to the growth in the labour force relative to the growth of capital and income. If the labour force grows at a rate that differs from the rate of growth of capital, there is a tendency for either labour shortages or, more likely, unemployment to develop.

Businesses do not have to be convinced that growth is desirable. The senior vice-president of a large American drug company put it succinctly: "The desire of this company is to be a growth company, the responsibility of this management is to make the company grow both here and abroad, to be a growth company. Otherwise we are not doing our job."[6] The need to grow knows no national boundaries. The multinational corporation has arisen to open up markets wherever they can be found. This statement by Jacques G. Maisonrouge, president of the IBM World Trade Corporation, testifies to this new kind of missionary work:

> It has been our constant desire to grow, and to grow by being president in every feasible market, that has led IBM to where it is today. Wanting growth has nothing to do with imperialistic motives. Rather, it is one of the conditions necessary to remain dynamic, to remain young, and to maintain a sound level of excellence. Through time, I am sure, we will have substantial changes in the structure of the company, but one thing that will remain is our desire to grow, our desire to develop the non-U.S. markets, and to be present, as much as we can, in all the countries of the world.[7]

The development craze of the business community is by now widely recognized. Businessmen support population growth and urbanization as these create larger markets and higher sales potential. The everyday experience of businessmen tells them that growth is essential for their survival. Moreover, growth does solve, for the time being, the problem of surplus absorption and unemployment. But growth is a short-run "fix." It satisfies present-day needs but at the same time it creates conditions that can only be satisfied by a still bigger "fix." Hence the problem of surplus absorption is forever enlarged and the tendency towards stagnation is deepened.

The business economy attempts to counteract the tendency to stagnation, which is a threat to the profitability of its capital, by expanding its domestic and foreign markets. Opening up branch-plants abroad has become the main vehicle for achieving the latter. As for the expansion of domestic markets, the unequal distribution of income precludes a widening of the consumption base. The alternative is to induce those who already can afford to buy what they want, to want more. This project is achieved by a vast sales effort supported by the expanded use of consumer credit. However, besides being wasteful, this effort by private capital to force-feed the domestic market and to enlarge its presence in international markets is also economically insufficient to absorb the surplus fully. Hence the intervention of the state.

Keynes expressed the belief that stagnation was the normal state of capitalist affairs unless government imposed itself in the investment market. Some of Keynes's disciples did not think it an exaggeration to say that "inflation and full employment are the normal conditions of a war-time economy and that deflation and unemployment are the normal conditions of a peace-time economy in the present stage of capitalist development."[8] What alone could save capitalism was government spending to take up the slack in the private sector. Even "pyramid-building, earthquakes, [or] . . . wars" could serve to bolster the economy if statesmen could not find anything better to do.[9] But Keynes was confident that achieving full employment did not have to involve warfare, capital destruction, or useless production. It could be realized by way of public works and expenditures on the general welfare that would increase incomes and jobs without enlarging savings or competing with private industry.

In a contemporary review of Keynes's *General Theory,* the eminent Oxford economist J. R. Hicks pointed out that if we accept Keynes's analysis then "either we must accept something like the policy he advocates, of stimulating investment and repressing savings by changes in social organization; or our once benevolent science becomes a paean to destruction, whose helpers are earthquake, war and conflagration, Atilla and Ghengis Khan, Great Raisers of the Marginal Efficiency of Capital and Creators of Employment."[10]

With a discomforting accuracy, the U.S.A. has chosen to take this second path over the past 30 years. A moment's reflection should indicate why. The mainspring of the economic system is private investment. Any assault on its privileged sanctuaries, whether these be public housing, public transit, or even redistributive tax measures, is likely to provoke instant retaliation by way of declines in new investment. A significant rise in welfare rates somewhere beyond the poverty line would threaten the incentive system by which businesses are able to maintain control over their workers. "In short, any attempt by the government to make up for the deficiency of demand which results from the inequalities generated by capitalist production relations must collide with the fact that these inequalities have their origin in a 'private' and unequal organization of power which runs all through capitalist society and cannot be altered by any one set of institutions within it."[11]

However there is one kind of government expenditure that sustains total demand without challenging the prerogative of private capital. That is military spending. Besides providing a seemingly limitless market for the products of giant industry, it also performs the vital service of protecting their expanding investments and markets abroad. The huge American arms budget has meant the difference between prosperity and stagnation. Two American economists have calculated the number of workers who were either unemployed in 1970 or directly and indirectly dependent on military spending. They added these figures and compared the result with the number of unemployed in 1938. Using conservative estimating methods in adjusting for hidden unemployment in both years, they found that 25 per cent of the labour force were either out of work or dependent on the war industry compared to 30 per cent in 1938. "All of which leads to the conclusion that, apart from military spending, things were a bit better in 1970 than in 1938 . . . but not much."[12]

A Permanent War Economy

War brings prosperity. An American consensus developed around this view, beginning with World War II which brought an end to the Great Depression. The editors of *U.S. News and World Report* made this discovery early on in the Cold War:

> The Government planners figure they have found the magic formula for almost endless good times . . . Cold War is the catalyst. Cold War is an automatic pump primer. Turn a spigot, the public clamours for more arms spending. Turn another, the clamour ceases. . . . Truman era of good times, the President is told, can run much beyond 1952. Cold War demands, if fully exploited, are almost limitless.[13]

Employed Americans numbered 46 million in 1939 and 53 million in 1945. Simultaneously the armed forces absorbed another 11 million persons. Since 1939 the main focus of the American state has been war or the preparation for war. Money for the Pentagon has been lavished without restraint. The military budget stood at $13 billion in 1950, reached $80 billion at the height of the Vietnam war and kept on soaring to $100 billion in 1975. Obviously Vietnam is only one event in a continuing program. The bill for past, present, and future military operations amounted to $125 billion in 1974, or 10 per cent of the American Gross National Product.

Even this 10 per cent figure understates the strategic economic importance of defense expenditures. While they comprise "only" 10 per cent of the GNP, they have a far greater impact on the volatile investment sector. The military budget supplies up to 40 per cent of the market for investment-type activities. The following will serve as examples: electronic components and accessories, 30 per cent; machine-shop products, 39 per cent; metal-working machinery and equipment, 21 per cent; materials-handling machinery and equipment, 17 per cent; engines and turbines, 20 per cent. These are 1958 figures and, if anything, are on the low side for today. But the extra 20 to 40 per cent of business provided by military markets still understates their importance, for they provide a much greater percentage of the total profits of the firms producing these goods. Businesses operate at a loss until production reaches a level sufficient to cover its overhead (fixed) costs. Once this "break-even" point is reached, profits surge ahead. The break-even point varies from industry to industry and from firm to firm, anywhere from 30 to 50 per cent of productive capacity. Therefore the 20 to 40 per cent of the sales provided by military purchases may yield as much as 50 to 75 per cent of the firms' profits.[14]

The assets of the U.S. military establishment constitute about 40 per cent of the assets of all U.S. industry.[15] Vast military budgets have been the primary vehicle of the state to stabilize economic growth at home and to establish U.S. economic growth abroad. When John F. Kennedy sought to get the economy "moving again" in 1961, his preferred instrument was enlargement of the military budget. The permanent war economy spawned many new industries. One of the most important was a university-based and media-centred industry that produced the fears and ideological justifications that lent legitimacy to the Cold War and its military and espionage activities.

As against this argument, our mainstream economists contend that, from an economic point of view, military spending is not essential to maintain prosperity; any government spending will do.

They further point to Europe, Japan, and Canada for that matter, where government spending has also increased dramatically but not primarily in war-related sectors. These contentions can scarcely bear serious scrutiny. Of course military spending is not the sole outlet for government intervention. There has never been any lack of worthy purposes for the economic controllers to turn their attention to. "From an economic point of view" there are no barriers to undertaking these worthy projects. But from a political-economic point of view, that is seen within the context of the reality of corporate power, the barriers are obvious. They are evident in the fact that despite its large military budget, the U.S.A. has had upwards of 5 per cent of the labour force unemployed in each of the past 5 years, and yet there was no effort to mobilize these idle resources to undertake the construction of mass transit systems, low-cost housing, pollution control, and other public necessities. As the eminent Keynesian Joan Robinson has noted:

> If there were no need for armament, it would be necessary to make useful investments and so to encroach upon the power and independence of the capitalists. The capitalists therefore prefer a situation in which armaments do seem necessary. This cure, most of us would agree, is even worse than the disease, and on the basis of Keynes' reasoning, it can be argued that capitalism will not save itself from the tendency to unemployment by any other means.[16]

Preoccupation with military affairs is not a new experience for the United States. Beginning with colonial and revolutionary days, U.S. history has been shaped by a continuous economic, political, and military expansionism. It has evolved through several stages. The first was one of consolidating a transcontinental nation by evicting or buying off competing colonial forces (France, England, Spain, and Russia), exterminating the Indians, and defeating Southern separatism. This stage lasted until well into the nineteenth century. In the second and third stages, the U.S. obtained control over the Caribbean area and a major position in the Pacific Ocean. In the fourth stage, post-World-War -II, the American empire became global, extending into Europe and all parts of the Third World. Its task was complicated by the rise of Communism. It became one of containing the spread of Communism, defeating it wherever possible, and preserving as much of the world as possible for "free enterprise." Adding up all the months that the U.S. has been engaged in military action from the time of the war of Independence to 1970 gives a total of 1,782 months out of a total of 2,340 months, or three-quarters of its history.[17]

Militarism is the right arm of imperialism. The two are insepar-able. Much of the expenditure on arms has been required to keep former European colonies that achieved political independence after World War II economically dependent on metropolitan cen-tres. According to retired U.S. General David Shoup, who should be in a position to know, this exercise involves 1,500,000 Americans in uniform in 119 overseas countries.[18] Aside from the operations in Vietnam, included in Shoup's estimate, U.S. overseas power is spread out over 429 major and 2,972 minor military bases. In addi-tion, 80 countries have received over $50 billion in American mili-tary aid since World War II.[19] Military bases overseas, military aid programs, military training, and advisory services are all part of the apparatus developed to bolster weak governments in the Third World and southern Europe that are under a constant threat of social revolution.

Harry Magdoff has summarized the role of post-World-War-II military expenditures as follows:

> The size of the "free" world and the degree of its "security" define the geographic boundaries where capital is relatively free to invest and trade. The widespread military bases, the far-flung military activities, and the accompanying complex of expendi-tures at home and abroad serve many purposes of special interest to the business community: (1) protecting present and potential sources of raw materials; (2) safeguarding foreign mar-kets and foreign investments; (3) conserving commercial sea and air routes; (4) preserving spheres of influence where United States business gets a competitive edge for investment and trade; (5) creating new foreign customers and investment opportunities via foreign military and economic aid; and, more generally (6) maintaining the structure of world markets not only directly for the United States but also for its junior partners among the industrialized nations . . .[20]

Thus military expenditures do more than provide lucrative cost-plus contracts for industry. As regards raw material, a further word is warranted. There is, of course, the growing dependency of the United States on foreign supplies of materials.. But there is also the dependency of giant business monopolies on the control of these supplies. In many instances their monopoly or quasi-mono-poly position arose precisely because of their control over the sources of raw materials. Whatever the views of the economic the-orists, the men who run these companies know that their ability to maintain positions on top of their industries depends on their suc-cess in gaining and retaining a commanding position as controllers of the world's raw materials.

In attempting to downplay the role of military expenditures (and foreign investment), our economists employ the method of separating out various parts of the economy. They assume that the elimination of any one part can do no harm providing it is replaced by the expansion of other parts. Any theoretical analysis which severs economics from politics and does not view the separate parts in the context of their interrelation must be held suspect by any but the most dogmatic of thinkers. The essential oneness of economic and political and military interests was no better expressed than by the vice-president of the Chase Manhattan Bank who supervises Far Eastern operations:

> In the past, foreign investors have been somewhat wary of the over-all political prospect for the [Southeast Asia] region. I must say, though, that the U.S. actions in Vietnam this year [1965] which have demonstrated that the U.S. will continue to give effective protection to the free nations of the region — have considerably reassured both Asian and Western investors. In fact, I see some reason for the same hope in the free economies of Asia that took place in Europe after the Truman Doctrine and after NATO provided a protective shield. The same thing also took place in Japan after the U.S. intervention in Korea removed investor doubts.[21]

As for the unquestionable observation that other advanced capitalist countries have not had the benefit of large military expenditures, our optimistic economists, perhaps because of their narrow orientation, forget that capitalism is a global system and not a collection of separate national economies. "What happens in any part of the system affects to some extent what happens in all the others; and if the part in question happens to be by far the largest in the system, as is the case with the United States in world capitalism, the effect on some of all of the other parts is likely to be large and even decisive."[22] This is unquestionably the case for Canada, but to a lesser degree it also holds true for Germany, Japan, and the whole of West Europe. The leaders of these countries are the last to deny that a prosperous United States is essential for their own prosperity. And, to the degree that American prosperity has depended upon vast government expenditures on war and war preparation, it can hardly be disputed that its impact extends far beyond the boundaries of the U.S.A. More particularly, under the Pax Americana countries like Japan and Germany, without having to pay their military dues, are special beneficiaries of American efforts to keep as much of the world as possible safe for free enterprise. Japan especially has benefited not only from an expanded American market but also from U.S. purchases for the Korean and Vietnamese wars.

An Elaboration

Conventional economic theory has discovered two causes of inflation: "demand-pull" and "cost-push." According to the first theory, which also goes under the rubric "too much money chasing too few goods," there are more dollars of spending coming on the market than can be supplied with the existing production capacity and labour force. Prices and wages rise such that the higher dollar spending will buy the same volume of goods and services.* According to the second theory, inflation is produced by trade unions demanding wage increases that exceed the growth of productivity. If these are granted by businesses who in turn raise their prices accordingly, a general inflation will result.

The two forces of "demand-pull" and "cost-push" are combined in the "Phillips curve" which expresses the "trade-off" between unemployment and inflation. According to this curve, the higher the rate of unemployment (or the lower the level of aggregate demand) the lower the rate of price increases, and vice versa. In Canada, the relationship between inflation and unemployment is not represented by the points on a curve, but by a "trade-off zone," reflecting the fact that the relationship in this country is also influenced by other factors such as inflation in the U.S.A. According to one version of the zone, a rate of unemployment of 2 per cent would produce a rate of inflation of 4 per cent to 7 per cent, a rate of unemployment of 4 per cent would produce price increases of 2 per cent to 4 per cent, while to get a zero price increase would require an unemployment rate of 7 per cent to 9 per cent. Samuelson-Scott comment:

> The zone shows a problem of choice. Policy makers or society as a whole cannot, in the present structure of the Canadian economy, have both price stability and high employment. Instead, compromises must be accepted, "trading-off" some departure from zero price change for some gain in employment.[23]

---

* Since wages are rising more than productivity, the inflation is commonly blamed on the greed of workers or in more polite circles, on their unreasonableness. Actually, whenever prices are rising, wages must rise by more than productivity as a matter of simple arithmetic, providing the relation between wages and profits remains the same. The fact that wages are outstripping productivity says nothing about the causes of inflation. Furthermore, real wages (money wages adjusted for price increases) that rise proportionately with the rise in productivity merely mean that workers are getting the same share of the total product that they were before. Contrary to the confused arithmetic of business apologists, it does not mean that labour is taking all the gains of technological progress for itself. Gains in real wages that are in line with increases in productivity mean that capital and labour are sharing the increased product in accordance with the previous division.

In practice, governments throughout the 1950s and 1960s accepted the inevitability of both permanent unemployment and permanent inflation, hoping through "fine-tuning" of the economy to avoid either extreme. Actually there is no stable relationship between unemployment and the degree of inflation. Historically there has been a rough correlation, but the terms of the correlation have varied frequently and by such wide margins that the Phillips curve has no predictive value. According to the trade-off zone derived in the mid-1960s, an unemployment rate of 8 per cent should produce a rate of inflation of zero to 2 per cent. Yet today the rate of unemployment is approaching 8 per cent and prices are rising by over 10 per cent.

The Phillips curve is only the latest intellectual weapon used against the working class. We are told that workers, by fighting for inflationary wage demands when unemployment is low, force the government to increase unemployment to eliminate undesirable inflation. This is a new version of the "iron law of wages." Since any wage demand that exceeds the growth of productivity is defined as inflationary, any attempt by workers to redistribute income between wages and profit is labelled by conventional theory as inflation. And as the trade-off relationship worsens, requiring more unemployment to lower price inflation, our economists again blame it on the working class. Either trade unions are becoming excessively strong, or increasing skill requirements make many workers functionally unemployable, leading to greater "structural unemployment." The latter theory has become the ideological rationale for the belief that the official unemployment rate is not the "real" unemployment rate as it increasingly includes many unemployable workers. This is the reason behind the mysterious increase in the "full employment unemployment rate" from 3 per cent in the early 1950s to 5½ per cent today.

According to Keynes's own account, his treatise The General Theory can be summed up by saying that "given the psychology of the public, the level of output and employment as a whole depends on the amount of investment."[24] What then determines the amount of investment? The answer given by neoclassical economic theory was the amount of saving. Saving, according to this theory, is deferred consumption. The amount of both saving and investment is determined by the rate of interest which is a reward for abstinence. If savings are too high, given available investment opportunities, then the rate of interest will fall and consumption will rise. Rising consumption will thus substitute for any shortfall in investment, thus maintaining the total level of output.

Such a theory was obviously contradicted by the actual path of development in capitalist economies. Keynes's breakthrough came from seeing that saving and investment are principally performed by capitalists whose motivation in savings has nothing to do with deferred consumption. Rather than being a reward for saving, Keynes viewed interest as a premium to induce savers not to hoard their money. Why should a premium be required to induce people to spend their money rather than hoarding it? His explanation lay in the existence of uncertainty regarding the future. The more uncertain is the future state of the economy, the higher the premium required to induce capitalists not to hoard their money. If investment does not offer a favourable prospective yield (in Keynes's terms, if the "marginal efficiency of capital" is low) there is always the alternative to the ownership of real capital assets, namely the ownership of money. But when capitalists find it profitable to hold their wealth in its money form, that is, to hoard their savings and withdraw them from circulation, a crisis ensues. The amount of savings exceeds the amount of investment, and output, income, and employment fall until savings have declined to a level equal to that level of desired investment.*

While capital accumulation as a social process is a means of creating use-values, that is, a means for meeting consumption needs, as a private activity of capitalists it is nothing more than a means for expanding business income. When investment outlets are saturated and do not offer satisfactory profit possibilities they cannot for the moment absorb all the savings generated by the prevailing level of income. Hence, paradoxically, "the abundance of capital interferes with the abundance of output, old wealth is a barrier to the production of new wealth."[25] † This of course explains why production slackens off in a depression despite the particularly grave needs of people during these times. Capital and labour are amply available to meet those needs, but real values cannot be transformed into money value because capitalists are unable to satisfy their profit requirements. It also explains why the advent of "affluence" is regarded as a menace to growth.

Dudley Dillard, a discipline of Keynes, observed a peculiar

---

* Not surprisingly, our conventional economics textbooks lay the blame for economic downturns on the saving habits of consumers. As people reach higher income levels they tend to save more of their income, we are told. This "paradox of thrift," as Samuelson-Scott call it, is the root of the problem. But as the above analysis shows, the root of the problem does not lie in the habits of people but in the behaviour of business. There is no "paradox of thrift," only a paradox of profits.

† In Marx's terms, *"the real barrier of capitalist production is capital itself.* It is the fact that capital and its self-expansion appear as the starting and closing point, as the motive and aim of production, that production is merely production for *capital,* and not vice versa....", *(Capital,* Vol. 3, p. 293.)

dichotomy between money and goods in the capitalist economy.

> Real goods appear to the individual producer as an artificial
> form of wealth until they are converted into money, which
> appears as real wealth to the individual producer . . . Real social
> wealth (stocks of goods) will be produced by entrepreneurs only
> if there is the expectation of transforming them into unreal social
> wealth (money). In brief, what is "real" to society is "unreal" to
> the individual producer; and what is "unreal" to society is "real"
> to the individual producer.[26]

It is the inability to convert goods into money that sets up a chain
reaction, bringing the economy "tumbling down."

The extent of the depression depends on the state of prospective
investment opportunities. In a path-breaking, but much neglected
article, Robert A. Gordon[27] makes a crucial distinction between
underlying investment opportunities and the inducement to exploit
these opportunities. The occurrence of an economic downturn does
not necessarily mean that the economy has exhausted all of its profitable investment opportunities. What may have happened is that
the inducement to exploit these opportunities may have been temporarily impaired. In the latter case, the downturn is bound to be
relatively mild and shortlived.

The major source of new and profitable investment opportunities is technological change, which changes the appropriate composition of output either by destroying the salability of some existing
products and creating new ones or by altering the method of producing existing products. When this occurs, equipment is rendered
obsolete and whole industries may be destroyed, thus altering the
appropriate composition of investment. War, preparations for war,
and reconstruction after war are other historically important
sources of new investment opportunities. They stimulate technological change and create new markets for industry. Less conse-
quential sources of new investment are the replacement of worn-
out plant and equipment and the implementation of minor technological variations. In Canada, the discovery of exploitable raw
materials has been a profoundly important source of long-time
investment opportunities.

An economy may well turn down before all investment opportunities are fully exhausted. Profit margins may be narrowed in
some sectors and cutbacks can reverberate throughout the
economy. There may be a too-rapid build-up of inventories which
have to be allowed to run down; the scarcity of money and the
resulting high rate of interest may discourage investment. In short,
the inducement to exploit existing investment opportunities may be

impaired, causing short recessions and rapid recoveries.

On the basis of this distinction, Gordon distinguishes between various kinds of business cycles. The first category assumes no reduction in real investment opportunities. In the first instance there may be no serious deterioration in the inducement to exploit these opportunities either. What occurs is a desire for liquidity (cash) and this can be achieved by cutting down on inventories. However, the decline is mild and brief, and recovery sets in as liquidity is restored and inventories are replaced. Aside from inventories, there has been no decline in investment spending.

In the second instance, what Gordon calls an intermediate downturn, short-term profit expectations are more severely impaired and the desire for liquidity is not so easily met by a simple reduction of inventory purchases. Other kinds of investment spending decline, and the impact on production and employment is greater. Recovery, though somewhat longer in coming, is nevertheless vigorous and sets in as inventories and equipment must be replaced and as the temporary squeeze on profits is corrected by lower interest rates, wages, and other costs.

As for the second category, major depressions, the immediate cause of the downturn may be the same as for the other ones, but the underlying situation is different since long-term investment opportunities have been exhausted. If this is not recognized early, investment spending will have greatly exceeded the profitable opportunities and the result is a large excess of capacity which makes the depression all the move severe and longer in duration. Furthermore, although the revival mechanisms — improved expectations, lower interest rates, and wages, etc. — bring about an upturn, they are not sufficiently powerful by themselves to produce a full recovery. The recovery is only partial, and may generate another downturn before full utilization of capacity has been achieved. Full recovery only occurs as the underlying investment opportunities change — primarily as a result of major technological changes, war, or massive government intervention.

Gordon has classified the cycles of 1923-4, 1927, 1949, and 1953-4 as minor cycles of the first variety. He classifies the cycles of 1907, 1921, and 1937-8 as intermediate cycles and the cycles of the 1870s, 1890s, and 1930s as major cycles.

What kind of a cycle are we now in? It is clearly either an intermediate cycle or a major cycle, but which one of these it is remains in doubt. It is possible to argue that the downturn of 1957 was the beginning of a major cycle, with the investment opportunities that emerged from World War II, its aftermath, and the Korean war being finally exhausted; that this was interrupted by the stimulating impact of the Vietnam War; and that with the end of American intervention the cycle is continuing. What would have disguised the major cycle is the existence of permanently high levels of government expenditures which were noticeably absent in the 1930s. In short, according to this hypothesis, a major depression has been repressed since 1957 by active government intervention.

On Aborting Depressions

In order to compensate for private capital's failure to maintain the level of investment, Keynes argued that government must undertake offsetting expenditures of its own. The "Keynesian Revolution" was manifested after World War II by government declarations that promised to avoid the massive social discontent of the 1930s by maintaining full employment. In the U.K., the Beveridge Report proposed a program of full employment based on the "socialization of demand without the socialization of production." In Canada, dedication to Keynesian prescriptions was enshrined in the White Paper on Employment and Income. Indeed, where full or nearly full use of productive resources has come about in the post-World-War-II era, it has been accomplished by the extension of government-induced production. At various times there have been attempts to operate with balanced budgets and even to gain surpluses (tax revenues in excess of government expenditures) to reduce some of the debt. But ensuing recessions forced a reversal of these policies. Any decrease in government spending led to the contraction of economic activity which could be altered only by the resumption of government pump-priming.

The new weight of government can be seen in the dramatic growth of the public sector. Whereas in the 1920s one out of 15 American workers was on some government payroll; now the proportion is one out of 6. The trend is similar in Canada. For both Canada and the U.S., whereas in 1929 less than one dollar in ten of national production owed its origin to government purchases, today about on dollar in five of all goods and services produced is sold to some branch of government. It was by way of expanding the supply of money, deficit financing, government-induced production, war preparations, and actual warfare — all inflation-producing policies — that the dominant capitalist nations reached some approximation to full employment through much of the post-war era. Even so, unemployment in North America has rarely been under 3 or 4 per-cent, particularly since the mid-1950s when the post-World-War-II-Korean-War booms spent themselves.

We can clarify the impact of government intervention à la Keynes

by tracing what happens in the trade cycle in the absence of government intrusion. In the early phase of the upswing in economic
activity, there is substantial unused productive capacity and unemployed labour — a legacy of the previous depression. Economic
activity is easily speeded up without generating excessive
inflationary pressures. There are few bottlenecks and large bodies
of workers prepared to work at prevailing wages. All of this permits
rapidly rising profits, which add income to the rich and allow for a
reinvestment in new productive capacity in both equipment and
inventories. Businesses are eager to expand to get their share of
rising profits, and new businesses multiply to stake their claims to
the profits bonanza. A boom psychology takes over the business
world. Many firms go into debt to finance their expansion. And
their sales are increasingly based on credit. Soon debts are rising
faster than real production and income. As paper values rise, they
become the basis for more borrowing and more spending, which in
turn induces further inflation of values. By now certain bottlenecks
appear and a shortage of materials develops. As the economy
approaches full employment, businesses cannot expand their operations except by bidding up the price of labour. Workers become
less manageable and more demanding. The inflation is now in full
swing, and wage increases begin catching up to price increases.
Profit margins are slipping. While businesses have increased their
productive capacity, they find themselves unable to sell their
swollen output at profitable prices. Consumption is constrained by
the capitalist law of profitability. Rising wages or reduced prices
would create the required consumer market, but that would impinge further on profit margins. At the height of prosperity, wage
increases which keep pace with or even outrun the rise in prices are
actually a sign of the approaching crisis.

With inflation eating up cash faster than expected and with sluggish collection of accounts receivable, corporations are turning
more and more to the banks. But as they further extend their lines
of bank credit, the short-term liability sections of their balance-
sheets reach dangerous proportions. This is "the swampy soft spot
and breeder of bankruptcy" in every enterprise, large and small, to
quote one economist. In the light of price inflation, banks are
forced to raise interest rates to attract new lenders. And they raise
their rates to borrowers — because of the shortage of loan money
and the expectation that they will be paid back in depreciated currency, and because of the higher risks they face due to the liquidity
problems faced by many of their borrowers. As interest rates rise
the paper value of business firms is subject to downward pressures.
The stock market is depressed and the cost of raising equity capital

through new stock issues is increased — causing them to seek more of their cash from banks and creating still more pressures on banks to raise their rates. The financial structure becomes more and more fragile. As business firms struggle to find liquid funds to pay their debts, competition becomes more cutthroat. Commitments made on the assumption of a continuous upward trend in sales increasingly cannot be met.

The crisis of production is at the same time a financial crisis. These are the self-inflicted wounds of every capitalist prosperity. In the absence of powerful government intervention, it would end up in an economic depression. Business firms would now cut down on production and lay off workers; new investment projects would be shelved; the stock market would decline dramatically; prices, wages and interest rates would fall off; there would be a long chain of business failures, including some bank failures.

However deadly it is to its victims, an economic depression has a healing effect on the capitalist economy. It creates a new economic environment which allows for a renewed upsurge in profitable economic activity. Most important, it recreates the "reserve army" of workers which weakens the bargaining position of labour and produces a price-wage relationship that is more favourable to the capitalist class. It also wipes out weak businesses and transfers their assets at bargain prices to larger and financially stronger firms. Inventories are drawn down to manageable proportions. Bank credit is available on easier terms. Money can be raised more cheaply on the stock market, at least for those firms whose profit potentials seem greatest. As production and employment pick up, demand increases and the excess of productive capacity is eliminated. In short, the stage is set for a new period of expanding production, investment and profit.

It is this natural rhythm of the capitalist organism that the Keynesian prescription interrupts. Its purpose and meaning is to provide a way to have full employment in the absence of war and genuine prosperity, to pass over depression through government-induced demand rather than overcoming it in the orthodox fashion of waging war or passively waiting until the storm of crisis finally passes. The Keynesian message goes something like this: don't fight the workers too hard over wages; above all, don't beat them down by dis-employing them. Within reason, give them whatever wages will keep them happy and then, when they're not looking, raise prices to re-establish acceptable profit-margins. Use inflation instead of unemployment to maintain your profits. The government will ensure the additional money and credit to maintain circulation at higher prices. And it will keep the economy buoyant by raising government spending, financed by deficits if necessary. Don't worry too much about competitors. They will all be following the same practice, in foreign countries as well as our own: prices, wages and profits will rise throughout, leaving relative competitive positions pretty much unchanged.

The Keynesian goal of full employment is laudable — even at the cost of 2, 3, 4 or 5 per cent inflation a year which it was thought it would produce. The demise of Keynes's capitalist safety-valve is nowhere better demonstrated, however, than in the 5 per cent to 9 per cent unemployment cum 10 per cent to 25 per cent inflation that much of the capitalist world has been experiencing over the past two years. As Jacob Morris has neatly summarized:

> . . . a condition of high employment is impossible in an economy which is perpetually on the verge of a financial nervous breakdown. . . . When inflation has finally reduced the capitalist system to a condition of more or less permanent internal chaos, it can no longer serve as an efficient substitute for the industrial reserve army. The system no longer responds well to inflationary drugs (which now seem to effect it as a poison), and it begins to heave convulsively as it attempts to restore the basic inner relationships and balances which it needs for continued survival.[28]

As Morris writes, the inflationary strategy worked well while it was an insider's strategy. Once it became general knowledge and all sorts of people started to do something about protecting themselves or taking advantage of it, it was bound to turn into an agency for chaos and disorder.* For one thing, after a few beatings, union

---

* It is interesting that the Economic Council of Canada in its Third Annual Report (1966) alluded to the possibility of a "creeping" inflation turning into a galloping inflation and dismissed it as a likely development. It cited various counterforces at work, in particular "the remarkable slowness of many persons and organizations who could with seeming ease get aboard the inflationary process to avail themselves of the opportunity." The ECC's treatment of this subject is worth quoting in full: "Twenty years ago, or even more recently, the drawing of a distinction between the evils of large and small inflations would have struck many economists as not only unnecessary but even dangerously misleading, on the grounds that small inflations had a strong inherent tendency to grow into large ones. Support for the view that acceleration is inevitable has diminished, however, in the light of post-war experience. Accelerative tendencies have indeed appeared, and maintain a constant potential threat; but to a greater degree than was anticipated they have run into powerful counterforces. One counterforce has no doubt been simply the resolve of people and their elected governments not to let indefinite acceleration happen, plus improved policy tools to make this decision effective. At some stage or other, especially when the balance of payments has gone wrong, an adequate consensus has developed for weighing in with sufficient force to bring acceleration to a halt. An additional and to some extent distinct factor, however, has been the remarkable slowness of many persons and organizations, who could with seeming ease get aboard the inflationary process, to

wage demands begin to take account not only of past losses in purchasing power but of future losses as well. While most workers today seem to accept the "normal" exploitation that occurs in the labour market where they are forced to give over a portion of the value they produce to fatten the profits of their employers, and while they also generally resign themselves to being fleeced again as consumers by monopolistic manufacturers, retailers, and other middlemen, their patience begins to run out when week after week they find their paycheques shrinking in buying power. Thus the current spread of wildcats and bitter strike confrontations throughout western Europe and North America.

While organized labour is battling furiously to stay up with the price spiral, and even to forge ahead of it in advance of further expected price increases, others are also caught up in the inflationary psychology — to build up inventories in anticipation of price increases, to speculate on land and commodities, to expand plants and equipment, office buildings, and luxury highrises, and to buy out other firms — and most of this on borrowed money. Banks and other moneylenders meanwhile are raising their interest changes in anticipation that loans will be paid off in depreciated currencies. Business firms that have made the right financial moves are swimming in profits, while many others are facing insolvency. To abort bankruptcy of major firms, heavy pressure is placed on government to relieve crises of liquidity by more inflation. The point is that "with the growth of speculative manias, the whole internal discipline of capitalist production is weakened: disproportions, bottlenecks, and a dozen varieties of impairment of normal functions grow apace."[29]

Credit Capitalism

"The U.S. economy stands atop a mountain of debt $2.5 trillion high — a mountain built of all the cars and houses, all the factories and machines that have made this the biggest richest economy in the history of the world." So begins a remarkably perceptive special

---

avail themselves of the opportunity. This has probably been in part a reflection of the high cost of 'moving out of money into goods,' except in an indirect and selective fashion: it can be very expensive to store goods in advance of need, especially when they are perishable, and of course services cannot be stored at all. Whether from this, or faith, or other causes, large numbers of people have refrained from rearranging their affairs in ways which would amount to placing a heavy bet on further inflation and thus helping to accelerate it." (p. 47)

report of *Business Week* magazine, titled "The Debt Economy."[30] Of the total, $1 trillion is in corporate debt, $600 billion in mortgage debt, $500 billion in U.S. government debt, $200 billion in state and local government debt, and $200 billion in consumer debt. This debt, averaging $200 million a day since the close of World War II, has fuelled the three decades of economic boom at home and exported it abroad. As the report remarks, "it would be an awesome burden of debt even if the world's economic climate were perfect. It is an ominously heavy burden with the world as it is today — ravaged by inflation, threatened with economic depression, torn apart by the massive redistribution of wealth that has accompanied the soaring price of oil." The authors ask two pertinent questions: can all the debt now outstanding be paid off or refinanced as it becomes due? Can the economy add enough new debt to keep growing at anything close to the rate of the post-war era?

In 1946, total U.S. debt was only $400 billion, and nearly 60 per cent of it represented debt incurred by the federal government to finance the war. After the war, consumers and businesses both raced through the liquid assets they had piled up and, having spent them, borrowed so that they could keep on buying. Corporate debt also soared, and federal government spending rose consistently to ward off any major slowdowns, much of it financed by borrowing money. While it took fifteen years for U.S. total debt to double from 1946 to 1960, it took only ten years to double again, from 1960 to 1970. Whereas Gross National Product, Personal Income, Corporate Profit and the like have all grown by about 500 per cent or so since World War II, public and private debt have grown by three and four times that amount.

The sharpest increases have come since 1960. Corporations have tripled their debt over the past fifteen years. Instalment debt, mortgage debt, and state and local government have all climbed by 200 per cent or more since 1960. As *Business Week* remarks, business abandoned every theory that it ever had about how much debt it could safely take on, and much the same is true of consumers. And for their part, lenders scrapped every theory they had about what constituted a safe burden of lending. Loans of commercial banks jumped twice as fast as deposits and risk assets (loans and investment) grew twice as fast as bank capital.

Debts of this order could be justified only on the assumption that personal income and corporate profit would rise sufficiently to allow them to be paid off and that government economic policy would remain expansionary. But inflation, while forcing consumers and business to borrow ever more, reduces the share of income that is available to pay off debts, and expansionary government policy only adds to the inflationary pressures. This is the bind governments find themselves in. They are forced by inflation to adopt policies of restraint, but effective anti-inflationary measures can crush borrowers and lenders alike. According to a Chicago banker quoted by *Business Week,* "A major downturn in business activity would cause a much sharper increase in liquidation and bankruptcies that at any time in the past 30 years." It is the extent of their cumulated debt that makes businesses so vulnerable to a contraction of sales. And because of the infinitely complicated web of exchange relationships there is, in the words of *Business Week,* "the specter of a chain reaction of defaults by borrowers and failures by lenders, thrusting the world into deep depression."[31]

The destruction of stock prices reflects, more than any other single factor, the build-up of debt. In particular, the market's weakness is due primarily to the soaring rise in interest rates. On top of the general state of uncertainty in the economy, the enormous yield available on debt instruments has made it difficult for equities to attract the investor. But as corporate debt continues to increase, corporate businesses find that their interest payments can exhaust or even exceed their profit earnings. Management is more preoccupied with the management of financial assets that it is with production, and corporations are being run for the benefit of creditors rather than stockholders.

The panic triggered by Penn Central's bankruptcy in 1970 was countered by a massive injection of Federal Reserve Credit. The same happened when the Franklin National Bank was threatened by bankruptcy. Con Edison was saved from bankruptcy when the State of New York took over its $500 million obligation on its nuclear power account. The British, French, and Italian governments have been forced to intervene to salvage several major corporations from financial wreckage. Both West Germany's Herstatt and Franklin National sustained heavy losses from foreign exchange dealings. The lack of profitable investment opportunities in productive areas forced these banking interests to meet their rising debt obligations by searching for profits in speculative ventures. David Rockefeller, chairman of the Chase Manhattan bank, confesses that money markets are increasingly unable to absorb the billions of dollars of "recycled" funds accumulated by oil producing countries. Where will the banks find sufficient profit outlets to secure then a rate of return that will allow them to make the interest payments to the oil producers? In the end, as one writer has observed,

> . . . only real profit from investment in the production of real goods can make viable the growing pyramid of financial paper. Lacking these productive investment outlets, financial interests

are given to passing these prices of financial paper among themselves, increasing new interest obligations to pay off the old debt, causing the total mass of paper to rise, the money supply to expand way beyond the ability of production to match. [32]

The New York Stock Exchange estimates that the amount of investment required for new plants, equipment, and inventories between 1975 and 1985 is $2.65 trillion. If this were raised in the proportion of the last five years, debts would soar by $750 billion. In *Business Week's* mild words, "since the resulting interest burden would certainly bring about — well before 1985 — the bankruptcy of most U.S. corporations it is something less than desirable."[33] *Business Week* lists two alternative strategies. The first is to reduce the level of investment expenditures. But "if this were taken far enough to bring down debt to safe levels, it would result in such painful unemployment —and hence such dislocations of world trade — as to be equally undesirable." The second alternative would be to correct the balance between equity and debt. This can be done by a drastic redistribution of income in favour of business profits: by large increases in personal taxes which would take governments out of the money markets where they compete with private industry and drive up interest rates; by raising profits through further acceleration of depreciation allowance; making equity investments more attractive by reducing the capital gains tax and making dividends tax deductible. Ultimately this scenario calls for a program of wage-price control whose effect would be to raise profit margins and cut back living standards.

One of the casualties of the economic crisis is the venerable principle of rewarding thrift. Savers now have the choice of losing purchasing power at a slower rate if they save through government instruments or at a faster rate if they save through the banks. Neither have been offering interest rates which are sufficient to fully compensate for the rise in prices.

Moreover, in most every country, governments have been overwhelming banking institutions by outbidding them in the interest rates they pay on savings.* Bankers everywhere complain

---

* In England, the government has adopted an index-linking system. Purchasers of government bonds and depositors in government savings accounts receive no interest, but the face amount of their savings is adjusted for increases in the cost of living. In real terms, the English scheme constitutes an interest-free loan to the government. Yet this is an improvement over what happens elsewhere, where governments and banks are paying back in purchasing power less than they borrow. Moreover, except in the English index-linking system, taxes are levied on the interest that is paid, compounding the theft of the buying-power of people's savings.

of the hemorrhaging of savings deposits. Consequently, business enterprisers have been finding it more difficult to raise debt capital, to say nothing of equity capital. One of the pressures on the banks to raise their lending rates has been the competition from governments. To attract savings they have to pay interest yields high enough to compete with the yields on government issues. They can do this only by raising the interest charges on loans they extend. These high interest charges, in turn, are one of the factors threatening the profitability of businesses.* Ultimately, high interest rates are shifted on to prices which in some instances have the effect of reducing sales.

What this amounts to is that the United States economy (with other economies not far behind) is on a collision course between government finance capital and private finance capital. This is precisely what U.S. Treasury Secretary William E. Simon expressed concern over as the American Congress began debating the size of the 1975-76 budget deficit.[34] In fulfilling their responsibility of keeping corporate capitalism viable, government have put the squeeze on the very businesses that their measures are intended to save. Hence the contradiction of some major corporations, reeling under the burden of accumulated debt — which in the first instance was aggravated by government policy — being rescued by government handout operations.

On Thin Ice

Except for agriculture, there are few major sectors of the American economy that are not in deep financial crisis. Take the real estate industry. Several of the large developers have been operating in the red for a dangerously long time. According to *Business Week,* "it is hard to see how the industry and the institutions that finance it, can escape from today's bind without some major write-offs and some stunning failures." [35] While the mortgage market consumes one-quarter to one-third of all the capital used in the U.S. economy, its institutional base is weak. Mortgage lenders are limited both by regulations and prudence in what they can pay for funds. During slow periods, when there is more money than takers, mortgage lenders get all that they want. When the economy is booming, mortgage lenders are skipped over as money passes into the hands of

---

* According to one calculation I have seen, corporations require a gross rate of return (including interest charges, depreciation and debt-retirement needs) of 24 to 25 per cent per annum on borrowed money if they are to earn an after-tax net return of 6 to 7 per cent for the borrowed money.

those who can command it, like the Treasury and government agencies, and those who are in a position to pay dearly for it, like the big commercial banks and giant corporations. Over the past eight years, the U.S. federal government has attempted to bolster the position of mortgage lenders by guaranteeing them funds. Between 1968 and 1974, federal agencies increased their holdings of mortgages by over 200 per cent compared to a 33 per cent gain by the private holders. Yet the intrusion of government into the field has evidently solved nothing, and while it has not done enough to improve the mortgage market, its borrowing has been heavy enough to cause trouble in the money market. "The effort, at best, has only prevented a disaster from turning into a catastrophe. Residential housing starts still have declined 45 per cent from the peak in 1972, and what all that borrowing by federal agencies to support the market seems to have done is push up the cost of money for everyone."[36]

Nobody knows what constitutes too much consumer debt. Certainly debt payments do not come anywhere near their ultimate limit of taking up 100 per cent of disposable income. Yet they are rising rapidly — from 4.5 per cent of disposible income in 1946 to 13.2 per cent in 1960, 15.5 per cent in 1970, and 17 per cent in 1974. While the number of households has risen by only 8 per cent since 1970, consumer instalment debt has risen by more than 50 per cent, resulting in a far larger debt burden per individual household. With such debt loads, many consumers think twice about going further into hock, and, as the recession spreads, more will have trouble meeting their loan payments. Either way, businesses that depend on installment buying can be severely affected. One such company, Sears, Roebuck, was pushed into the red in 1973 and remained there in 1974 because of bad debt, slowing sales, and soaring interest rates.

What is far more worrisome to business and government leaders is the critical state of the U.S. banking system. The banks are accessories in the attempts by business to maintain their viability through borrowing. As corporations edge closer and closer to the brink of insolvency, the banks are also drawn nearer to the same edge. The harder it becomes for corporations to repay their bank loans, the more the banks are forced to grant them further loans to prevent them from going under and defaulting on the backlog of loans. But they can lend at a furious rate only by impairing their own liquidity.[37] Concern over the banking crisis has been expressed by the chairman of the Federal Reserve Board, Arthur F. Burns:

This year, for the first time in decades, questions have been raised about the strength of the nation's, and indeed the world's banking system. . . . [Moreover] for the first time since the General Depression, the availability of liquidity from the central banks has become . . . an essential ingredient in maintaining confidence in the commercial banking system. Faith in our banks . . . now rests unduly on the fact that troubled banks can turn to a government lender of last resort.[38]

As a percentage of the GNP,* bank loans rose only slightly from 1950 to 1960, from 12.1 per cent to 13.8 per cent. A decisive change began with 1960 and accelerated further after 1970, as bank loans were growing far faster than business activity. By 1970, bank loans grew to 19.9 per cent of GNP, and by the first half of 1974 to 25.2 per cent. Banks act as a depository of money. They accept deposits because it gives them access to funds from which they can profit by making loans or purchasing bonds. However, to meet day-to-day withdrawals by depositors they are required to keep a reserve of cash and to invest a portion of the deposits in short-term government bonds that can be converted almost instantaneously into cash should withdrawals suddenly increase. The banks are now approaching the absolute limit (100 per cent) of the deposits that can be loaned out. By the end of 1974 they had committed 82 per cent of their deposits to loans. By comparison, the proportion in 1929 was 73.1 per cent.**

The liquidity of the banks is stretched to the limit. In 1950, they held 54 per cent of their deposits in the form of cash and U.S. Treasury notes. This fell to 34.7 per cent in 1960, 18.3 per cent in 1970, and 13.6 per cent in 1974. What is extraordinary from the 1960s on is the extent to which the banks have themselves borrowed money in order in turn to loan the funds to others.† This process has allowed the banks to escape the regulations of the monetary authorities. "In the process they have created a complex network of borrowing and lending throughout the business world which not only further stimulated the inflationary process, but also resulted in a kind of delicately balanced debt structure that is constantly in danger of breaking down."[39]

The banks discovered another way of getting around government regulations: switching their money to their foreign branches

---

* More precisely, the GNP originating in nonfinancial corporations.

** The balance-sheets of the banks actually understate the extent of their loan commitments. They omit a variety of obligations taken on by the banks such as "standby letters of credit." For a fee they guarantee the IOUs issued and sold by big corporations. Should these corporations default on these IOUs, the banks guarantee to pay the borrowed money.

† In 1950, short-term borrowing of the banks accounted for only 2.2 per cent of bank loans; this rose slightly to 4.5 per cent in 1960, to 28.7 per cent in 1970, and to 48.5 per cent in 1974.

operating in the Eurodollar market. Once the money was converted to Eurodollars,* the back home office "borrowed" it, thus maintaining its deposit base. By 1969 the annual volume of money making this round-trip had grown to $15 billion. Eurodollars can support a lot more loans than conventional term deposits because there are no reserve requirements on Eurodollar deposits. They also have no interest-rate ceilings. Furthermore, any bank can get into the market. Many did. Sixty banks set up London offices over the two-year period 1972-3. The major source of deposits was money borrowed from other banks. From 1968 to mid 1974 Eurodollar market deposits rose by 30 per cent a year. By the end of that period there was something like $200 billion in the system. The quadrupling of oil prices brought the banks all the investors they could have wished for. These included many European governments which used the Eurodollar market as a source of money to finance their mounting balance-of-payments deficits. France borrowed $2.9 billion in the first half of 1974; Britain, $4.8 billion. The government of Italy, the market's single greatest debtor, had over $9 billion in outstanding Eurodollar loans. With inflation rates and Eurodollar totals both rising furiously, many economists came to view the market as a monster that was out of control. But growth came to an abrupt halt in the summer of 1974 as the failure of the Herstatt bank reduced the number of participants in the market and sobered the judgement of those lenders who remained in it. The question that remains concerns the health of the loans made in the last few years in view of the worldwide recession, and the ability of corporate borrowers to find alternative sources as their loans come due for payment.

The banks are gambling that businesses will be able to repay their loans despite their declining corporate liquidity. Government regulatory agencies have been forced to go along with this dangerous situation because to disturb this intricately interrelated debt structure now could easily bring it all crashing down. The "fine tuning" that economists have been talking about since the end of World War II has proved incapable of handling the conflicting pressures on the economy.

---

* A Eurodollar is any currency that is deposited in another country's bank.

Priming the Pump:
The Canadian Way

In Canada it is the Treasury Board and the Bank of Canada that prime the pump that keeps our economy afloat with more and more money. Over the last few years these venerable institutions have been working overtime. Take for example the growth of debt, reflecting the pumping activity of the credit system. Through the upswing of the 1960s the average rate-of-increase of bank loans was 12 per cent. This was already 30 per cent more than the average annual increase in output. Between 1972 and 1974, bank loan increases averaged 23.4 per cent, almost four times the average annual increase in output.[40]

Or take consumer instalment credit, which over the post-war period has tended to double every six or seven years, a rate of increase well above the growth of the economy as a whole. Between 1972 and 1974, loans to consumers expanded by 50 per cent, much more than in any three-year time-span during the 1960s. Consumer indebtedness has been rising steadily in relation to disposable income — from 14 per cent in 1960 to 24 per cent in 1974. Whereas debts absorbed less than 6 cents of the average consumer's take-home dollar just after the war, today they absorb about 25 cents. And in the mortgage loan field, too, debts have tripled since 1969. No one knows exactly what the outside limit of instalment credit may be. While average Canadian consumers are still a long way from having to spend 100 percent of their income for debt payments, excessive debt is already engulfing thousands of families. Certainly the need for especially heavy repayments depresses consumers' willingness to commit themselves to further instalment buying.

Neither Canadian corporations nor Canadian chartered banks appear to be facing the degree of liquidity squeeze being experienced by their U.S. counterparts. Nevertheless the ice is getting thinner. For example, bank loans constituted 61 per cent of deposits in 1973 compared to 44 per cent ten years earlier, and their liquid asset ratio (the percentage of deposits that can be got hold of quickly) fell sharply from 33.6 per cent in 1964 to 21.5 per cent in 1974.

Government finances can operate either to inflate or deflate the economy. When government spends more than it takes in, it can either print up more money to cover the difference or, as is more common, borrow what it needs from the banks. Either way the money supply expands. Until the mid-1950s the Canadian government had a decidedly restraining impact on the economy. Taking all levels of government into account, there were only two deficit years in the ten-year period between 1947 and 1956. The total accumulated surplus in the period was 3.3 billion dollars. The following seven years were years of continuous deficits. The accumulated deficit over the seven years was 4.5 billion dollars. These were followed by eight surplus years (1964-1971) (total accumulated surplus of 4.2 billion dollars), while the last four years have had deficits totalling in excess of 6 billion dollars.*

The overall role of government in Canada has increased remarkably in recent years. Total expenditures of the three levels of governments combined (including both government purchases and transfer payments) represented 22 per cent of GNP at the start of the 1950s, grew progressively to 31 per cent up to 1966, and then rapidly to 40 per cent by 1974. While it took 16 years to increase the share of public spending from 22 to 31 per cent, it took only eight years to climb from 31 per cent to 40 per cent! While this spectacular increase in expenditures has been matched by increases in revenue through most of the sixties, governments will increasingly have to resort to priming the pump through deficit financing to maintain these bloated expenditures in the seventies.

Conservative criticism of government spending has always contained an element of truth. Expanded government spending on armaments, administration, and welfare is partly responsible for the phenomenon of permanent inflation. It creates purchasing power in exactly the same way that production of consumer goods or capital goods does — wages, welfare increases, and profit — but this supplementary buying power is not matched by a corresponding supplementary merchandise placed on the market. Parallel with the creation of buying power in the private sector is the appearance of merchandise which absorbs this purchasing power. In contrast, the creation of purchasing power in the government sector has no compensatory increase in the supply of merchandise whose sale can absorb the extra purchasing power. Only if the expansion of government spending were more than matched by taxation of the private sector would the effect of government be safely non-inflationary.

The Bank of Canada, which controls the money supply, has also been working overtime in recent years. Throughout the 1960s it increased the money supply by about 8 per cent each year. This has been raised to an average of over 15 per cent a year in the seventies.

---

* By contrast, U.S. government finances have been far more expansionary. Over the last ten years only one showed a surplus, and the cumulative deficit of the first four years of the 1970s is more than 80 per cent greater than the cumulative deficit of the last four years of the 1960s.

In fact, the money supply has almost doubled since 1969 — a rate of increase of money far greater than the rate of increase in real output.* The central bank has been using its facilities to support the massive inflationary tide.

The upshot of all this, and what needs repeating, is that ever since World War II, and particularly since the mid-1950s, governments have been aborting recessions by letting loose the Keynesian prescription of deficit financing, money expansion, and credit. Creeping inflation of 2, 3, or 4 per cent a year was considered a bargain compared to massive unemployment. What was ignored is the resulting increase in the debt structure, and the parallel decline in corporate and individual liquidity.

A Recapitulation

A recapitulation of what I have attempted to argue thus far begins with the general statement that the making and remaking of profit is the key to any understanding of the path of growth in a capitalist economy. The ultimate source of all profit is the value of things that workers produce over and above the wages and salaries they receive. The hazards that get in the way of stable growth are numerous. On the one hand, capitalists may seek to earn higher profits by squeezing the value of the wages they dispense relative to the value of the things that are produced. In the first instance, this can be done by depressing wages or speeding up the work process. When many follow this course, they run the risk that workers may not be able to purchase all the commodities that are produced. The source of profits may be the point of production, but profits are finally realized in the market place. If businesses are unable to sell all that they produce, they must eventually cut back on production and see their profits diminish. What can offset this tendency is the opening up of new markets by the discovery of new customers abroad or the development of new products. For a time individual capitalists may postpone a decline in their profits by squeezing their smaller rivals. Giant corporations can extract extra profits from the smaller companies they buy from or sell to, or from taking over the markets of competing companies.

Another hazard surfaces when the economy is expanding too

Between 1965 and 1974, Canada's volume of goods and services rose by 56 per cent while the money supply tripled. The volume of production rose 3.7 per cent, 6.8 per cent, and 5.8 per cent in 1971, 1972, and 1973, while the money supply was rising by 14.5 per cent, 16 per cent, and 18 per cent in those years. For every dollar's worth of Canadian production in 1965 there was about 35 cents in the money supply. For every dollar of 1974 production (measured in 1965 prices) there was more than 65 cents in money supply.

rapidly, creating shortages (particularly of labour), the over-working of equipment, and the paying of overtime. On the one hand labour productivity falls off, not only because of the over-utilization of plant and equipment, but also because of the increasing amount of time loss due to strikes as workers become more militant. On the other hand wages are bid up. With labour costs rising, profits begin to slip. Employers may try to offset this tendency by replacing workers with machines. This response may backfire in the end. Individual capitalists earn profits only on the basis of "value-added" within their own enterprises. Machines cannot add value to their purchasers because they must pay the producers of the machines their full worth, or nearly so. Their full worth, reflected in their price, takes into account the costs that their purchasers save in using less labour.* Aside from their dealings with weaker capitalists, the only exchange on which producers may earn some extra money is in the purchase of the labour time of workers. The fewer the workers that are employed, the narrower the base for profit accumulation. Again, this squeeze on profits can be offset by finding ways of raising the productivity of their declining numbers of workers.

These are some of the permanent contradictions that face individual capitalists and the economy in the aggregate. They were easily overcome in the aftermath of World War II. The Depression, the war, and the Cold War created conditions for rapid expansion: new and growing markets and rapid technological changes that greatly increased labour productivity. But the expansion of these markets was bound to slow and the most dramatic impact of the technological innovations of the period were bound at some point to be exhausted, or nearly so. And with the unions struggling for a bigger share of the productivity gains, the shares of profits in national income were therefore bound to show a declining tendency.[41]

A few years before Keynes wrote his *General Theory*, a Polish economist, Michael Kalecki, writing within the Marxist framework, wrote three essays that contained the essentials of Keynes's great work.[42] Subsequently, in 1943, he became the first major economist to show the fallacies of the Keynesian notion that government stimulation is sufficient to guarantee full employment. He argued that policies that maintained continuous full employment are inconsistent with the political and social requirements of liberal capitalism:

---

* For a time, the price of the new equipment may be less than their full value, but when a machine contributes more value over its lifetime than it costs, many firms are bound to purchase it, ultimately bidding up its price until it approximates the full value.

The assumption that a Government will maintain full employment in a capitalist economy if it only knows how to do it is fallacious. . . . The *maintenance* of full employment would cause social and political changes which would give a new impetus to the opposition of the business leaders. Indeed, under a regime of permanent full employment, the "sack" would cease to play its role as a disciplinary measure. The social position of the boss would be undermined and the self-assurance of the working class would grow. Strikes for wage increases and improvements in the conditions of work would create political tensions. . . . [The] class instincts of business leaders tell them that lasting full employment is unsound from their point of view and that unemployment is an integral part of the normal capitalist system.[43]

Kalecki's writings, which were regarded as antiquated in the 1950s and 1960s, provide the best theoretical guide to today's economic crisis.

Economists who observe what happens to wages and profits during the course of the business cycle note that halfway through the typical expansion the economy experiences a pronounced decline in the ratio of profits to wages.[44] (See accompanying chart.) The level of profits also comes under severe pressure at the same juncture and typically falls thereafter.* This is what one would expect from the contradictory forces at work. In the early phase of an expansion, unit labour costs (determined by the relationship between wages and productivity) decline relative to prices but typically overtake prices after the mid-point of the expansion. Profits are high, growing rapidly in the first phase, slow down and decline in the second. They are lowest during the recession, a fact that is often used to counter the argument that corporations need a recession. Certainly they would like to be able to avoid a recession. Yet, as stated earlier, recession is a necessary condition for achieving the highly profitable first phase of the expansion and for avoiding the highly unprofitable consequences of sustained full employment.

Up to the stagnation years that followed 1957, North America enjoyed twelve years of sustained expansion. The business cycles that occurred in this period featured long vigorous expansion phases and brief mild contraction phases. Long-term investment opportunities were ample enough that mere slow-downs were sufficient to create the slack in the labour forces and reductions in inventory that permitted quick recovery. The "automatic stabilizers," largely a product of the large government sector, were able to do the rest. By the end of the 1950s, the early post-war

---

* To some extent monopoly-sharing corporations are able to protect their profits even during downturns, by being able to hold up or raise their prices. The greatest pressures fall upon the more competitive sectors.

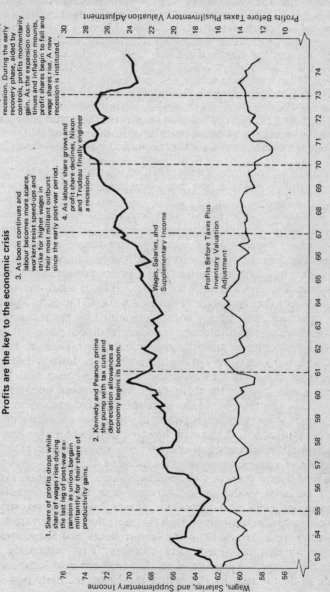

Figure 10
Profits are the key to the economic crisis

1. Share of profits drops while share of wages rises during the last leg of post-war expansion as unions bargain militantly for their share of productivity gains.

2. Kennedy and Pearson prime the pump with tax cuts and depreciation allowances as economy begins its boom.

3. As boom continues and labour becomes more scarce, workers resist speed-ups and strike for higher wages in their most militant outburst since the early post-war period.

4. As labour share grows and profit share declines, Nixon and Trudeau finally engineer a recession.

5. They shrink from sustained recession. During the early recovery phase, aided by controls, profits momentarily gain. As the expansion continues and inflation mounts, profit shares begin to fall and wage shares rise. A new recession is instituted.

Wages, Salaries, and Supplementary Income

Profits Before Taxes Plus Inventory Valuation Adjustment

Sources: *Royal Bank of Canada, Statistics Canada.*

expansionary forces had run their course, and as a result the economic recession that began in 1957 was severe and sustained. Immediately upon taking office, the Kennedy Administration substantially raised military spending and shortly thereafter enacted investment tax credits, liberalized depreciation allowances, and personal tax cuts. The combination of these stimulating policies and a badly weakened labour force led to the substantial economic growth, super profits, and falling share of labour income of the mid-1960s. As a sub-economy of the United States, Canada, after experiencing the same stagnation, underwent the same expansion with the same consequences for profits and income shares.*

By late 1965 (late 1964 in Canada), as profit margins peaked and the trade surplus declined (trade deficit increased in Canada), business clearly required a recession. But by this time the U.S.A. was just beginning its escalation of the war in Vietnam, and, unlike the case of World War II and the Korean War, the demands of war and domestic economic requirements did not mesh. Unable to reduce military expenditures and unwilling to stir up more opposition by raising taxes, the Johnson administration let the economy run its inflationary course. With sustained full employment, a new phase of labour militancy emerged, and while profit margins slipped badly, labour's share of the national income rose. Squeezed of profits, businesses were forced to go increasingly into debt to finance their operations. A long and severe recession was clearly required to end the dislocation generated by eight years of continuous expansion and five years of tight labour markets.

In 1969 the incoming Nixon administration set about to follow this course by instituting a policy of fiscal and monetary restraint. It was joined in this approach by Pierre Trudeau. Unemployment rose sharply in both countries. But the recession was aborted long before it was allowed to complete its painful task. Looking forward to the 1972 presidential election, Nixon surmised that continuation of a policy of restriction would have raised unemployment to politically unacceptable levels. Businesses, squeezed by five years of tight labour markets and then by the initial impact of recession, screamed for relief. Many were so deeply in debt that a prolonged recession might have forced bankruptcy on them. Trudeau again followed Nixon's lead, but while the American President instituted his New Economic Policy, a full-scale program to pull United States capital out of its dilemma, Trudeau set up an ineffective program of price and income guidelines.

---

* With a similar expansionary fiscal policy, Canada also enjoyed the additional stimulus of a devalued dollar and large wheat sales to the U.S.S.R. and China.

By the early 1970s U.S. capital required at one and the same time an expansionary policy to stimulate investment and keep unemployment from rising too high, a restrictive policy to curb inflation, raise interest rates, and get labour fully under control, and an international policy that would improve deteriorating trade balances. No combination of Keynesian "fine tuning" could achieve these results. Until the distortions it produced became unbearable, profits recovered momentarily under the program of wage and price controls. The series of dollar devaluations, along with the wheat agreement with the U.S.S.R., gave an enormous boost to American exports, helped turn around the balance of payments deficit, and gave an impetus to investment and employment — so much so that serious shortages began to surface. When the Phase IV guidelines were finally lifted in early 1974, the price explosion was felt around the world. As prices skyrocketed, workers struggled to recover their wage losses and strike activity surged. This time the entire capitalist world, much more closely integrated than it was a decade and two earlier, was engulfed in the same dilemma — ultimately the consequence of postponing a severe recession in the mid-1960s. Corporations borrowed money frantically, in the hopes of staying ahead of the profit squeeze. With consumers and governments responding to their cash shortages in similar fashion, banks were straining to meet the demand for loans, and the supply of money was allowed to continue its great climb. To protect themselves against the effects of inflation, banks were forced to raise their interest rates — which in turn put more pressure on the level of prices. What this adds up to is that North American growth has been constructed over the past 15 years almost like a house of credit cards. As the tremors increase, there is always the threat that the house will crumble.

A prolonged and severe recession was desperately needed now to rid the economy of its excess baggage and to bring some discipline to the labour force — in short, to complete the task of the aborted recession of 1969, that much the greater now because of four added years of wild expansion that included a food crisis and an energy crisis and growing instability in the international order. Most political leaders followed the dictates of the economic system and brought on an economic downturn which, in terms of both breadth and depth, is the most severe the world has seen since the days of the Great Depression. Large declines in industrial production reduced the volume of imports, improved the balance of payments of nations that had been struck with extraordinary oil bills, and forced a sharp reduction of the prices of most primary commodities. Massive layoffs of workers seem to have delivered the effects expected of them — reduced wage demands, reduced worker militancy,

reduced time loss due to work stoppages, strikes, and absenteeism.*
Price inflation fell off most everywhere, although monopoly-
sharing enterprises have slowed down the adjustment process by
substituting extraordinary production cut-backs rather than accept
price declines.

The business economy needs much more contraction — at least
another 18 to 36 months of sustained recession and sustained
unemployment — to eliminate the accumulated distortions of the
previous decade and a half, and to fully subdue the labour force. It
also needs to open up new areas of profitable investment to stimu-
late a level of investment spending that would fully absorb the savings produced in a rapidly growing economy. If neither of these
conditions are present then the worldwide recovery will be sporadic
and partial and soon lead to another sharp contraction. It appears
that vast new investment opportunities are in fact opening up in the
field of energy exploration and production. What they require to
make them profitable are government subsidies and a program to
hold up the price of conventional oil.** What remains in doubt is the
willingness of governments to allow the recession to run its course
and fulfil its essential mission.

It seems that political leaders are much more aware of the full
dimensions of the crisis today than they were in 1969 and they have
shown much greater tenacity in stretching out the economic downturn that they originally set in motion. Yet, by the first quarter of
1975 many of them were already showing signs of bowing to
internal pressures of organized labour and business and easing into
a more expansionary monetary and fiscal policy.† Should they
fully surrender to these pressures another round of inflation will
again be upon us. What would normally follow, as should be clear
by now, is yet another round of recession. This is the nature of the
script we are now following. What could change the plot —with no
changing of the characters and hence no alteration in the substance
of the script — is a full-fledged plan of price and wage control and
government allocation of scarce materials. Whatever the guise in
which it is introduced, the underlying purpose of state planning
would be to engineer a sustained expansion while redistributing
income shares from labour to capital. This is the central challenge
facing workers in the years ahead. Defeat lies ahead unless workers

---

* The exception to this generalization is the public sector, where job tenure is more
  secure.
** Just such a strategy is in fact being instituted. See Part V.
† Some of them, President Ford included, were undoubtedly thinking of forthcoming elections that would test their popularity.

can organize defensively simply to protect their interests against those of the corporations. Beyond the defensive struggle lies the task of liberation from capitalist instabilities, securing an even and balanced growth in output and income shares and greater controls over their working and political lives.

V/The Declining U.S. Empire

Most major economic crises are international in character. This is because capitalism is an international system. There can be differences in timing. The crisis begins in one country or a group of countries, then spreads to the others, sometimes after a long interval. It is transmitted through trade, capital movements and currency transactions. Typically, when a country does not have the international reserves to make payments that are due and demanded by foreign creditors, it will adopt policies that depress its economy so as to shrink its imports. European bankers urged this solution on the U.S. government through the 1960s as the pending crisis in international finance became evident. Instead, the U.S. followed a different course which contributed to worldwide inflation and depression.

The three pillars of a nation's power are economic, political, and military. These pillars stand or fall together. In the summer of 1973 they began to fall together for the United States of America.

In mid-August the American bombs stopped falling in Cambodia, 23 years after the first American military mission arrived in South Vietnam and 12 years after the first American GI died fighting there. In all, the Americans spent 140 billion dollars, 46,079 dead in battle, and over 300,000 wounded, in a vain effort to control the destiny of Indo-China. Even in the defeat, the salvage expenses continued to mount: 621 million dollars in 1973 for South Vietnam and 295 million dollars in Cambodia.

An energy crisis burst on the scene in the winter of 1973 and a food crisis in the summer, accompanied by the wildest inflation in recent history and a catastrophic collapse of the American dollar. None of the calamities happened overnight, nor were they isolated from each other or from the war in Indo-China. While the United States was squandering its resources on imperial adventures and military bases on all corners of the globe, its European and Japanese rivals gathered their strength.

Finally there is Watergate, "the superbowl of political scandals." Watergate is the final denouement of the myth of American exceptionalism. For most liberally-minded Americans, the outrageous lies of the Kennedy-Johnson era ended whatever trust still remained in the American political system. What the Kennedy-Johnson era of deception did for liberals, the Watergate era has done for the "silent majority." Solid consensus, so crucial to American conduct during the Cold War when the Communist bogeyman was needed to shroud the imperial project, can no longer be taken for granted. Indeed, the new detente with China and Russia, so important to Nixon's electoral victory, robbed him of his perennial weapon to contain his domestic critics. He could not use the threat of international Communism to stop the Watergate investigation. While the ruse of "national security" was used to thwart a full investigation into the Kennedy assassination, Nixon found himself ideologically defenseless.

The Roman Empire enjoyed a long period of decline, over 500 years. Once in decline the British Empire disintegrated in less than 50 years. We can with confidence expect to witness the eclipse of the American Empire by the turn of this century. We are already beginning to observe its disintegration, but like a wounded beast in the forest, the American giant is showing a fierce resistance in its struggle to stave off defeat. And its capacity for survival remains formidable.

America's rise to affluence and power rested on the flow of people and capital from the cramped lands of England and Europe. Traditions held over from the feudal era limited the scope of capitalists there and gave little hope to labourers of ever owning the land they worked or earning sufficient income to set about establishing their own businesses. By comparison, the opportunities for both labourers and capitalists seemed boundless in America. The attractive forces of an expanding agriculture, increasing population and markets, and high rewards to industrial and commercial capital caused capital and skilled labour to flow irresistibly from England, Germany, France and elsewhere.

As land grew scarcer and giant corporations developed and cornered the market, these boundless horizons drew to their limits. Immigration began to be unwelcome, and in the 1920s strict quantitative limits were imposed. But with war and the threat of war enveloping the world, the United States became the recipient of a flood of new capital from Europe and Asia — seeking safety more than rewards. This time the inflow took the form of gold. From 1934 to 1941 the U.S. stock of gold grew by $14.5 billion. By 1950 it had risen to more than $24.2 billion; almost two-thirds of the nation's total money stock. With so vast a liquidity, growth in private and public debt seemed trivial. Simultaneously, undamaged by a war that ravaged the rest of the world, the United States underwent an amazing multiplication of its productive capacity, not only in manufacturing but also in agriculture. The United States could feed its own people and much of the world besides. This was to become decisive in the 1970s, when the U.S.A. was to use its cereal surpluses, a renewable resource, in exchange for the non-renewable mineral and energy resources of the Third World.

The unquestioned industrial and agricultural supremacy of the United States, backed up by its possession of most of the world's gold stock, made it inevitable that the dollar would act, with gold, as the world's monetary reserve. This suited the needs of the rest of the capitalist world until well into the 1950s, but as the economies of Europe and Japan revived, the accumulated dollar reserves, which had been used by the United States to pay for direct overseas military expenditures and to purchase foreign assets, became an unmitigated burden. In effect, the rest of the world was financing America's global empire by accepting increasing amounts of dollars that were not matched by American exports. Because dollars could be printed faster than gold could be dug out of the ground, the gold cover began to shrink. A fear developed that the payments of gold in exchange for dollars, as guaranteed by the Bretton Woods agreement, would have to be suspended. A gold drain set in when foreigners began to mistrust the value of the dollars they had been accumulating. The American gold stock fell from $22.8 billion in 1957 to $15.4 billion in 1964, to $10.4 billion in 1968. The inflows of capital, people and gold which had been the foundation of American affluence now turned into an outflow — the first sign of her descent.

Like England at the turn of the century, the U.S.A. is fighting to remain on top of the capitalist world. Her problems are severe. In 1972, the U.S. purchased almost $7 billion more from the rest of the world than she sold to them. On top of this trade deficit, there was a deficit of $3 billion in military aid, $4 billion in "economic" aid, $2 billion in tourism, and $2 billion in foreign investment. Together this came to $17 billion. Unlike England's at the height of the British Empire, U.S. returns from foreign investment are not large enough to cover this deficit. They amount to $6 billion. What was still left to be paid for was $11 billion.

In 1971 the U.S. was compelled to embargo gold payments, but dollar outflows continued to rise to pay for her rising foreign indebtedness. By the end of 1972, total U.S. liabilities abroad were $83 billion, and rose to above $90 billion in 1973, when Europe finally closed its foreign exchange windows to further dollar debt payments. These dollar exports really represented the export of American inflation. Exchanged for foreign currencies, they raised the supply of foreign money and increased price levels abroad, improving the competitive position of American products in foreign markets. When Europe compelled the dollar to float, the dollar ceased being the world's one reserve currency. The dollar could no longer be used to finace U.S. military and economic activities abroad. The United States was put in the same position as other countries, of having to pay for its place in the world by increasing its exports relative to its domestic consumption. The end of easy affluence in North America is the direct consequence of the changing shape of the world economy.

But this was only the beginning of her problems. Strategists were already beginning to calculate the enormous costs of importing the vast amounts of resource the U.S. would have to import to supply her industrial and military systems. The Interior Department estimated that the annual gap between domestic production and consumption of all minerals, including energy materials, would grow, *in constant dollars,* from $8.6 billion in 1970 to $31 billion in 1985 and $64 billion by the turn of the century. By 1980, imports of oil from the Middle East alone would run to 16 billion dollars a year, assuming the pre-October war prices. Left to take its natural course, the trade deficit would then increase two or three times in the space of a very few years. This was deemed an impossible course to sustain.

The steps taken by President Nixon in 1971 to restrict imports into the U.S.A. and devalue the American dollar were just the first round in the American fight to re-order the flow of world trade to her advantage. The policy of allowing the value of the U.S. dollar to fall relative to the currencies of other capitalist countries was accompanied by vigorous efforts to restrict the imports of manufactured goods to the U.S.A. A third element in the Nixon strategy has been the attempts to expand exports to the U.S.S.R. and China. To a very large degree this is what the dramatic reconciliation with the U.S.A.'s former enemies is all about. Nixon's eagerness to conclude the wheat export trade with them was part of his effort to find the foreign currency to cover the U.S. deficits on trade, military expenses, foreign investment, and the rest. Illustrative of the way all points in the economy inter-relate, it was the same export deals to the U.S.S.R. and China that were partially responsible for the shortage of wheat and feed grains in North America and the dramatic rise in food prices. The devaluation of the American-Canadian dollar made North American wheat a bargain that the Communist world and Japan were happy to take advantage of.

The energy crisis, engineered by OPEC and the oil companies, was instrumental in raising the price of crude oil to a level which makes it possible to develop costly conventional and non-conventional sources of energy. However much it has damaged U.S. industries within the domestic economy, by equalling the price of fuel between North America, Europe, and Japan, it has vastly improved their competitive position in the world economy. More important, the energy crisis enabled Presidents Nixon and Ford to launch Project Independence, which aims to make the United States self-sufficient in energy consumption by the year 2000.

These policies, designed by the Nixon administration and further developed by the Ford administration, aim to put the United States back in the saddle of world capitalism. The obstacles in its path are formidable. The goal can be achieved by (1) thwarting the aspirations of the Third World for a fairer division of the world's product, (2) maintaining a division of world trade among the industrialized capitalist nations that is favourable to the United States, (3) redividing the income flows within the United Sates in a manner that sends a greater proportion to the giant corporations. The struggles around these questions will occupy the attention of world politics for the next quarter of a century.

The Challenge

The cumulative impact of the Keynesian Revolution would not have been nearly so devastating were it not for the changing constellation of international forces. The integration of world capitalism has reached new heights. The record expansion of international trade and international investment has resulted in the rapid spread of inflation and unemployment from one country to another. For most of the post-war era, any one country undergoing momentary recessions could substitute rising foreign markets for declining domestic ones, and multinational corporations would shift their capital from depressed areas to prosperous ones. The increasing international integration of world capitalism removes this safety-valve. The prospects for a severe contraction or a severe inflation are all the greater because these become international in scope.

At the end of World War II, the U.S.A. was the only really strong country among the leading capitalist nations. It had most of the productive capacity and most of the gold reserves. The famous Bretton Woods agreement recognized the superior position of the U.S.A. by establishing the gold exchange standard which requires that every capitalist nation define the the value of its currency in terms of gold or the dollar. Literally, the dollar was "as good as gold." The value of the dollar in relation to gold was set at $35.00 an ounce, and the U.S. agreed to buy gold or sell gold at that price. The International Monetary Fund was established to administer these arrangements.

During the post-war era of dollar shortage, the U.S. pumped money into Europe via the Marshall Plan, $12 billion worth. The Marshall Plan was anything but charity. In order to block the expansion of Communism in Western Europe, the U.S. had to build up the economies of these countries, including its recent enemies as well as its allies. And the expansion of the U.S. economy was seen to depend on the revitalization of world trade and the reopening of opportunities for foreign investment, both of which required rebuilding the economies of West Europe and Japan. It was the American deficit that helped to create the miracle economies of Western Europe. By 1958, the year of the Common Market, a remarkable shift had occurred. Fourteen years of "dollar gap" gave way to a period of dollar surplus as the economic growth of Germany, Italy, France, and Japan dramatically outpaced the growth of the U.S. economy. Between 1955 and 1970, the industrial production of Japan had increased eight-fold. Italy's and Germany's production rose more than three-fold. By contrast, U.S. (and Canadian) production failed to double (while British production rose by only two-thirds) in the same sixteen-year period.

Because of its pre-eminent position it was possible for the U.S. to re-establish an international order which had been lacking for over half a century — since the time when other nations had begun to challenge British pre-eminence fifty years before. But good times for America could not last forever because the successful operation of the new order was from the outset leading to its own destruction. Success for the U.S.A. required stability and prosperity in the capitalist world, but this allowed its rivals to re-establish themselves.

America's relative economic decline is confirmed by every important economic indicator. (See the accompanying tables). In the years immediately following World War II, the gross domestic product (GDP) of the U.S.A. was about equal to that of the rest of the nations of the world combined. The combined GDP of the other five leading capitalist countries was less than 40 per cent that of the U.S. Since the fifties, the relative postion of the U.S. has declined steadily. By 1972, the combined GDP of the other five leading capitalist countries was almost 90 per cent that of the United States. The most extraordinary gains are by Western Germany and Japan. West German GDP was only 8 per cent of the U.S. GDP in 1950. By 1972 it was 22 per cent as great. Japan's relative position grew from less than 4 per cent to 24 per cent. On a percapita basis, the relative decline of the U.S.A. is even more striking. And this evidence is further supported by the much more rapidly rising wage level being experienced outside the U.S.

Table 8
GDP as a Percentage of U.S. Gross Domestic Product

	1950	1955	1960	1965	1969	1972
France	9.7	12.3	12.0	14.3	15.1	16.5
West Germany	8.1	10.7	14.1	16.7	16.5	22.2
Italy	4.9	5.6	6.8	8.5	8.8	10.1
Japan	3.8	5.7	8.5	12.8	18.0	23.9
United Kingdom	12.6	13.5	14.0	14.3	11.7	13.6
All five	39.1	47.8	55.4	66.6	70.1	86.3

Source: United Nations, *Yearbook of National Account Statistics,* various years; and International Monetary Fund, *International Financial Statistics,* April 1973.

Table 9
GDP Per Capita as a Percentage of U.S. GDP Per Capita

	1950	1955	1960	1965	1969	1972
France	35.3	47.2	47.4	57.1	60.8	66.6
West Germany	25.8	35.5	46.1	55.0	55.0	76.5
Italy	15.8	19.1	24.9	31.9	33.6	38.6
Japan	7.0	10.1	16.4	25.4	35.7	47.2
United Kingdom	38.0	43.9	48.4	51.2	42.7	50.7

Source: United Nations, *Yearbook of National Account Statistics,* various years; and International Monetary Fund, *International Financial Statistics,* April 1973.

Table 10
Wages in Manufacturing as a Percentage of U.S. Wages in Manufacturing (Per Week)

	1950	1955	1960	1965	1970
France	17.6	24.1	21.5	26.0	29.0
West Germany	24.7	26.3	31.5	42.1	53.5

(continued)

Italy	17.4	17.4	18.5	25.9	32.7
Japan	9.8	13.9	15.9	21.4	34.3
United Kingdom	31.6	35.7	39.2	43.9	43.3

Source: United Nations, *U.N. Statistical Yearbook,* various years.

Table 11
Production of Passenger Vehicles (percentage of World Total)

	1950	1955	1960	1965	1970
France	3.1	5.1	8.7	7.2	11.0
West Germany	2.6	6.5	14.2	14.3	15.7
Italy	1.2	2.1	4.7	5.8	7.7
Japan	.02	.1	1.3	3.6	14.2
United Kingdom	6.4	8.2	10.6	9.0	7.3
USA	81.6	72.5	52.2	48.7	29.2

Source: United Nations, *U.N. Statistical Yearbook,* various years.

Table 12
Steel Production as a Percentage of U.S. Steel Production

	1950	1955	1960	1965	1970
France	9.9	11.9	19.2	16.4	19.9
West Germany	15.9	23.2	37.8	30.8	37.7
Italy	2.6	5.1	9.1	10.6	14.5
Japan	5.5	8.9	24.5	34.5	78.2
United Kingdom	18.9	18.9	27.4	23.0	23.7
USSR	30.5	42.7	72.5	76.3	97.2
USA/World	54.5	39.4	26.1	26.0	20.1

Source: United Nations, *U.N. Statistical Yearbook,* various years.

Table 13
Exports as a Percentage of U.S. Exports

	1948	1953	1959	1965	1969	1972
France	16.8	25.7	32.4	37.0	39.7	53.8
West Germany	6.2	30.3	57.1	65.8	77.6	95.1
Italy	8.6	9.6	16.7	26.5	31.3	37.8
Japan	2.1	8.1	19.8	31.1	42.7	58.4
United Kingdom	50.2	45.7	54.9	48.7	45.1	49.6
EEC (Original 6)	53.2	93.7	146	176	202	254
Centrally Planned Economies	29.5	50.4	81.3	79.8	79.3	—

Source: *Yearbook of International Trade Statistics,* various years; and International Monetary Fund, *International Financial Statistics,* April 1973.

The evidence of relative economic decline can also be illustrated by production statistics for such basic industrial goods as passenger cars and steel. In 1950, the U.S. produced 82 per cent of all passenger cars in the world. By 1970, this had fallen to 29 per cent. Japan, which produced only 6 per cent as much steel as the U.S. in 1950, produced about 80 per cent as much in 1970. All the other leading capitalist countries except the United Kingdom increased their share of steel and automobile production relative to the U.S.A.

Similar trends are observable in the export field. All the major capitalist countries, except the United Kingdom, have been rapidly closing the gap in their share of world exports, most spectacularly West Germany and Japan.

Seymour Melman, an industrial engineer at Columbia University, has given life to these statistical trends in a recently published book called *The Permanent War Economy, American Capitalism in Decline.* The foundation of a modern industrial economy is composed of efficient systems of transportation, communication, and power generation. Melman cites pages and pages of evidence of breakdown in these strategic areas.

- While President Nixon was hailing the manned lunar landing in August 1969 as "the greatest week since the Creation," a rather different technological drama was enacted in America's largest city. Millions of New Yorkers were suffering the effects of breakdowns in basic industrial services. Firms that could no longer be reached by phone placed ads in the newspapers to announce that they were still in business. The telephone service, normally taken for granted, seemed to be falling apart as ordinary local and long distance calling became annoyingly difficult. At the same time the gradually-deteriorating commuter railroads into New York City reached a new low in unacceptable performance with collisions, casualties, train cancellations, and delays.[1]

- Even more disastrous for normal functioning in modern urban life were the successive breakdowns in electric power generating plants of Consolidated Edison during the August heatwaves, leaving buildings without air-conditioning, elevator services or proper illumination.[2]

- During 1969 new railroad equipment was delivered to the Long Island and to the Penn Central Railroad. According to the New York Times, August 6, 1969, "The Long Island Railroad accepts 94 new cars and finds mechanical defects in all 94. . . . Because of breakdowns, it takes a standby fleet of 10 replacement cars to keep an average of 18 cars moving on the

New York to Washington Metroliner. Two of the new Metroliner cars must be scrapped for spare parts. Twenty additional cars are delivered more than 6 months behind schedule and they also have serious defects." "It seems nobody knows how to make a passenger car anymore," complains one railroad executive.[3]

● The steel industry of the United States has become a major center of industrial depletion with about 18% of the domestic market being serviced from abroad. . . . About 80% of the Japanese steel industry makes use of the basic oxygen process whereas only about 50% of the U.S. industry is so equipped. The U.S. industry's managements have failed to do research and development on a scale necessary to offset cost differentials between U.S. steel industry which have risen to a level making imported steel saleable at from $20 to $40 per ton less than domestic steel.[4]

● The case of civilian electronics is perhaps the most striking example of industrial depletion in the United States. The design and manufacture of small radio receivers and most TV sets has dropped sharply. And civilian electronic firms, with close ties to the burgeoning military-space electronics field, have managed to avoid technological options which could help make U.S.-based production economically viable.[5]

In what is perhaps even a more basic industry, machine production, Melman notes that the price of machinery has been rising more than the price of labour, causing businesses to continue using their existing equipment rather than discarding it for more productive labour-saving equipment. The reason is the drop in productivity within the machine tool industry that produces the drills, lathes, etc. The net effect of using obsolete equipment is a slowdown of industrial productivity in the economy as a whole. Almost two-thirds of the metal working equipment used in American factories is ten years old or over, contrasting sharply with the newer equipment in West Germany, the U.S.S.R., and Japan.

What explains America's speedily deteriorating economic position? A major cause is that while the U.S. was squandering her resources on military armaments throughout the 1950s and was bogged down in a hopeless war in the sixties, the European countries and Japan were recovering from the devastation of World War II and developing their own industrial and technological capability. They were able to plow back a much greater proportion of their resources into research and development and new productive capacity. The Common Market countries, for example, employ fewer resources in research than does the United States but one-third more researchers for purposes of economic development and civilian industrial technology. When the U.S. defense and space programs attract the most capable scientists and engineers to design military rocket motors and naval vessels, they are not available to design trains, mass transit systems, a more efficient motor car, or an effective merchant marine. The "high-technology" goods whose U.S. Manufacturers have until recently enjoyed world pre-eminence are showing signs of competitive weakness as the accompanying table reveals.

Table 14
U.S. Imports of "High-Technology" Goods, 1960-70

	1960	1970	Per cent increase
	(millions of Dollars)		
Chemicals	808	1,450	79.6
Nonelectrical machinery	438	3,102	608.2
Electrical Apparatus	286	2,272	694.4
Transport Equipment	742	5,797	681.3

Source: U.S. Bureau of the Census, *Statistical Abstract of the United States,* 1971, cited in Melman, p. 92.

A permanent war economy has had the contradictory result of saving the U.S. from a prolonged depression while at the same time exhausting her energies and resources in the economic battle to stay on top of the industrial world. As much was observed by the Wall Street Journal in an article which appeared on October 6, 1971:

Corporate expenditures for new plants and equipment are . . . climbing. . . . But not enough to give the U.S. much help in maintaining its faltering position. . . . For, in terms of reinvestment of earned capital, the U.S. has fallen behind other industrial nations. . . . What concerns some economists is that, despite the expected rise in U.S. capital spending, this country still won't be plowing back a big enough chunk of its [GNP] to keep pace with its increasingly competitive foreign rivals. . . . "This country appears to have forgotten the basic lesson taught in every economics classroom — that a country's industrial development is determined by its capital formation" says . . . a private economist. "Our balance of payments problem, inflation problem, employment problem and economic growth problem all are really the exact same problem — the inadequacy of capital growth" . . . [says another]. "It makes for a scary situation. You've got them [U.S. rivals] putting in new stuff while we're sitting here with so much excess capacity we don't feel the need to expand and we can't afford to anyway. Our plants are getting older, meanwhile, and we're going to the point where the quality of stuff coming off their lines is now better than ours. We're still king of the heap, but I don't know for how much longer."

This line of thinking is supported by the data in the accompanying table.

Table 15
Output per man/hour 1965-1970

Country	average annual % incr.
Japan	15.0
Netherlands	9.1
Sweden	7.9
Belgium	6.8
France	6.6
Switzerland	6.2
Germany	5.3
Italy	5.1
United Kingdom	3.6
Canada	3.5
U.S.A.	2.1

Source:*Monthly Labour Review,* August 1971.

Unit labour costs, which depend on productivity, wages, and currency valuation also show U.S. and Canadian industry to be in a poor competitive position compared to their rivals. Canadian labour costs rose faster than any other. This was not because wages were rising faster than elsewhere. In fact, Canadian wages were among the slowest rising. As in the U.S.A., the reason why unit labour costs in Canada were rising so rapidly was due to the absence of significant productivity gains. These points are confirmed in the next table.

Table 16

Country	Hourly Compensation 1965-1970 Average annual % Change	Unit Labour Costs 1965-1970 Average annual % Change
Canada	8.4	5.1
Germany	17.0	4.7
U.S.A.	6.8	3.9
Italy	18.8	3.8
Netherlands	10.4	2.5
Sweden	12.7	2.5
Belgium	11.7	1.4

(continued)

Japan	17.0	0.8
France	10.5	0.6
Switzerland	6.6	0.0
United Kingdom	14.2	-0.2

Source: *Monthly Labour Review,* August 1971.

The burden of Canada's dependent status is nowhere better revealed than in these productivity figures. The source of most innovation in this country is the U.S. multinational corporation, which exports its new designs and techniques to its branch-plants when and to the extent that it sees fit. When American productivity lags behind Europe and Japan, Canada necessarily finds itself in the same postion, a helpless and pitiful victim of America's economic decline.

The Consequences of Vietnam

By the late fifties and early sixties it had become clear that Japanese and West European goods were beginning to compete effectively with U.S. products. If the only challenge had come from rival capitalist nations, it seems likely that the U.S.A. would have maintained its dominant position for many more years. But this was not the only challenge.

Up to the end of World War II the imperial system of colonies and dependencies had several metropolitan centres. As a result of its economic and military strength and and the destruction inflicted on its rivals by the war, the United States had the opportunity of becoming the sole leader of a new imperial system. In the words of Eugene V. Rostow, Undersecretary of State for Political Affairs, "... in many ways the whole post-war history has been a process of American movement to take over possessions ... of security which Britain, France, the Netherlands and Belgium had previously held."[6]

The value of U.S. direct investment abroad grew from $11 billion in 1950 to $30 billion in 1960 to $70 billion in 1970. United States presence in Latin America, the Middle East, and Asia and throughout the European colonial world became dominant as U.S. ambassadors began to replace European colonial administrators as the dominant political figures. As World War II stretched into the Cold War, British and French military networks were replaced by U.S.-centred "alliances" such as SEATO and CENTO. These were components of a new international police force maintained by the U.S.A. to keep "law and order" throughout the capitalist world. And along with NATO they were designed to contain and harass the Communist world. By 1957 the United States had a total of 275 major base complexes in 31 countries, and more than 1,400 foreign bases. These bases cost nearly $4 billion and were manned by a million American troops.[7]

According to Harry Magdoff,

> ... what matters to the business community, and to the business system as a whole is that the option of foreign investment (and foreign trade) should remain available. For this to be meaningful, the business system requires, as a minimum, that the political and economic principles of capitalism should prevail and that the door be fully open for foreign capital at all times. Even more, it seeks a privileged open door for the capital of the home country in preference to capital from competing industrial nations. How much or how little an open door may be exploited at any given time is not the issue. The principle must be maintained, especially for a capitalist super-power like the United States, and especially when it is being challenged widely and openly (by the forces of national liberation).[8]

Maintaining the open-door policy is not without its problems in an era of social revolution. In some areas, conflict has been contained without resorting to the open exercise of military force. Military and economic assistance to bolster "reliable" and "friendly" regimes and employment of the ubiquitous CIA are often sufficient. In other instances, the U.S. government has been obliged to engage in direct and indirect encounters: Greece, Iran, Guatemala, Lebanon, and the Dominican Republic, only begin the list of nations that have felt the impact of American coercive actions. Indo-China, however, presented a different story. The liberation forces of Vietnam and Cambodia were not so easily contained. U.S. leaders invested vast sums of money to wage the war in Vietnam. These expenditures were never balanced against the limited business opportunities in Vietnam itself. Rather they were weighed against the much wider U.S. interests in Asia and, more generally still, the need to make an example of Vietnam to discourage popular liberation forces throughout the U.S. economic empire. But the war in Indo-China drained the American economy to the point where it was less and less able to pursue a successful military policy.

By the late 1960s a particular kind of dialectical process had unfolded, combining the conflicts between the U.S.A. and rival industrial nations and conflicts between the U.S.A. and the Third World. It is the combined operation of these two conflicts that has ended the brief era of U.S. hegemony.

The erosion of America's economic domination had to be

reflected in her balance of payments.* Since the 1940s there have been only two years in which the United States has had a favourable balance of payments. The major deficit items have always been military expenditures abroad, foreign aid, and foreign investment. But until the early 1970s there had always been a large trade surplus of exports over imports. In the period 1960 through 1965, the trade surplus averaged $5.8 billion. In 1968 for the first time in this century, non-farm imports exceeded non-farm exports. For the 1966 to 1970 period, the over-all trade surplus averaged only $1.4 billion. In 1971, despite a 2-billion-dollar surplus in agricultural exports, the over-all foreign trade was in deficit to the tune of $2.7 billion, rising to $6.9 billion in 1972.

Long-term competitive trends which had been working against the U.S. position were severely aggravated by the economic consequences of the Vietnam War. Instead of financing the war by way of taxation, a policy that would have fanned the anti-war sentiments, the government paid for it by way of large deficits. The consequent inflation worsened the competitive strength of American industry both at home and abroad. For example, U.S. export prices rose 10 per cent from 1964 to 1968, while the average for all industrial countries rose only 3 per cent. Before the Americanization of the Vietnam War, the U.S. had a robust export surplus of approximately $6 billion (1964). This had largely disappeared by 1969, causing a drastic weakening of the U.S. balance of payments position.

The increasing cost of policing the empire placed an additional burden on the balance of payments. From 1960 to 1965, U.S. expenditures on aid and military operations averaged $5.5 billion a year. During the height of the Vietnam War it rose to $7 billion a year.

The old British Empire was always able to pay for its import surpluses as well as its colonial administrative and military expenses by the profits extracted from its foreign investments. The American empire has not been quite so lucrative. Increasing profits from foreign investments, though almost always in excess of new investment outflows, were seldom if ever large enough to cover expenditures on military and aid operations. By the end of the 1960s the

---

* A country's balance of payments is the summation of all of its international transactions (receipts and expenditures) in a given period. Exports and imports of merchandise are the largest item. Others include capital exports and imports, profits and interest on foreign investments, spending on foreign military bases, and receipts and expenditures of tourists and shipping. If a country's receipts exceed its expenditures it has a surplus. If the expenditures are larger, it has a deficit. Traditionally, settlements of deficits are made in gold, the one universally-recognized money commodity.

cumulative amount of dollars paid out in excess of the amount taken in was already $55 to $60 billion. When trade surpluses turned into deficits in 1971 the gap between total receipts and total expenditures in the U.S. balance of payments could no longer be ignored.

Why were other nations for so long willing to accept U.S. IOU dollars? For that is what has financed these continuous deficits. By accepting U.S. IOU dollars, these nations allowed the U.S. to expand its economic empire through foreign investment and to protect it through military bases and armed warfare — at a nominal interest cost. By not demanding American exports or gold, which would have represented the real payment, they were permitting the Americans to acquire and maintain their post-World-War-II empire virtually for nothing. What explains this remarkable generosity?

The dollar was valued as an international medium of exchange, a reserve currency, treated the same way as gold. As national economies grow and world trade expands, the need for monetary reserves also expands. Because of the shortage in the supply of gold, the need for reserves was increasingly filled by U.S. dollars. The mechanism by which U.S. dollars have been added to the world's monetary reserves has been nothing else but the continuing deficits in the U.S. balance of payments. De Gaulle once talked of dethroning the dollar and returning to the gold standard, but this was and could be no more than talk. The capitalist world needed the steady outflow of U.S. dollars to facilitate its trade. What was convenient and profitable for the United States was also convenient and profitable for the rest of the capitalist world. Yet, the outflow of dollars that followed the Americanization of the Vietnam War was far in excess of what was required for monetary reserves. Still the other capitalist powers acquiesced in this situation for some years before it finally became intolerable.

The ghetto uprisings in the hot summers between 1964 and 1968 were cause for concern in the U.S.A. Should a severe recession be allowed to occur, such as would cut down imports and thereby eliminate the payments deficit, the resulting dislocation might unleash forces that could not be easily controlled. A story in the *New York Times* of November 18, 1969 (datelined Basel, Switzerland) casts a revealing light on how both American and European powers viewed the situation:

> The United States, at a meeting here of central bankers from ten major nations, has linked its continuing deficit in the balance of payments to the problem of black unrest in the country.
> Central bankers from the United States have told their

Western European and Japanese counterparts that the United States cannot accept the social cost implicit in getting rid of the balance-of-payments issue.

The most effective way to eliminate the payments deficit is by prescribing a recession, but the Americans argue that the first men to be laid off, acccording to traditional employment patterns, would be unskilled black workers. This, they say, would provoke an intolerable aggravation of racial disquiet.

The argument is not a new one, but it is unusual for it to be raised in international monetary discussions ...

The reaction of the European and Japanese was said by the same sources to have been sympathetic. Their attitude was summed up as follows:

Since the growth of international trade depends on the healthy evolution of the American economy — the richest market in the world — little can be gained by having this economy slip into a recession torn by violence.[9]

In short, the European powers recognized the U.S.A. as the bastion of world capitalism around which their economies revolved, and it made no sense to weaken it. Moreover, European and Japanese corporations benefited handsomely from the arrangement. The American war machine kept the Third World safe for capitalist trade and investment, including European and Japanese trade and investment. And since they did not have to bear any of the direct costs of policing the Third World they might well feel some obligation in absorbing the outflow of American dollars, one of its by-products.

U.S. liabilities abroad, essentially the foreign-held dollars which stood at $16 billion at the end of 1957, jumped during the height of the Vietnam War to $38 billion at the end of 1968 and to $63 billion in 1971, 4½ times the U.S. stock of gold. Until then the crisis was staved off by the willingness of European central banks to accumulate paper dollars. However, the gross imbalance in international finance could not go unresolved indefinitely. The American dollar, so eagerly sought after in the immediate aftermath of World War II, had turned into a heavy burden. When Bretton Woods established the dollar as an alternative parity standard to gold, it trapped other countries into supporting the dollar under all circumstances. When banks (and, through them, individuals and corporations,) presented their dollars to the central banks of West Germany, Britain and France, for example, they could demand payment in deutschmarks, pounds, and francs at the official parity. The swelling flood of deutschmarks and other currencies paid out in exchange for dollars became a source of monetary domestic inflation in these countries. Had the U.S. been forced to sell exports to pay for the economic empire it was building and defending, much of this inflationary pressure would have been internalized upon itself. Victor Perlo is not off the mark when he writes that countries like West Germany, France and Japan were in effect subsidizing U.S. imperialism to the tune of billions of dollars every year and doing themselves untold harm in the process.[10]

Nixonomics

The day of reckoning was approaching. In July 1971 came the news of the U.S. trade deficit. Within days a wave of speculation of unprecedented proportions erupted as many U.S. firms anticipated a reduction in the value of the dollar. Led by U.S. multinational corporations, this wave saw $16 billion of flight capital shift from dollars to other currencies, a direct and massive export of inflation. It had the effect of a self-fulfilling prophecy, for it ended whatever willingness European banks still may have had to hold onto surplus American dollars. They began to cash in their dollar holdings for U.S. Treasury gold. Had gold convertibility been retained, the U.S. supply of gold would have been wiped out.

On August 15, 1971, President Nixon announced that the U.S. was formally abandoning convertability of the dollar into gold. Bretton Woods was dead. Currencies were allowed to float in the international exchange markets to find their own values as central banks were freed from further obligations to support the dollar. A round of devaluations of the U.S. dollar followed. By May 1973, the Federal Reserve Board could calculate the following appreciations of foreign currencies against the dollar as compared to April 1971:

Australia	up	26.3%
Belgium-Luxembourg	up	27.7%
Britain	up	6.4%
Canada	up	0.8%
France	up	25.0%
Germany	up	31.6%
Italy	up	6.2%
Japan	up	36.2%

What these figures mean is that (all other things remaining equal) the prices of Japanese products in the U.S.A. were 36 per cent higher in 1973 compared to 1971 and the prices of American products in Japan were 36 per cent lower. The changes in the terms of exchange with Germany and France were only slightly less advantageous for the U.S.

Nixon's plan was simple. Rather than bringing about a sharp reduction in U.S. imports by allowing the U.S. to slip into a deep recession, he launched a major attack on America's economic rivals by forcing trade losses on them. The exchange rate realignment was designed to improve the U.S. international payments position and to help the U.S. recapture its dominant economic position. More precisely, Nixonomics was aimed at regaining the large trade surpluses of the 1950's, which could pay the bill, or most of it, for continuing foreign investment by U.S. corporations, overseas military expenditures by the Pentagon, and foreign "aid" activities by the State Department, the Agency for International Development (AID) and the CIA. In fact, the devaluations in December 1971 and February 1973 did succeed in cheapening the prices of U.S. goods relative to those of her major overseas rivals and U.S. exports did once again rise above imports. Thus *Business Week* magazine reported on July 6, 1973, that "U.S. exports of goods and services as a percentage of GNP have almost doubled — to nearly 8 per cent in the last ten years."

But the devaluations had a dual impact. They influenced the pattern of world trade by increasing U.S. exports and reducing her imports, and they both directly and indirectly contributed to the inflation that erupted in the U.S. in 1973. The direct contribution came from raising the prices of foreign goods in the U.S. market. This was actually doubly inflationary because it also took the edge off foreign competition, allowing U.S. businesses to raise their own prices. The indirect contribution to U.S. inflation stemmed from the soaring exports that created sudden major shortages in the American economy.

It is important to recall the world economic context at this point. The years 1970 and 1971 had seen mild recessions in most countries. The dampening of wage demands, selling off of inventories, and government deficit-spending paved the way for a new world upswing. In fact, 1972-73 saw a simultaneous rise of the economies of all countries, resulting in an upsurge of demand and trade. This was happening as the two dollar-devaluations were cheapening U.S. goods. The worldwide demand for American products soon surpassed U.S. productive capacities in certain crucial industries, aggravated by the sluggish growth of investment in the U.S. economy. The situation was vividly described by *Fortune* magazine:

The overvalued dollar had repressed the growth of many producers, directly by creating new competition for them in the U.S. market, and indirectly by eroding the overseas market of their manufactures customers. It took the double devaluation of the dollar — which raised the price of foreign goods by as much as 50 percent — to reverse these devastating trends. But when the reversal finally took place, basic manufactures in the U.S. suddenly found that they had the lowest prices in the world. And they also had the longest list of customers.[11]

It can be added that since the Canadian dollar is closely tied to the American dollar, the Canadian dollar has also depreciated in value compared to European and Japanese currencies, setting in place the same direct and indirect inflationary pressures. However, the scramble for raw materials and the resulting boom in commodity prices make Canada somewhat more inflation-prone in view of the disproportionate role of resource production in the Canadian economy.

The New Trade Wars

The Nixon administration did not rely on the devaluations alone to reverse the tide against the American economy. This was only one part of a multi-pronged program. The U.S. Department of Defense came up with a plan for enlarging world sales of armaments, increasing American exports from $925 million's worth in 1970 to $3.8 billion's worth in 1973. Negotiations were undertaken with the U.S.S.R. for large sales of agricultural produce, and in the spring of 1972 the administration launched a co-ordinated campaign of harassment against its major trading partners.[12]

On April 20, 1972, the U.S. Tariff Commission ruled that imports of heavy electrical transformers from Japan, Britain, France, Italy, and Switzerland were "injuring domestic producers," clearing the way for the Treasury to impose anti-dumping duties. The next day, Treasury made public findings of dumping wire mesh for concrete reinforcement from Belgium and hand-pallet-trucks from France. On April 24, President Nixon hiked tariffs on imported ceramic dinnerware and related items — $22 million work in 1971 — judged to be "injuring domestic producers of earthenware table articles." In May, Treasury announced investigations into dumping of sulphur and aluminum ingots in Canada; imports of the ingots alone totalled $216 million in 1971, making this the second anti-dumping case ever looked into by the Treasury. A day later, Treasury revealed that it was looking into a whole series of Japanese government tax subsidies for exports of electronic products, with an eye toward putting "countervailing duties" on them. In June, the Agriculture Department set forth details of new dairy-import quotas aimed at curbing rising imports of less expensive cheeses from ten European countries and New Zealand; Treasury stated that it was launching dumping inquiries into imports of hardwood craft pulp from Canada, cast iron soil pipe from Poland, dry cleaning machinery from West Germany, and zippers and permanent magnets from Japan. On August 3, Treasury charged Japan with dumping cadmium in the United States. This marked the first time that any U.S. government agency had ever ruled that tax incentive and other grants to spur the development of new industries in poorer regions of the country were to be subject to penalty as unfair practice. On February 20, Treasury formally accused Canada of dumping its aluminum ingots. The suspect ingots are valued at $350 million, making this potentially the largest dumping case in U.S. Treasury Department history.

On January 7, 1973, in a precedent-setting decision, the Treasury Department ruled that the Canadian government is unfairly subsidizing the manufacture of radial auto tires by Michelin in two Nova Scotia plants. Contending the "substantial majority" of the plants' output is exported to the U.S., Treasury held that the subsidies to Michelin to locate in Nova Scotia constitute "bounties or grants" to encourage exports.

The campaign continued through 1973. In March, the report of the President's Council on International Economic Policy accused the EEC and Japan of having an export "surplus syndrome" that discriminated against U.S. goods. It hinted at tariff reprisals. One week after the publication of this report Herbert Stein, chairman of the Council of Economic Advisors, further underscored the necessity for removing foreign barriers to the expansion of U.S. exports. "We have an obligation to behave in a way that permits us to earn [a trade surplus]," Stein declared, "and others have an interest in permitting us to do so." In Nixon's May 3 "State of the World" message to the U.S. Congress, the President invited Europe to help devise new economic arrangements "more equitable for the United States" and bluntly informed European leaders that their otherwise welcome goal of closer economic integration could not be at the expense of American exports.

When the Nixon administration accused Japan, the EEC, and Canada of unfairly subsidizing exports, it could have been reminded that a number of state governments in the U.S.A. offer tax incentives and other subsidies to attract businesses that ultimately export some of their output. The Export-Import Bank has long furnished credit and risk guarantees for Americans doing business abroad, and has made loans to foreigners to help them purchase U.S. goods. The avowedly export-promoting DISC (Domestic International Sales Corporation), passed in December

1971 as part of Nixon's "new economic policy," authorizes U.S. companies to set up special export-sales dummy subsidies, half of whose profits are granted an indefinite deferral of their corporate income taxes. By the summer of 1973, 3,500 U.S. corporations, among them virtually all the giants, had already taken advantage of the law and reaped tax savings of $150 million — and these figures have risen since.

It should come as no surprise, that the EEC and Japan refused to take the American trade-putsch lying down. On February 14, two days after the last dollar devaluation, the EEC Council agreed to take action against the DISC program as an unfair export-promoting scheme that violated all existing international trade conventions. In 1972, shortly after the Nixon Administration kicked off its "anti-dumping" campaign, the EEC also struck back by raising import duties 11 per cent on U.S. corn and levying its own "compensatory tax" on edible by-products of pigs and chickens.

Nixon's reconciliation with China and the Soviet Union, and the attempts by the U.S., the EEC countries, and Japan to break into the Communist markets, have to be seen in the light of the trade war that is raging within the capitalist world. In a world of endemic inflation, there are restraints on the fiscal measures governments can take to maintain business prosperity and employment. This is why they are all turning to one form or another of "beggar-my-neighbour" policies. (That phrase, which is commonly used to describe efforts by one country to improve its individual position by pushing exports or restricting imports, such as to worsen the position of other countries, is the name of an old card-game in which you try to capture all the cards.) Unfortunately for those who would play the game, the value of world trade barely rose at all in 1974 and 1975, thus narrowing the room for manoeuvring in this field and reducing the gains that can be made from it.

The Economics of Detente

Whereas the Truman Doctrine, signalling the beginning of the Cold War, was designed to answer the needs of an expanding American Empire, the Nixon Doctrine, signalling the beginning of detente with the U.S.S.R. and China, was a response to the needs of an empire that was in the early stage of disintegration. What has happened in the quarter-century that passed between these major policy-pronouncements? Surely it is naive to believe that in the early 1970s the United States suddenly discovered that China was not a military threat after all, and that it must finally negotiate with the U.S.S.R. Since the Cultural Revolution, China has become more "communistic" than ever before, and the Soviet Union barely had an economy, let alone nuclear weapons, when the campaign of containment and confrontation was first launched.

We now know that at the Yalta, Potsdam, and Tehran conferences the Soviet Union, whose Red Army was already occupying most of Eastern Europe, was allocated that region, and the United States and its allies were allocated the rest of the world. The American objective in the Cold War was to undo this understanding. A campaign of confrontation was launched not because the Soviet Union was strong but because it was weak. Panicking at the prospect of a revival of German militarism, the U.S.S.R. wanted a buffer zone on its eastern flank. Given the fact that she had been invaded twice in a generation through this area, it was realistic that she should wish to exercise a dominant influence in its political organization, and as she already controlled it militarily, the western nations had little choice but to accede to her demands. In return, the U.S.S.R. gave up the struggle in those places where Communism was a real political force. The French and Italian Communist Parties were instructed to lay down their arms and participate in the highly manipulated parliamentary politics of the immediate postwar period. The Greek and Philippine guerrilla movements were abandoned to the mercies of the American and English occupying forces. Tito's Yugoslav liberation forces were refused support; likewise Ho Chi Minh in Vietnam. The Communist Chinese were issued a go-slow order. The American Communist Party was instructed to support the Democractic Party and the Canadian Communist Party was instructed to support the Liberals. Stalin lived up to his side of the bargain in the years immediately following the war.*

Contrary to the official utterances of Churchill, Truman, Acheson, and their mouthpieces in editorial offices across the continent, and the efforts of the academic community, the threat posed by Communism was never a military one, but rather economic, political, and ideological. After the war, the U.S.S.R. lay bleeding and prostrate, desperately short of manpower for reconstruction,

---

* To be sure, the Russians had agreed to establish "democratic" as well as "friendly" governments in Eastern Europe, but they did so with the clear understanding that the democratic process would be allowed scope only insofar as it was compatible with their security interests — which did not include extending democratic rights to "fascist" elements. What precipitated the Cold War conflict was the attempt by western powers to violate the sphere-of-influence agreement by turning the region into an anti-Soviet sphere.

let alone for armed conquest and occupation. Much of her territory was a wasteland. The United States, by contrast, having doubled its economic capacity during the war, and having sustained relatively little loss of manpower, was never stronger. Moreover, she had possession of the new atomic bomb. Even George Kennan, the formulator of the famous "containment" policy, rejected the idea that the U.S.S.R. was an aggressive power in the sense that Hitler's Germany was. In his 1957 Reith lectures, Kennan frankly admitted that at the time of the formation of NATO, the U.S. State Department's policy planners considered "the Communist danger in its most threatening form as an *internal* problem, that is of Western Society." To make it perfectly plain, he added, "it was perfectly clear to anyone with even a rudimentary knowledge of the Russia of that day [1947], that the Soviet leaders had no intention of attempting to advance their cause by launching military attacks with their own armed forces across frontiers." In the words of W. S. Schlamm, an editor of *Fortune* magazine who advocated nuclear ultimatums as a way of getting the Russians out of Eastern Europe, "Communism *thrives* on peace, *wants* peace, *triumphs* in peace."[13]

Kennan held a parallel view of the Chinese "threat." "The weapons with which the Chinese are operating here [in Southeast Asia]," he wrote, "are primarily the political reactions of the people of the threatened areas themselves: their inherent resentments [against the Western powers], their fears, their weariness, and such error and prejudice against ourselves and their own regimes as can artificially be pumped into their minds."[14] A British expert on Chinese military capability confirms Kennan's estimate. "China" he said, "has shown no signs of wishing to carry out physical expansion. Its armed forces are ill-equipped to mount any sustained operations beyond Chinese frontiers and their equipment, training and development suggest an intense pre-occupation with defense. Its navy has no offensive capability to speak of, and that of its air force is inconsiderable."[15]

The post-war project aimed at containing the fire of revolution among the "have-not" peoples, many of whom had recently emerged from colonialism, and at containing Communism in Western Europe and eliminating it in Eastern Europe. It was launched under the guise of "self-determination " and "freedom," hence the creation of the foreign devil — "International Communism." Its real purpose was to re-establish the hegemony of western capitalism.

Up to a point it worked. Anti-communism united all groups and classes in a new crusade that saw radicals purged from the labour movement and the universities. It became unworkable when the

Bay of Pigs invasion and the Vietnam War finally exposed the pretenses of the "containment of aggression" policy, and more particularly when the cost of policing the empire became economically and politically unbearable. Anti-communism had now become a divisive force, and it was dropped as abruptly as it had been taken up 25 years earlier. In Nixon's words:

> Our experience in the 1960s has underlined the fact that we should not do more abroad than domestic opinion can sustain . . . . To continue our predominant contribution might not have been beyond our physical resources — though our domestic programs summoned them. But it certainly would have exceeded our psychological resources.[16]

— "psychological" meaning that the American people refused to make sacrifices any longer for the sake of the empire.

The new course is anything but isolationist. It does not abandon the goal of global domination, but rather aims at what Nixon called

> . . . a new, more subtle form of leadership . . . . We do not rule out new commitments, but we will relate them to our interests . . . . Our objective, in the first instance, is to support our *interests* over the long run with a sound foreign policy . . . . Our interests must shape our commitments.[17]

What are those interests? Immediately, they comprise the need to secure vital raw materials and to correct the U.S. balance of payments position. Insofar as U.S.A.-U.S.S.R. relations are concerned, these "interests" mean detente. For 25 years the United States has boycotted and sought to get its allies to boycott trade with the Communist world. This is no longer the case. William J. Casey, U.S. Undersecretary of State for Economic Affairs, explains the rationale for "economic relations with state-controlled economies" in terms of its contribution to reducing U.S. volume of payments problems. For 1973, American trade with the U.S.S.R. and China ran four-to-one in favour of the U.S., providing a surplus of $2 billion which, in Casey's words, "has made a major contribution to working our way out of the enormous trade and payments deficit we sustained last year."*[18] Casey refers specifically to the vast investment opportunities open to American capitalists in providing technology, capital and management skills to exploit "the large ore and gas deposits and great forest resources which exist within the Soviet Union." Besides opening up markets for "massive exports of American capital equipment," the U.S.S.R. in return "could supply

---

* U.S. exports to China jumped from $5 million in 1971 to $840 million in 1973. U.S. exports to the U.S.S.R. exceeded $1.2 billion, triple the 1972 figure.

us with long-term supplies of energy and raw materials to replace depleted domestic sources." The major constraint of "the Soviet determination to seek partnership with the West" is a political one: "economic normalization is linked with progress towards the improvement of political relations." The pace of expanded economic relations is "regulated by the pace of advancement in the political sphere."

This turn in trade policy had been advocated by the Committee for Economic Development when that prestigious body released its report "A New Trade Policy Toward Communist Countries" in September 1972. * The CED stressed the edge that America's West European and Japanese rivals had already gained with the Communist bloc. " . . . The maintenance of restrictions by the United States is a gesture in futility since other trading nations have relaxed their restrictions . . . American business firms and their foreign subsidiaries have been deprived of numerous export opportunities. These have been seized by European and Japanese business competitors."

The report of a Special Presidential Commission, † *United States International Policy in an Interdependent World,* set forth the guidelines by which the U.S.A. could improve its deteriorating balance of payments position, largely caused, in the words of the commission, by "the overseas responsibilities the United States has assumed as the major power of the non-Communist world." Its principal proposal was a program to expand agricultural exports — by negotiating special arrangements with foreign governments, and structuring domestic prices to favour agriculture. The Soviet grain deal was conceived as the first major step in the direction of the Commission's proposal. The exemption of raw agricultural products and exports from Nixon's price-wage controls was a related measure that encouraged both the growth of agricultural output

---

* It should be noted that the board of trustees of the CED consists of the directors of the most powerful U.S. corporations. For example, its Chairman is E. G. Colado, executive vice-president of Standard Oil of New Jersey; two of its five vice-chairmen are Fred Burch, head of General Electric and John D. Harper, Chairman of the Aluminum Co. of America. These three men represent the Rockefeller, J. P. Morgan and Mellon interests of American finance capital.

† The President's Commission on International Policy in an Interdependent World was established in May 1970, at a time when there was substantial warning of pending crisis in international finance. Chairman of the Commission was Albert L. Williams, of IBM. Others on the Commission included Fred Borch of General Electric, Richard Gerstenberg of General Motors, Lee Stinebower of Exxon, and William Pearce of Cargill. The two labour representatives were Lloyd Smith, international president of the International Association of Machinists and Aerospace Workers, and I. W. Abel, president of the United Steel Workers of America.

and its sale on foreign markets. The program was successful.

The deal with the U.S.S.R. saw 440 million bushels of wheat and 267 million bushels of other grains sold to the Soviet Union. The wheat sale absorbed 25 per cent of the total crop. Exports of corn and soybeans, used not only for human consumption but for livestock feed as well, also reached mammoth proportions. One-fifth of the corn crop and over half of the soybean crop were earmarked for export, including to the Soviet Union. In 1973, the value of agricultural exports rose by 80 per cent, compared to the year before — from $9.9 to $17.7 billion. By that year U.S. exporters held contracts totalling more than half the annual production of wheat.*

This explosion of wheat sales did wonders for the United States and its balance of payments position. The 1973 agricultural trade surplus of $9.3 billion offset the non-agricultural trade deficit of $7.6 billion.

"The fundamental reason for the sudden jump in food prices," one researcher has confirmed, "was that agricultural surpluses and basic stocks were pressed into service when the value of the dollar slipped in the late 1960s and began to tumble rapidly in the first two years of this decade."[19] By employing its two-price system, whereby prices for export are lower than the prices in the domestic market, the U.S. government, in accordance with stated policy, made food a critical factor in overcoming sagging trade balances. Despite government price-support schemes, the international clamour for U.S. grains helped force domestic prices up. The rapid increase in food prices in 1973 was a central element in fuelling the general inflation. It was not confined to items like bread and spaghetti. Rising exports of grain, that would otherwise have been used for livestock feed, forced cattle growers to pay more at home for feed, forcing prices of beef, pork, and chicken to new levels. Actually, livestock raisers found that, until Nixon's price controls on meat were lifted, it was cheaper to slaughter cattle and poultry and use them for feed

---

* The role of monopoly speculators in the Russian wheat deal is worthy of note. A few insiders bought up a large part of the U.S. harvest at rock bottom prices in anticipation of the Soviet purchase. According to the *New York Times* (December 13, 1973): "James A. MacHale, Secretary of Agriculture for Pennsylvania, testified ... that corporations had enjoyed economic profits as a result of being able to 'corner and manipulate scarcities in the grain market'. Grain dealers, he said, made 13 times their normal profit on the $1.1 billion Russian grain deal. He also said that some companies bought up grain supplies last year for resale this year at higher prices. Three large grain export companies — Cargill, Continental and Cook — bought up 90 per cent of the 1972-73 soybean harvest by last January for $4 a bushel, sending domestic prices up to $10 a bushel a few months later ..."

than to prepare them for market. In effect they went on strike. When the controls were lifted in the spring of 1973, meat prices went sky-high.

While it is true that U.S. trade with the U.S.S.R. represents less than 2 per cent of her total foreign trade (the U.S. imports as much in a week from Canada as it imports in a year from the U.S.S.R.), the long-term effects of detente are bound to increase the importance of their trade. Already New York's two largest banks, the First National City Bank and the Chase Manhattan Bank, have opened branches in Moscow. The Russians have recently signed some 100 contracts with 40 U.S. companies for more than $500 million worth of equipment and machinery as part of the new Kama truck complex, "the largest industrial project in the world."[20] U.S. involvement in this project had been turned down on orders from the Pentagon when the Russians first approached Henry Ford about it in 1967. The Pentagon's opposition to Kama was overruled as the Nixon Administration's policy of detente crystallized in 1971.

More generally, as a sign of things to come, Eugene Guccione, senior editor of *Engineering and Mining Journal,* notes that the U.S.S.R. accounts for 57 per cent of the world's coal reserves, 40 per cent of the iron ore, at least one-third of all national gas and oil, and respectable percentages of the world's reserves in nonmetallic minerals. He notes that these reserves are mostly located in Siberia and Kazakhstan, and are almost untapped because of the Soviet shortage of development capital and technology. According to one projected plan, U.S. firms will be contracted to build 1,500 miles of pipelines to transmit gas and construct a plant at the port of Murmansk to liquify the gas for shipment to the east coast of the United States. The project would also include building 20 tankers. The total cost to the U.S.S.R. would be on the order of $6 to $7 billion. As Guccione says, "the magnitude of potential deals with Russia can be grasped when considering that within the next ten years the Soviet Union will expand its mineral industry output to as much as $60 billion or $65 billion, of which $20 billion to $25 billion may be available for export."[21]

Reviving the Pax Americana

Henry Kissinger's "new Atlantic Charter" signalled Washington's first efforts to revive the post-war order of American supremacy. When he proposed his concept of "a revitalized Atlantic partnership" on April 23, 1973, Kissinger admitted that the West European

countries had become strong competitors of the U.S.A., thus giving
rise to certain frictions and requiring a readjustment in the alliance.
On the other hand, he insisted that in the readjusted alliance,
Europe would play a "regional" role and the U.S. a "global" one.
The two, he added, are not "automatically identical." Thus, "the
United States . . . must act as part of and be responsible for a wider
international trade and monetary system." But reconstruction of an
effective international monetary system, along with maintenance
of U.S. troops in Europe and America's worldwide obligation,
depends upon European acknowledgment of the "special role" of
the U.S. as the ultimate guarantor of the "Free World" (that is, the
world capitalist system).

In effect, Kissinger was asking the NATO countries to commit
themselves to granting the "guarantor" trade advantage in view of
her heavy international burdens. As much was said a month earlier
by Herbert Stein, Chairman of the Council of Economic Advisors:
"we have an obligation to behave in a way that permits us to earn [a
trade surplus], and others have an interest in permitting us to do
so." Kissinger pointed out that "for us European unity is what it has
always been — not an end in itself but a means to the strengthening
of the West." In short, European unity must be subordinated to an
"Atlantic ensemble" that is organized and co-ordinated by Washington.

However, in their response, written up as a draft entitled
"Declaration of Principles between the U.S.A. and the European
Community," the Europeans insisted that the EEC would function
"in world affairs as a distinct entity" and would co-operate with the
United States, but "on an equal basis."

On a more limited scale, this time at the height of the energy crisis,
Kissinger again tried to work out a modus vivendi with Europe.
This time he had no choice. He had to block an attempt on the part
of the EEC to work out a new relationship with the Middle East oil-
producing countries. The EEC had conceived of the idea of creating a new Mediterranean super-power in which countries like
Iran, Iraq, Saudia Arabia, Kuwait, Lebanon, Egypt, Libya,
Algeria, Morocco, Turkey, the Sudan, and Zambia would be
invited to join as members or associates of the Common Market.
The Common Market — its European component embracing a
quarter of a billion people with the world's largest aggregation of
industrial and manufacturing facilities and the largest market for
new materials and energy — would then also include the Near East
and its vast petroleum deposits and North Africa with its vast store
of yet-to-be-developed raw materials and tropical products. The
Arab nations would be invited to invest their inflated budgets in

Europe, thus easing Europe's new balance of payments problem, while European business would help them with their much-desired industrialization.

Kissinger knew that talks between the parties were already underway and he understood the urgency of aborting this new challenge to American hegemony and persuading the Arabs to invest their money in the U.S. He had some inkling of the possibility of this emerging economic colossus back in April 1973 when he complained that "in trade the natural economic weight of a market of 250 million people has pressed other states to seek special arrangements to protect their access to it. The prospect of a closed trading system embracing the European community and a growing number of other nations in Europe, the Mediterranean and Africa appears to be at the expense of the United States and other nations which are excluded." This made clear his real intention which is best expressed not as the Year of Europe, but the Year for Keeping Europe in Line. Europe showed in 1973 that it had no intention of being kept in line and, though in a weakened state a year later, it still balked at accepting Washington's leadership. France was the only nation at the February 1974 conference to challenge the United States directly. The French delegation refused to agree to key sections of the communique issued at the end of the conference that were critical of bilateral arrangements between oil-consuming and oil-producing nations. Instead of following the American course of "consumer solidarity," France made special deals directly with various Middle East countries for long-term oil purchases in return for French armaments and technological assistance. Japan and other European countries have also made their own deals, bypassing the monopoly of the major oil companies.

But as the energy crisis deepened and many of the countries of West Europe faced increasingly severe economic difficulties, their ability to resist American leadership began to evaporate. This change in attitude, "a 180-degree turn in one year," was noted by Kissinger in his January 1975 interview with *Business Week*. Having found the new ground for extracting concessions from America's industrial rivals, Kissinger did not hesitate to compromise on his demand for a "new Atlantic Charter." What he now insisted upon was that all oil-importing nations commit themselves to "solidarity" — which means that in all future deals with the oil-producing countries they will be represented by a U.S.-sponsored and led International Energy Agency. At the same time, Kissinger insisted that a "Special Fund for Financial Products of Petroleum" be set up. Underwritten by the U.S. Treasury, it will administer a $25 billion fund to recycle some of the petrodollars to the nations with large deficits. It is understood that only countries that comply with Washington's energy strategy are eligible to receive these funds.

What all the capitalist countries are aware of is that with the $100 billion of investable surpluses the OPEC nations could play havoc with the international monetary system — and the total could rise to almost 500 billion by 1980. Although all importing countries transfer wealth to OPEC, there is the crucial question of how OPEC distributes the surpluses among the deficit nations. As the import capacities of the OPEC countries are limited in the short run, most of the surpluses now take the form of short-term foreign investments. Ultimately they will use their surpluses to build up their own industrial capacities, which will make some of them major exporters of industrial products. In the short run, it is highly unlikely that they will choose to invest their money in and buy their imports from each deficit country in proportion to the payments each needs to eliminate strains in their balance of payments. The point is made by Gerald Pollack, a Senior Economic Advisor at Exxon Corporation: "The Achilles heel of the entire world economy may turn out to be the international payments system. The financial flows associated with more expensive oil are so immense as to threaten intolerable balance of payments strains and currency instability."[22]

Looking at it from the point of view of the Third World nations, Kissinger is obviously trying to shape an alliance of rich industrial countries to force a conciliatory stance upon them in the face of the worldwide shortage of resources. But if the world's hewers of wood and drawers of water suddenly discover that in fact they possess a public utility of vital importance, they are not likely to respond by simply producing more. Rather they are more likely to ask themselves how they can use their new-found advantage to get a larger share of the world product.

This was precisely the view taken by Carlos Andres Perez, President of Venezuela, in his candid response to President Ford's September 23 speech at the United Nations.*

The establishment of the Organization of Petroleum Exporting Countries (OPEC) was a direct consequence of the developed countries' use of a policy of outrageously low prices for our raw materials as a weapon of economic oppression. In a sense, this fact demonstrates the truth of your statement to the United Nations that any attempt by a country to use a product for political purposes will inevitably tempt other countries to use their

---

* The response was published in an open letter full-page advertisement in the *New York Times,* September 25.

products for their own purposes.

. . . Venezuela has not used and will not use its energy resources as a political weapon . . . rather, its purpose was to protect the basic wealth extracted from our subsoil at prices that have never compensated for the costs of our imports and of the technology needed for our development.

. . . Venezuela is an oil country producing and selling an increasingly valuable, scarce and strategically vital commodity. We see no other way to confront the economic totalitarianism that has been coming to the fore in business and world trade and portends as much evil for the world as was threatened by political totalitarianism in the form of Nazi Fascism.

To cite the particular case of Venezuela, petroleum prices showed a steady decline for many years, while our country was obliged to purchase manufactured goods from the United States at ever-higher prices, which day after day, restricted even further the possibilities of development and well-being for Venezuelans.

Whatever their limitations, and they are substantial, the leaders of the OPEC nations have wisely determined that it is suicidal for them to co-operate in any acceleration of trade whereby their exhaustible resources are exchanged for the perpetually renewable foodstuffs and other renewable resources of the United States. The foodstuffs the United States ships abroad one year are regrown the next but the nonrenewable resources of the Third World, once shipped out, vanish forever. The OPEC nations have attempted to reverse the flow of wealth in their favour. Other resource-exporting countries are attempting to do likewise. Their success will depend on their unity as against the unity that Henry Kissinger is seeking for the industrial nations of the West, and also on their ability to use their temporary advantage to forge economies of self-sustaining development.

VI / Food, Energy, Population: A Critique of the Ecological Analysis

The conjunction of rapid economic growth founded on the ethos of the consumer society on the one hand and increasingly scarce resources on the other defines one element of the continuing crisis that is now overtaking us. At the root of much of the inflationary pressures of this era and at the root of the growing conflicts between nations and classes lie the elements of this ultimate contradiction.

The industrial and technological bases of the British Empire were coal, iron, and the steam engine. Upon this base, the British controlled the trade, commerce, and finance of the eighteenth and nineteenth century world. Colonies were an important source of wealth and raw materials, but by the mid-nineteenth century Britain had become so much more proficient than all of her rivals that free access to world markets became more important to her than maintaining and expanding her colonial system. Ruling circles became convinced that colonies were often more of a burden than an aid to British prosperity. The colonial system was loosened, and new colonies were added only where informal ties failed to achieve her economic objectives.

Developments toward the end of the century forced her to alter her strategy. Britain was now being rivalled by new industrial giants like Germany and the U.S.A. Her resources were gradually depleting and her technology was stagnating. In a desperate effort to remain top nation of the capitalist world, she began to search for new colonies to guarantee new markets for her goods, new outlets for her investment, and new sources of raw materials. Thus began the invasion of Africa and Asia and a new scramble with the French, Germans, Japanese, and Americans to divide up China, Africa, and Southeast Asia. By the turn of the century, Britain was accumulating large and permanent trade deficits (including food and other strategic materials) with the rest of the world. She was able to pay for these only by the earnings on her foreign investments. World War I was the ultimate consequence of the inter-imperialist competition for commercial supremacy. In order to bankroll her participation in the war, Britain was forced to cash in many of her foreign assets. This was the first sign of the crumbling of the British Empire. Between the two world wars, she had to follow a policy of draining India and her other colonies to avoid total collapse.

A parallel may be drawn with the U.S.A. in our own time. The industrial and technological base of the American economic empire is petroleum, hydroelectric power, and certain base metals. Because of her rapid industrial growth in this past quarter-century, large-scale military commitments around the globe and a total neglect of elementary conservation, her resources are being rapidly depleted.

Table 17
The Shift in U.S. Imports of Resources

	Imports as percentage of U.S. consumption		
Material	1937-39 Average	1950	1970
Zinc	6.3	37	60
Manganese	—	77	94
Titanium	N.A.	32	47
Aluminum*	N.A.	71	86

(continued)

Petroleum	0.5	8	22
Iron ore	2.6	6	14
Platinum	N.A.	91	98
Cobalt	N.A.	92	96
Natural Gas	0	0	3
Chromium	100	100	100
Columbium	100	100	100
Tin	100	100	100
Timber	N.A.	11	8
Nickel	99.2	99	91
Lead	0.2	59	40
Copper	0.3	35	8
Tungsten	41.8	80	40
Mercury	N.A.	92	38

* Includes bauxite and alumina.
Data: National Commission on Materials Policy.

Of the 62 materials on the U.S. Defense Department list which it uses for its stockpiling program, 38 need to be imported to the extent of between 80 per cent and 100 per cent of total requirements. For 52 of them, at least 40 per cent of the U.S. supply has to be imported. Thus the U.S. is especially vulnerable in these strategic materials.

For some of the 62 materials, perhaps for most of them, the problem is not one of actual scarcity. The raw materials are there in great supply. Rather, the problem is economic. A recent report of the Geological Survey estimated the extent of U.S. resources, its total supply of mineral deposits that may some day become recoverable. The report indicates that the U.S. has potential reserves to meet cumulative demands for many of its imported mineral commodities well beyond the end of the century (though only a few are plentiful enough to last hundreds of years). Converting these potential resources into real resources is the problem. Many are still hypothetical. Costly and time-consuming exploration is needed to prove that they even exist. Others are of such low grade that prices will have to rise a lot more and technology will have to be further developed before they can be mined. Taking environmental concerns seriously would create obstacles to the development of many of the deposits. So for some decades, the report indicates, the U.S. will have to rely on other countries to provide cheap and accessible supplies of many minerals. While the U.S.A. was squandering her resources on armaments and military adventures throughout the fifties, sixties, and seventies, the European countries and Japan were recovering from the devastation of World War II and developing their own industrial and technological capability. The result has been a massive turn-about in the economic strength of the leading capitalist nations, with new strains and a rivalry within the "free world" — a throwback to earlier times.

But the full dimensions of the conflict go beyond the rivalry between industrialized nations. Caught in between are the Third World nations. They possess the reserves of resource requirements upon which imperial dynasties have always rested. Continual access to these reserves, on terms favourable to the on-going expansion of the capitalist world, has now become a central issue in world politics. The "have-not" nations are attempting to capitalize on the growing scarcity of their resource possessions to engineer a turn-about in the distribution of the world's wealth, and break the monopoly on economic development now being exercised by the western world. The United States, its strategy masterminded by Henry Kissinger, is attempting to forge a coalition of industrialized countries to thwart these efforts.

While predictions of a global ecological armageddon may be misplaced, famine and shortages of catastrophic proportions are already occurring in parts of the Third World. The issue at hand is not that the world is running out of resources, but rather how a diminishing supply of resources will be distributed and who will pay the cost of developing new sources. Ultimately this comes down to a question of power, not only between nations, but also within nations. The dramatic inflation of the past few years is a reflection of the struggle for power between nations and between social classes. What we are likely to see in the years ahead are policies of various kinds that would impose "restraint" on the working class in every nation. By repressing the living standards of the underlying populations, giant corporations are to be afforded the profits to develop their new resources base. This "internal imperialism" is a new dimension to the external imperialism whose practice is also bound to intensify in the coming years.

During the Middle Ages, a life of scarcity was tolerated because the real purpose of life was not material abundance but salvation. Each person had a part in the scheme of things because all accepted the grand religious design that gave that society cohesion. Modern industrial society undermined the traditional foundation of solidarity. In place of the religious community, the Enlightenment substituted the religion of rational self-interest. The Industrial Revolution created an era of an unprecedented interdependence. But interdependence does not by itself breed solidarity. Together with rational self-interest it gives rise to Adam Smith's "invisible hand,"

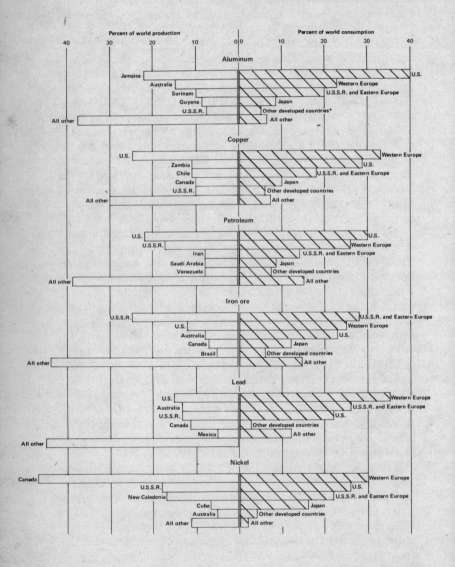

Figure 11
Resource Production and Consumption, by Country

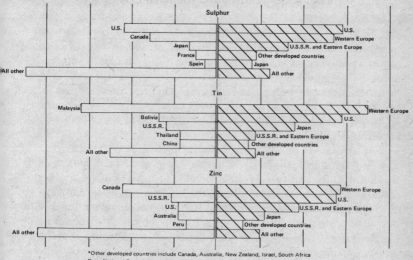

Sulphur

Tin

Zinc

*Other developed countries include Canada, Australia, New Zealand, Israel, South Africa

Data: National Commission on Materials Policy; Interior Dept.; American Metal

Market; Engineering & Mining Journal; American Petroleum Institute. Based on data from 1966 to 1970 a social instrument that works reasonably well in periods of rapid growth, but not very well at all during periods of stagnation and decline where questions of distribution rise to the fore. The modern economy is highly vulnerable to breakdown and paralysis which can be provoked by a number of small minorities of capitalists or workers. The possibility of economic and social breakdown is all the more marked because of the absence of a widespread sense of community solidarity. What usually follows breakdown is a dramatic increase in the use of the only other instrument of social cohesion — force. And that force may be applied as easily by the right as by the left. In the event of a breakdown, barbarism and socialism are equally possible.

The advantage of socialism is that if offers the possibility of a new foundation of solidarity, one that can give social cohesion in this age of interdependence. In a socialist economy, where market forces are replaced by comprehensive planning and private owner-ship of the means of production is replaced by social ownership, the degree of growth can become a matter of choice since the economic engine is not driven by the need for continuous expansion. Yet the Soviet experience cautions that this too can be a mirage. The U.S.S.R. and the other centrally-planned economies of Eastern Europe seem as growth-oriented as western capitalism. In fact it is the old familiar consumerism that they have substituted for the coercion of the early period. The socialist revolution that only accomplishes a transfer of ownership is a truncated socialism that cannot resolve the contradictions of capitalism. It must work towards revolutionizing the relationship between work and personal gain, an end to the fetishism of commodities — or end up facing some of the same dilemmas as corporate capitalism.

The Food Crisis

The conventional explanation for the sudden rise in food prices is that bad crops created temporary shortages. This is the argument of the optimists. The pessimists, some call them doomsayers, say that our ability to grow food has been overtaken by our ability to procreate; the world's population has finally begun to outrun the supply of food. The mouths have won the food vs. mouths race.

An argument can be made for both views, but neither goes to the root of the matter. There were some bad crop years in the early 1970's* but even these were not due solely to the weather. Marine

---

* In 1972, drought and typhoons decimated rice and maize crops in the Philip-pines, and drought continued in sub-Sahara Africa, India's monsoon rains

biologists, for example, contend that overfishing, depleted stocks, and declining catches are affecting the haddock fishing of the northwest Atlantic and the anchovy fishing along the western coast of Latin America. Mercury pollution has seriously affected fresh-water fish on Canadian lakes. The Peruvian anchovy fishery, the world's richest, yielded as much as 12 million tons, or one-fifth of the world fish catch, during the late sixties. Largely because of over-fishing, the catch fell to scarcely 2 million tons in 1973. Overgrazing and deforestation in the sub-Sahara have encouraged the advance-ment of the desert at rates up to 30 miles per year along the desert's 3,500-mile southern fringe stretch from Senegal to northern Ethi-opia. As the desert expands southward, Africa, which has one of the highest population growth rates of all the continents, is in danger of losing much of its food producing capacity.[1]

Most countries produce less food than they consume. Only three produce significant surpluses — the United States, Canada, and Australia, and of these three, the U.S. is by far the most important, accounting for 60 per cent of the wheat trade, 75 per cent of the corn trade, and 90 per cent of the soybean trade. More important, the world's only significant grain reserve lies in the U.S.A. Aside from the enormous power this gives to the U.S.A., the danger it poses arises from the irrational character of capitalist food production.

Beginning in the 1920s and 1930s the North American economy experienced periodical gluts of food supplies in which the world market was incapable of purchasing the total agricultural product at prevailing prices. Prices fell to levels which could not sustain farm producers. It fell upon governments to take measures that would restrict farm production and hold prices up. Monopoly sharing enterprises in the manufacturing sphere long ago had dis-covered this ploy of artificial scarcity (Veblen called it the "con-scious withdrawal of efficiency"). Thus, government-sanctioned and government-organized agricultural sabotage were now added to the industrial sabotage that was already commonplace. This absurdity reached its most glaring heights during the leanest years of the Great Depression, when huge quantities of food were des-troyed in order to insulate it from the market.

For the next 40 years, U.S. agricultural policy was devoted to reducing food production. Mountains of wheat and other grains were burned, more was placed in storage, cattle and poultry were slaughtered, and farmers were paid to withhold crop land from pro-duction. 33 million acres were removed from cultivation by 1949.

---

dropped below normal, wet weather cut into the fall maize and soybean harvest in the United States, and grain crops in the Soviet Union, Argentina, and Austra-lia fell because of inadequate rains.

Secretary of Agriculture Earl Butz ordered another 60 million acres into retirement in 1971. A year earlier his Canadian counterpart, Otto Lang, had introduced the LIFT program (Lower Inventories for Tomorrow), which paid farmers $6.00 an acre for land taken out of production. Canadian farmers cut their wheat acreage in half between 1969 and 1970 with a corresponding reduction in bushels (from 665 million to 313 million).*

Professor Edwin P. Reubens has calculated the effects of these restrictive policies.[2] The broken line of his chart represents the level of food production that could have been obtained if the major food-producing countries had utilized as much acreage in later years as they had in 1967. His production gap understates the degree of lost food output since he arbitrarily selected the acreage planted in 1967 as a maximum figure. In the U.S. alone, over 50 million metric tons of grain were not produced that year because of idled crop land that farmers were paid not to farm. Reubens contends that

> ... the causes of fluctuation in these countries [the United States, Canada, and Australia] are not to be found in any failure of yields. . . . Actually, yields were rising steadily and strongly in almost all cases. . . . The largest single factor appears to have been cutbacks in acreage. The most extreme of them was in Canada, where 1970 acreage of wheat was just half of the 1969 average, which in turn was slightly below that in 1968 and 1967. Australia's acreage of wheat in 1970 was only 60 per cent of the 1968 acreage. The U.S. figure for 1970 was 80 per cent of 1968, and only 74 per cent of 1967; it was actually back to the 1948 - 1952 level...
>
> To put it more bluntly, the plentiful food supplies of 1968 were piling up surpluses and tending to drive prices down. . . . The U.S. Department of Agriculture . . . stepped up its system of "required set-asides and payments for voluntary diversions." Similar policies were implemented by the Canadian and Australian governments.

The cycle of "overproduction" and cutbacks in the late sixties and early seventies led to a tightening of the world food supply that was exacerbated by the poor world harvests in 1972. The double devaluation of the dollar that cheapened North American food for foreign buyers, the simultaneous upswing of the business cycle throughout the capitalist world, and the U.S.-Soviet wheat deal so increased the demand for food relative to the reduced supply that the world's reserves of grain all but disappeared.

The absolute decline of cereal production during the 1972-73

---

* Wheat acreage averaged around 29,000,000 in the period 1963 to 1969. Throughout the 1950s and early 1960s it averaged about 25,000,000. The 12,500,-000 acres it plummeted to in 1970 is the lowest on record since the year 1945.

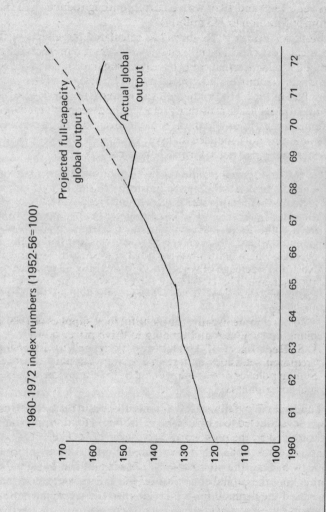

Figure 12

Actual and Potential Production of All Foods

1960-1972 index numbers (1952-56=100)

Projected full-capacity global output

Actual global output

crop year of 35 million tons, when combined with the increases of world cereal demand of 25 to 30 million tons a year, created a shortfall of nearly 60 million tons. In 1961, reserves of grain amounted to 222 million tons or 95 days of world consumption. By 1972 they had declined to about 60 days and by 1974 to 26 days. According to Lester Brown, the world food supply-demand equation was precariously balanced in mid-1974.[3] A poor harvest in any major producing country — the United States, the Soviet Union, India, or China — would send economic shockwaves not only throughout the food sector of the world economy but, as it fuelled the fires of inflation, throughout its other sectors as well.

Since 1966, costs of wheat soared 325 per cent; since 1967, rice prices climbed 361 per cent and soybean prices jumped 233 per cent. In January 1974 the price of winter wheat was $6.00 a bushel, $3.30 over the 1973 price level. According to the U.S. Department of Agriculture, the cuts in production together with the unprecedented surge in farm exports that drained domestic supplies added $2 billion to U.S. food bills in 1973 alone, or 15 per cent of the year's increase in retail food prices.

By the most conservative estimates, 500 million people are threatened with starvation today.[4] At least 10 million died in 1974 — most of them children under five years old. Prophecies of growing famine abound. The U.S.A. possessed the world's only significant food reserves, the sole buffer against world famine. The liquidation of those reserves, a move described by U.S. Agriculture Secretary Earl Butz as "getting the government out of the grain business," has made the world fully dependent on the success of the current crop.

The perverse nature of the capitalist system of organizing the supply and distribution of food is underlined by the fact that the disastrous harvest of 1972 was hailed as a great boon by American agribusiness, and that *Forbes,* a business magazine, warned that the number-one pitfall that might undermine agribusiness's "rosy projections" for 1974 was "good weather conditions around the world."[5]

1973 and 1974 were years of bumper crops. Another record crop in 1975 will probably send farm prices tumbling, but supermarket prices will continue their rise or will fall by far less. Monopoly sharing arrangements at the supermarket level and among the major food processors result in a price structure that is flexible in an upward direction but sticky in a downward direction.[6]

At the crest of the agricultural cycle, the giant grain handling and agribusiness corporations reap the greatest proportion of the profits since they control most of the trade and production. When prices fall, as they must, they have the storage capacity to hoard some of their grain until prices become more attractive. The small independent farmers cannot sit out a downswing in farm prices so easily. Many of them are squeezed out under the circumstances as their land, buildings, and equipment are taken over by agribusiness.

Cutbacks in crop acreage in the early 1970s were paralleled by cutbacks in the production of fertilizer that created shortages, higher prices, and consequently reduced food output, particularly in the Third World. The fertilizer industry follows the same boom-and-bust cycle as agriculture. Fertilizer companies over-expanded during the 1960s to take advantage of the worldwide "green revolution." Fertilizer prices dropped when manufacturing capacity outran demand. The companies stopped building new plants and cut back on the maintenance of old ones. After the lifting of U.S. price controls in October 1973, the three major U.S. producers raised their prices an average of 65 per cent within three months. Costs on the world market climbed even higher. The price of urea fertilizer, which sold at $40 a ton in 1971, soared to $260 on the world market by April 1974. The higher prices for petroleum and natural gas, key ingredients in the production of fertilizer, were a contributory factor.

At such high prices, many of the Third World nations still dependent on imports of chemical fertilizer, could not afford even the minimal amounts they had been using. The jump in fertilizer prices was the principal reason for the 7-million-ton short-fall in India's 1974 wheat harvest. The FAO has estimated that the 2-million-ton drop in fertilizer used in Third World countries caused a loss in grain production of 20 million tons, sufficient to feed 100 million persons. Third World peoples are caught in a vicious circle: They cannot afford the higher-priced imported fertilizer that their agriculture depends upon; consequently their crop yields decline, requiring more food imports. But with food prices jumping to astronomical levels, they cannot afford to maintain even their current levels of imports, let alone increase them.

Only the rich countries can afford to purchase fertilizer at the prevailing prices. Consequently they tend to absorb most of what is available. An additional pound of fertilizer in countries like the United States and Canada, which are already well fertilized, yields only about five more pounds of grain, compared to the ten or twelve pounds it would yield if it were applied to the nutrient-starved fields of Asia, Africa, and Latin America. Still more perverse is the fact that "Americans are applying some three million tons of nutrients to lawns, gardens, cemeteries and golf courses — more than used by all the farmers in India and half again as much as the current shortage in developing countries."[7] One of the oldest and most tenacious laws of capitalist economics is that use is dictated not in accordance with need but in accordance with dollar demand, and that depends on who has the cash.

At the World Food Conference in Rome, the U.S. delegation proposed a resolution to restrict the non-agricultural use of fertilizer. Things would certainly be simple if such regulations would lead to the transfer of resources from the rich countries to the poor. Unfortunately, as any beginning student in economics knows, there are no such easy solutions in the market economy. By restricting non-agricultural uses of fertilizer, demand for it is reduced and therefore prices. Theoretically this would be of some temporary benefit to the farmer in Bangladesh, for he could then buy more fertilizer with the same money, if he had any money. But in all but the shortest run, the lower price would mean that less fertilizer would be produced, for it would reduce the profitability of supplying this commodity. In commenting on this proposal the *Wall Street Journal* concluded that "it would be comforting to believe that eating less here would provide more for the hungry abroad, but instead it will mean lower prices and lower production. . . . Doing penance with a brown lawn may for all we know, save your soul and eating less is likely to save your heart. But neither has much to do with feeding Bangladesh; for that we need policies attuned not to the next world but to the harsh but inescapable economies of this one."[8] The harsh and inescapable economies of the market economy prescribe that the consumption of foods, fertilizer, and everything else depends on one's income, because production is organized to fulfil profit expectations, not to satisfy human needs.

The Energy Crisis

The energy crisis is just as real as the food crisis. Of that there can be no doubt. Shortages, long lines at gas pumps, rationing in several countries, and sharp rises in fuel prices everywhere were real events. Exactly why this crisis took place, and why in the 1970s, is not fully clear even now, but with the benefit of hindsight it is possible to trace some of the forces that led to the crisis.

What seems quite clear is that in this crisis, as in previous ones,*

---

* In the twenties, for example, the major oil companies used the threat of an impending oil shortage to panic the U.S. Congress into passing the system of depletion allowances. Though the U.S. at the time was in no danger of running out of oil, the enactment of this allowance greatly enriched the coffers of the oil companies, provided a lucrative tax haven for existing millionaires, and helped create

the profits of the oil companies have zoomed upwards and the companies have obtained legislation that is favourable to their interests. Exxon Corporation enjoyed after-tax profits in 1973 of $2.44 billion, up 59 per cent over 1972. The profits of Royal Dutch Shell, the second biggest oil corporation, were up 153 per cent from a year earlier. Among the five U.S. international oil companies, after-tax profits totalled $6.2 billion in 1973, up 56 per cent from a year earlier. Because of the crisis, the U.S. oil companies received practically everything they wanted: higher prices, the approval of the Alaskan pipeline, and an easing of environmental restrictions.

The immediate catalyst that allegedly triggered the oil shortage was the Arab boycott and the cutback of Middle East production. There are various facts that cast doubt on this explanation. The Arabs account for only 7 per cent of all crude oil consumed in the U.S. in 1973. It seems unlikely that reduced shipment could have produced such swift results in the fall of 1973 requiring gas stations to close on Sundays. The Shah of Iran blew this cover when he announced over American television in February 1974 that shipments had not in fact been reduced notwithstanding the alleged boycotts.* If they were not finding their way to U.S. refineries where were they going? The answer to this question was given by the British magazine, *The Economist,* which reported the presence of large numbers of super tankers off the British coast. According to *The Economist,* the oil companies also paid service station owners to keep their tanks full.⁹ These manoeuvres were aimed at holding onto oil supplies until the expected price increase materialized, after which they could realize sensational speculative profits.

Oil industry figures confirm that large quantities of oil went into storage rather than to consumers. Production in the non-Communist world rose by 9.2 per cent compared to a rise of only 4.5 per cent in 1972. Since consumption in 1973 is estimated to have increased

---

many new millionaires. Again, after the Arab-Israeli war of 1956-57 the oil companies induced the U.S. government to impose quotas on oil imports to encourage exploration in the U.S. To what extent this was actually achieved is uncertain, but the import quotas did keep U.S. (and Canadian) oil prices higher than in the rest of the world and protected the position of the established international companies against competition from new entrants into the market. (Edward Shaffer, "A Global Perspective on Energy," *Canadian Dimension,* Vol. II No. 2.)

* U.S. government officials continued to complain of real shortages. Federal energy chief William Simon put the amount of the shortfall on gasoline at 15 per cent in February 1974. The available evidence suggests that the boycott was at best minimally effective before it was lifted in March 1974. According to *The Economist* (December 15, 1973), tonnages of tankers leaving Kuwait and Iraq were up 39 and 43 per cent respectively in early December 1973 when the Arab countries were supposed to have cut back production by 20 per cent. The tonnage sailing from Saudi Arabia was also up 39 per cent.

by only about 7 per cent, some 320 million barrels must have gone into storage during the embargo.[10]

A third indication that the Arab oil boycott was not the crux of the matter surfaced with the allegations made in the report of U.S. Senator Henry M. Jackson's investigating committee. According to its findings, the reasons for the shortages and subsequent price rises are mainly related to the drive of the major oil companies, which control 70 per cent of domestic production and marketing of crude and refined oil, to take over the remaining 30 per cent controlled by independent refineries and marketers. The large oil companies are accused of generating shortages of crude oil to starve the refineries and marketing facilities of the independents so as to make them vulnerable to takeovers. Since the independents receive more than 50 per cent of their requirements from the majors, any limitation in oil supplies places a severe burden on their capacity to survive.

Ever since the 1930s, seven international oil companies have been operating as a cartel* to regulate Middle East production and European refineries. These five American and two British-Dutch companies dominated the industry through ownership of most of the world's low-cost oil as well as their vertical integration into the refining, marketing, and transporting of oil. The economic power of the Big Seven was backed by the home governments. For example, in 1951 the government of Mohammed Mosadeh nationalized Iran's oil industry. The majors promptly retaliated by shutting Iranian oil out of world markets while raising output in other Middle eastern countries to make up the difference. Economic sanctions were backed two years later by "a coup engineered by the U.S. Central Intelligence Agency."[11] The new government retained formal ownership of the oil industry but handed it over to a consortium of the major oil companies.[12]

However, throughout the late 1950s and sixties the market power of the seven sisters diminished. Small independent companies and state oil companies like Italy's ENI opened up new concessions, giving governments better deals. Between 1963 and 1968 the cartel's share of world production fell from 81 per cent to 77 per cent, its share of world refining capacity fell from 65 to 60 per cent, and its share of marketing fell from 62 per cent to 55 per cent. Without credit cards, games, and coupons, the independents have been able to deliver gas at lower prices. Over half of the pre-tax retail price of gas at the pump is for marketing costs. Without the burden of carrying a brand name, the independents have been able

---

* Standard oil of New Jersey (now called Exxon), Royal Dutch Shell, Texaco, Gulf, Mobil, Standard Oil of California, British Petroleum.

to undercut the majors. 1972 was apparently the year the majors chose to fight back.

This competition had forced a steady decline in the market price of crude oil throughout the 1960s. It was during this period that the Organization of Petroleum Exporting Countries (OPEC) was born. OPEC was at this time a relatively weak organization, but it was sufficiently strong to stop the oil companies from cutting their prices any further, so that government revenues per barrel remained constant and the declines in market prices were reflected in declining per barrel profits for the companies. According to *Fortune* magazine, their profits on crude oil in the Middle East plummeted from 18.2 per cent in 1957 to 11.2 per cent in 1970.

OPEC's power really emerged with the coming to power of Colonel Muammariel-Quddafi in Libya in September 1969. The closing of the Suez Canal in 1967, the subsequent rise in tanker prices, and the blockage of the Trans Arabian Pipeline (TAPLINE) by Syria in 1970 thrust Libya into an extremely favourable position. Because of her proximity to Europe she was less affected by the higher tanker rates. Libya bargained with companies one by one, and she enforced cutbacks in production until companies agreed to the concessions that were demanded. With the initial moves by Libya, other nations followed suit. The concessions won by Libya were used as a standard for the Tehran and Tripoli Agreement of February 1971. There is some evidence that Quddafi's aggressive moves were not strongly resisted by the major oil companies or the U.S. government. This may have been because the company immediately affected was Occidental Petroleum, one of the new interlopers in the industry. Or it may have been because the majors favoured a rise in the price of crude. According to the testimony of an oil company insider, the critical turning point in the early Libyan negotiations was the refusal of the major international oil companies to help Occidental resist Quddafi's demands. Occidental had requested the major internationals to provide it with crude petroleum to tide it over while the Libyan government enforced production cutbacks. The majors refused, forcing Occidental to cave in to Libya's demands for increased prices and royalties, which demands the majors would predictably be called upon to meet.[13]

There is additional evidence that the international majors were themselves interested in increasing foreign crude oil prices. In particular, it was clearly evident that the United States would require much more imports of oil in the 1970s than heretofore. There was increasing pressure to end the U.S. oil import quota law which had kept the price of domestic crude oil more than $1 a barrel above that of foreign crude oil.* It was clear that if the price of foreign crude was increased to the level of U.S. crude, then the oil import quotas could be abolished without threatening the profits of the U.S. majors. This was in fact accomplished six months before the October war, thanks to the rises in foreign crude oil prices engineered by OPEC.

The agreements of 1971 and 1972 mark a new phase of monopolistic control of petroleum, this time a shared arrangement between the seven majors and the OPEC governments. The agreements gave the OPEC governments a sharp raise in oil revenues as well as minority shares of the oil companies' production, with the promise of majority share by the early 1980s. By controlling the supply of oil, the agreements allowed prices of crude oil to soar, providing the companies with unprecedented profits. In 1969, the market price of oil was $1.25 per barrel, of which about 10 cents was cost, 95 cents government taxes and 20 cents company profits. By the middle of 1973, the market price had risen to $2.50 per barrel, of which $1.50 went to the government and 80 cents to the company. Both parties had made significant gains, government revenues per barrel increased by three-fifths, company profit per barrel increased four-fold. Government participation measures reduced the pressure for total nationalization while the companies' monopoly over sales was secured by the "buy-back" provisions of the agreement. With the governments selling back most of the "participation oil" rather than undertaking refining and marketing themselves, they are still largely tax collectors, and not much of a threat to the majors.

The October War produced a substantial shake-up in these arrangements. In the context of the skyrocketing prices created by the energy scare, the OPEC countries fixed the divisions of crude oil resources between themselves and the company at 84 to 16 in their own favour. In two stages the posted price (upon which tax revenues are based) was raised from $3.00 per barrel before the war to over $11 by December 1973. Government revenue leaped from less than $2.00 per barrel to over $7 per barrel. This blow to the oil companies was further sustained by the Iraqian nationalization of all U.S. and Dutch oil interests. On the other hand, the new split in profits still left the companies $1.20 per barrel or 50 per cent more than what they received before the October War. Nor is it certain that the acceleration of the ownership transfer called for in the new arrangement will hurt the companies. Providing the oil is sold back

---

* U.S. crude oil, with production cost of $3.00 a barrel, could hold its own in the American market only because of the quota. Middle Eastern crude could be processed and shipped to the same markets for less than $1.50 a barrel.

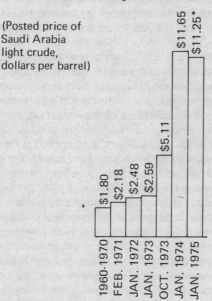

Figure 13
Change in Oil Prices

(Posted price of
Saudi Arabia
light crude,
dollars per barrel)

*Drop in price reflects realignment of tax and royalty payments.

to them for refining and marketing, they seem quite willing to
accede on questions of legal title. What they fear is nationalization
in which the OPEC nations take command over the oil supplies and
set up their own refining and marketing facilities.

Aside from the rest of the Third World,* the major losers in these
events are the Japanese and Western Europeans who depend
almost entirely on Middle East oil supplies. Western Europe's oil

---

* According to a report released on March 17, OPEC gave 17 billion dollars in aid
to Third World countries in 1974. The $17 billion, which represents 10.2 per cent
of the gross national product of the 13 OPEC member nations, amounts to an aid
total many times greater than that given by the industrialized countries over a
period of several years. $4 billion of the aid was transferred in cash, and the re-
maining $13 billion in credit and other forms.

By contrast, the industrialized countries have so far refused to honour the resolution of the sixth extraordinary session of the UN, which states that industrialized nations must allocate one per cent of their GNP to finance development
programs in Third World countries.

imports, which amounted to $10 billion in 1969, rose to $20 billion in 1973; the figure in 1974 is expected to be in the range of $50 - $60 billion. This means that Western Europe's oil imports, which took 10 per cent of its total export revenues in 1973, absorbed 20-25 per cent in 1974. The situation is even worse for Japan, where oil imports rose from $2 billion in 1969 to $7 billion in 1973, at which point they already took over 20 per cent of total export earnings; in 1974 the proportion is close to one-third. U.S. oil imports have also risen— from $3 billion in 1969 to $8 billion in 1973 and an expected $25 billion in 1974, which would amount to about one-quarter of total exports. However, with more than $10 billion returning to the U.S. in oil profits from abroad, American oil imports are a far smaller burden on her balance of payments compared to Europe and Japan. The changes in world oil arising from the energy crisis have therefore resulted in a drastic shift in economic power from Western Europe and Japan to the United States.

It has been frequently suggested that Washington has not been averse to this aspect of the energy crisis and even lent it passive, if not active, support — at least in its early stages. By raising the price of fuel to European and Japanese manufacturers to levels which are equal to or even higher than the price that U.S. industries have to pay, the energy crisis strengthened the competitive positions of U.S. industry in international markets. This is one of the key explanations given to the energy crisis by the French journalist Michael Bosquet:

> It was in the interest of the United States to induce a high increase in the price of non-American crude oil in 1970 in order to re-balance their own situation, to reduce the commercial advantage of their Japanese and European competitors . . . And it is not by chance that none other than the Shah of Iran made himself the spokesman for the producing countries, successfully shepherding their demands in the direction wished for by the U.S. He induced a rise in the price of non-American crude, miraculously equal to the gap existing between Middle Eastern and American crude oil.[14]

Rather than being a plot hatched in Washington, the energy crisis more likely resulted from joint and separate actions taken by the oil companies and the OPEC nations that Washington chose not to interfere with. To a remarkable degree the three elements — OPEC, the oil companies and big business in the U.S.A. — enjoyed a coincidence of interests in the immediate run. However, there were some conflicts too. Even though American auto, steel, and chemical companies benefit internationally from the far worse fate of Western European and Japanese industrialists, they are forced to scramble to protect their positions within the American economy. Domestic industries like automobiles and electrical and gas utilities, as well as the leisure industries dependent upon travel, are important losers. Up until now, the oil-military complex has had the dominant say in American ruling circles but the tensions are there, as reflected, for example, in the demands of many members of Congress for a more active government role in the oil industry.

The American Counter-Attack

Until recent years, the United States has been virtually self-sufficient in energy resources. That situation has begun to change. By 1975, over one-third of all crude oil was imported. Without moving dramatically towards a new course, this would probably reach two-thirds of all supplies by the 1980s. This is the crux of the matter. To avoid an impossible balance of payments deficit, the U.S. would have to increase its export of manufactured goods on a truly mammoth scale. With Europe and Japan facing an even greater balance of payments squeeze and with markets for manufactured goods in Middle East countries being severely limited, the prospect of a sufficient expansion of exports abroad is not encouraging. Aside from oil, the U.S. will be facing an enormous import bill to pay for her supplies of other raw materials. The alternative choices so far as energy is concerned are the achievement of self-sufficiency or a military invasion and occupation of a Middle East oil producing country. The latter is always a last resort possibility and has been alluded to by both President Ford and Henry Kissinger.

The dimensions of the crisis, as seen from the American perspective, were laid out by Henry Kissinger in his November 14 (1974) speech at the University of Chicago:

> The oil producers now enjoy a surplus . . . far beyond their payments or development needs and manifestly more than they can invest. Enormous unabsorbed surplus revenues now jeopardize the very functioning of the international monetary system. Yet this is only the first year of inflated oil prices. The full brunt of the petrodollar flood is yet to come. If current economic trends continue, we face further and mounting worldwide shortages, unemployment, poverty, and hunger.
>
> An economic crisis of such magnitude would inevitably produce dangerous political consequences. Mounting inflation and recession — brought on by remote decisions over which consumers have no influence — will fuel the frustration of all whose hopes for economic progress are suddenly and cruelly rebuffed. This is fertile ground for social conflict and political turmoil.

Moderate governments and moderate solutions will be under severe attack. Democratic societies could become vulnerable to extremist pressures from right or left to a degree not experienced since the twenties and thirties. The great achievements of this generation in preserving our institutions and constructing an international order will be imperiled. . . .

The potentially most serious international consequences could occur in relations between North America, Europe and Japan. If the energy crisis is permitted to continue unchecked, some countries will be tempted to secure unilateral benefit through separate arrangements with producers at the expense of the collaboration that offers the only hope for survival over the long term. Such unilateral arrangements are guaranteed to enshrine inflated prices, dilute the bargaining power of the consumers, and perpetuate the economic burden for all. . . .

Nor can consumers finance their oil bill by going into debt to the producers without making their domestic structure hostage to the decisions of others. Already, producers have the power to cause major financial upheavals simply by shifting investment funds from one country to another or even from one institution to another. The political implications are ominous and unpredictable. Those who wield financial power would sooner or later seek to dictate the political terms of the new relationships.

Kissinger called for measures that would reduce the West's imports of energy resources from one-third of total consumption to one-fifth by 1985, and the United States to less than 2 per cent. The effect of this reduced dependence would be "crucial," in his words. By holding imports from the OPEC nations static, it would cut down their revenues and force them to reduce their prices in order to gain greater access to western markets.

The achievement of self-sufficiency can be realized only through massive investment in and rapid development of North America's conventional and non-conventional petroleum resources. In Kissinger's words "it represents the investment of hundreds of billions of dollars, public and private — dwarfing our moon-landing program and the Manhattan project, two previous examples of American technology mobilized for a great goal. Project independence demonstrates that the United States will never permit itself to be held hostage — politically or economically."

"Project independence" suits the major oil companies very well. Seeing that the end of cheap oil is in sight (not long after the year 2000) their intention is to extract maximum profits from existing oil production to finance their own conversion to new sources of energy over which they will exercise monopolistic control. According to Michael Bosquet:

. . . for the big American companies which are the only ones to have a long-term strategy to "organize the end of oil," this is the goal: To instigate an almost vertical rise in the price of Persian Gulf crude oil, and to make crude oil so expensive that the exploitation of Alaska, of the bottom of the sea, of the asphastic shists of Colorado, and the sand of Athabaska will become profitable. Thus the United States will retain its independence in the matter of energy, and with the huge profits from the little oil that is left prepare the new kingdom of coal — coal which will have become less expensive than oil and which will give back to the U.S. its supremacy. Afterwards it will be the era of nuclear, geothermic, and solar energy.

This is not idle dreaming. American oil companies already control 48 per cent of the world's uranium reserves. It took only two years for them to buy a third of American coal mines. There is in the U.S. five times more coal than the total oil reserves in the world. And when a barrel of crude oil will be worth eight to ten dollars, the automated extraction of coal and its processing will become a highly profitable business. The United States will have regained its self-sufficiency in energy, while Europe and Japan will continue to be dependent upon the oil from the Gulf, oil which will cost them more than the American processed coal (and the U.S. will see to that).[15]

Bosquet exaggerates. At present prices of oil, Western Europe and Japan will be badly hurt in the next few years while the United States will be strengthened by comparison. Yet since the U.S. has a big stake in Western Europe and Japan, a collapse there is not to her interest. What the U.S. must do is to walk a tightrope of benefiting from Europe's and Japan's weakened position while not allowing their positions to deteriorate to the point of collapse.

These countries are not, of course, sitting idly by watching their treasuries being emptied. Contrary to Kissinger's admonitions, France, West Germany, Britain, and Japan have been working out deals with various Arab countries and Iran to trade jets, arms, and industrial equipment for crude oil. Western Europe has the option of importing Soviet oil and natural gas on a significant scale.* West Germany has vast reserves of relatively cheap coal. Oil discoveries

---

* Several West European countries are already exercising this option. In December 1969, the U.S.S.R. agreed to supply West Germany with natural gas over a period of twenty years involving a delivery of 3 billion cubic metres of natural gas per annum by 1978. In May 1973, the two countries signed a ten-year pact providing for economic, industrial, and technological co-operation with the U.S.S.R. to provide the West Germans with petroleum, natural gas, and other industrial raw materials. In December 1974, France and the U.S.S.R. signed an agreement whereby the Soviets would supply France with 2.5 billion cubic metres of natural gas per year to 1980 and 4 billion cubic metres annually thereafter. In 1969, Italy signed a twenty-year $3 billion contract for the import of 100 billion cubic metres of Soviet natural gas over the life of the contract.

in the North Sea are expected to provide Western Europe with 15 per cent of its needs by 1980. All of west Europe and Japan are accelerating their nuclear programs.

It is nevertheless true that while hard times lie ahead for every nation because of energy price increases, the United States can look forward to important gains over her industrial rivals. Moreover, it is Europe and Japan that are paying and will continue to pay a significant part of the gigantic sums that are required to develop North America's future energy supplies. About three-quarters of the profits made by Exxon and the other majors come from their earnings on sales to Japan and Western Europe.[16]

America's "project independence" incorporates two essential and related goals. The first is self-sufficiency for the United States, and this requires sustained high level prices for petroleum. The second is to break the power of OPEC, which has caused such a drastic redistribution of the flow of wealth within the capitalist world and has placed countries like Italy and Great Britain in financial jeopardy. This requires that the price of Middle East oil be forced down. The dual nature of the project was hinted at by Henry Kissinger in his January 1975 interview with *Business Week* magazine. When asked to list the objective conditions required to bring down the price of oil, he mentioned "consumer solidarity," presumably under U.S. leadership, but "most important [the need] to bring in alternative sources of energy as rapidly as possible so that the combination of new discoveries of oil, new oil-producing countries, and new sources of energy create a supply situation in which it will be increasingly difficult for the [OPEC] cartel to operate."[17]This dual policy was made explicit by Thomas Enders, Assistant Secretary of State for economic and business affairs, who is a member of a special committee established by Kissinger to deal with the international implications of the oil crisis. Enders disclosed the essence of the U.S. administration's oil policy at a forum at Yale University. *New York Times* international monetary expert Leonard Silk, who attended the forum, reported that "the startling news broken by Mr. Enders at Yale — startling against the background of repeated declarations of high American officials that OPEC nations must reduce their exorbitant high prices — is that the United States is now founding its strategy on the $11 price."[18] (The "$11 price" is roughly the price for oil now prevailing in world markets.) The $11 price has evidently started a worldwide oil boom that will soon force the OPEC producing nations to cut their production to such low levels that "the cartel could fall apart." "Paradoxically," said Silk, "the United States is worried that a downward break in world prices could come too soon, and be devastating for heavy American and other Western investment in the development of alternative energy sources, based on the assumption of a continued 'real' oil price of $11 a barrel."

What Enders also revealed in his address is that when foreign oil prices have been forced down, it is expected that the oil companies will be allowed to maintain domestic prices at the current high rate. This envisions a "two-tier cost structure for energy." "One [tier]," Enders explained, "that assures consuming countries their desired degree of independence; the other [tier] balances a constant demand and growing supply for imported oil at prices that diminished, or even reversed, the accumulation of assets by producers." In short, the first tier means high prices in North America, Europe and Japan so that the oil trusts are able to continue to produce from higher-cost energy sources; the second tier means that the underdeveloped oil-producing nations will be deprived of their share of the take from their own oil resources, preferably to the point where they are forced to sell off some of their accumulated assets in order to finance their imports.

In his January 1975 message to the American congress, President Ford outlined some of the projects which are to take effect over the next ten years:

—200 major nuclear power plants
—250 major new coal mines
—150 major coal-fired power plants
—30 major new oil refineries
—20 major new synthetic fuel plants
—the drilling of many thousands of new oil wells
—the construction of millions of new automobiles, trucks, and buses that use less fuel.

To implement these programs, he asked Congress to modify automotive pollution standards, to amend the Clean Air Act such as to allow greater coal use, and to pass less restrictive strip-mining legislation. He also asked Congress for an investment tax-credit program that would encourage utilities to accelerate their planned nuclear expansion.* Furthermore, he raised the fee on imported crude oil and petroleum products and asked Congress to establish "tariffs, import quotas or price floors to protect our energy prices at levels which will achieve energy independence."

---

*. The concerns of scientists not employed by the Atomic Energy Commission about a "pace of construction [which] has far outstripped the pace at which safety technology has been developed," have evidently been waved aside. (See the testimony of nuclear physicist Henry W. Kendall, speaking before the American Congress, *Congressional Quarterly*, July 15, 1973.)

The goals that President Ford reiterated in his speech are revealing of the overall American strategy: (1) immediate step-by-step reductions of oil imports; (2) "end vulnerability to economic disruption by foreign supplies by 1985"; (3) and develop energy resources to the point that by the turn of the century the U.S. has "the ability to supply a significant share of the energy needs of the free world."

Capitalism seems to work best when there is a universally recognized leader nation that establishes a global system around its orbit — witness the flowering of international capitalism under the aegis of Great Britain from 1800 to 1914 and in "the world the dollar built" from 1945 to 1970. That world began to crumble in the late 1960s, and Nixon's aggressive acts of August 1971 ushered in a period of uncertainty and dissension within the ranks. They were meant to recoup American leadership, but their immediate effect was to cause a swift breakdown of the old order and a jockeying around for new leadership roles. The energy crisis, which leaves the U.S. strong relative to Europe and Japan, may catapult the Americans into the leadership role again. Certainly, if the United States is in a position to "supply a significant share of the energy needs of the free world" by the end of the century, her predominant role would seem secure. But a lot can happen between now and the year 2000.

The Kissinger-Ford scenario rests on the assumption that the United States will be successful in subordinating Western Europe and Japan to her own global designs; that she will be successful in squelching the the aspirations of the Third World for balanced and diversified economic development; that she will be successful in diverting an increasing share of her domestic product away from wages and salaries of working people to the profits of the multinational resource companies. It takes no genius to recognize that these are formidable obstacles in the path of the efforts to retain American supremacy. That they cannot be overcome without considerable internal and external conflict is a certainty. That they cannot be overcome at all remains a distinct possibility.

A Role for Canada

In the spring of 1973 the U.S. Treasury Department called in one hundred prominent Canadian businessmen and newspaper editors for a series of top-level meetings. Likely similar meetings were conducted for other nationals around the same time. Clive Baxter of the *Financial Post,* who was present at these meetings, reported that the U.S. Treasury Department spokesman laid down three general propositions that summarized U.S. goals for the immediate future: to absorb massive imports of resources for an indefinite period; to bring the U.S. international balance of payments into balance; and to remain "the fountainhead of new world capital."

In short, the U.S.A. has no intention of giving up its position as the leading power in the capitalist world. Unlike England in World War I, U.S. business will not sell off its assets abroad to clear up the debts. Rather, her "free world" partners are expected to accommodate American objectives by restructuring their economies and adjusting their trade flows.

What this means in concrete terms is that in order for the U.S.A. to be able to buy massive supplies of resource materials over the indefinite future, and at the same time keep her economic empire intact, she will have to pay for them by selling similar amounts of manufactured goods abroad. Thus Europe, Canada, and Japan are being asked to reduce their share of world output of manufactured goods by selling less around the world and buying more from American manufacturers. The devaluations and the imports restrictions were the initial designated means by which the U.S. government hoped to achieve this objective. A redistribution of secondary manufacturing jobs is already under way. For example, Canadian General Electric has been laying off Canadian production workers in Rexdale, Ontario, and bringing in their products from General Electric plants in the U.S. The massive turn-about in automotive trade is a further indication of things to come.

Since the launching of Nixonomics in August 1971, the U.S.A. has had two overriding objectives in its dealings with Canada: to increase Canadian imports of American manufactured products; to secure access to increasing amounts of Canadian resources. Facing serious competition from Western Europe and Japan, the U.S. has been compelled to rationalize her relationship with Canada. The good old days of "special status" for Canada are ending. What this means in concrete terms is that Canada must adjust itself further to being a market for U.S.-made manufactured goods and a supplier of resources to feed U.S. industrial mills.

The United States government is also requiring multinational corporations to finance their expansions abroad by borrowing in the countries they are located in rather than reinvesting branch-plant earnings. Branch-plant earnings are expected to be returned to the U.S. parent company to a far greater degree than in the past. In Canada, heretofore, half of their profits are normally sent back to the U.S. and half have been reinvested to expand branch-plant operations. Already 85 per cent of U.S. investment in Canada is financed with Canadian funds. Branch-plants are under instruction to raise this percentage still further.

It is not expected that Canada should phase down its secondary manufacturing sector and receive nothing in return. What Washington offers is unlimited access to the American market for all the energy resources we can supply them with — at good prices. They're still operating on Walter Hickel's plan, revealed in 1970, for pooling Canadian and American oil, natural gas, coal, water, and hydroelectric capacity. Many Americans believe there is a natural fit between an energy-deficient country and an energy-surplus country. They believe it is our duty as good citizens of the world to help solve their shortages. They have long coveted our northern water resource in particular, from time to time remarking how marvellous the world would be if nations stopped being so possessive about God's bounty on earth.

Aware of their growing dependence on outside supplies of strategic raw materials, American strategists are cognisant of the fact that there are few places left in the world which have large untapped resources whose people are friendly to the U.S.A. They haven't written off any part of the globe. Even the U.S.S.R. seems accessible now. But they know that there are few reliable and stable regimes that they can depend upon for steady supplies at reasonable prices. Canada is one such case. That is why Nixon chose Canada as a prime external supplier to meet U.S. energy needs.*

This position has not exactly been foisted upon Canada. Canadian ruling circles, both government and industry, have been manoeuvring to occupy this role for about a hundred years. They have always seen their role as being one of facilitating the movement of resources into and out of Canada. Once the British lost interest in Canadian resources, the merchants, bankers, railwaymen, and political leaders — who together decide what happens to Canada — were determined to link their futures with the U.S.A.

It took many years before their plans were fully realized. From the beginning, American economic policy was designed to restrict the imports of manufactured goods from other countries. Tariffs on most raw materials were kept low, but the U.S.A. was for many years self-sufficient in all or most basic resources. Indeed, she was a

---

* This was the justification offered by the U.S. Cabinet Task Force on Oil Import Controls for its recommendations of a "harmonized energy policy" with Canada: "The risk of political instability or animosity is generally conceded to be very low in Canada. The risk of physical interruption or diversion of Canadian oil to other export markets in an emergency is also minimal . . .."

large exporter. This began to give way when her forests were unable to satisfy the demands of the U.S. daily press. The export of pulp and paper early in the twentieth century gave Canada's merchants, industrialists, bankers, and railway tycoons their first real chance of cashing in on the vast American market. Other opportunities arose during World War I and the 1920s, particularly in the new metals like copper, nickel, and zinc. By this time most foreign investment in Canada was U.S.-owned and the Canadian economy was largely organized to assist a north-south flow of trade.

But the real break for Canadian capitalists came after World War II. The oil strike at Leduc and a pipeline down the west coast built to accommodate Seattle's and California's feared shortages during the Korean War were the first signals that the long-laid plans for a thorough continental trade network were going to be realized. This was confirmed a few years later by the opening up of large iron ore mines in Quebec and Labrador and government construction of the St. Lawrence Seaway to bring the ore down to U.S. steel mills. Then Inco's second nickel-copper complex opened in Thompson, Manitoba. The 1964 Columbia River Treaty gave the U.S.A. one-quarter of the Columbia River waters that flowed from Canada. By the late 1960s, one-third of Alberta's known gas resources were already committed for export to the U.S.

This is only a capsule summary of some of the major developments that made Canada's northland a frontier for America's resource-depleting economy. But a pattern was emerging by the fifties and sixties which has relevance for the even more dramatic developments slated for the last quarter of this century.

While the export of most Canadian resource materials continues to flow uninterrupted, the National Energy Board discovered in 1974 that Canada had its own energy crisis and recommended that exports of petroleum be phased down and eliminated by 1982 until the new sources of conventional and non-conventional energy are developed. This came as a rude shock, as just three-and-a-half years earlier (June 2, 1971) while speaking to the Canadian Institute of Mining and Metallurgy the then Minister of Energy, Mines and Resources, Joe Greene, assured us that "Canada's total oil reserves were 469 billion barrels at the end of 1970, while total natural gas reserves were 725 trillion feet. At 1970 rates of production, these reserves represent 923 years supply of oil and 392 years of gas."

In 1961, exports to the U.S. of crude oil and natural gas liquids averaged 185,000 barrels a day, about 45 per cent of Canadian consumption totals. On the basis of Greene's assurances, the National Energy Board permitted an increase of natural gas exports by 50 per cent as well as large increases in petroleum exports. By 1971, for the first time, more Canadian crude and liquids were exported than consumed and, in 1973, the year of the "energy crisis," the pace of exports continued to climb, reaching 1,175,000 barrels a day compared to 805,000 barrels of Canadian crude and liquids consumed by Canadians.[19] Now we are told that there is about nine years' supply of conventional oil in the ground and that we will soon be faced with deficits that will cost billions of dollars a year in imported oil.

Mr. Greene, of course, had meant to speak of potential reserves, but it is these centuries of hypothetical reserves that have consistently misled Canadian policy-makers. The source of the Cabinet's information regarding reserves, and the only source of the National Energy Board as well, is the industry itself. Precisely the same people who lulled our politicians and civil servants to sleep with their comfortable and misleading reserve figures, so that they could accelerate their exports of our oil and gas, now warn that we are quickly running short and that we must allow them to raise their prices so that they can earn sufficient profits to explore and develop more costly reserves.

Is it a mere coincidence that in 1973 the oil companies guaranteed us that they would produce enough oil to meet our domestic needs for the next 80 years, while a year later, with the international price of oil having increased from $3.00 a barrel to $11.00, they predicted that Canada would face a domestic oil shortage in only eight years? With their monopoly of information the oil companies hold both the public and government agencies to ransom as they manipulate petroleum reserve data to serve their own interests. It did not take them long to resolve to destroy the two-price system established by the federal government in September 1973.

The two-price system consisted of a fixed domestic price and an export price that moved upward with the international price. The domestic price was initially set at $4.00 a barrel — and an export tax was imposed on oil exports based on the difference between the Canadian price and the prevailing price that oil sold at in the Chicago market.* From the moment the system was established, the Canadian petroleum industry was determined to break it and force the domestic oil price up to export levels.

From the point of view of the oil companies, Canada was an unattractive location so long as Canada's price was frozen below the world level. With higher profits to be made elsewhere, they announced a shrinking of the size of Canadian reserves worth their

---

* The export tax began at 40 cents a barrel, then rose to $1.90 a barrel in December 1973, to $2.20 a barrel in January 1974 and to $6.40 a barrel in February 1974.

while developing. Hence the sudden discovery of an oil shortage in Canada, confirmed by the National Energy board report of October 1974. The previous report of the Board had concluded that "there is little question that Canada can satisfy her needs easily until the year 2050 at oil prices reaching $7 or $8." Somehow, between June 1973 and October 1974 a comfortable surplus had been converted into a dangerous shortage. During the intervening five months the oil industry had put its publicity department into action, laying the basis for an attack upon the two-price system.* In the spring of 1974, the price of crude in the domestic market was raised from $4.00 to $6.50 a barrel. It was the beginning of the end for the two-price system. A year later, in June 1975, the finance Minister announced measures to raise the domestic price in steps until it approached the world level.

The companies are evidently making a determined bid to appropriate as much of the economic rent from oil as they can. The federal government's Energy Board estimates that "a reasonable rate of return" is a 20 per cent rate of profit on capital invested. But, over and above the costs of exploration, production, and transportation and the "reasonable rate of return," the Board's report explains that there may be a considerable rent that can be collected when the price is raised to prevailing international levels. Rent is another way of expressing "windfall profit." The report noted that federal and provincial governments collected only a small proportion of this rent compared to what other governments were taking.

Since the report, both levels of government have increased their stake substantially, but it is still only a part of what is available. As the chart makes very clear, Imperial Oil, with profits rising from $151 million in 1972 to $290 million in 1974, has been able to clear extraordinary profits. Industry profits for the past two years (1973-1974) are more than $1 billion more than total exploration and development expenditures and more than all the revenues the province of Alberta has received in the 25 years since Leduc. Gulf's profits in 1974 were about 90 per cent above the previous year, while Shell's profits about doubled. After all the taxes, royalties, and various adjustments were made, the industry received about $2.25 per barrel in profit, which is 80 per cent of the 1972 well head price! †

---

* The two-price system also came under the attack of the U.S. government. Washington did not expect Canada to sell oil to the U.S. at less than the world price. What concerned the Americans was that with the low domestic price of oil, Canadian industry would have an "unfair" advantage over U.S. manufacturers, and with large-scale surplus industrial capacity beginning to surface in the U.S.A. this was not an attractive development.

† John Turner's aborted budget of May 1974 had cancelled the oil companies'

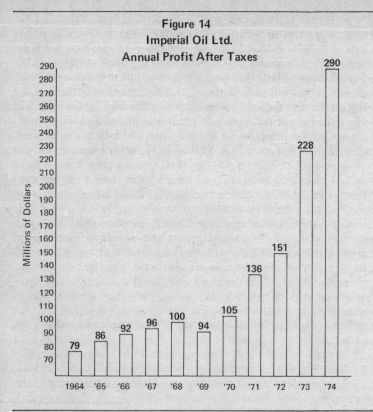

Figure 14
Imperial Oil Ltd.
Annual Profit After Taxes

In the fall of 1973, the Alberta Government, with most of its information and research coming from within the industry, produced a comprehensive oil sands viability study. Syncrude would claim to deduct provincial royalty payments as expenses against their federal taxes. At prevailing prices this would mean a transfer to the federal government of a billion dollars from the oil industry. On the other hand, Turner added a provision which would allow the industry to write off 70 per cent of exploration expenses against federal taxes. His November budget extended the exploration write-off to 100 per cent. These concessions, along with further ones presented in the June 1975 budget, gave the industry back an estimated $225 million in 1975 or something in excess of $15 billion over the life of Alberta's proven reserves of 6 billion barrels. Meanwhile the premier of Alberta, under some pressure from the industry, had backed down in the battle with Ottawa, agreeing to refund to the oil companies a sum equal to the amount flowing to Alberta as a result of the federal taxation of provincial royalties. As well, he lowered the province's effective royalties. The oil industry estimated that Alberta's measures would place $250 to $300 million in its hands. Adding together this sum with federal funds, the industry was able to reduce the original $1 billion federal tax bite to about $500 million between May 1974 and June 1975.

be profitable, it concluded, at $4.85 a barrel in 1978 and at $7.10 in 1986, adjusting for inflation. A few months later, Ottawa's policy makers were told that 15 billion barrels of tar sands oil could be profitably produced at $5.00 a barrel and 35 billion barrels at $6.00. Less than a year later the Syncrude consortium threw down an ultimatum that it would close down the project unless at the outset it was guaranteed the international price of $11.50-$12.00 a barrel. In 1972, the bill for the Syncrude plant was placed at $500 million. One year later it was raised 100 per cent to $1 billion and the next year another 100 per cent to $2 billion—a 400 per cent increase in 30 months. The Alberta, Ontario and Ottawa governments have agreed to put up $600 millions which gives them a 30 per cent interest in the project. The province of Alberta has also agreed to put up $200 million in loans as well as investing between $500 million and $600 million in a power plant, pipeline and housing to serve the project. The federal government agreed to exempt Syncrude from tax provisions that prevent oil firms from writing off provincial royalties when calculating federal taxes.

According to J. C. Russell, an Edmonton scientist, ". . . the project is controlled by the Exxon group (Imperial) and reflects its interests. The costs are being ballooned upwards rapidly so that profits will accrue from the building of the project and refining the product. With an agreement to split any profits with Alberta on a 50:50 basis, it is in the companies' interest to show no operating profit."[20] The project is being constructed by Bechtel Canada Ltd., a subsidiary of a U.S. firm that also got the contract to build the James Bay hydroelectric development project. It is Bechtel that is largely responsible for submitting the escalating cost figures which include its own engineering fees. Much of the profit from a large-scale industrial project is controlled by procurement practices, and arises from the manufacture and supply of components. Bechtel is doing 80 per cent of the engineering itself and has contracted much of the technical work to U.S. companies, who will end up receiving royalties on top of their fees. Virtually all of the heavy equipment is contracted out to U.S.companies. Therefore, aside from the labour costs on the construction side, it is likely that most of the $2 billion investment will actually be made in the U.S.A.

Oil company executives have taken to calling the oil sands "Canada's Middle East." Recoverable oil from the sands is estimated to be more than 300 billion barrels to the year 2000. Total Canadian consumption of oil will absorb no more than 30 billion barrels. The vice president of Shell Canada Ltd. says that he can foresee his company operating 30 heavy-oil and oil-sands plants by the year 2000.[21] As the Alberta government report on oil sands

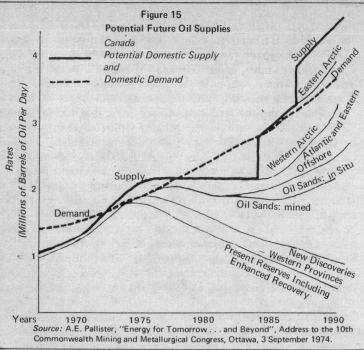

Figure 15
Potential Future Oil Supplies
Canada

Potential Domestic Supply
and
Domestic Demand

Source: A.E. Pallister, "Energy for Tomorrow . . . and Beyond", Address to the 10th Commonwealth Mining and Metallurgical Congress, Ottawa, 3 September 1974.

development makes clear, "The pressure to develop synthetic crude from the tar sands emanates from markets external to Canada."[22]

In announcing the phasing down of oil exports to the U.S., Energy Minister Donald Macdonald made it clear that this is only a temporary phase to tide us over between now and the late 1980s when Arctic and tar sands oil would bring about "a resurgence" of production and export sales can resume.* (See accompanying chart.)

In the words of one writer, "although not a work of great vision, this country's energy policy has not been without a centre of gravity. The oil companies have provided the direction and the statesmanship . . . For the oil companies the future lies in gigantic projects that respond to continental rather than Canada's demand for energy."[23] Up to now, some 16 billion barrels of oil have been found in western Canada, of which 6 billion barrels have been produced. According to estimates of the Geological Survey of Canada, 7 to 22 billion barrels remain undiscovered in the Western provinces. Approximately 75 to 95 billion barrels are thought to be

---

* The reasons offered for not cutting off exports immediately were: "an immediate halt to exports would be disruptive to Canadian-U.S. trade relations"; and an immediate cut-off would mean a drastic reduction in oil company income; besides, it would "only" extend Canadian self-sufficiency for 18 months to two years.

present in the arctic and off the east coast and 300 billion barrels of recoverable oil from the tar sands. But much of this (about 190 billion barrels) depends on the development of technology still being developed. As noted earlier, Canada will use only about 30 billion barrels between now and the year 2000, assuming a standard 4 per cent increase a year. We may safely presume then, that most of the production from the tar sands and the arctic is slated for export. The same may be said for natural gas, with recoverable potential reserves estimated at between 712 trillion cubic feet and 835 trillion cubic feet — 350 to 400 years' supply at the 1972 level of output.

The Mackenzie Valley Pipeline was conceived as a project to bring natural gas from Alaska and the Canadian arctic down to southern Canada and the American midwest. Its construction would cost about 6 billion dollars. The project is subject to approval by the National Energy Board and is also being subjected to hearings conducted by B.C. Judge Thomas Berger. But the Liberal Cabinet decided years ago that it supported it. The Prime Minister has likened it to the Canadian Pacific Railway, "too big a project for Canada . . . only in the view of those who have lost faith in what Canada is about."[24]

If the CPR was the "National Dream," the Mackenzie Valley Pipeline is clearly the "Continental Dream." This is the conception of both the industry and the government. In a letter written to U.S. Interior Secretary, Roger Morton, Donald Macdonald assured the Americans that "Canada has an interest in the energy security of your country, and this land route for Alaska crude oil would enhance that security of supply to deficient areas in the United States." Presumably the same argument would apply to natural gas. Imperial Oil's W.O. Twaits has said that "it [the arctic] would not be economic to explore at all if we're looking at Canadian demand only."[25]

The consortium promoting the pipeline warns that without it Canada would run out of natural gas by the end of this decade. The pipeline would assure Canada of adequate supplies and could furthermore give the country the benefit of economics of scale because it is conceived in terms of American as well as Canadian markets. The economics of scale argument is indisputable. What is in dispute is whether Canada requires arctic gas at this time. A Calgary petroleum engineer has written that the shallow Milk River gas potential in southeastern Alberta and southwestern Saskatchewan could alone be more than sufficient to meet Canadian needs into the next century.[26] This is confirmed by the estimates of the Geological Survey of Canada. According to these sources, Canadians would not be hurt if, for the present, a moritorium on the Mackenzie Valley Pipeline were to be called. However, the federal government appears to be hell-bent in co-operating with the industry in getting this and other projects underway.*

Some Consequences

It is apparent that we are locked into an energy investment boom that will carry us to the mid or late 1980s, by which time most of the new energy projects will be in place. The total cost of the James Bay development for the period 1972-1985 is $12 billion (in 1974 dollars). As mentioned, the estimated capital requirement for the Mackenzie Valley Gas Pipeline is $6 billion. The Alberta Energy Resources Conservation Board placed the cost of each 100,000-barrels-per-day tar sands plant at between $800 million to $1 billion. The companies now insist on a cost of $2 billion. Each plant would require approximately 5,000 man-years of construction labour and 800 man-years of design and professional services.

The Eleventh Annual Report of the Economic Council of Canada lays out three different scenarios of resource development, each one reflecting a different price level for oil and gas. At current price levels (option A), the Mackenzie Valley Pipeline and all but two tar sands plants would be deterred; at an intermediate price level (option B), the Mackenzie Valley Pipeline would begin construction by 1977 and four tar sands plants would be built by 1985; at high level prices (option C), an additional four synthetic crude plants would be built.

Energy Investment 1975 - 1982 (billions of current dollars)

Option A	Option B	Option C
$73.4	$85.2	$93.9

The ECC does not include in these totals the $12 billion James Bay development, nor the east coast developments, nor, for that matter, Manitoba's Churchill River diversion. And tar sands plants were costed at half the current demand price of $2 billion. Accordingly, investment in energy will require between $90 billion and $120 billion over the next ten years. This does not include the uranium enrichment plant that the government of Quebec is negotiating

---

* I do not mean to suggest that a substantial amount of investment in energy resources is not required to meet Canadian needs. If we can believe the statistics that have been compiled on the state of oil reserves in established regions, new sources of fuel have to be developed in the near future. However, the extent of development now going forward or just over the horizon appears to be far in excess of Canadian requirements, and because of the industry's appetite for profits, the amount of investment and public subsidization — in the form of both high prices and government moneys — exceeds that which is economically necessary to undertake these new profits.

with France. If brought to fruition, this plant would require another $6 billion and absorb one-fifth to one-third the James Bay hydro-electric potential.

It is apparent that Canada cannot sustain such a heavy investment in energy, on top of all of our other investment requirements, without continued inflation of prices. Even the ECC admits that these projects will have to be financed, to a significant degree, by foreign capital. Inflation is a crude rationing device. The labour, capital, and materials attracted to the resources project will be drawn away from housing and other government programs, which the ECC projects will fall off. The increase in the value of the Canadian dollar brought about by the large inflow of foreign capital will reduce the competitiveness of Canadian manufacturing, particularly exports, whose growth rate will also decline, according to ECC projections. In the ECC's carefully chosen words:

> In the longer run, the size of prospective investments in Canadian resource industries will tend to sustain or raise the exchange value of the Canadian dollar and to shift economic activity towards primary and processing production of resource products.[27]

One economist has estimated that a 5 per cent increase in the value of the Canadian dollar compared to the American dollar would cause a $715 million negative trade shift for Canada with the U.S., resulting from decreased exports and increased imports; a 10 per cent increase would cause a $1.6 billion negative trade shift.[28] Upward re-evaluations of the Canadian dollar would also cause losses with other trading partners.*

A secret federal government document on the Mackenzie Valley Pipeline prepared by the Department of Finance leaked to the public in the spring of 1973 was not overly enthusiastic about the impact of the project, concluding that "[it] would likely prove to be a mixed blessing to Canada." It pointed to the inflationary pressures that would be exerted by the pipeline, upward pressures on the value of the Canadian dollar, a relatively small contribution to taxes ($73 million a year), and "a potentially serious upward pressure on the level of Canadian energy prices." Finally, it pointed out that only 150 to 200 permanent jobs would result from the project.[29]

Long before these new energy developments were underway, it was already apparent that manufacturing engaged a relatively small percentage of the work force. In 1960, only 24.5 per cent of non-agricultural workers were employed in manufacturing. By

---

* To the extent that foreign capital raised for these projects is spent directly on purchasing equipment, the Canadian exchange rate will not be affected. But, in this event, few of the jobs will be created in Canada.

1973, the percentage had dropped to 22.4 per cent. Among western countries only Greece and Ireland have a lower percentage of their work force employed in manufacturing. The squeeze on manufacturing was already well underway by the late 1960s. A study of 72 manufacturing firms employing more than 100 workers in Hamilton in 1966 showed that 12 of these had shut down by 1972, while only four new ones had opened in their place. While Hamilton's labour force had risen by 20 per cent in the interim, the number of manufacturing jobs had decisively fallen.[30] What James Laxer has aptly called the process of "de-industrialization" is bound to deepen under the onslaught of the energy investment boom. As the relative postion of manufacturing shrinks still further, an even larger portion of the work force will have to find jobs in the service industries. The service industries already employ about two-thirds of the labour force, the highest proportion of any country in the world. Over-supply has already created a squeeze on salaries in this sector, the lowest paid of any in the economy. "It is no accident," Laxer remarks, "that white-collar workers, teachers and civil servants are becoming increasingly militant as their livelihood and economic security are threatened by the effects of Canada's stagnant manufacturing sector."[31]

In short, as pointed out in an earlier chapter, the energy investment boom will chart a very uneven development pattern for Canada over the next decade. There will be raging growth and shortages in certain hinterland regions, while metropolitan regions will find themselves with surplus capacity and labour. It is safe to predict that over the next decade we will be seeing a boom in resource development largely designed to supply American requirements of raw materials, fuelling a domestic inflation that squeezes out our manufacturing sector and increasing the number of temporary construction jobs at the expense of permanent jobs in manufacturing.

Canadians were worried about this infamous trade-off a few years ago when the debate over the Mackenzie Valley pipeline started in earnest. It is the logical outcome of the "pooling of resources" policy that has been an established practice despite denials to the contrary by the government of Canada. Continental energy and resources sharing is the final realization of the dream of the early Canadian business tycoons who chose to hitch their wagons to the American economy. A powerful alliance of vested interest groups emerges to actively campaign for each and every project that aims to sell Canadian resources to the U.S.A. These include the multinational corporations who sponsor the projects; the banks and finance companies that help finance them; the railway companies and pipeline companies that carry the resource products to American markets; the local businessmen and chambers of commerce in hinterland communities who profit from any new activity in their region; and the provincial and federal governments who are prepared to invest vast amounts of public funds to support private developers.

After the construction stage is completed, the approximately $100 billion invested in resource development will have created only about 250,000 new jobs. By contrast, an equivalent investment in manufacturing would have created about 1,500,000 new jobs. More to the point is that many of the new jobs in the resources sector are not permanent. It is relevant to ask what will be left of these hinterland communities once the resources are depleted. We already have many historic examples of ghost towns and ghost regions. The Ottawa Valley, the site of the great nineteenth-century lumber trade, encouraged some local development in agriculture and commerce, but once the resource was depleted the population was stranded. In the long run, says Pierre Bourgault in a study done for the Science Council of Canada, if we keep on this path, "before the children of today could reach middle age most of the resources would be gone, leaving Canada with a resource-based economy and no resources."[32]

This trade-off between the production of raw materials and the production of manufactured goods is clearly revealed in Canadian trade statistics. In 1974 Canada had a net deficit of $7 billion in the field of high-technology (that is, sophisticated manufactured) products. This deficit has risen steadily. In 1960 it was under $2 billion, rising to $3 billion in 1965 and just over $5 billion in 1973. (See accompanying chart.) Trade officials are candid about the explanation: If we are going to run continuous surpluses in raw materials and in food products "we can hardly expect to have a net gain in advanced technology as well. There has to be some move toward over-all balance." The officials are also candid in admitting that "with foreign ownership of Canadian industry so widespread — particularly in the high technology field — it may not be realistic to expect foreign companies to pump much new work in here if they can do it at home."[33]

The Science Council of Canada issued a clear warning about this problem in its background study, "The Multinational Firm, Foreign Direct Investment and Canadian Science Policy," published in 1971. The most common type of research performed in subsidiary firms involves little more than adapting American products to Canadian tastes and/or climatic conditions or to scale down parent production technology that was designed for longer production runs. When full research capability is established in subsidiary firms, "the critical aspect of a laboratory of this type is that, while it

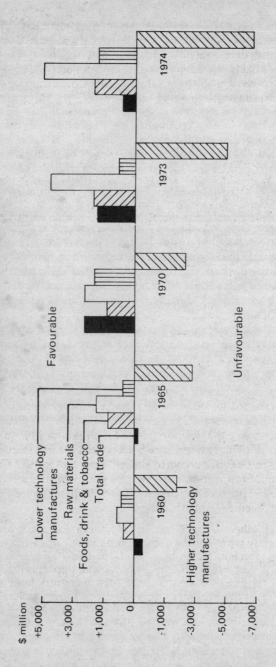

Figure 16

Canadian International Trade Balance in Merchandise Goods

Source: Department of Science & Technology

is physically in Canada and may be located adjacent to the plant site, there may in fact be little interaction between the R and D (research and development) personnel and the plant management." More likely, the Canadian laboratory reports directly to the parent company. On this score the Science Council quotes Professor J. B. Quinn of Dartmouth College:

> If the laboratories work on problems of the local environment, participate in university programs, enter joint research relationships with other national laboratories, or rotate their personnel to other company locations for training, the country gains greatly from the laboratories' presence.
>
> But if the laboratories merely work in isolation and transmit their results to the parent company for worldwide exploitation, the country gains little more than some jobs for its science graduates. It may actually sustain a net loss if these graduates' services could have been better used on other problems of higher priority in the country.[34]

The Science Council cites the case of Northern Electric, an independent company which until 1956 had imported most of its technology from Western Electric and Bell Telephone Laboratories of the United States. Because of a United States anti-trust ruling in that year Northern was put into a position of having to gradually develop its own technology. In 1960, about 90 per cent of the new product designs originated from the United States. By 1970, foreign designs accounted for only about 1 per cent of the overall total. Research staff grew from 153 in 1960 to 2,000 in 1970. Research and development expenses rose from $2.5 million in 1960 to over $37 million in 1970. Exports, which accounted for less than 3 per cent of sales in 1960, had grown to almost 18 per cent in 1970. Canadian control of raw material and components, which had been 88 per cent and 62 per cent respectively, rose to 93 per cent and 85 per cent. As the Science Council report concludes:

> This and other changes seen in Northern Electric's performances may represent the "opportunity costs" of extreme reliance on foreign technology in Canadian "science-based" industry. Northern's gain in employment opportunities and export activities gives a measure of what a country loses when many firms rely on sources abroad to develop its technology. Stating it another way, the Northern Electric case appears to be an interesting example of possible gains to Canada from indigenous science-based industry.[35]

Being "hewers of wood and drawers of water" is a three-centuries-old story for Canada. What charts the future of a nation is precisely how its capital investment is being used today. We have learned very well how to extract wealth out of nature. But when the resources of nature are non-renewable, once out of the ground they are lost to us forever.* Meanwhile, unless the wealth that is gained is carefully martialled to develop and expand other sectors of the economy — such as agriculture and manufacturing — whose processes are not self-destructing, we will find ourselves without an economic base upon which to survive and prosper. What is required is an industrial development strategy that aims to conserve our supply of non-renewable resources and plans its use in a way that assures us of economic continuity.

Unfortunately there is little evidence to suggest that existing governmental and economic institutions are capable of devising and implementing such a strategy. Our resources policy and our industrial strategy are presently being designed according to the global concerns of multinational corporations. The oil companies have teamed up to scare us into accepting development schemes that do not suit our needs. Faced with threats to regulate their prices and raise their taxes, they respond by engaging in counter-threats of an investment strike. With the co-operation of successive Canadian governments and the backing of our capitalist elite, the multi-nationals have successfully converted Canada into their northern frontier. The next quarter-century will see a gigantic struggle for power among the giant industrial nations. The American economic empire is under attack. So far as the U.S. multi-nationals are concerned, Canadian resources are part of the arsenal at their disposal in their efforts to keep it intact.

It requires no great imagination to see that the pace of resource development in Canada and the way resources are utilized would take a radically different course if they were subject to a plan designed to meet the needs of the majority of Canadians.

Every experience with planning resource use has demonstrated that planning without ownership is an exercise in futility. None other than Winston Churchill recognized this principle. When he was first Lord of the Admiralty, shortly before the outbreak of World War I, Churchill decided to convert the British navy from coal to oil. Britain had no oil, but a British company, the Anglo-Persian Oil Company, had obtained a huge concession in Persia (now Iran). Churchill induced the British government to invest 2 million pounds in this company in exchange for majority ownership. To this day, the British government has held onto its stock in

---

* Some can be recollected and recycled, of course, but at costs which are steep, if not prohibitive.

the company, now called British Petroleum. Churchill was aware that if the company had attempted to raise the capital in the money market, it was likely that American and/or German interests would buy its shares. Despite his devotion to free enterprise, he understood that "we [Britain] must become the owners ... at the source of at least a portion of the supply of national oil which we require."[36] Government ownership was the only vehicle that could assure British control at the time and he therefore became its leading proponent.

The U.S.A. has similarly showed no hesitation in using its ownership of oil resources to shape world politics. In this case, government ownership was not required, but government support was in ample evidence. An example that may be cited occurred in the era of the Marshall Plan. Oil was the single largest expenditure of the Marshall Plan. The U.S. granted the European countries millions of dollars to import oil from U.S.-owned companies in the Middle East, but no money whatever to finance refineries to process crude oil unless these refineries were American-owned. This policy not only gave the U.S. internationals a decided advantage over Shell and British Petroleum in the European markets, it also assured, or so it seemed at the time, U.S. hegemony over Europe. Having encouraged Europe to shift from a coal-based to an oil-based economy, with the oil coming from U.S. companies in the Middle East, the United States had in its possession an economic weapon of considerable power.[37]

The point of both of these examples is, of course, that ownership confers power, and more particularly that resources are inevitably used by their possessors as a means of influencing events in their own interests. If we wish our energy resources to be used to suit our needs and priorities, we will have to face the fact that we must take possession of them. This can mean nothing else than taking them into public ownership. Under the British North American Act, most of our resources are already part of the public domain. They have been leased out to companies for private exploitation, but their ownership has never been alienated. What alone is privately owned is the structures that have been built and the equipment that has been purchased to extract and refine the resources.

Public ownership of the resource industries makes sense only as one aspect of a comprehensive industrial strategy. With resource exports phased down, resources, labour and capital can be released to expand our manufacturing and agricultural industries. Manufacturing industries, in particular, would need to be reorganized and freed of their branch-plant status to take full advantage of the comparatively low-cost energy and material supplies available for them. Massive training programs for the development of a full range of skills, including research and the development of appropriate technology, would be a necessary priority. The effort that would be required to transform Canada from a satellite economy to an economy that directly aims to meet our needs is admittedly monumental, involving the mobilization of all our potential talent and energies. Whether Canadians are prepared to undertake this task is a question that will require an answer in the course of the decades ahead.

Wants, Needs, and the "Limits to Growth"

"Growing to Beat '70" was the slogan employed by the Manitoba government to summarize its policies as the sixties were giving way to the seventies. Such expressions are unpopular today, but throughout the 1950s and 1960s rapid economic growth was enshrined as the top priority of every government in every land. Growth was universally celebrated as the solution for poverty, hunger, unemployment, inflation and all manner of woes inflicted upon mankind.

Economic texts have been purged of their most gross expressions of the growth panacea, but illustrations to the contrary still litter their pages. An example occurs in Samuelson-Scott's *Economics, Third Canadian Edition*.[38] The authors consider the possibility of automation making the labour force 30 per cent more productive. The same output can be produced by far fewer workers. If nothing else happens, there would be massive unemployment. Their answer to this program is contained in a sub-section titled "New Economics to the Rescue." The solution? Expand output by stimulating growth through new government spending or tax cuts. "By proper policy we have converted the machine from a curse to a blessing. People now enjoy 30 per cent more output without being forced into breadlines. They are not made to work shorter hours and do not have to take Monday off because the limited work has to be shared." The authors do not ask whether or not we need 30 per cent more output, or 50 per cent, or 100 per cent. It is assumed that we have unlimited capacity to consume more things and that the resource capacity of the continent and the globe is also unlimited. It is assumed that a shorter work-week is unwanted and an undesirable way to channel increased productivity, that people must experience their increased incomes in the form of the increased number of products they can buy rather than by having more time to enjoy the things that they produce as well as more time to spend with their families or in community, athletic, cultural, educational, or political activities. The only desirable solution to technological unemployment is increased output through more growth. That there may be institutional restraints which make this the only desirable solution in the context of a capitalistic economy is not mentioned by the authors.

Economic growth is also put forward as the painless solution to poverty. Poverty in its absolute sense would be eradicated overnight by a moderate redistribution of wealth and income, but this would be painful for the rich. Growth, on the other hand, channels income to the "have-nots" without penalizing the "haves." However indignant we might be over the fact that the owners and managers of Imperial Oil and the Bank of Montreal will benefit more from growth than the poor, we might be comforted if poverty were being eliminated, even if inequality were not. But there is no clear evidence that poverty is being eliminated as a consequence of general economic growth. The fact that the trickle-down process has not touched the poorest classes* has apparently made little impact among the proponents of growth. An American economist, Herman Miller, puts forward the proposition that, by the year 2000, output per-man-hour will be three times as great as it is today, with average family incomes equalling $18,000 in 1965 prices. "With this kind of leverage," he contends, "the allocation of a small additional fraction of the national income to the eradication of poverty becomes a real possibility."[39] The reallocation *today* of a large fraction of the national income to programs that aim to eradicate poverty is precluded on the grounds that the rich will not give up a significant portion of their income. Indeed, were they forced to, the incentive system upon which the capitalistic mode of production is founded would be seriously damaged. Therefore the poor must wait for their "growth dividend." On the way to the year 2000, vast amounts of resources must be absorbed in meeting the wants of the affluent. By that year the costs of food, shelter, and other basics will be so high that the economists will no doubt have to find another explanation in their tool kit as to why poverty must persist for a little while longer.

But also on the way to the year 2000, while biological needs will have remained unchanged, socially-defined needs will have expanded as fast, or faster than income. As long as people consider themselves poor when their living standards lag behind the average in their community, then with per-capita incomes twice their

---

* See "Who Benefits from Inflation," in Part VIII.

present level, 20 per cent of the population will still be living in poverty — *even if* their incomes advance along with the rest of the population. And if their real incomes grow less rapidly than the national average, the proportion of the population living in "poverty" will have increased. Evidently, growth has a tendency to increase poverty!

This conclusion, absurd by any common-sense standards, is not absurd at all by the logic of capitalist sociology. Anthropologists tell us that everyone in every civilization and society expresses a need to find acceptability and honour among peers. Different societies and different civilizations provide radically different avenues to its members for achieving acceptability and honour: religion, fighting, politics, art, and wealth are examples. It is no accident that in the capitalist society the accumulation of individual wealth and the possession of things are the most universal measures of personal rank.

The capitalist economic order, as its most aggressive proponents now insist with increasing vehemence, rests on the drive for profit. The drive for profit is necessarily a drive for expansion, the insatiable search for additional money and wealth achieved through continuous growth of the economy. Consumers cannot be allowed to lag behind in their wants and desires. They cannot be allowed to enjoy what they have. They have to be made forever dissatisfied. They are therefore prodded, teased, and conned into wanting more. If there were ever a sense of "enough", capitalism would sputter and die. An unchanged pattern of wants would not absorb the continuous increase of new consumer goods that flow off the production lines of industry each year. As the British economist Edward Mishan has written, "keep a man covetous and he may be kept running hard to the last day of his life."[40]

It is the conjuncture of rapid growth and increasingly scarce resources that defines the character of the continuing crisis that is now overtaking us. However, even the most pessimistic prophets of doom do not see an ecological catastrophe immediately ahead. What is known about existing reserves indicates that the question of finite resources does not pose the likelihood of an immediate global disaster. Even if world consumption were to rise by a phenomenal 10 per cent a year, the world would have enough coal to last for 55 years, enough conventional oil to last for 16 years, and enough natural gas to last for 17 years. The known supplies of most other minerals have somewhat greater longevity. As new reserves are discovered and the tar sands and shale oil are developed, the life-span for fossil fuels will be correspondingly lengthened. While this lengthening of the life-span will merely postpone, rather than eliminate, the day of reckoning, it buys time to make the transition to the era of nonfossil fuel — nuclear energy, solar energy, tidal power, and wind power.

The limiting factor is not the physical availability of resources. It is the cost of their development, the distribution of the burden of these costs, and the distribution of the resources themselves. The ultimate question is not a biological one, or at least it is not alone biological: it is economic, social, and political. It comes down to resource use, and finally to power. I do not intend by this to sweep away the prognosis of the ecologists. They are undoubtedly right when they say that we are not confronted today with the problem of abundance, but with that of survival. It is completely absurd to speak in terms of a "society of super-abundance" or of the abolition of wants. But the matter of survival comes down to whose survival and at what level of subsistence.

Most of the Marxists still accept the traditional view that the development of "the productive forces" is by itself positive. They are persuaded that capitalism, in the course of its development, provides a material and technological base which, when taken over, will provide the material means for a society that can function in the "realm of freedom" rather than the "realm of necessity." This view must now be discarded. For as nature is increasingly damaged in irreversible ways, the Marxist idea of a free society loses its meaning. The affluence of the over-developed industrial societies of the West, insofar as it is not a mirage for a part of the population, is the result of "a wave of plunder and privilege unparalleled in history; its victims are, on the one hand, the peoples of the Third World and, on the other, the men and women of the future." It is therefore a kind of affluence that produces unimaginable want. [41]

The ecologists, however, exaggerate the extent of the problem when they use the average per-capita consumption of resources of a U.S. citizen as a standard toward which the rest of the world is reaching. On this standard, even at today's population level, the world production of energy would be seven times as great as at present, and the thermal, atmospheric, and radioactive pollution would increase to such a degree that the consequences might well be catastrophic and the available reserves of fossil fuels would disappear. The problem with this kind of scenario is that Third World peoples do not have to come anywhere near the U.S. per-capita energy consumption to achieve comparable living standards. Per-capita energy consumption in the U.S. is more than three times that in Western Europe. Yet the American standard of living is nowhere near three times the West European. Looking at energy consumption over a longer time-frame, per-capita energy use in the

U.S. in 1925 was significantly higher than in both present-day Western Europe and the U.S.S.R. Living standards are notoriously difficult to measure, especially over time and between continents, but it is surely questionable whether they were that much higher in the U.S. in 1925 than they are almost a half-century later in the U.S.S.R. and Western Europe.

The problem with using U.S. patterns as a standard is that U.S. energy consumption is wasteful in the sense that increases in consumption do not bring equivalent increases in living standards. For example, though military expenses absorb only about 10 per cent of the U.S. Gross National Product, they use a quarter of all manufactured goods and two-fifths of the durable goods. These are energy-intensive industries. This use of energy enables the U.S. to maintain its power position in the world, but its contribution to the well-being of the majority of Americans is nil.

More so than any other country in the world, the U.S. economy is geared to the use of the automobile. Not only is this directly wasteful of energy through a high fuel consumption, but it is indirectly even more wasteful through the enormous quantities of energy used in producing the automobile itself* as well as the complementing facilities like roads, garages, parking lots, gasoline stations, and the like. In the typical North American city, the automobile absorbs a full quarter of the land space in streets, driveways, garages, parking lots, service stations, car washes, etc., whereas parks seldom occupy more than one per cent of the space. There are more registered mechanics per car than there are physicians per person. As for efficiency, on a one-lane highway, automobiles can carry a maximum of 3,600 passengers per hour while half-filled buses can carry 60,000 people per hour. Lewis Mumford reminds us that before there was any mass transit in London, 50,000 people an hour used to pass over the London Bridge on their way to work, whereas our best expressways, using far more space, cannot move more than 4,000-6,000 cars in the same length of time.[42] The waste is compounded by the proliferation of models (360) produced every year. It is questionable to what extent the sundry shapes, sizes, and styles have anything to do with increased car value. Because they contain so much gadgetry, they tend to break down more frequently and are much more costly to repair. The policy of forced obsolescence both reduces quality and increases energy consumption. But the problems caused by current reductions in automobile

---

* The U.S. automotive industry uses up over 20 per cent of steel consumed in the U.S.A., 55 per cent of the lead, 20 per cent of the natural rubber, 37 per cent of the zinc, etc., etc. (1970 Automobile Facts and Figures.)

production show that, given the North American economic and social structure, we cannot function without it.

E. L. Dale, Jr., a financial writer for the *New York Times,* asserts that the private enterprise economic system operates according to "iron laws" dominated by the law of accelerating growth in productivity and output, which cannot be halted because "the profit motive will almost always propel individual daily decisions in the direction of higher productivity."[43] Barry Commoner shows how this "iron law" has been carried to its most extreme conclusion in the U.S.A. since World War II. In industry after industry, high energy-using and pollutant-creating technologies and materials displaced older productive techniques and older products, e.g. aluminum and plastics for steel and lumber, detergents for soap. While they improved the profits to investment they added little or nothing to quality or use-values to the consumer. And their greater profitability was largely due to the fact that the costs of environmental degradation that they produced were chiefly borne not by the producers but by society as a whole in the form of "externalities" that are not caught by the price system.[44]

The over-use of the automobile, the new post-World-War-II technologies, and the overwhelming presence of the military sector illustrate a few key points that deserve to be stressed. The first is that these industries absorb far more energy and raw materials than they return in the form of use-values to the public. It would likely be possible to approach North American living standards and do so with far less pollution while utilizing one-half to one-third less energy consumption per person. The ecologists over-state their case of resource exhaustion when they project world consumption to American levels. The second point is that the energy crisis, to the extent that it is caused by this sort of waste, is essentially a social crisis.

Another strand in ecological thinking blames pollution on the personal habits of North Americans who are pictured as piggish slobs and who are exhorted to shop wisely, avoid waste, and stop cluttering the city streets and highways with orange peels, cigarette butts, and garbage. There is nothing wrong with clean-up campaigns, but the exhorters seem to forget that the ordinary worker does not dump industrial waste into the air and water. And the ordinary worker does not benefit from or demand planned obsolescence or elaborate packaging, or energy-intensive technology, or the waste that these produce. Nor is the ordinary worker responsible for the equipment and buildings that lie idle or under-utilized as a result of recession, or for the massive use of American and Canadian resources for the American war machine, or for the $25 billion of advertising in North America that bombards working-class homes and clutters the streets and highways.

Appeals to the individual cult of responsibility is part of the culture of capitalism and mirrors the capitalist organization of society itself. Rather than emphasizing the social character of the problem, and hence the social character of the solution, we are told that we are to blame and that we, as individuals, can effect basic change by "cleaning up our own act." Changing people's attitudes and behaviour is no such simple task. As R. D. Laing has pointed out, "our behaviour is a function of our experience. We act according to the way we see things . . . If our experience is destroyed, our behaviour will be destructive." While it would be absurd to insist that individuals are completely moulded, shaped, and determined by society, it would be even more absurd to argue that individuals are not significantly influenced by the institutions of that society — schools, churches, advertising, family, politics.

Just how an individual's life is shaped by the universal human condition on the one hand, and by society's particular institutional orders on the other hand, is from far a simple question. The liberal view of corporate man, and the view commonly espoused by many leftists, is helpful neither in understanding what is wrong with corporate capitalism nor in sifting through alternative remedies. Thus, imbalances between private goods and public goods are attributed to the conscious policies of individuals in large corporations rather than by the impersonal forces of the market. By focusing on personal decision-making, that is, by assigning imbalances and waste to individuals, it is alleged that the resulting distortions can be markedly reduced because individuals are after all susceptible to change. Thus Galbraith ends up assigning to his university-trained technostructure, so different from the robber barons of old, the task of delivering a sense of social responsibility to the corporations.

The populist view that corporation executives are malevolent creatures, deliberately engaged in devious practices to rob the people, is equally simplistic. Some of them are, but most are not. They are harried men driven by the necessity of each corporation to expand. Their careers depend on their success in helping their corporations grow. They must succeed or give way to others. What is rewarding behaviour within the corporate world is beyond their control. Whatever scope there may be for personal choice disappears altogether when corporations are compelled by their indebtedness and dwindling markets to devise whatever techniques are necessary to penetrate new markets and expand in old ones.

Moreover, the corporation is not the only prop on which the consumer civilization rests. No institution creates the spiritual conditions for its own existence. Advertising works not just because of its sheer quantity or because of the cleverness of the ad men. Our appetite for consumer goods is so vast because the human need to feel important, to win acceptance, to express individuality has no other equally accessible outlet. In the words of Andre Gorz, "[It is] the nature of capitalist society . . . to constrain the individual to buy back individually, as a consumer, the means of satisfaction of which the society has deprived him."[46] We have a fetish about the possession of commodities because of the way capitalist society breaks down the sense of community. An atomized public will always clamour for individual commodities. Collective needs can only be defined collectively. While there is a chance of obtaining an automobile and even a better one, there appears to be little chance, through individual pressure, of obtaining a decent public transit system. The corporation is the ultimate expression of this atomization, at the same time that it intensifies it. The last point has been expressed very well by the eminent British economist Joan Robinson:

> . . . What is it that should grow? What is national wealth? [As it appears in the official accounts] it is the volume of sales of goods and services. . . . It is what is SOLD that counts. "Productive" investment is investment that creates capacity to increase sales. Cleaning up slums, improving health and education, preserving wild country, are not counted as "productive" activities. The issue is not between what is useful to society and what is not, but between what creates a field for profitable enterprise and what does not. [47]

The point that I wish to stress, however, is that the constant renewal and recreation of consumer commodities that so shapes our experience is not due simply to the existence of a class of owners. The root of infinite consumerism is the peculiar network of social relationships between human beings created by the much broader capitalist mode of production. This system of production cannot be done away with by dispossessing private capitalists, however much their dispossession is a necessary step. A transfer of ownership leading to a more just distribution of income, which still leaves other relationships alienated, will not remove the soil from which consumerism grows. It is in precisely this sense that the capitalist mode of production continues to exist in Soviet Russia. Atomization of life and material incentives persist as the main character of social and economic organizations. Social ownership superimposed upon a capitalist mode of production does not fundamentally alter the relations between human beings and the relationship between rulers and ruled. Nor, consequently, has it altered the relationship between people and things and man and nature.

Ecology and Class

The ecologists like to speak of the "spaceship earth," a closed and global ecosystem that we overtax at our own peril. What is denied in this metaphor is any distinction between first-class passengers and second-class passengers. The image of global brotherliness carefully avoids the obvious point that some can afford to plan for growth in the "spaceship earth" and actually draw profits from the elimination of the damage that they do, while others certainly can not.

The eco-industrial complex has found a way to profit in two ways. It produces the consumer and military hardware that pollutes the environment and it is hired to repair the environment by control techniques that are financed by the public or passed on to consumers in the form of higher prices. According to the calculations of the American Council of Environmental Quality, at least a million dollars is pocketed in the course of the elimination of $3 million worth of damage to the environment. Thus the recognition of the problems that result from profit-propelled growth has served to create a new growth industry that is another source of profits for the giant corporations.

With mounting pressure from environmental groups the large corporations have found it necessary to join the ecological movement so as to be able to constrain it within acceptable limits. The advance guard of corporation executives, who see that the legitimacy of corporate capitalism is being seriously questioned from this front, are among the leading reformers.* In concert with technocrats at all levels of government — the conflicts between them are usually over timing, not substance — they actively seek the speediest solutions to specific problems — quick "technological fixes."

Citizens' groups are overwhelmingly members of the middle class, particularly young professionals, whose activities range from harmless litter-cleanup and boycotts of non-returnable bottles to more potentially explosive actions such as preventing the construction of an expressway, oil refinery, airport, or high-rise development. The urgency of the environmental issue imposes itself upon

---

* The growing role played by business in promoting ecological campaigns such as Earth Day and the liaison between business and governments are analysed in James Ridgeway, *The Politics of Ecology*, pp. 207-211.

the middle class at this time because the environmental damages that industrialization brings with it have begun to invade their life-styles. Congestion and pollution, which have been the everyday reality of the working class since the beginning of the industrial revolution, have become universalized, or nearly so. The super-rich can still escape to their mansions and private beaches and employ maidservants and chauffeurs, but for the middle class expenditures of this order are unthinkable.

On the other hand, despite the fact that industrial workers bear much of the burden of environmental damage, working-class support for liberal reform measures is sparse. The reason is simple enough. In the absence of comprehensive planning programs which can assure them of alternative employment and guarantee that their living standards would not be severely reduced, pollution abatement measures harm their material welfare. Zoning by-laws which reduce density in downtown areas force up the price of land, housing and rent. The imposition of an effluent tax or stringent abatement regulations would result in mass lay-offs in a number of industries. Besides bearing most of the unemployment effects of liberal reform, working people are hard hit by price increases when abatement costs are shifted onto consumers. Alternatively they are hit by speed-ups and stretch-outs when employers attempt to shift these costs back to workers by forcing up their productivity. The invisible social costs of private enterprise are rising immeasurably. Already they are being passed on in higher prices, rents, taxes, and deteriorating working conditions. Under these circumstances it is easy to understand that the blue-collar working class is not prepared to support environmental campaigns unless they involve measures that would directly improve their working and living conditions.

Moral appeals addressed to the people living in over-developed countries to lower their standard of living may be noble, but they are futile.* To ask the individual wage-earner to differentiate

---

* Prime Minister Trudeau is one who has lent his name to such pleas. In a speech given back in 1971 he asked why western governments "continue to worship at the temple of the gross national product without taking into account resource depletion as well as harmful environmental and social effects."

In its January 1973 report, the Science Council of Canada recommended that Canada "begin the transition from a consumer society preoccupied with resource exploitation to a conserver society engaged in more constructive endeavours." Nearly one-third of the Council's 1975 budget is earmarked for the purpose of exploring the transition to a "conserver society".

between his "real" and his "artificial" needs is to totally misunderstand the nature of the political economy of capitalism. In a society where labour is mobilized by material incentives, and motivated by invidious comparisons, where work is a means to purchase consumer satisfaction and has little or no enjoyment in itself, appeals to cut down on "artificial" needs are mischievous at best and cynical at worst. Hunger for commodities is not an expression of greed but rather an expression of emptiness. Within the context of the existing mode of production it could only be suppressed by force.

In fact, shortages — of food, land, energy, and energy-using commodities — have begun to appear. There is no question of a "just" distribution of these commodities. Shortages are being handled in the classical fashion of supply and demand, with the supply being firmly under the control of monopoly-sharing enterprises. Rationing of want through the price system ensures that the richest elements will preserve their share of what is available without any guarantees for the rest of society. While the best-organized part of the work force battles ferociously to avoid losses, the vast majority of workers, without unions to protect their living standards, face significant declines.

As the crisis persists, the process of what has been called "internal imperialism" will likely increase, along with a more aggressive practice of external imperialism. The ensuing chaos that results as organized workers attempt to protect their living standards will give rise to appeals for a more orderly management of scarcity, namely more widespread resort to the authoritarian instruments of the state. Under the aegis of corporate capitalism, the "limits to growth" leads to fascism. Among its supporters could well be the mass of unprotected workers who are easy prey for anti-union demagoguery. The proposals of the ecologists would then end up in the hands of forces and be used in ways quite unintended by their authors.

This is one scenario of "the limits to growth." It may be the one that is not far from the minds of the corporate backers of the Club of Rome. There are other scenarios, one of which is that the shock of hardship and repression after years of relative prosperity will spur socialist revolutions everywhere in the industrialized world. The likelihood of this happening depends on the degree of politicization and organization achieved over the next few decades and the extent to which it encompasses all branches of the working class. But it would be facile to count on such a development, for as Lenin once wrote:

It would be erroneous to believe . . . that revolutionary classes always have sufficient strength for the accomplishment of the overturn at the time at which the conditions of the socio-economic development have rendered the need for that overturn entirely ripe. No, human society is not arranged so rationally and so "conveniently" for its progressive elements. The need for the overturn may become ripe, but the strength of the revolutionary creators of that overturn may turn out to be inadequate for carrying it out. Under such conditions, society rots and this rotting sometimes lasts for entire decades.

Food, Famine, and the Population Explosion

In his famous *Essay on the Principles of Population* (1803), Thomas Robert Malthus wrote: "A man who is born into a world already possessed, if he cannot get subsistence from his parents on whom he has a just demand, and if society does not want his labour, has no claim of *right* to the smallest portion of food, and in fact, has no business to be where he is." Malthus opposed relief for the poor because, he pointed out, it would only encourage them to multiply, an evil to be avoided at all cost.

Virtually nobody took Malthus seriously for 175 years, but he is very much in vogue today. His philosophy, now fully embraced by the leadership of the western world, was persistently articulated by western spokesmen at the United Nations-sponsored World Food Conference in Rome. It has also been embraced by various ecologists, most notably by Paul Ehrlich and Garrett Hardin. Hardin employs the world-as-a-lifeboat analogy. He says that we should view the world as a lifeboat in which there are only so many spaces. Those in the lifeboat—mainly people in the economically advanced nations—have to decide whom they can admit without swamping the boat, and let the rest drown. "Our survival is then possible, although we shall have to guard against boarding parties. Some say they feel guilty about their good luck. My reply is simply: 'Get out and yield your place to others'." Hardin has called for an end to all aid programs. Saving lives in India and Bangladesh not only adds to world population pressures, it hurts other Indians and Bengalis. He admits that his philosophy would turn the richer countries into fortress states repelling the power of the world at their borders. "But modern warfare is so expensive only the rich nations can afford it. Terrorism against the rich countries is a possibility but we have to find operational answers to terrorism." If people shrink from these hard choices, "they had better get used to it. We just don't have what it takes to save the world." Here, only faintly masked, is barbarism.

Paul Ehrlich, somewhat less extreme in his views, calls for a consortium of the world's most powerful nations making the basic political decisions for the have-nots: "simultaneous population control, agricultural development, and where resources warrant it, industrialization of selected countries. The bedrock of this program would be population control, necessarily including migration control to prevent swamping of aided areas by the less fortunate."[48]

The idea that the superpowers could disinterestedly make these decisions in the world's best interests is too naive to warrant comment. The criteria that would be used have already been amply demonstrated. When India asked desperately for 10 million tons of grain from the U.S., Secretary of State Kissinger said they might be able to find half a million tons. Soon afterwards, the U.S. had no trouble finding grain for Syria, which it wanted to help for strategic reasons. Of the $1 billion worth of U.S. food that was shipped abroad, the National Security Council insisted that almost half should go to bolster the military strength of Cambodia and South Vietnam. Or to take yet another example, three days before President Salvadore Allende of Chile was overthrown and killed, his government charged that the United States had refused to sell it vitally needed supplies of wheat *for rash.* Less than a month after the coup, the U.S. government approved a credit sale of wheat to the junta in an amount eight times the total commodity credit offered to Chile in the Allende years.[49]

The theories of Malthus and his apostles have repeatedly been proven wrong by the tremendous advances in agricultural technology. Roger Revelle, director of the Centre for Population Studies at Harvard, has noted that the world's population increased by less than 50 per cent between 1951 and 1971, while world production of cereal grain, the main food staple, more than doubled, a rise of cereal supplies per person of 40 per cent over the 20-year period.[50] This gain in food supplies was not evenly distributed. More than half of it was absorbed by the rich countries which account for 30 per cent of the population. But the problem has less to do with the "population bomb" than with over-fill in the rich nations and the low level of agricultural productivity, employment, and industrial development in the Third World. Revelle is not one who believes in theory of "overpopulation" as the primary cause of food shortages in the Third World. He believes that by increasing the land area under cultivation and by applying technology and intensive labour "a diet based on 4000 to 5000 kilocalories* of edible plant material

---

* A kilocalorie is the same as a large calorie. The minimum daily caloric intake advised by the U.N. Food and Agriculture Organization is 2,300.

could be provided for between 38 and 48 billion people, between 10 and 13 times the present population of the earth."

If India and Bangladesh and Nigerian farmers obtained the same yield per acre as Japanese farmers, their rice production would jump more than three-fold; corn yields in Thailand and Brazil are less than one-third those of the United States. Brazil, by doubling its present cultivated area, a possible feat, could produce an additional 22 million tons of grain even if its current low yields were not improved. Most of the land in Latin America is owned by a tiny aristocracy, and significant portions of it remain uncultivated. Colonialism converted most of Africa, Asia, and Latin America into one-crop export-oriented economies. The best land and most agricultural investment is still being used to grow bananas, coffee, peanuts, and other such foods and delicacies for the export market. In some instances poor nations export food that is needed at home. More meat is being produced in Central America than ever before; it seems, however, to be ending up in McDonald hamburgers more than in the stomachs of Latin Americans. For example, a recent 40 per cent rise in meat production in Guatemala was accompanied by a 6 per cent decline in the average meat consumption of Guatemalans.[51] A 92 per cent increase in Costa Rica was accompanied by a 26 per cent decline in per capita consumption.

This pattern of imposed development, justified by the economists under the guise of the "law of comparative advantage", may be advantageous for the United Fruit Company, but it can hardly be said to serve the best interests of Third World peasants and workers who are forced to depend on imports for much of their daily food. There is no law of comparative international efficiency that can explain these perverse results. Rather, they are reflections of the laws of international power that remove control over the use of local and national resources from the local population to metropolitan enterprises. This has been the driving force of the relations between rich and poor countries since the dawn of Western colonialism. The economic devices and the political forms of imperialism have altered over the years, but the substance of the relationship — the extraction of wealth by the metropolitan regions while the poor countries themselves become ever poorer and underdeveloped — has remained the same. There is no reason to believe that, in the absence of basic structural changes in both metropolitan and hinterland economies, things will be any different in the future.

Not much imagination is required to discover the reasons behind the U.S.A.'s frenetic efforts to export birth control to the countries of the Third World. It has less to do with international charity than with the fear that the white races will soon be a small minority when compared with the rest of the world and that population size can become a source of political and military power. On the other hand it would be wrong to dismiss all arguments for family planning as simply an imperialist trick whose purpose is to perpetuate cultural genocide among the coloured races. Statements like the following from Fidel Castro substitute irrational hopes for the none too disguised racism of the imperialist nations.

> In certain countries they are saying that only birth control provides a solution to the problem. Only capitalists, the exploiters, can speak like that; for no one who in conscience of what man can achieve with the help of technology and science will wish to set a limit to the number of human beings who can live on the earth. . . . *We shall never be too numerous,* however, many of us there are, if only we all together place our efforts and our intelligence at the service of mankind, and mankind which will be freed from the exploitation of man by man.[52]

While conceding that overpopulation is not the primary problem and that birth control by itself does not provide the entire answer, such a view is based more on wishful thinking than a materialist analysis of possibilities and limits.

The question of overpopulation is more complicated than the statistics of catastrophic growth allow for. Limitations of space permit only a few observations. One is that, in terms of present food intake, a cogent case can be made that if there is an overpopulation problem it lies in North America more than it does in the Third World. With our 6 per cent of the world's population we consume over 30 per cent of the world's food. While Indians on the average consume about 7 pounds of meat per person per year, the Japanese and Chinese 25-50 pounds, the Russians about 80 pounds and the west Europeans about 110 pounds, Canadians and Americans consume nearly 200 pounds each. Grain consumption also reflects our rich diets. It is over four times as high per person here as it is in the Third World, and more than 80 per cent of it is first fed to the animals from which we get our meat, poultry, eggs, and dairy products. With our livestock feeding methods, it takes about three pounds of grain to produce one pound of pork, and ten for one of beef. The grains and high protein supplements fed to Canadian and American cattle, pigs, and poultry would go a long way to alleviate hunger among people around the world. The shame of this incredible waste is that much of it is unnecessary. Cattle and sheep need not be fed the same food as people. They can be raised on forage unsuitable for human consumption grown on land unsuitable for human crops. But agriculture, like other economic activities, is not governed by human needs, or by the principles of maximizing the use of valuable resources like soil, water, and grain.

Given the low price of feed-grains and protein supplements, the meat, dairy, and poultry businesses found that they could maximize their profits by using the mixtures that would produce the heaviest animals in the shortest time.

Our method of agriculture not only wastes food resources, it is a gluttonous consumer of energy. The accompanying table gives a breakdown of where the energy is used between the farm and the dinner table.

Table 18
Food Energy Budget (1963)

Activity	% of Energy Consumed
Agriculture	18.3
Food processing	32.9
Transportation	2.4
Wholesale and Retail Trade	15.9
Home (storage and cooking)	30.5

Source: Eric Hirst, *National History*. Reprinted in P. Ehrlich, *The End of Affluence*, p. 199

Widespread use of synthetic fertilizers is the greatest single drain of energy in agricultural production. Yet a superior natural fertilizer exists in abundance — the sewage from livestock feedlots and human sewage, most of which is dumped into our rivers. Windmills, a form of free energy, could be used to supply power for irrigation and to meet the electrical needs of farmers. Processed foods use three times as much energy as fresh foods. They are less nutritious and usually more expensive and they are more often wrapped in energy- and resource-absorbing packaging. The typical supermarket store is a lumbering over-sized inefficient mausoleum that stocks 8,000 to 12,000 different food items, most of which duplicate each other in every respect except the packaging — and displays them in acres of open freezer and refrigerator cases that waste enormous amounts of energy. The excess capacity of these supermarkets alone costs the consumer about 4c on the food dollar; while the luxurious displays, lighting effects, and other comforts cost another 3c on the food dollar.[53] Individual transport of food from the supermarket to the home is yet another waste of valuable energy. Carpool shopping or a revival of grocery-store delivery services are obvious solutions.

By this brief description of our eating habits, I mean no harangue about the inherent piggishness of human kind. It is well to recall here Barry Commoner's discovery that in terms of caloric intake, just as in terms of household space and clothing, we are consuming little more than we were 25 years ago.* We are consuming differently, and this has more to do with the imperatives of profit-making than with gluttony.

As regards the prophets of a population armageddon, Commoner advises that "the scientific evidence regarding the *future* course of world population is by no means unambiguous or conclusive."[54] There is much evidence that confirms this statement. For example in an increasing number of poor countries birth rates have dropped off sharply despite relatively low per-capita income and despite the absence or relative newness of family planning programs. Examination of countries like China, Sri Lanka (formerly Ceylon), Cuba, South Korea, and North Korea suggests a common factor. In each of these countries a large portion of the population has gained access to education, health, food and employment — to a far greater degree than in most poor countries or in most western countries during comparative periods of development. The latter point is important in view of the common practice of extrapolating onto present population levels future levels based on past historical experience.

Fertility levels fall as education levels rise. In a number of societies, the attainment of literacy brings with it a sharp decline in fertility. Several studies show that as women acquire literacy they reduce their number of children by one-third. In Chile, for example, the average number of children born to a woman with no education is 4.9 while the average number born to a woman with just an elementary education is 1.3.[55] Birth rates also tend to decline as life expectancy rises and infant mortality rates decline. The provision of adequate health services in rural areas of Korea, Sri Lanka, Cuba, and China has drastically reduced infant mortality to half the rate in other poor countries and added several additional years to life expectancy. Parents generally wish to ensure the survival of at least one son to care for them in their old age and to carry on the family name. Where a woman must bear six or more children to be certain that one son survives to adulthood, the birth rate is bound to be extraordinary. On the other hand, where death rates are low and declining and life expectancy approaches 50 years, studies indicate that each additional reduction in the death rate leads to a dramatic decline in the birth rate and a slower over-all population growth. Similarly an assured and widely distributed food supply helps to reduce birth rates. "It is no coincidence that virtually all well-fed societies have low fertility, and poorly fed societies

---

* "Total calories actually declined somewhat, from about 3,380 per person per day in 1946 to about 3,250 per person per day in 1968 . . . Protein available [also] represents a slight decline from 1946 to 1968." (B. Commoner, *Closing of the Circle*, p. 134.)

have high fertility . . . Where malnutrition is widespread, it is virtually impossible to achieve low infant mortality rates."[56] Finally, the absence of full-time employment opportunities* prohibits the economy from producing at a level that can support full-fledged educational and health facilities and guaranteed adequate food supplies.

Ecology In China

While I have a tendency to be naturally suspicious of the enthusiastic reports of people who, upon returning from a visit to the People's Republic of China, extol the virtues of that country in a manner akin to a new religious faith, the near-universal consensus that Mao's China has conquered the population and food problem cannot be easily dismissed. The Chinese appear to be taking care of their people using a very small proportion of world-resource consumption. China is about the same size as Canada. Only 10 per cent of her land can be farmed, but in most years the Chinese are able to draw enough food from this soil to feed 800 million people, about one-fifth of the world's population. Despite periodic natural disasters, most notably in the years 1959 to 1961, there has never been even a hint of famine. While the population has gone from 500 million in the early 1950s to today's approximately 800 million, a 60 per cent increase, food production has more than doubled. According to the Chinese this bears out the truth of Mao's saying that "revolution plus production can solve the problem of feeding the population."[57]

The American author Lester Brown, an internationally respected authority on agricultural development, offers some explanations for the Chinese success:

> The planned obsolescence of everything from fashions to automobiles built into economic systems in the more affluent nations does not exist in China. A well-developed public transportation system combined with the extensive use of bicycles provides effective personal mobility without the tremendous environmental, mineral, and energy costs of an automobile-based transport system. Through the direct consumption of soybeans and reliance on pork and poultry to the almost total exclusion of beef and dairy products, China has achieved a remarkably high level of nutrition for a nation of 800 million people with a per capita income of perhaps $160 a year.

---

* In Latin America, for example, the real unemployment rate varies from 20 per cent in some countries to over 50 per cent in others.

Unlike many developing countries now experiencing rising levels of unemployment as a result of the postwar population explosion, China has harnessed the energies of its people to undertake some of the most extensive public works projects in human history. Many of these have centered on the development and conservation of water resources. More recently, human labor has been mobilized on a large scale to cope with environmental problems. Millions have participated in projects designed to reforest land that has been denuded over the centuries.[58]

The Chinese have not rejected growth. They have tailored it to meet the needs of the people using a minimum of resources and spreading industry throughout the country rather than intensifying urbanization. This is being accomplished by encouraging industrial self-sufficiency in rural areas and the cultivation of food around urban areas. City workers regularly aid in farm work, and use waste and old materials from nearby industries to help build industry workshops in rural communes.

In what follows, as I have no first-hand knowledge of the Chinese approach, I have drawn upon the observations of others and the accounts of the Chinese themselves.

The use of urban sewage for irrigation and fertilization is well advanced over the practices in other countries. The city of Changchun in northern China, for instance, built a 10-kilometre-long canal which brings 52,000 tons of sewage water from the city's factories and living quarters to drain off and irrigate the cropland of a nearby commune which saves a total of about 3,000 tons of chemical fertilizer a year. [59] Water conservation has been given notable attention by the Chinese. A phenomenal 60 per cent of their cultivated land is now being irrigated. They now have more than 2,000 large and medium-sized reservoirs. Power irrigation and drainable capacity totals more than 30 million horsepower, about four times that of 1965, the year preceding the Great Cultural Revolution. In the same period, the number of power-pump wells has risen from 100,000 to 1,300,000. It is said that every winter and spring, tens of millions of people work on building water conservation projects and removing millions of metres of earth and stone.

The Huai, Yellow and Haiho Rivers, the three most troublesome, have been harnessed according to an overall plan. One-third of China's population and more than one-third of its arable land are to be found in the drainage basins of these rivers. An endless procession of droughts and floods accompanied the history of reactionary rule in China. Prior to liberation, there were no less than 1,029 serious floods and 1,056 serious droughts in about 2,000 years. When the Yellow River breached its dykes in

1933, it flooded 11,000 square kilometres and inflicted sufferings on some 3.6 million people. When drought struck five provinces in north China in 1920, it brought widespread starvation, directly affected 20 million people, of whom half a million died. . . . Today these rivers which wreaked so much past havoc have been tamed to serve industry and agriculture. Once known as "China's Sorrow," the Yellow River has been made safe for the past quarter century without once breaching its banks thanks to the work put into protecting the dykes against savage torrents. Its waters are being led in a planned way to irrigate fields.[60]

The Chinese success in eliminating the age-long problem of famine is not due only to raising production levels. Local flooding and droughts still occur, and the national disaster that struck the country in 1959 was the worst in recent recorded history. By carefully managing their trade balance, they have been able to build up foreign reserves to purchase grain on occasion. They also keep on hand a large supply of grain reserves to supplement the production of disaster-prone areas. But more important than these measures is the revolutionary change in distribution methods they have introduced, whereby grain surpluses from some regions can be quickly transported to other regions that face local flooding and droughts. In past eras these regions would have suffered certain famine. According to their own accounts:

Supplying relief grain to areas stricken by natural calamities was one of the most serious social problems which, throughout China's past history, the ruling classes of successive dynasties were unable to cope with. Though most of the harvests in the 25 years since the founding of New China have been good, there were setbacks in some years resulting from serious natural disasters. Because of China's vast expanse and complex geographical conditions, even in a bumper harvest year drops in output were inevitable in a few areas affected by bad weather. The Party and the People's Government always show great concern for production and the people's livelihood, and they see to it that those in the afflicted areas get enough food. During China's First Five-Year Plan (1953-57), the state provided such areas with 15 million tons of grain. When the worst flood in a century occurred in the Yangtze River valley, the state helped the people in the stricken areas tide over their difficulties in production and everyday life by sending in five million tons of grain from over 20 provinces and regions, including northernmost Heilungkiang, southernmost Kwangtung and Szechuan in the southwest. The people said: "This is the biggest flood in a century, but we have the best government in China's history." The provinces of Hopei, Shantung and Honan, prone to natural disasters over the centuries, received state grain every year until they became self-sufficient. Over ten million tons of grain were sent to Hopei Province alone during 1949-67, with all freight costs borne by the state. This fully demonstrates the spirit of "co-ordinating the efforts of the whole nation as in a chess game" and demonstrates the superiority of the socialist system.[61]

Balance is clearly a motivating principle of Chinese development. One example is the industrial city of Shenyang in Northeast China. A few years ago, as many as 17 or 18 provinces were required to supply Shenyang with grains and vegetables. In accordance with the Chinese view of balanced development between city and countryside, agriculture and industry, workers and peasants, Shenyang set out to become self-reliant in agriculture, rather than extending the specialization of industry. The consequence was increased over-all production. While achieving self-sufficiency in grain and vegetables, the city increased the area under cultivation by three times from 1966 to 1970.[62]

The Chinese view the question of population and food supply not simply as an economic or engineering one, but also as a political one. Evidently that does not mean chanting the words of Mao Tse Tung, but mobilizing the energies and resourcefulness of the whole population to conquer famine, disease, malnutrition, and illiteracy and relentless propagandizing on the advantages of birth control. Over-population is regarded as a serious problem but not the primary problem. "Our government has always advocated family planning, and the publicity, education and other necessary measures adopted over the years have begun to produce some effects. [But] it is wholly groundless to think that population growth in itself will bring about pollution and damage of the environment and give rise to poverty and backwardness."[63]

This balanced perspective on population is further elaborated in a recent issue of the *Peking Review:*

Of all things in the world, people are the most precious. Once the people become masters of their own destiny, every miracle can be performed. As working people, human beings are first of all producers and then consumers . . .

China pursues a policy of developing its national economy in a planned way, including the policy of planned population growth. We do not approve of anarchy either in material production or in human reproduction.

Man should control himself as well as nature. In order to realize planned population growth, what we are doing is, on the basis of energetically developing production and improving the people's living standards, to develop medical and health services throughout the rural and urban areas and strengthen our work in maternity and child-care, so as to reduce the mortality rate on the one hand and regulate the birth rate by birth planning on the other.

What we mean by birth planning is not just practising birth control, but taking different measures in the light of different circumstances. In densely populated areas where the birth rate is high, marriage at later age and birth control are advocated. However, active medical treatment is provided for those suffering from sterility.[64]

In his profoundly pessimistic *Inquiry Into the Human Prospect*, the renowned author Robert Heilbroner predicts that "the torrent of human growth" will produce intolerable social strains on the peoples of the Third World and hideous individual costs. He can see only two outcomes, neither of which he finds palatable. One is "the descent of large portions of the underdeveloped world into steadily worsening social order marked by shorter life expectancies, further stunting of physical and mental capabilities and political apathy intermingled with riots and pillaging when crops fail." These countries will be ruled over by dictatorial regimes serving the interest of the small upper class while repressing the rest of the people into a state of powerlessness and hopeless submission. Indeed, this outcome is already beginning to emerge on the African and Asian continents.

The second outcome visualized by Heilbroner is the emergence of governments "capable of halting the descent into hell." The source of Heilbroner's misgivings about such governments is that they will not stop at birth control. "A reorganization of agriculture, both technically and socially, the provision of employment by massive public works, and above all the resurrection of hope in a demoralized and apathetic people are logical next steps for any regime that is able to bring about social changes so fundamental as limitations in family size." This statement reveals more about Heilbroner's surprising lack of understanding of effective birth control than about the process of social and economic development, a subject about which he has written profoundly in the past.[65] Forced birth control, short of compulsory sterilization, simply does not work. It seems obvious that, to be effective, birth control must be *combined* with the very changes he predicts as the "logical next steps." A demoralized, apathetic, unhealthy, and insecure people will not practise birth control. To be effective, birth control must flow from their real situation and from their understanding of its use and necessity.

"The problem," as Heilbroner sees it, is that such changes "are likely to require a revolutionary government, not only because they will incur the opposition of those who benefit from the existing organization of society, but also because only a revolutionary government is apt to have the determination to ram many needed changes, including birth control itself, down the throats of an uncomprehending and perhaps resistive peasantry."[66]

This statement again reveals a shallow understanding of the revolutionary process. Changes of this order certainly cannot be brought about via the parliamentary system. But neither can they be simply "rammed down the throats of an uncomprehending" or resistant peasantry. If China is a prototype of the kind of regime Heilbroner is referring to he has, according to my reading of the literature, totally misunderstood its essential character. Contrary to ramming changes "down the throats of an uncomprehending and perhaps resistive peasantry," the revolutionary government of China stresses its very opposite: widespread and active participation and discussion at all levels of decision-making; breaking down of specialization, and dismantling of remote bureaucracies.

The principles of Maoist economic development have been elaborated by Professor John Gurley of Stanford University, a former president of the American Economic Association.[67] There are three basic principles. The first is that development must be egalitarian. According to this principle, development is not worth much unless everyone rises together. No one is to be left behind, either economically or culturally. Attached to this principle is the belief that rapid development is not likely to occur *unless* everyone rises together — a rejection of the trickle-down process. While capitalism builds on the "best" — hires the best and most skilled workers, locates its factories in the most profitable centres, devotes most of its educational resources to the best prepared students, etc., etc., — the Chinese way, while seeking material security, in numerous ways builds on "the worst." Experts must take into account the views of workers and peasants; new plants are located in rural areas; the educational system is oriented to the disadvantaged; new products are produced domestically rather than being imported more cheaply. According to Maoist belief, the massive effort spent on building on the basis of "the worst," leaving nobody behind, will eventually pay off not only by enormously raising labour productivity, but in creating a society of men and women who are able to respond intelligently to the world around them and who come to understand that they can best help themselves and achieve happiness by helping others.

The second principle is that economic development can be best promoted by breaking down specialization, by undermining the growth of bureaucracies, experts, and technicians who have a tendency to command change rather than generate change from the active participation of the mass of people. According to this principle, people learn best by doing: ". . . only through personal participation in the practical struggle to change reality can you uncover the essence of that thing or class of things and comprehend them. . . . If you want knowledge, you must take part in the practice of changing reality. . . ."[68] When people actively participate in decision-making, "dare to do" new things, learn to reason things out and become good at presenting their ideas, when they criticize others and themselves, in short when they are mobilized and aroused and taking conscious actions — then "the socialist initiative latent in the masses [will] burst out with volcanic force and a rapid change [will take] place in production."[69]

The third principle is that each person should be devoted to "serving the people" rather than reaching out with "grasping hands everywhere to seek fame, material gain, power, position and limelight."[70] It is believed that a person who is selfish will resist criticism and suggestions and is likely to become an elitist. That is why the Chinese are de-emphasizing material incentives.

While these are only principles, they are more than mere guidelines. They comprise the basic values that affect the organization of economic and cultural activity in China today. And while there is always a tendency to backslide and for bureaucratic methods to emerge* so that the practice can not possibly conform everywhere and always to these principles, the revolution that Heilbroner is apprehensive about appears to me to be not only a way out of the dilemma he so elegantly describes, but also the embryo of a society that many people everywhere would find desirable. John Gurley's evaluation of the past twenty years concludes that "Communist China is certainly not a paradise, but it is now engaged in perhaps the most interesting economic and social experiment ever

---

* Mao has observed that even under a socialist regime there is a "selfish spontaneous tendency towards capitalism." Karl Marx suggested the reason for this over a hundred years ago: "the tradition of all the dead generations weighs like a nightmare on the brain of the living. And just when they seem engaged in revolutionizing themselves and things, in creating something that has never yet existed, precisely in such periods of revolutionary crisis they anxiously conjure up the spirit of the past to their service. . ." (Marx and Engels, *Selected Works* Vol. I, p. 398.) Seeing that the leadership of the U.S.S.R had become the captive of "the traditions of dead generations" in their drive to catch up with the West and fearing the same outcome in China, Mao Tse Tung launched the Cultural Revolution. But he was moved to emphasize that "the present Cultural Revolution is only the first; there will inevitably be many more in the future." *(Peking Review,* September 29, 1969.)

attempted, in which tremendous efforts are being made to achieve an egalitarian development, an industrial development without dehumanization, one that involves everyone and affects everyone."[71]

VII / The Future of Democratic Capitalism: Lessons from Europe

The United States is widely recognized as the linchpin in the political economy of world capitalism. Not only the future of Canada but also those of Europe, Japan, and the lesser states of Asia and Africa and Latin America are tied in lesser or greater degrees to the health and sickness of the American economy, to the economic policies set down in Washington and to the decisions made in the board rooms of American multinational corporations. Yet each country has its own place in the tottering world of monopoly capitalism. Each has its own historic and recent past, each has its own peculiar economic and social structure, and therefore each will experience the crisis differently and have its own response to it. While I am unable to provide a full description and a detailed analysis of these responses and their consequences, it seems important to attempt a broad panorama of some of them as they appear to be developing outside North America.

The Europe of the eighteenth century was swept up by an immense optimism born of the dynamic potential of industrial technology and of democratic aspirations. No one voiced it more enthusiastically than the philosopher-historian Condorcet: "There is no limit set to the perfecting of the powers of man. The progress of this perfectionability, henceforth independent of any power that might wish to stop it, has no other limit than the duration of the globe upon which nature has placed us."[1] Confidence in the forces of technology and democracy waned in the nineteenth century, but it was a century of vigorous expansion that fairly easily deflected the new-found doubts. It was finally the cataclysmic events of the first half of the twentieth century that brought an end to European optimism. In the words of Robert Heilbroner:

> From 1914 through 1945 Europe experienced a compression of horror without parallel in history: the carnage of the First World War, the exhaustion of the Depression, the agonizing descent of Germany into its fascist nightmare, the suicide of Spain, the humiliation of Italy, the French decay, the English decline — and finally the culminating fury of World War II. Before the cumulative tragedy of these years all optimistic views failed. Indeed the obvious question was no longer whether the forces of technology, democracy, and capitalism were the agents of a promising future, but the degree to which they should be held responsible for the unspeakably malevolent outcome of the past.[2]

Until recently, optimism in the United States emerged unscathed from these miscarriages of hope. Geographically isolated, materially independent, unburdened by the weight of a feudal past, American soil gave full vent to the historical forces of technology, democracy and capitalism. Only the Great Depression gave cause for doubt. But with the return to a sustained period of prosperity unprecedented in its duration, the Great Depression could be easily treated as a momentary aberration that would never again be repeated.

The remarkable recovery of Western Europe after World War II gave rise to new optimism. It was destined to be short-lived. And the pall of gloom that has now spread over Europe has also cast its shadow over North America.

Writing from Paris, *New York Times* columnist C. L. Sulzberger drew together some of the evidence that illustrates the symptoms of crisis:

> We appear to be on or over the brink of a collapse like that of the 1930s. France, traditionally Europe's most prosperous land, has more unemployment than any time since World War II and

work stoppages ripple across the country. England is flat broke, floundering economically and caught in an endless Irish conflict, last battle of the seventeenth-century religious wars.

Italy is mired in chaos. Portugal hovers on the edge of tumult and Spain may soon approach a similar border when Generalissimo Franco dies. Japan's dynamism shows signs of dissolving like a wet noodle; South Asia is disintegrating; much of Africa starves; and the richest oil sheiks have accumulated so much money that they don't know even how to budget it.

Sulzberger added that "it is considered axiomatic by many so-called experts that no democracy can for long survive an inflation rate exceeding 20 per cent."[3]

In the spring of 1974, the *Financial Times* listed no fewer than twenty countries (excluding Latin America, the Middle East, and Africa) which were "politically unstable." In every case the basis of instability, it suggested, was economic. Depending on how you count the musical chairs of Italian politics, there were nine or ten changes of government leadership in Europe and Japan in 1974, and election winners have prevailed by only the narrowest of margins or, as in Britain, Denmark, Germany, Norway, and Sweden, had to form governments without absolute parliamentary majorities. As one writer put it, "If there is a political equivalent of a nervous breakdown, Europe is in the midst of it."[4]

Until the early 1960s, most of Europe was preoccupied with reconstruction, industrial transformation and massive population shifts from rural to urban areas. These changes made possible and necessary a sharp elevation of educational standards. There was a general breakdown of old institutions and old attitudes and the inevitable competition among new ones. The very rapidity of change was bound to create social tensions and conflict among contending classes. The restiveness that has characterized much of Europe since the late 1960s reflects the large and growing presence of a new generation that has not known war, depressions, or catastrophic inflation and that is unmoved by traditional appeals to nationalism and national harmony. Young workers and students have come to reject traditional hierarchical arrangements and to demand a more equalitarian and libertarian organization of society, demands that are not easily co-opted within a capitalist order. The widespread outbreak of wildcat strikes reflect the wide gap that exists between workers of the new generation and the older men who constitute the leadership of the unions.

While European capitalism has made a remarkable recovery since the war, to the point where it is challenging American hegemony, growth has been very uneven. Per-capita income exceeds $5,000 a year in Hamburg while in western Ireland and southern Italy it is less than $1,000. Some countries have remained strong throughout the current crisis while others face possible insolvency. This unevenness threatens the future of the European Common Market. Weak nations are inclined to opt for protectionist measures and the strong ones are hesitant to bail them out. The "miracle" days are over in Western Europe. Efforts at national planning have proven to be only marginally effective, and supranational planning is non-existent. As the accounts of development in Great Britain, Italy, France, and the European Common Market show, the future of democratic capitalism in Europe is precarious.

Great Britain

"The 'Sicily of the North Sea' or the 'Pakistan of Europe' — as the British have been referring to their island of late — is sinking into her deepest post-war recession against a background of apprehension, despondency and resignation," wrote the *New York Times'* Clyde Farnsworth reporting from London.[5] Over the past ten years the increase in real take-home pay (adjusted for inflation and taxes) has been only 11 per cent for the average worker. Living standards dropped 5 per cent in 1974. Most estimates suggested a further 10 per cent cut in the following year or 18 months. The question, it appears, was not whether or not this would happen, but how the losses should be distributed. As seen by *The Nation* magazine's London correspondent, Raymond Williams, the Labour government's Social Contract with the unions was "the last real chance for capitalist democracy in Britain."[6] It was a formula to cut real personal wages in return for an increased social wage — food, fuel, and housing subsidies and welfare benefits. The cut in money wages was meant to improve the competitiveness of British industry along with increased industrial investment by direct state involvement and control.

While the Trades Union Council, Britain's federation of unions, accepted the Social Contract, it could do nothing to restrain its member unions. In its first year wage increases averaged 30 per cent, well above the bounds set by the Social Contract. With Britain's version of the consumer price index rising by 48 per cent between March and May of 1975 and unemployment growing to a million, the Social Contract was all but dead.

Matters came to a head in July when Chancellor of the Exchequer Denis Healey announced the government's policy of drastically cutting inflation to 10 per cent over the next 12 months. There was something ironic in this pronouncement, for a few hours earlier the Prime Minister, Harold Wilson, had told an audience at a farm show that "we reject panic solutions. We reject the advice of those who want to see us thrashing about wildly for some melodramatic solution which would not work." Wilson was apparently unaware that while he was speaking about the need to avoid panic solutions, the governor of the Bank of England was issuing Healey an ultimatum to save the pound. It stood at 29 per cent below the value fixed by agreement with Britain's main trading partners at the end of 1971. Large-scale withdrawal of funds by nervous Arab depositors had caused a sudden and major drop in the value of the pound. Once again British capital called upon a Labour government to shore up its weakening position. Under similar circumstances in 1966 Wilson froze wages and scrapped socialist policies for orthodox treasury deflation and lost the next election. This time, Labour's controversial Industry Bill, which had vast powers to take over firms and to set investment and production targets, was set aside. The wage policy, lifted holus-bolus from the Liberal Party's election manifesto, would limit wage increases to 10 per cent and forbid firms to hand on in higher prices any wage-settlement costs above 10 per cent. This policy was calculated to reduce the real value of the British worker's pay cheque by at least 5 per cent over the year, while shoring up the dwindling profits of British capitalists. Cash ceilings on public sector wage bills, another part of the Labour program, would shift the brunt of inflationary settlements onto employment. Unemployment was calculated to rise to 1.5 million by the spring of 1976.

Indicative of the point of the exercise, the London stock market rejoiced at the announcement of the new program. The *Financial Times* index rose a phenomenal 8 per cent on the day it was announced. *The Economist* magazine titled one of its lead articles "Hey Chaps, Denis is one of us." The last time Labour imposed wage controls on British workers, it cost them the government. When the Conservatives moved to statutory wage control in November 1972 it led to a confrontation with striking coal miners, the three-day week for industry, and ultimately to a general election which the Conservatives also lost. The crisis of the British economy is obviously a long-standing one. It is a crisis of British capitalism challenged by an increasingly aggressive working class.

Before the advent of Keynesian economics, British income was regulated by the so-called foreign trade multiplier — which means that output and employment tended to be at the level at which the demand for imports (which varies with the level of domestic income) was equal to the demand for British exports. Income and employment were allowed to fluctuate to ensure a continual external balance between imports and exports. With post-war governments all obeying the prescriptions of the Keynesian revolution, the level of domestic income was managed so as to achieve continuous full employment levels. The effect of the new system was to convert the chronic pre-war unemployment problem into a chronic post-war balance of payments problem.

What underlies Britain's post-war stagnation is the slow growth of industrial exports, an inability to maintain its share of growing world trade. This in turn can be traced to the weak competitive position of British industry, with an average annual rate of growth in productivity of only 2.6 percent between 1950 and 1970 compared to rates of 5.6 percent for France, 4.7 percent for Germany, and 6.9 percent for Italy. While Germany was allocating from 23 to 27 percent of its GNP to investment, France 20 to 26 percent and Japan 30 to 35 percent, Britain was only allocating 16 to 18 percent in the same period (1960-1972). Because of the low rate of investment, British plant capacity is inadequate. The result is a flood of imports whenever there is a business upswing. For example, when the Tory government promoted consumer spending in 1972, the market share of imported cars shot up from 8 per cent to 25 per cent.

These underlying economic weaknesses have caused Great Britain to tumble from fifth place among the twelve leading capitalist nations in 1958 to eleventh place by 1973, measured in terms of per-capita income.

Historically, home-based industrial capitalism has not been the dominant force within the British ruling class. Economic pre-eminence has been in the hands of finance capital, symbolized by and centred in the City of London. The policies of Tory governments have been shaped by its needs. This was shown in the return to the gold standard after World War I to maintain the value of the pound, with disastrous effects on domestic industry and exports. Maintenance of an inflated exchange rate after 1945 again protected British investment abroad and crippled industrial exports. The maintenance of military forces in East Asia and the Arab Gulf at a cost vastly beyond Britain's financial capacity and an alliance not with Europe but with the United States, the only possible military protector of British foreign investments, are other expressions of a policy suited to the needs of financial capitalists at the expense of industry.

It was Britain's burgeoning empire that gave pre-eminence to the City of London over the industrial bourgeoisie. But Britain's dominant role in the world economy also had profound implications for the whole fabric of British society. The rewards of empire allowed British capital to make concessions to a well-organized working class which helped dampen class conflict. It also assured an uninterrupted parliamentary democracy between the two world wars when other capitalist regimes were forced to resort to military and Fascist solutions to maintain their rule.

By the turn of the century, precisely because of its weak home base, Britain did not have the capacity to defend its markets against the encroachments of rival nations — Germany, Japan, and most notably, the U.S.A. The wreckage of World War I forced the British to divest themselves of major portions of their portfolio Empire. After 1945 they could no longer afford to sustain a foreign military system that far exceeded that of any other capitalist power save the U.S.A.

Even as late at 1968, on a far smaller Gross National Product, Britain still invested over twice as much abroad as West Germany and four times as much as Japan. These figures go a long way in explaining the smaller rate of British home investment compared to other capitalist countries and the consequent weakness of British industry. By the early 1960s it was finally clear to all that the old pattern of British economic development was no longer viable. The net outcome of all these developments was a deteriorating performance in every important economic index — rate of profit, rate of investment, rate of industrial growth, productivity. It was now clear that the Empire could no longer compensate for domestic deficiencies.

A radical reorientation toward an industrial strategy seemed to be the way out — meaning mergers of weak enterprises, mammoth rationalization, an orderly system of industrial relations, and entry into the European Common Market. What blocked this strategy was the failure of the big industrialists to gain control of the Tory Party in the leadership crisis following the illness of Harold Macmillan. Faced with this situation, decisive sections of Britain's industrial bourgeoisie moved to support the Labour Party in the 1964 elections, including Lord Stokes, head of Leyland Motors, Lord Kearton, head of Courtaulds, and *The Economist* magazine. But Harold Wilson was unable to deliver the British working class to them. Besides his slavish support for the U.S. in Vietnam, Wilson did manage to cut away some welfare legislation, reintroduced the medical care payments that he had abolished at the beginning of his term, withdrew free milk for school children, and the like, as part of an economy drive. But his attempt to impose an income policy under the banner "In Place of Strife" failed as it led to massive resistance including a strike of 90,000 workers on May Day, 1969. The lesson learned from the failure of the "In Place of Strife" program was that there would be no peaceful integration of the working class. Open confrontation was the only way. By this time the Tories had dumped the ineffective Hume and replaced him with Edward Heath, a clear representative of industrial capitalism.

Heath moved quickly to ready the British economy for entry into the Common market. His attack on inflation began with retrenchment in public expenditures, with lots of mean little savings in school meals and health charges. Welfare programs reverted to the old Poor Law principle of conditional welfare for the few with the return of means tests. Housing subsidies were reduced by raising rents on publicly owned houses to so-called "fair" levels. Unemployment was allowed to soar to over a million persons. To reverse the shocking trend of falling profit shares (as a proportion of total national income, profits had gradually declined from 25.2 per cent in 1950-54 to 22.8 per cent in 1955-59, to 21 per cent in 1960-4, then drastically to 16.8 per cent in 1968 and 14.2 per cent in 1969), Heath introduced tax changes in his first budget that shifted 355 pounds to the top third of income receivers. But most crucial to his strategy of breaking the back of the increasingly militant working class was the Industrial Relations Act and the incomes policy.

Heath's Industrial Relations Act (IRA) was modeled on the North American system. Collective bargaining was to be transformed from a daily struggle on the shop floor lead by rank-and-file elected shop stewards to periodic, highly regulated, and extremely legalistic bargaining led by "responsible" national officers and their coterie of legal experts, with the long ritual of conciliations, mediations, and personal intervention by a "kindly" Minister of Labour. The agreements were to be legally enforceable with stiff penalties for any breaches and with the union officers being turned into policemen of the agreement. All unions were to have to register with the state, and their constitutions would require state approval. Only constitutions which give full control to national officers would be approved, making mandatory the hierarchial North American union structure. Again as in North America, sympathy strikes would be outlawed, thus dividing labour into thousands of isolated groups unable to act together. The whole package would be administered by a series of bureaucratic agencies, like our labour boards, so that to get justice the worker would have to rely on lawyers at every turn. In the main, the IRA was aimed at destroying the power of the British shop stewards, who were elected directly by their co-workers and represented them on a day-to-day basis in negotiating not only grievances but also wages and working conditions. The Tories recognized that the rank and file posed a greater threat to management control of industry than did the official union leaders, who were thought to be more capable of seeing management's side and more open to the persuasions of mediators and government ministers.

The union leadership was forced to take action against the Bill. There were four one-day strikes against the Bill between December 1970 and March 1971. For a country with no tradition of political strikes, these work stoppages had some significance. But one-day strikes are by definition symbolic actions, regularly used by union leaders in France and Italy as a safety-valve for mass worker discontent. The Trades Union Congress was not prepared to use its full industrial strength to defeat the Bill, although there was substantial rank-and-file support for an all-out campaign. In July 1972, five dockers, jailed for refusing to appear before the Industrial Relations Court, were released after escalating rank-and-file action forced the General Council of the Trades Union Congress to call a general strike, the first since 1926. Jack Jones, head of Britain's biggest union, the Transport and General Workers, said in defense of the call for a general strike, "If we don't do something, then the leadership will be in the hands of unofficial elements." For the moment the Tories capitulated, but the trade union leadership, having gained the upper hand, never again took the offensive to force a repeal of the legislation. Instead, it agreed to discuss Heath's suggestion on inflation at No. 10 Downing Street.

The key issue for Heath was wages. Within months of his taking office he was met with the rising tide of strikes that had plagued Wilson in his last years. Although the dockers, and then the municipal workers, broke through Heath's strategy, he claimed his first victories when the power workers were defeated in the winter of 1970. Then in the spring of 1971 the lowly-paid postal workers were smashed. Heath's policy of "n-1", each major pay settlement to be one per cent lower than the preceding one, appeared to be succeeding. But the tide soon turned when the closures and mass layoffs, products of his policy of retrenchment, began to affect the key industrial sectors. When the Tories announced the closure of the Upper Clyde Shipbuilders, threatening 6,000 jobs directly and another 20,000 indirectly dependent on the yards, the UCS shop stewards responded with a work-in beginning in July 1971. The example of the work-in triggered a series of other actions, including sit-in occupations and other work-ins. While the work-in at Clyde and elsewhere did not yield a complete victory and the ultimate settlements involved considerable concessions, they succeeded in stopping a number of plant closures and saving thousands of jobs. In the opinion of Ken Coates of the Institute of Workers Control:

The electric appeal of the idea of a 'work-in' exists because it can explain for millions of ordinary workers that workers' control of dismissals is entirely possible, that workers can veto manpower policies of which they disapprove, and that the power of management is only unchallenged where trade unionists have decided not to challenge it.[7]

For every work-in there were numerous sit-ins, some aimed at halting plant closures, others like the occupation of 30 Lancashire factories in March, 1972, aimed at supporting wage demands. Factory occupations which had been widely used by French workers in 1968, were virtually unknown in Britain before 1971. They spelled defeat for Heath's policy of austerity. During the spring and summer of 1972, British workers scored victory after victory, including the dramatic mines strike that closed down scores of Birmingham factories.

With unemployment soaring, industrial investment falling, and inflation unchecked, Heath reversed gears. The new policy consisted of expanding domestic demand through lower taxation, higher public expenditures, and easy credit. It soon led to a balance of payments crisis. The large tax reductions and easy credit policy set off a tremendous boom in spending, but most of it went into services and property which absorbed the unemployed in sectors that added nothing to industrial capacity or exports. As the balance of payments deteriorated from +1,000 pounds in 1971 to zero in 1972 to -3,025 pounds in the third quarter of 1973, and as inflation reached record levels, it became evident to all that governmental fiscal and monetary policies must again by sharply reversed. The incomes policy, confrontation with the miners, the stage-managed three-day week, and the snap election finally brought an end to a government that the noted British economist Nicholas Kaldor called "one of the worst which Britain ever had."[8]

At first it seemed that Heath would survive. Phase I of the Incomes Policy, a virutal three-month freeze on wages, followed by Phase II which was little better, found no united opposition. The share of profits in the national income had risen at the expense of wages and salaries. But now came Phase III and the demands of the coal miners for a raise in pay outside the legal limits. The miners' strategy of a ban on overtime brought forth Heath's declaration of a state of emergency, the three-day week, and major cuts in public expenditures on health, education, and other social services. By imposing a loss of earnings of up to 40 per cent, Heath hoped that British workers would blame the miners for their plight. When the miners decided in favour of strike action (81 per cent in favour) the Tories had three options. The first was to capitulate to the miners as a special case, and hope to hold back the rest of the working class, as pledged by the TUC. The Tories judged, probably correctly, that the miners' dispute could not be dealt with in isolation. It was by now the locus around which the total relation of class forces was lining up. The second option was to attempt to break the miners by repression. This was judged to be too risky a venture. Support for the miners was widespread, and a show of force might provoke a general strike. A general election was the third option. In spite of its reluctant leadership, the colossal organizational strength of the British working class succeeded in bringing down a government. What it will do with Harold Wilson's Labour government is an open question. Raymond Williams may well be right when he says that the Labour government is the last real chance for capitalistic democracy. With a massive balance of payments deficit to be overcome ($10 billion in 1975),* soaring inflation (20-25 per cent or more), together with widespread unemployment (about 1 million unemployed in 1975) and a heavy cut in living standards seen as unavoidable, Wilson's ability to govern is as tenuous as was Heath's.

Standards of health, education, and housing are declining at an even sharper rate than the fall in the real value of wages. Inflation and direct cuts in local government expenditures have eroded most sectors of the welfare state. While almost one-fifth of British housing units can be described as "unfit dwellings," a polite term for slums, housing construction has fallen by nearly 20 per cent since 1973.

With wage increases running over 30 per cent above a year ago, inflation entering the 20-25 per cent range, and firms being squeezed by increased profit taxes, British industry faced severe liquidity problems. The rate of bankruptcy rose by 15 per cent in 1974. One thousand firms are said to be lined up for government aid. The Labour government was forced to invest $115 million to $230 million in the British Leyland Motor Corporation to save that company from bankruptcy. It also bailed out Ferranti, a major electrical engineering firm, and Alfred Herbert, a large machine-tool firm. Other sick industries like aerospace and shipyards are slated for nationalization. Gone is the former talk of nationalizing the profitable sectors of the economy. Instead Wilson set up the National Enterprise Board, which was slated to take shares in companies that it aids and operate as an industrial holding company. Companies remaining in private hands would be invited to sign so-called planning agreements with the Government and their workers. These agreements would deal with investment decisions,

---

* About 60 per cent of the deficit is attributable to oil. Eliminating the part of the deficit not accounted for by oil would still imply a reduction of total consumption by about 5 per cent.

exports, and prices. The incentive to sign would be access to extra financial aid from government.*

In November, Wilson told a banquet sponsored by the Lord Mayor of London that "the crisis can be conquered only by the nation, all the nation, as one nation, taking up the challenge in a spirit of total commitment." At the same time he warned the British people that they would have to tighten their belts as more income must be diverted into investment and exports. Whether the British working class is prepared to make further sacrifices "for the good of the nation" waits to be seen.

With a balance of payment crisis looming ahead, Wilson opened the New Year by declaring that he would not bail out industries whose losses are caused by "avoidable" strikes. His speech had special force coming in the middle of the strike at British Leyland. The new line was implicit recognition that the "social contract" was failing. This was given official recognition when the Chancellor of the Exchequer, Denis Healey, brought down his April budget, which took away in extra taxes some of the gains British workers had earned over and above inflation. The budget also brought cuts in public expenditures, with further promises of further cuts in 1976. The budget was admittedly designed to increase unemployment and thereby reduce wage demands. However, with trade union strength still unbroken (and labour continuing to improve its share of the national income) the pound inevitably floated down as the British trade deficit worsened. This helped exports to compete but it exacerbated domestic inflation and spurred Britain's working class to still greater militancy. The crunch finally arrived in July 1975 when Healey introduced his new incomes policy.

A survey conducted by the London *Daily Telegraph* in the fall of 1974 "revealed a nation that senses instinctively that it could be on the brink of one of the greatest social and economic upheavals in history; a nation afraid that it is careening along out of control, going it knows not where; a nation that feels split from top to bottom...."[9]

While some trade union leaders and some industrialists refused to go along with what they called "the imminent catastrophe theory," others freely predicted the end of democratic capitalism in Great Britain. "What we have to decide during the next year," Adrian Cadbury, deputy chairman of Cadbury-Schweppes, is reported having said, "is whether we are prepared to back a democratic solution to our problem. If we just go bumbling on as we are, there are

---

* These arrangements were temporarily set aside when Denis Healey introduced his new incomes policy in the summer of 1975.

forces which will push us either to a Marxist state or a government of the right — and the Marxist alternative is the most likely." A local Labour councillor and pit miner concurs. "I think we are beginning to see the end of the capitalist system. The working class is more united than it's ever been. Just look into the crystal ball and you'll see that it's the working man who's going to control the interests of the entire country."

The workers quoted in the survey dismissed the "economic disaster line" of the Wilson administration. "That's just part of the brainwashing middle class people are always trying to do. They've been crying wolf for so long to brainwash us into believing things are so bad we must become passive again. . . . Should there come a recession there won't be the same religious influence there was last time when people passively accepted disaster. . . . This time their attitude would be we're going to have it by hook or by crook."

There does not seem to be very much disagreement about the direction in which Britain is going. The question that remains to be answered is whether Harold Wilson can stop the process from going beyond the regime of state capitalism that he is forging or whether it will finally burst these historical bounds.

Italy

Italy's economy is the most fragile in Europe. In 1974 prices rose at an annual rate just short of 25 percent. Runaway inflation in 1973, devaluation of the lira, and mounting fuel bills created an annual trade deficit of $13 billion. To finance the deficit, the Italian government has been borrowing heavily abroad and has committed itself to $1 billion in annual interest payments. Throughout 1974, Italy's ruling Christian Democrats were playing a game of musical chairs with Cabinet portfolios. By the fall of that year there was every indication that Italy would be the first western country to suffer actual financial collapse. The response of the government and the more stable Bank of Italy has been to engineer a general recession that would cool off imports and bring the balance of payments into line. Real growth in 1974 fell off; unemployment rose to one million people (6 per cent of the work force) and is expected to rise to 1.2 million before the end of 1975. This does not include the tens of thousands of Italian "guest workers" who are returning from Switzerland and West Germany because they are not needed there. Some 15,000 retail concerns have gone bankrupt in the past year, with more failures sure to follow. The future of Italy, as elsewhere in Europe, depends on the ability of the state to contain the popular protests that its policies are provoking.

The roots of the Italian crisis are not to be found in the 1970s nor even in the so-called "hot autumn" of 1969. They lie in the pattern of development that set in after World War II leading to the Italian "miracle" of the late fifties and the reversal that came about in the mid-sixties. In the best treatment of the subject I have seen, Michele Salvatti divides the post-war history into three periods: 1945-47, the period of reconstruction; 1948-1962, the period of "repressive" development; 1964-present, the period of "precocious maturity."[10]

In the first period, the war-devastated economy was repaired and the social structure that had been shattered by the resistance movement and the defeat of fascism was re-established. All over the country, anti-fascist groups who had been armed since the time of the Resistance were persuaded to lay down their weapons. Instead they were given a seat in the government. But once the threat of armed insurrection was out of the way, the Communists and Socialists were quickly ousted.

The second period coincides with the governments of the Centre and a harsh repression of the political, social, and trade-union strength of the workers' movement. The governments followed a tight monetary and fiscal policy and a liberalization of international trade. This had the effect of eliminating weak firms and inducing Italian capitalists to modernize. Consumption spending was kept down to channel growth into exports. An abundance of cheap labour (about 1 million people migrated from South to North between 1959 to 1963) and repressive measures against trade unions meant that wages rose by less than productivity, and profits increased substantially. While the rise in consumption was held down to 80 per cent between 1950 and 1962, exports rose four-fold and investment three-fold. Wage costs per unit of output fell from 100 in 1953 to 85 in 1960.

By the early sixties the era of cheap labour had come to an end and *Il boom* was in trouble. The 1960s marked a turning point all over Europe: the rate of growth slowed down, wages began to push upwards at the expense of profits, and, especially in France and Italy, there was a marked revival of workers' struggles. The period of "precocious maturity" following 1964 is to Italy what the period of "relative stagnation" (1958-1961) was to the U.S. and Canada. Investment practically stopped increasing, and the share of profits in the GNP never recovered the levels of the 1950s. The investment boom of 1959-1963 created a shortage of workers as registered unemployment fell from a level of one and three-quarter million in the 1950s to half a million; wage increases and a decline in the growth of productivity caused a rise in labour costs only partially offset by a rise in prices as Italian capitalists, faced with international competition, had to accept a reduction in profit margins; land prices and rents skyrocketed due to mass urbanization; the rising cost of living gave an extra push to wages; imports rose relative to exports, causing a deterioration in the balance of payments. The government response was a classical exercise in monetary and fiscal restraint, "a model of correct economic policy" according to the OECD. The planned recession worked, re-creating general unemployment and bringing the inflation under control.

By now (1963), the Centre Left government had been formed. The famous "opening to the left" made sense to the more intelligent elements of the Italian bourgeoisie. Now that the most flexible labour reserves were exhausted, a more sophisticated model of economic development was required based on a new electoral consensus, wage truce, social reforms, and Keynesian economics. But the Centre Left coalition never really worked. Conservative and reformist forces were so deadlocked as to impede any clear direction of the economy. By 1968 it was "no more than an empty parliamentary formula which could not discipline the actions of the various social forces, including the trade unions."[11] Between 1964 and 1969, in the absence of any increase of investment, increased output was literally squeezed out of labour through crazy speedups and depressed wages. It was only in 1969 that the level of industrial employment reached in 1963 was again recovered. Profits rose, but with lagging investments the capitalists exported their capital abroad. "The hesitant signs of recovery were, however, enough to give rise to the greatest wave of workers struggles in the history of the Italian trade union movement."[12] Growing discontent with living conditions, both inside the factory and outside — worsening conditions of work and a deterioration in housing, the rising cost of living, poor transportation, the growing weight of unemployment — brought matters to a head in the autumn of 1969. "There was a moment in which this rage exploded, encouraged by more diffuse social agitation."[13]

To place this "moment of rage" in a broad political context, it is necessary to recall that from the late 1950s onwards Italy's Communist party (PCI), the largest in Europe, and the CGIL, the main trade union which it dominates, had worked out a new strategy after several dismal years marked by repression and defeat. On the political front, even before the monumental 20th Congress of the Soviet Communist Party, the PCI declared that it would follow its own path to socialism — promoting structural reforms within the parliamentary system and within the capitalist order. These comprised "intermediate solutions" for agrarian reform, regional development, and reorganization of firms due to close — all measures which could mobilize wide support — as well as preparing the ground for new advances through a constructive opposition that would lead the Communist Party, in league with the non-Communist left, to an electoral victory. Even leaders of the non-Communist left admit that the PCI's commitment to the parliamentary system and to a socialism which guarantees political pluralism is genuine and not just a tactical expediency.

The CGIL decided that it could no longer focus its struggle upon general claims in regard to wages and working conditions, and it decentralized its operation to encourage union branches in the factories to formulate specific demands on the basis of local conditions. The first application of this strategy on a major scale was the 42-day rotating strike of about a million engineering workers. The national agreement for the metal industry signed in February 1963 brought within the province of the union such matters as the classification of skills, work speeds, and to a degree, the organization of production. This was a bold advance over previous agreements and set the stage for the struggles that ensued in the following years leading up to the "hot autumn" of 1969, struggles that were to extend well beyond the "intermediate" boundaries set by the CGIL.

In 1969 many of the important three-year labour contracts in the vital metal working and automobile industries were due to expire. The large firms were eager to negotiate new terms and settle with the unions as peacefully as possible. For their part, the trade unions and the PCI were ready to make a deal. In exchange for industrial peace, they asked for higher wages and the promise of social reform. But the workers wanted far more than that. Not much has been written about the "hot autumn" of 1969, but here is one description of some of the events:

> When the workers at Fiat were called out on a one-day token strike protesti᠎g the killing of a Southern worker during the rioting at Battipaglia, they refused to leave the factory, and started to take it over instead. Very quickly people began to develop aims, tactics, and organization which had nothing to do with what the unions were after. They didn't just want a wage increase — they wanted the abolition of the grading system, equal pay raises for all, and a drastic reduction in work speed. Rather than passively coming out on strike, as the unions wanted them to, they began to organize a struggle inside the factories, with mass meetings on the job, rotating strikes in different sections which brought production to a stand-still, marches through factories involving a lot of damage to plants, and direct

confrontation with management. New organizations began to take control of the struggle — base committees at Pirelli (Milan) and at the chemical works in Porto Marghera, and the worker-student assembly at Fiat Mirafiori (Turin). Factory newspapers began to appear. Links were established with groups of students, and meetings were held regularly at factory gates.[14]

A Fiat worker speaking at the national Conference of Worker's Base Committees in Turin in July 1969 describes the growing tensions between the workers themselves and their trade unions:

> We know what the contracts mean for the unions and the employers. They are their way of ensuring that workers only fight once in every three years, and that after that, they sit still and behave like good children. The contracts are a sort of cage, in which the worker is locked up, and the union given the keys and told to make sure that the cage stays shut. But in the last years, in hundreds of factories all over Italy, it has become clear that workers don't accept orders from bosses or from unions.
>
> The sort of strikes that the union intends to call for the autumn are the sort that cost us the most and cost the employers the least — the sort where the employer has plenty of warning of the strike, and can organize himself so as not to be hit too hard — and the sort that gives us precious little help to get together and organize ourselves. But in the strikes at Mirafiori, and previously at the Pirelli rubber factory in Milan, as well as in many other advanced struggles recently, we have been able to organize in new ways. We have understood that if the factory is the heart of the employer's power, then it can and must become the centre of our power. We have understood that organizing and fighting inside the factory allows us to come together to discuss and organize much more than was the case when we all just used to go home for the day....[15]

Days lost in work stoppage per thousand of employees amounted to 4,100 in 1969 compared to an average of 1,400 over the previous decade. In the hope of bringing some industrial peace the owners now desperately made big concessions on wages. Between 1969 and 1970, wages went up 23.4 per cent compared with an annual average increase of 9 per cent over the previous 10 years. Since productivity first dropped and then no more than regained its 1969 level, labour costs soared, prices escalated, exports fell off and imports rose. To bring the deficit in the balance of payments under control, the government took hundreds of millions of lire out of the economy in what was another planned recession. Massive layoffs, expulsion from the labour market of peripheral elements — women, old people, and youth, decreased work mobility — these were the efforts made to break down the strength of the workers' movement.

Yet the wage pressure continued. With productivity virtually stagnant, wages rose by fully 16.6 per cent in 1971 and cut still deeper into profit margins. By year's end, Italy's central bank, the Bank of Italy, revealed that a 670-billion-lire increase in the value of production was swallowed up by a 1,500-billion-lire increase in wages and salaries. "There was no capital accumulation in Italy in 1971," boasted Potere Operaio ("Worker's Power"), a large radical formation that sprang up during the "hot autumn." By now the "Centre Left" coalition was finished and the government that emerged from the 1972 elections was a "Centre Right" coalition, including among its ministers several Christian Democratic neanderthals from the fifties.

The new governments, starting with Adreotti in January 1972, moved from economic repression to a systematic campaign of political repression. The police force was modernized and enlarged; hundreds of radicals were jailed; right-wing terrorists were allowed a free hand including the assassination of the revolutionary publisher Fetrinelli. The unions were now told to keep the workers under control or else bear the burden of continued recession. A wage ceiling was set as a precondition to economic recovery. But as Potere Operaio says, years of open autonomous struggle made it unlikely that the unions could guarantee the collaboration of the working class. Here is its account of the resistance as it developed in late 1972 and 1973:

> Since the Turin general strike of September 1972, the struggle has grown out of control in terms of both violence and generalization. Throughout the fall, the Fiat workers stepped up their *cortei interni* (inside-the-factory militant marches that proceed from shop to shop busting doors and gates and sweeping away foremen, strike breakers, and guards). On January 22, the Lancia auto workers launched a sit-down and battled with the police when the latter tried to enter the factory. (One worker was killed by the police.) On January 26, striking students joined picket lines and workers' marches in Milan. (One student was severely wounded by the police.) On February 2, some 20,000 Fiat workers staged a one-day occupation of Fiat-Mirafiori that triggered a wave of factory occupations in the following months. By February 9, nearly half a million workers had congregated in Rome for the largest working-class demonstration to take place since World War II. Their slogans were "Power to the Workers" and "Factory, School, Community — Our Struggle Is for Power."

Once again Fiat workers have led the way with an absenteeism rate of 28 per cent. This means that each day 30,000 Fiat workers do not go to be exploited by the capitalist factory; that the average real work-week at Fiat has been self-reduced by workers to a little over 30 hours. Through their absenteeism and sick leaves, the 100,000 Fiat workers of Turin have reappropriated 45 billion lire ($90,000,000) — nine times the net profit that Fiat posted for 1972 — *without work*. And absenteeism, far from being a substitute for other forms of struggle, has been growing together with other forms of the workers' revolt — strikes, picket lines, factory occupations, and mass demonstrations.[16]

Contracts were finally signed in the spring of 1973, but there was no way the unions could deliver an end to "permanent conflict" as demanded by Fiat's chief, Gianni Agnelli. Absenteeism did not subside, nor was discipline restored. According to Potere Operaio, "signing the contract did not put an end to the struggles. For the workers' struggle has been beyond the contract all long." The most recent outbreaks at Fiat bear out this analysis.

Facing a situation of national bankruptcy, Italy was able to negotiate a $2 billion loan with West Germany, but only by guaranteeing the Germans one-sixth of Italy's gold reserves. The interest on this massive loan is on top of the $700 million in interest that Italy pays out each year on previous foreign loans. In announcing the surprise loan, West German Chancellor Schmidt said that a solvent Italy "lies in Germany's own economic interests," which indicates that the German government is acting to protect the position of German banking interests and financial groups that must have made large loans to Italy. The U.S. Office of the Controller of Currency has alerted its bank examiners to view all medium and long-term loans to Italian government agencies and Italian banks and companies as "problematical."

To combat the raging inflation and counteract mounting fuel bills, the Italian government has restricted credit, cut public expenditures, and raised taxes and tariffs. On October 14, the Fiat Company, the country's largest employer, announced that due to the energy crisis it would cut back production to 200,000 vehicles and reduce the work-week to 24 hours for 40 per cent of its employees. Three days later, in the midst of a general political crisis, 10 million Italian workers staged a strike in protest against the massive layoffs as well as against inflation and the government's measures to combat it by repressing their living standards.

Employers are using the crisis to eliminate the gains made during the past years by the workers' struggles in the factories. In particular, they are hoping that, threatened with unemployment, the workers will desist from their practice of passive protest in the form of absenteeism.

A feature of the Italian situation which receives much attention in the western press is the overbloated, inefficient, and corrupt character of the state bureaucracy. With some 40 per cent of the economy in the state sector, much of it parasitic, Italy operates under a severe handicap in the international economy. The presence of this parasitic sector was no great burden in boom times. In fact it fostered the spread of a middle social stratum that constituted a large market for durable consumer goods. However when the boom was exhausted, restricting the room for fiscal manoeuvring, and when international competition tightened, it became an intolerable weight on the economy which has yet to be removed.

The Andreotti government fell after the vigorous struggles of 1972 and early 1973. The new Rumor government, since replaced, was more moderate in composition, with the Socialist party replacing the right-wing Liberal party. It has been the various governments headed up by Rumor and others that engineered the Italian economy through the oil crisis, the squeeze in balance of payments, and yet another planned recession.*

At first the trade unions and the Communist Party adopted a "constructive" opposition, but it was not long before Italian workers balked at the truce, leaving the official leaders of the left with a dilemma. The Communist Party, which formerly followed a strategy of forming a government that would include itself in coalition with the Socialists and the left-wing of the Christian Democrats, has now made what it itself calls a "historic compromise" with the Christian Democrats. With the backing of some of the major industrialists and the promise of industrial peace, it is pressing for a place in a national unity government, a broader Centre-Left coalition that would include itself and the Catholic-supported CDP. The Italian Communist leader Enrico Berlinguer has asserted that the party would not challenge Italy's membership in the European Common Market. One of its spokesmen has even assured the U.S. that the party would not undermine Italy's membership in NATO, suggesting that the U.S. ought to prefer "economic and political efficiency and security" to an Italy threatened by instability. This implied that the Communists could, through their control of the largest trade unions and their popularity in the

---

* At the cost of stagnant output and investment and heavy unemployment, Italy managed to engineer a remarkable turnaround. Inflation slowed from 25 per cent in 1974 to under 15 per cent in 1975, and the deficit in her balance of payments fell by half. By April of 1975, international banks had removed Italy from the list of countries from which they demand a high-risk premium on loan interest rates.

industrial areas, enforce labour discipline and thereby strengthen economic production.

This assessment is questioned by some of the more radical left formations. In the opinion of Potere Operaio, "to the extent that reformism has been defeated, there has been little that capital and the Communist Party could offer each other. [Italian] capitalism has no margin for reforms . . . and the Communist Party has been in no position to guarantee control over workers' behaviour." But perhaps, as Guilo Viale has written, "if it is true that Italy is the 'weakest link' in the chain of capitalist powers, it is also true that this chain cannot break except in the face of much stronger tensions which would then place the rest of Europe in the same condition as Italy."[17]

France

The economic situation in France is less critical than in most other countries. Little has been done to reduce a 15 per cent a year rate of inflation, but the general recession was relatively mild, and France's rate of growth continued at a respectable rate to the summer of 1974. Between August and January 1975, however, industrial production fell by 10 per cent. The government of Giscard d'Estaing has moved vigorously to solve the oil-induced balance of payments deficit that plagues nearly all of Europe. Giscard's strategy has been to capture new markets in the Middle East and Algeria by means of massive trade agreements. However, this requires a major restructuring of the French economy away from its heavy emphasis on consumption goods towards the heavy equipment sector. This is being accomplished by measures that aim to reduce consumption spending and encourage a greater concentration of industry. Tight credit policies and a surtax on increased wages and prices have mainly hit small and medium-size businesses, and their failure rate has reached record proportions. A hard line on salary negotiations in the public sector has had its effect in stabilizing, if not reducing, purchasing power.

At the same time the government accepted the inevitability of high unemployment, up 40 per cent within a year. Unemployment is a necessary adjunct to Giscard's strategy of restructuring the economy. It provides for a mobile labour force, and so far it has served to discourage a more militant response by the working class against the efforts being made to erode its purchasing power. Nevertheless, to avoid a head-on confrontation, the government has forced the major enterprises to sign an agreement with the labour federation guaranteeing laid-off workers 90 per cent of their salary for one year.* When unemployment began to approach the politically unacceptable level of one million, the government switched gears and adopted a reflationary fiscal program, following the pattern already in effect elsewhere in the capitalist world.

Giscard d'Estaing emerged with a slight majority in the March 1973 general election, narrowly defeating the electoral alliance of the Communist Party and the Socialist Party. "Giscard is the living embodiment of France's financial elite," observes George Weisz, *Canadian Dimension's* Paris correspondent.[18] His maternal family, the Bardoux, were prominent in Third Republic politics and in colonial business ventures in North Africa. Giscard's father and brother are on the boards of administration of numerous companies including such multinationals as IBM and ITT. His wife, however, has even more impressive credentials. She is the granddaughter of Eugene Schneider, perhaps the single most important industrialist in turn-of-the-century France. All this capitalist breeding, writes Weisz, was trained in technocracy at the prestigious Ecole Polytechnique and Ecole Nationale d'Administration.

Giscard's cabinet is primarily composed of technocrats, many from the banking sector with which Giscard has so many intimate ties. Writing in the summer of 1974, Weisz was pessimistic about his chances for survival:

> The new government is hardly in an enviable position. That more than 49 per cent of the electorate voted for social change will force Giscard toward some measure of social reform. But in the absence of structural changes, such reforms are likely to exacerbate inflation and further the deterioration of the troubled economy. Such social concessions are not likely to be viewed favourably by the largely conservative social groups that elected Giscard and that remain primarily concerned with maintaining privileges. Neither is it likely to win the support of the left while the government pursues austerity policies in response to economic problems. To rule effectively moreover, the President must depend on the Gaullists, helpless at present but unlikely to acquiesce to their political destruction. Finally he must somehow hold together an alliance born of fear, between a capitalist class seeking economic concentration and rationalization and small shopkeepers and peasants trying desperately to prevent this process. In the face of such difficulties, neither Giscard's unquestionable speaking ability nor his efforts to generate

---

* By the spring of 1974, because of the many inroads the employers made against the application of the agreement, the number of workers actually benefiting from the agreement included only 2 per cent of those unemployed.

a Kennedy-style charisma, are likely to succeed. The coming autumn promises to bring a resumption of the labour problems and social unrest which abated temporarily after Pompidou's death.[19]

But there were, in fact, only some hesitant signs of a resumption of open labour unrest. The insecurity resulting from the economic situation dampened working-class combativity. Only in the public sector, where a degree of job security exists, was there intense activity. In November, postal workers demanding higher wages and the hiring of more workers to improve services went out on strike and more or less crippled the country for several weeks. They were joined by garbage collectors, state television workers and briefly by railway workers. But the strike never went much further despite large demonstrations of support and two limited general strikes. Sensing the isolation of the postal workers, the government took a hard line and the strikers were eventually pressed back to work with none of their primary demands having been met.

Despite this defeat, the French bourgeoisie is still haunted by the ghost of May 1968 — that spontaneous movement of workers and students that brought the country to the point of revolution. What was missing then was a revolutionary party that could synthesize and merge the specific actions and demands of the millions of strikers in a program of radical change. In its hour of crisis the bourgeoisie was saved by none other than the Communist Party, the dominant party of the French left, which turned out to be the pillar of law and order.

It was a student revolt that led to the largest strike in French history. Since the war the French economy has been expanding at an average rate of 4 to 5 per cent a year, but the growth has been uneven. Most of the expansion has been concentrated in the industrial sectors which have undergone extensive modernization under the guiding hand of the state. The public sector has been allowed to deteriorate badly, including the University. The huge influx of students generated by the economic expansion arrived at the university to confront inadequate facilities manned by inadequate staffs totally incapable of providing the skills and training needed to equip them for jobs in the new economy. As one author puts it, "It tried to contain within its nineteenth (some say eighteenth) century structures, the social forces generated by a rapidly expanding neo-capitalist economy . . . . All it would take would be the slightest spark to trigger, not just an outburst from a small group of radicals protesting distant injustice, or making demands that the average student would not consider worth getting excited about, but a massive protest movement firmly rooted in the great majority of students demanding what they felt to be vital, legitimate and long overdue reforms."[20] Triggered by a series of small incidents at Nanterre University, and responding to repressive measures by University officials to squelch the rebellion, ever-larger numbers of students were mobilized, politicized and radicalized far beyond the original demands. The movement spread, first to the Sorbonne, then to the other French universities, then to the high schools, to important segments of the adult intelligentsia, and finally to nine million workers.

At least one thing about the strike is certain: it did not begin in the executive councils of the unions. It was a chain reaction of wildcats. During the night of May 10 there was a particularly bloody battle between students and police in a barricaded street in the Latin Quarter of Paris. The Communist Party, through its union, the Confederation Generale du Travail (CGT) decided to reassert its leadership over the rebellion by seizing the initiative from the students and calling for a 24-hour strike. On May 13, 700,000 workers and students demonstrated in Paris alone. But control soon passed from the Communist Party to the base. The Sorbonne was occupied by students that night. Twelve hours later, workers at Suld-Aviation (Nantes) struck and occupied the factory, writing "Yesterday Slaves — Today Free Men" on the walls of the factory. The next day, the big Renault plant at Cleon was occupied. Within four days, 5 million workers were on strike and, by the end of the following week, this grew to 8 to 10 million, many of them occupying their factories and offices on a rotating basis over the next few weeks.

No strike of such proportions could arise from a series of overnight grievances or from sympathy for the plight of students. It rested on a solid base of cumulative grievances that had produced numerous wildcat strikes and lockouts over the preceding few years. The Fourth and Fifth French economic plans, about which I will have more to say, deliberately constrained consumption in order to build up profits and investment. Rising prices were eating up increases in wages. Planned unemployment produced by government austerity measures and a series of massive layoffs due to "redundancies" raised the question of job security. Working hours were among the longest in Europe. Serious regional disparities, low starting wages for young workers and long apprenticeship programs, a cut in social security benefits — these bread and butter issues were enough to generate a major strike once the students had shown the way.

But the May events were more than an economic strike for higher wages and shorter hours. They were also a political strike against traditional structures of authority. There were not only the traditional demands for nationalization. Many of the plants occupied, such as Renault, were already publicly owned. Workers were calling for the democratization of decision-making. "Democratic structures based on 'autogestion' (self-management) must be substituted for industrial and administrative monarchy," read one statement issued by a strike committee on May 16.

The CGT desperately tried to recapture control of the strike movement. After well over a million workers had gone on strike on their own, it called an official general strike from above. Then it set about "de-adventurizing" the strike, labelling the political demands for worker control as "meaningless," and a sell-out of the workers' "real interests." Student leaders were called "infantile leftists" and "provacateurs," Cohn-Bendit "a German Anarchist." Every effort was made to minimize the contact between workers and student revolutionaries.

The uprising had caught everyone by surprise, but the Communist Party was intent on proving that revolution is impossible. The Communist Party in France as elsewhere had long ago abandoned revolution for the "peaceful road to socialism." Peaceful means legal, and legal means electoral — an electoral alliance with the non-Communist left to form an "anti-monopoly" popular front within the parliamentary system. The Gaullist foreign policy had helped the Communist Party to escape from its Cold War isolation. To keep its electoral strategy intact, it was desperate to confine the uprising to the traditional 24-hour strike-and-parade and to reduce revolutionary demands to ones advocating improved wages and university reforms. But the students were declaring a revolutionary situation and, in part, their ideology, which was in direct contradiction to party strategy, was catching on with the workers. The CGT rushed to negotiate an end to the strike and signed the Grenelle Accords which "limited the workers' victory to purely 'economic' gains that were hardly commensurate with the scale and intensity of the greatest strike in French history."[21] But in factory after factory the workers rejected the Grenelle agreements.

At this point the situation was entirely out of hand, and most observers agreed that dramatic political changes were inevitable. General De Gaulle had disappeared from sight and the non-Communist left announced that it was ready to accede to power. But the General soon reappeared and went on the attack, calling for a massive demonstration in support of law and order and himself. He got the demonstration, and with the tacit support of the Communists he succeeded in shifting the crisis to the safety of the electoral plane. The denouncement was swift in coming. With its security regained, the Gaullist government promised university reform. France would have its Berkeleys and U. of T.s. In response to the demand for fundamental change, it also promised "Participation," a high sounding formula but essentially without definition, a program for preserving the existing distribution of power disguised as an elaborate *tour de force* of change. As for the role of the Communist Party, "there is no doubt that it played a crucial role in preventing major political changes in and saving the Gaullist Fifth Republic" — and serving its own strategy of achieving political power peacefully and legally.[22]

The new Communist strategy is against mass insurrection but in other, more basic ways it still follows the old model of a top-down revolution that will begin miraculously the day after the Party takes power. The revolutionary process remains that of substituting a socialist bureaucracy which acts on behalf of the people for the old bureaucracy that acts on behalf of the capitalists.

In the short run, at least, the Communist Party was successful in dampening and re-directing the revolutionary surge back towards the electoral process. Yet the experience of the May events was not lost. Rising prices were soon eating away most of the Grenelle wage increases.

The most dramatic indication that the spirit of May 1968 was not dead was the celebrated occupation of the LIP watch factory in the spring of 1973. Workers in the plant, located in the town of Besancor, one of the centres of the May uprising, discovered that the 107-year-old enterprise was about to be carved up and reduced to an assembly operation. The entire region would be faced with mass unemployment as many of the small dependent firms in the area would go under. Slow-downs and work stoppages and demonstrations finally ended in an occupation of the plant in June when workers stormed the office and discovered the confidential documents that detailed the massive redundancies and wage cuts that were being planned with governmental approval. The government planned to postpone execution until the March general elections. Faced with the prospect of no wages, the workers decided to start up production on their own to ensure a survival wage for everyone. In mid-August, the Government sent in riot police to invade the factory. The LIP workers, by now supported by national union leaderships, set up shop elsewhere and carried on production. All through these months there were large demonstrations, the biggest one bringing 100,000 people together from all corners of France and abroad, and joint meetings and actions with Italian and Swiss workers. An agreement was finally worked out in mid-January to reopen the plant which, after renovations, would re-employ the entire work force.

The continuing crisis in France attests to the ultimate failure of France's famed economic planning. Just about all of the European countries have adopted some form of national planning — France, Britain, Italy, Sweden, Norway, Holland, Belgium, and Austria. As Andrew Schonfeld wrote in 1965, "the degree of commitment to the exercise varies greatly with France at one extreme and Italy, judged at any rate by the performance to date, least committed to the practice of central economic planning."[23] But Italy too, under its "Centre-Left" government, turned to economic planning in a more serious way. Economic planning, once the preserve of the Communist states, is intended to go beyond the use of Keynesian measures to control the business cycle. The modern corporation, with millions of dollars invested in specific products and specialized equipment cannot afford to rely entirely on the free market to assure itself of vital supplies and markets. It sets up its own internal planning system, conducts massive advertising to guarantee markets for its products, and vertically integrates backwards and forwards. Yet even these measures are not sufficient in the age of monopoly capitalism. Therefore most countries now practise some degree of central economic planning — and in this France has set the pace.

According to official accounts, the French planning process begins with the Planning Commission preparing several preliminary growth targets relating to the GNP, investments, and foreign trade. The government chooses a general plan of development from among these. The outline plan then goes to the modernization commissions — roundtables of planners, government officials, businessmen, trade unionists, and experts where detailed investment and output programmes are filled in for each major industry. These industry programmes are then checked against one another for consistency so as to achieve full co-ordination of the economy. Such is the planning process in principle. "The reality," as Cohen writes, "is something else."[24]

In practice, French planning is little else than the co-ordination of investment plans already drawn up by private companies, adjusted to take into account one another's goals and to eliminate bottlenecks and duplications that are discovered. None of the targets and programs is enforceable by law. Business, including the many important nationalized industries, is under no legal obligation to follow the plan as it effects it. As Cohen relates, bargaining in the modernization commissions is not a series of conflicts. It takes place in the context of fundamental agreement. "The planners, the ranking civil servants and the managers of big business share the same attitudes, the same mode of thought and expression, the same outlook. . . . Indeed to an alarming extent, they are the same people" shifting in and out of the civil service to executive positions in the largest industrial companies and banks. "The modernization commissions are part of a partnership, part of a cooperative venture between the managers of big business and the manager of the state. ... The plan does not wish to run the firm. It wishes to guide the firm to its own true interest and it believes that that interest ... is the National interest."[25] When the plan wants a firm to locate in a special region, it is willing to pay for such a favour by providing various incentives. As economist David Granick succinctly puts it, "the essence of French planning... is the planning of each industry by its own members, acting as a great cartel, with the civil service sitting in on the game and sweetening the pot."[26]

Except for the co-ordination and mutual adjustment of existing investment plans of giant industrial firms, economic planning is really a misnomer for what is practised in France. In reality the plan does not direct development. It cannot be used to orient growth in a direction much different from that which would have prevailed in the absence of the plan. The French experience is a good illustration that economic planning is unable to fulfill its potential in a capitalist economy. As a source of important social change, it poses a threat to business interests. Properly speaking, economic planning should bring under collective decision the composition and distribution of goods, services, efforts and rewards. When removed from the framework of the market and subjected to a democratic political process, these would be bound to change. Certainly an explicitly planned income distribution would differ markedly from the present one. The independence and power of business would be severely curtailed. To achieve their own goals, large enterprises need the active participation of the state in the management of the economy. That is why they co-operate fully in the modernization commissions, while opposing expanding the parameters of the plan and opening its administration to popular participation.

For exactly the same reason, French economic planning has failed to attract active involvement of the trade unions. Of 612 persons who sat on the 19 commissions for the third plan, only 57, less than 10 per cent, were trade union representatives.[27] Trade unions in France may be partway along the road to reformism, but the socialist tradition still has a strong enough hold in France to preclude working-class organizations from co-operating with big business and the state in an exercise that solidifies the strength of capitalism. As seen by the left, "planning could only be democratic when workers ... had sufficient power in the planning process to make working class priorities prevail. ... As planning presently exists, trade unions have no real power over decision-making, thus their presence on planning bodies is decorative at best, compromising at worst."[28]

Aside from the absence of any democratic involvement in the planning process, a matter of no great concern to the planners, there is the *de facto* absence from the planning process of most governmental programmes — social security, housing, transportation, health, education, foreign policy, military expenditures, and the like — and the fact that government fiscal and monetary policy lies outside the discipline of the plan. These are matters of great concern for the planners because, without their being fully incorporated into the plan and executed as planned, there is no way that market forces can steer the rest of the economy to the planned targets.

In practice, although the commissions have been useful to the big industrialists, the planned patterns of development have never been realized. The past 25 years have been marked by recurrent inflations, foreign exchange crises, devaluations, deliberate recessions, regional imbalances and class strife.

The first plan, the Monnet Plan, set out to rehabilitate the French economy from the ravages of war and twenty years of pre-war neglect. It had the co-operation of the CGT, the Communist-dominated union, in the heady days of post-war collaboration. The Plan concentrated on a few basic industries largely within the nationalized sector, and much of its energy was devoted to rationalizing the use of Marshall Plan aid which accounted for over one-third of the investment funds in the late 1940s. It could do nothing about the rampant inflation. Wages, which had been repressed by the occupying power and the Vichy government, never did catch up. Prices rose by over 400 percent from 1946 to 1949 while wages rose by less than 300 percent. De Gaulle's military budget absorbed an inordinate amount of the resources. Heavy industry and defence received the bulk of the investment at the expense of housing, consumption, and agriculture, but rationing was done through inflation rather than by means of controls or heavy taxation.

The second plan, put into effect in 1954, following France's first post-war recession, was truly a partnership between big business and the state. It concentrated on increasing productivity through mergers and specialization among independent producers. Easy credit was offered for mergers; *ententes* were encouraged to permit small firms to specialize in one line of production rather than competing along diversified lines; industry was encouraged to set up industry-wide purchasing and marketing agencies; exports were tax exempt. The plan established modest output targets which were largely ignored and, by the time the third plan was set in place in 1958, the planners observed that "France finds herself in a severe financial crisis, the expression of a profound economic disequilibrium."[29] In 1957, prices rose by 12 per cent and so did wages. It was a classic inflation involving an excess of demand over supply, with prices, wages, imports, and the government deficit out of control. The length of the average work-week rose to 46 hours, and foreign workers, mostly from North Africa, were brought in by the thousands.

In large part, inflation and the trade deficit were products of the Algerian War, which in many respects had the same economic and political impact in France as the Vietnam War had on the United States ten years later. General de Gaulle finally pulled France out of Algeria, much as Richard Nixon reluctantly pulled the U.S.A. out of Vietnam. And it was the Gaullist government that was able to put through a massive deflation to end the inflationary spiral. Coupled with a devaluation of the franc and drop in real wages, this gave France a decisive competitive advantage in international trade as economic expansion resumed in 1961.

Growth was spectacular in 1962 and 1963, the first two years of the fourth plan, far in advance of the targets set for the plan. Inevitably this fired up the inflationary motor as prices, wages and imports again rose to dangerous heights and investment began to stagnate. The government's response, outlined by Finance Minister Valerey Giscard d'Estaing, was a deflationary program of increased taxes, reduced consumer credit, and reduced tariffs. Giscard's stabilization plan succeeded in slowing down prices and wages, but it also produced a stagnation in industrial production over the next 18 months as well as a 50 per cent rise in unemployment. The principle objective of the fourth plan — steady expansion with price stability — was not achieved. In fact, Giscard's stabilization plan had for practical purposes replaced "the plan."

As many are now prepared to admit, French planning (aside from the work of the Commission) has been reduced to little more than mere forecasting. In its heyday, advocates of French-style planning insisted that it offered something intermediate between the free enterprise economy and state socialism, a way out of a "false dilemma" and a means of closing "an old issue." Vera Lutz, a dispassionate observer, after undertaking an exhaustive evaluation of French planning, disagrees:

I have concluded on both empirical and logical grounds that French planning never had worked in France — nor could have worked there or anywhere else — as a largely "non-interventionist" form of integral central planning. . . . The view that it is possible to graft certain features of the centrally-planned economy on to the market economy so as to form the perfect hybrid ... must, we conclude, be dismissed in favour of the traditional views that this aim is impossible. Thus the "dilemma" persists and the "ideological issue" remains open. There is nothing in French-style planning, or in related conceptions of "modern capitalism," which dispenses with the need for us, as citizens of our respective "western" countries, to decide which of two opposite directions we prefer to take.[30]

By which Ms. Lutz means, of course, capitalism or socialism.

It was inside one of the frequent rounds of rapid growth, rising prices, deliberate deflation, and stagnation that the May events broke out in 1968. And now the French economy is reeling from yet another round of the deflationary, reflationary dialectic with Giscard d'Estaing as its executioner once again.

The May uprising raised the spectre of revolution. The bourgeoisie is now fearful that it will be raised again in the light of the new economic crisis. But for the moment the cold war that has developed between the Communist Party and the Socialist Party, partners in the narrowly defeated 1973 electoral alliance, has destroyed any possibility of political action to exploit the government's weakness.[31]

West Germany and the European Common Market

One of the victims of the new economic crisis could well turn out to be the European Common Market. In an article ominously titled "Can the Common Market Survive?", *Time* magazine quotes West German Chancellor Helmut Schmidt as saying "The European community is breaking up."[32] Schmidt's prediction seems premature but the crisis strikes at the root of the EEC's fundamental weakness.

The EEC is a transitory phenomenon, a hybrid creation that cannot remain in its present state. While the nine-member countries have agreed to allow unlimited trade and capital flows within their national borders, they have established neither a common state, nor a common currency. Neither the EEC Commission nor the Council of Ministers has the power to enforce its decisions on any government. Ernest Mandel, a Belgian economist, has been predicting for some years that the fundamental contradictions of this hybrid institution would break to the surface when there was a generalized recession in Europe. An economic recession is the precise moment when the state must intervene to bolster the system. The capitalist leaders of the member states are now faced with a clear alternative, according to Mandel: "Either create a real European super-state capable of working out an anti-crisis policy on an international scale, or fall back on an anti-crisis policy on a national scale. In either case, the Common Market (as we now know it) goes by the boards."[33]

It seems obvious that, in the face of a generalized recession, the European multinational trusts that were formed with the inception of the EEC would attempt to promote a superstate that alone could effectively serve their interests. On the other hand, the Europeanization of capital has penetrated only certain industries, leaving many capitalist groups still organized around their national states. In any event, in the absence of a superstate, the most likely response of the capitalists in each country is to press their separate governments to act against recession on a purely national level, that is, towards protectionist measures. Italy and Denmark have already moved in this direction, imposing limitations on imports in general, but also on imports originating from Common Market countries.

At the base of the current crisis is the uneven pattern of weakness and strength among the member nations. While the average annual rate of inflation in consumer prices has climbed to about 20 per cent in the major nations of Britain, France, Germany, and Italy, the dispersal around this average is wide and continues to grow, so that inflation in Germany is less than half what it is in France, Britain and Italy. And while German exports exceeded imports by between 30 and 40 per cent, the deficit of imports to exports grew to 15 per cent in France and to more than 30 per cent in Britain and Italy. Germany controls one-half of the total foreign exchange reserves in Europe.

In concrete terms, the survival of the EEC through the present crisis and its transformation toward a superstate may be in the hands of the government of West Germany. The Italian, Danish, and British governments have been obliged to resort to protectionist measures because of their huge balance of payments deficits. If West Germany's spectacular surpluses were pooled for the use of all member countries, resort to protectionist measures would be unnecessary. But as Mandel writes, "Such a 'pooling' of exchange reserves is obviously unthinkable without a common currency and a common economic, monetary and fiscal policy, and a common employment policy; that is, without a common government and a common "superstate".[34] However, Bonn agreed to bail out Italy with an extensive loan backed up by guaranteed access to a sizeable portion of Italy's gold supply. And as 1974 came to a close, it reluctantly agreed to contribute to a $9.5 billion Market fund to pump resources into the weaker areas.

Mandel describes the dilemma faced by West Germany: "If it opts for a "new push for the Common Market," it will have to absorb the balance of payments deficits and the effects of accelerated inflation of its major partners." If Chancellor Helmut Schmidt decides against footing the bill, the consequences for Bonn are equally serious. Protectionist measures would threaten to spread to other member countries and "the cumulative effects of these measures . . . would deal a decisive blow to the singular pillar of the "prosperity" of West German capitalists: soaring exports."* In short, according to Mandel, Germany's position "would then certainly succeed in "exporting" the recession to West Germany if West Germany did not export its exchange reserves to its neighbours."[35]

Of all the major capitalist nations, West Germany, with the lowest rate of inflation, least unemployment, largest balance of payments surpluses, and abundant coal supplies, has been so far the least affected by the economic crisis. Nevertheless it has not been trouble-free. Restrictive government policy in 1973 held down the rate of growth and caused increased unemployment. With wage increases running ahead of prices, there has been a squeeze on profits. The failure of three West German banks within two weeks in August gave cause for concern. By the winter of 1974, the general recession was beginning to have an impact on Germany, with car production down 25 per cent from the year before and chemicals and machine goods, Germany's other major export commodities, also well down. Nearly a quarter of West German production goes for export. With the rest of the capitalist world being overtaken by a recession, West Germany's export boom was bound to collapse. By the spring of 1975, industrial output was 10 per cent lower than 12 months earlier, and unemployment stood at over a million (5 per cent), with almost another million workers on reduced hours.

With West Germany herself absorbing over 50 per cent of the exports of the other eight nations in the Common Market, Chancellor Schmidt came under heavy pressure from them to reflate the German economy. However, with a budget already well in the red the government could not raise its deficit without adding to inflationary pressures. An expansionary fiscal program was nevertheless adopted with income-tax cuts, expanded public works, and new investment tax credits. These measures had remarkably

---

* German industry exports just under 25 per cent of its output and 50 per cent of its export market is in the Common Market.

little initial impact on production and employment, unable as they were to overcome the far more powerful external recessionary tendencies. Their major effect was to re-inflate the economy from the 5 per cent level it had fallen to at the beginning of 1975 to over 7 per cent mid-way through the year.

Until now, at least, the German bourgeoisie have had one marked advantage over their counterparts in the rest of Europe: a lethargic trade union movement. This goes back to the early days of the allied occupation when German industrialists found themselves, in spite of the destruction of 20 per cent of their productive machinery, with an industrial empire without equal in the rest of Europe. They had the support of American and British trustees who vetoed any efforts by local and regional bodies to nationalize basic industry such as coal and steel and dismissed the workers' councils that had sprung up to begin production again in the functioning plants. They could also count on the support of the Catholic Church, which led an ideological crusade against Communists and Social Democrats.

But most important was the weakness of the German labour movement: half of the old Communist Party membership had been arrested, killed, or imprisoned by the Nazis; many others had emigrated; still others had been removed by Stalin's purges of 1938-39. Even so, membership in the Communist Party expanded sharply in both zones after the war. A series of blunders, capitulation to a political line dictated by the U.S.S.R., and genuine fear that Communist advocacy for a united Germany meant Sovietization from above along the lines inaugurated in the People's Democracies, eroded the early strength of the party. Appealing to middle-class groups it thought were ready to accept a reunified Germany, the Party became little more than a mouthpiece for Soviet diplomacy, and lost all contact with working class objectives. By 1952 it was only a shadow of its 1945 self. When it was made illegal in 1956, the event evoked little reaction from the working class.

The Social Democratic Party (SPD) had a much more promising beginning. Under the dynamic leadership of Kurt Schumacher, the party displayed great vitality from 1945 onwards. It advocated nationalization of major industry, agrarian reform involving redistribution of land, and comprehensive economic planning, and it assumed a critical position towards the Allies, fingering them as the supporters of "our political and class enemies." But the SPD refused to utilize strikes for political purposes although they were numerous in 1947-48. The 1948 monetary reform and Marshall Plan aid robbed the Social Democrats of their political initiative. Defeated in the first elections in 1949 and again in 1953, the left

wing of the party yielded ground to the right, which was already
making its peace with the dominant forces of post-war German
society.

In context, then, "the German miracle" is no miracle at all, but
the product of the relative strength between social classes. The
weakness and disorganization of the German working class, barely
recovered from Nazi persecution, permitted German industrialists
to produce at low cost and thereby carve out for itself a leading
position in the world market while waiting for the gradual expansion of the domestic market. Through the early fifties, while production was expanding rapidly, workers' consumption was held
down. By 1951 it was still less than it was in 1936. The regular flow
of East German refugees, lasting until 1961, provided a large reser-
voir of trained workers who helped keep wages low. The alleged
threat of Soviet invasion was a handy tool used by the wily Ade-
nauer to repress any opposition arising in Parliament or the daily
press.

Not until the mid-1960s did German capitalism begin to feel the
negative aspects of full employment. In 1965, wages rose by 11.4
per cent; in 1966 by 7.4 per cent. The working class was finally
increasing its share of the national income, and capitalists found it
increasingly difficult to pass on wage increases without provoking a
fall in exports and consumer sales. In 1965 and 1966, prices rose by
4 per cent as against the international level of 2-3 per cent, and gross
profits were falling. Rising material costs due to the Vietnam War
and the heavy influx of American dollars were other sources of the
inflationary spiral. Like its counterparts elsewhere, the German
government was finally forced to invoke a deliberate recession,
ending two decades of virtually uninterrupted steady growth.
German capitalists now wanted planning of the sort that was well
underway in the rest of Europe, but Erhard's orthodoxy stood in
the way. The answer seemed to lie in a Christian-Social-
Democratic coalition of the kind already achieved in Italy and in a
different way by the Labour government in Britain. The mouthpiece of big business in Germany, the *Industrial Review*, clearly
understood the task of the "Grand Coalition":

> The SPD must fulfill a very special function within the govern-
> ment. . . . Its close contacts with the trade unions, which have
> hitherto served as a means for the trade unions to influence the
> welfare policies of the SPD, must now, on the contrary, serve as a
> means for the SPD to influence the trade union leaders. Both the
> governing parties must closely adhere to their decision to avoid
> all spending that would serve to promote consumption and thus
> reduce the reservoir out of which investments are financed.

The new government followed this advice. The Social Democrats' Minister for Economic Affairs, Schiller, pruned public spending, raised taxes on several consumer goods, offered special tax allowances on investment, and persuaded the trade unions to agree to a voluntary wage vetting. Little has changed in the Social-Democratic-Liberal Party coalition that has governed Germany under the chancellorship of Willy Brandt and his successor Helmut Schmidt, except for Brandt's courageous detente with East Germany and the U.S.S.R. Indeed, this detente has helped to open the door to a revitalized radical element within the SPD which the leadership is now trying desperately to bury.

With the appearance of growing economic difficulties, there are also some signs of political instability. The October 27, 1974, elections in the states of Hessen and Bavaria witnessed significant gains by the Christian Social Union (CSU) of Franz Josef Strauss, the Bavarian partner of the national Christian Democratic Union. Disgraced from public office twelve years ago in the infamous *Der Spiegel* affair, the authoritarian Herr Strauss is well on his way to a political comeback. In an article datelined Munich, titled "Germany Edges To the Right," American correspondent Herbert S. Levine writes, "His program consisted, as it always has, of little more than a continual harping on the Red Menace. And with his thumping beer-hall oratory, he was able to produce the greatest victory any party has ever won in a state election in the Federal Republic."[36] It is commonly believed that Strauss will make a bid to become the CDU/CSU candidate for chancellor in 1976. West Germany's ruling Social Democratic Party, besides its difficult decision regarding the Common Market, is wracked with scandal and draining its energies on an internal campaign to purge the party of its Marxist elements. As Levine warns:

> The leadership of the SPD, in its desperate attempt to cleanse the party of Marxists, is only playing Strauss's game for him, and by his rules. . . . Attempts by the CDU to set up the Communist scarecrow failed dismally through 1972, as long as German prosperity held. Now that the voters fear the loss of their recently won economic security, they are more willing to listen to the slickly-produced, well-financed propaganda spewed out by the Strauss machine."[37]

This chilling commentary from a highly reputable reporter lends weight to an earlier prediction by Willy Brandt shortly before he resigned from office, namely that Western Europe will soon slide, engineless and rudderless into dictatorship. In Herr Brandt's view it matters little whether the dictatorship comes from "a politbureau or a junta." Some will disagree that it makes no difference.

Certainly we can recognize that we have come to the end of an era in monopoly capitalism where the U.S. reigned supreme as the recognized leader of a fairly stable and harmonious alliance of capitalist nations. We are passing into a new era, the form and dimensions of which are impossible to predict. But the main areas of conflict can be outlined:

(1) inter-capitalist rivalries in the form of trade wars, the competition for scarce raw materials, and attempts to carve up new alliances, with the United States, Western Europe, and Japan struggling for the leadership of the capitalist world.

(2) continued struggles for national liberation in the Third World.

(3) heightened class warfare as the ruling class throughout the capitalist world attempts to control inflation by extending state control — placing a lid on wages and diluting free collective bargaining and the right to strike in "essential" industries.

What emerges from these conflicts will depend in large part on the kind of defensive struggles mounted by labour, on its ability to move from the defensive to the offensive, that is, to go beyond mere wage demands, and to co-ordinate its efforts on an international basis. While we have no reason to be optimistic on these counts, neither can we afford to be pessimistic and resign ourselves to some form of necessary despotism.

VIII / What Can Be Done?

The inflation-depression dialectic produces uneven results over the population. The majority of people have suffered to some degree in the past two years and the worst is yet to come. There are no recent precedents for a sustained and generalized reduction of living standards. There have been four recessions since the end of World War II, but these were relatively short-lived. Canadians have been taught to believe that economic prosperity is a permanent feature of our economic system. Capitalism has been legitimized because of its capacity to "deliver the goods" to most of the people: most of us have come to take food, clothing, and shelter for granted. In the past thirty years the idea of scarcity has been far removed from everyday consciousness. It has made a swift and unexpected comeback. One of the features of the seventies is that food and housing alone absorb half or more of most families' incomes. These together with clothing and transportation now take up 70 to 75 per cent of many family incomes. It is possible that the food and energy crises of 1973-74 were preparations for a long-term reduction of living standards.

The Vietnam War and Watergate have shaken the confidence of Americans, and also of Canadians and others, in the activities of government. The economic crisis and the general price gouging that accompanies it have cast a shadow of suspicion on the heretofore unblemished reputation of the giant corporations. As the economy becomes more and more shaky, the public begins to explore or is at least open to new possibilities in politics. Increasingly we come to see that the corporations and their government allies are at the centre of what ails society, be it the destruction of the environment, skyrocketing food prices, or plant closures.

The striking shift of public opinion is illustrated by a poll conducted by Gallup in May of 1974. Shortly after Arnold Toynbee commented on the probable demise of the free enterprise system due to plundering of the earth's irreplaceable natural resources, Gallup interviewers questioned Canadians about this. 40 per cent said that free enterprise was on the way out and 4 per cent said that it had already gone.

Similar shifts are occurring in the United States, as demonstrated by a recent Harris survey. According to the *New York Times* account:

> "In 1967," Mr. Harris observed in an interview, "substantial majorities of our sample — 60 to 75 per cent — thought the following people were 'dangerous or harmful to the country': people who didn't believe in God, black militants, student demonstrators, prostitutes, homosexuals. In the fall of 1973 we couldn't find a majority to say that any one of those groups was dangerous."
>
> "Today," he continued, "the people considered 'dangerous' by a majority of Americans are these: people who hire political spies (52 per cent); generals who conduct secret bombing raids (67 per cent); politicians who engage in secret wiretapping (71 per cent); businessmen who make illegal political contributions (81 per cent); and politicians who try to use the Central Intelligence Agency, the Federal Bureau of Investigation and the Secret Service for political purposes or to try to restrict freedom (88 per cent)." "That," Mr. Harris said, "is what has happened in America."[1]

If over 80 per cent of the American people now find corporate control over their history a danger it means that they have finally regained their collective sense and that serious concern over real enemies is replacing paranoia about foreign and domestic devils.

Basic economic and political as well as social questions that lay dormant during the "ecstasy" of the fifties and early sixties have now been thrown into the public domain. The public has abundant information, and experiences the crisis in everyday life. But without a political framework the new information is just so much scary data, leading to helplessness and cynicism rather than action. There is a danger that we will make ourselves into spectators of an anticipated economic and political disaster. We can escape from this predicament by making the crisis the subject of political debate and actions that centre on issues and concrete programs. And for this we require an active and organized left political force that can bring together all those in this country who recognize that the obstacle to making a decent society lies in corporate capitalism at home and corporate imperialism throughout the world.

Within a highly centralized and monopolistic economy there is no effective way of controlling inflation short of inflicting mass unemployment or repressing living standards. And without a war or an easily identifiable external enemy, it is highly unlikely that Canadians will accept either mass unemployment or a decline in living standards without a struggle. Since the war in Vietnam and the detente have eliminated the old bugaboos of the "red peril" and the "yellow peril," the major efforts of government and the corporations must turn towards the elimination of internal sources of opposition. * Employers are demanding increased productivity through speed-ups and stretch-outs. There is already pressure to pass laws outlawing strikes in "essential" industries and to introduce an incomes policy whose effect would be to prevent workers from increasing or even maintaining real purchasing power. For certain, the disruption of work caused by strikes, particularly those directed at the erosion of living standards, will take on an increasingly political colouration.

The new inflationary conditions, shortages in essential commodities and services, and the resulting shift in the pattern of consumption have blocked many of the conventional avenues open to trade unions to protect real wages. Cost-of-living allowances usually have upper limits beyond which the employer is not obliged to go. They fail to compensate adequately for the rise in the price of essentials. The garden-variety collective agreement does not deal with plant closures, mass lay-offs, or even speed-ups. Even the strong dose of worker militancy that is already evident cannot stem the tide if it continues to be bottled up in fragmented and isolated struggles that mark the way trade unions operate in North America. New strategies are necessary, as well as new alliances, if the forces of what has come to be called "friendly fascism" are not to overtake us all.

Who Benefits from Inflation?

Economists admit that inflation produces what they call "perverse income transfers." What that means in layman's language is that, over the past few years, inflation has been inflicting financial ruin

---

* While a major assault is being launched against unions throughout Canada, the old tactic of divide and conquer has also begun to resurface with new investigations into the role of immigration in the economy. As unemployment mounts and workers becom particularly job-conscious, the state, by bringing the question of immigration into the public limelight at this time, is hoping that the working class will turn on recent immigrants as the cause of its growing insecurity, rather than on the employers, government, and the capitalist system itself.

on the old, the disabled, the unemployed, on fatherless families on welfare, and on workers earning the minimum wage or employed in declining industries and declining regions. Recent increases in government social-welfare programs like old age pensions and family allowance, as well as increases in minimum wage rates and unemployment insurance, offset only some of the damage. Even workers in strong unions fall behind. They are barely touched by these government programs, and they end up paying for a disproportional amount of the taxes that finance them. As for people in middle and high level incomes, the impact of inflation can vary greatly:

> It works out as a heavy confiscatory property tax on all savers and investors who are, economically speaking, slow footed and slow thinking. It victimizes all creatures of habit and all practitioners of ancient capitalist virtues, like those who have faith in life insurance and in savings accounts and who would be horrified at the notion of confiscatory taxes on accumulated wealth. Prominent among the beneficiaries of inflation are individuals and business firms of the alert heavy-borrowing, fast-moving speculative type, and more generally, all the sly, swift killers of the business and financial jungles.[2]

As the chart indicates, 1974's price rise has given capitalists the largest share of national income that they have received in a quarter of a century. The level of corporation profits more than doubled between 1970 and 1974 ($8 billion to $19 billion). Corporate profits rose by 32 per cent in 1974 on top of a 36 per cent rise in 1973, a 21 per cent increase in 1972 and a 16 per cent increase in 1971.* In each period these gains have exceeded the rate of growth of the gross national product, so that the share of the GNP going to profits rose consistently from 1971 up to 1975. These extraordinary gains of the capitalist class came at the expense of Canadian workers, whose share of the GNP has dropped to 70 per cent, the lowest it has been since 1966.

Like all capitalist countries, Canada has always suffered from a grossly unequal distribution of income. By the mid-1970s, this inequality has grown even greater. Contrary to popular mythology, the distribution of income has become increasingly unequal over the past 20 years. In 1951 the bottom 20 per cent of Canada's population received only 4.4 per cent of the total income (welfare payments included). In 1971 their share fell to 3.6 per cent. On the other

---

* "After tax and excluding inventory gains attributable to rising prices, corporate profits rose 25.1 per cent in 1973, after having increased 23.8 per cent and 5.5 per cent in 1972 and 1971 respectively."(Economic Council of Canada, *Eleventh Annual Review.*)

Figure 17
Profit as a Per Cent of Canada's National Income

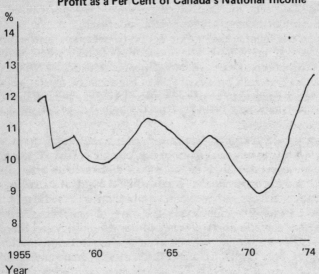

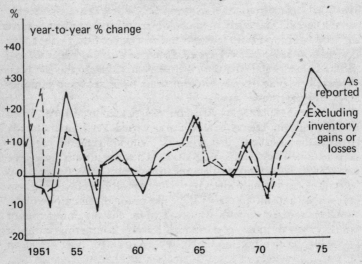

Source: Statistics Canada.

hand, the top 20 per cent took 42.8 per cent of the income in 1951 and this had risen to 43.3 per cent by 1971. Undoubtedly the mammoth 140 per cent increase in profit since 1970 has caused a dramatic shift of income in favour of the super-rich.

Among the biggest gainers are property owners — owners of land, buildings, machinery, and inventories of goods whose value rises in proportion to prices. National income statistics do not measure this type of gain because it takes the form of capital gains which are not deemed to be part of income. To this extent, statistics which show the relative share of labour and capital in national income are misleading.

As is generally recognized, inflation shifts wealth from creditors to debtors who can pay back loans in depreciable dollars. That part of the population that holds its savings in dollars, bank accounts, pension funds, mortgages, etc., tends to be robbed of its savings. Interest payments can provide some compensation to creditors, but inflation has tended to outpace the rate of interest. Almost everyone has some financial assets and some liabilities and therefore is winning and losing simultaneously when inflation accelerates. But it is only the net debtors as a group who come out ahead. The two biggest net debtors are government and corporations. Broadly speaking, the only net creditors are households.

Small businessmen and farmers are perennial victims of inflation. Their product is sold in competitive markets while their purchases take place in monopolistic markets where prices rise steeply with inflation. The effect is not uniform. Farmer's incomes have increased disproportionately over the past three years, owing to the dramatic increase in food prices. Pensioners and others on fixed incomes are especially hard hit by inflation, although this has been tempered to some degree in recent years by increases in pensions and welfare assistance levels.

While living standards of working people tend to be undermined by inflation, the effects here are also varied. As I have already stressed, the so-called "dirty workers," who are generally unorganized, are double victims of inflation. They are usually low-wage earners with little or no margin to reduce savings or delay purchases when the prices of necessities rise. They are also the first to be laid off when anti-inflationary policies produce unemployment. Among organized workers, whether real purchasing power rises or falls depends on the success unions have in countering inflation through collective bargaining. In the early stages they are at an obvious disadvantage, since businesses are free to change their prices without notice, whereas unions are bound to two- and three-year contracts. Many of them will do little better than catch up with lost income, although all attempt to win contracts that anticipate further price increases. As a result of its wage struggles, during the final stages of the upswing in the typical business cycle labour is usually successful in improving its income shares. This stage was reached at the end of 1974. It is no coincidence that the Liberal government began promoting its program of wage restraints soon after.

In the inflation of 1971-1973, compensation movements failed to dent the dramatic shift of wealth to the capitalist sector. Corporate profit rose nearly 2½ times as fast as gross national product. The statistical category called "wages, salaries, and supplementary labour income" includes the salaries of senior management and corporate executives and also includes various amounts of income not actually received by workers. Nevertheless, its share of the national income has declined. Moreover, much of the increase in labour income is owing to the increase in the size of the paid work force. On a per-worker basis, the increase in labour income was only .1 per cent between 1971 and 1973 — barely keeping up with the rise in the consumer price index over the same period. In 1973 and much of 1974, earnings per worker actually fell behind the rise in consumer prices. By the end of 1973, the average Canadian worker was losing $5.50 a week in real purchasing power, compared to a year earlier. These losses continued until mid-way through 1974 when wage increases finally caught up with price increases.

Table 19
Who Benefits From Inflation?

	1971	1973	% increase
	(millions of current dollars)		
Total GNP	93,307	118,702	27.6
Corporation profits	8,692	14,275	64.3
Interest	3,810	5,180	33.3
Farm Income	1,464	3,014	111.1
Unincorporated Business	5,861	6,803	16.1
Wages, Salaries and Supplementary Labour Income	51,342	64,108	·24.9

An incontestable consequence of the accelerated inflation since 1971 has been the widening of the gap between rich and poor in this country. While proof of this trend is not fully available, there are significant indications that this is so. As is well known, the pattern of family expenditure varies with income class. Lower income families spend much more of their income on necessities such as food and shelter. Indeed, the Economic Council of Canada uses this criterion to identify poverty.* It is the price of necessities, particularly food and shelter, that has risen most since 1971. The three basics, food, shelter, and clothing, account for about 80 per cent of the price rise since 1971.** When families are classed according to income, the poorest 20 per cent, with incomes under $5,000 a year, spend about 65 per cent of their income on food and shelter, compared to about 35 per cent by the richest fifth, with incomes over $15,000. A family that receives under $5,000 would have had to raise its income by about 35 per cent between 1971 and 1974 just to retain its standard of living, compared to something less than 25 per cent for a family receiving over $15,000. Only a radical redistribution of income in this period could have assured that the gap between rich and poor would not have been widened. There is no indication that this has occurred. If past history is any guide, whatever redistribution of income has occurred flows the other way from the poor to the rich.

The rapid growth in gross national product over the past 30 years and the increase in income levels of the average family disguise the ever-widening gap between rich and poor and the fact that many Canadians, even before the recent inflation, were actually worse off in an absolute sense than they were a decade and more ago. Figures to confirm this gloomy story will not be found in any economic textbook or government study. Caught up in the magic of economic growth and fixated on averages, our professional economists have successfully avoided the question of income distribution for a quarter of a century. Nevertheless, the figures speak for themselves. They can be found in a little pamphlet prepared by Leo Johnson, a Marxist historian, and published by a tiny publishing venture called New Hogtown Press.[3]

The figures show that the average Canadian worker receives very little money for his labour — half of them received less than $4,810 in 1971. The purchasing power of the lowest tenth of all income receivers fell off by 41 per cent between 1946 and 1971; the second lowest decile dropped by 3.5 per cent and even the third lowest dropped between 1966 and 1971.[†] According to Johnson:

---

* Where basic necessities take 70 per cent or more of a family's budget, it is assumed that the family has so little income left over for medical use, education, recreation, and the like, that it may be considered impoverished.

** The price of food rose by about 53 per cent between 1971 and 1974, the price of shelter by about 23 per cent. The price of all consumer goods, excluding food, rose by just under 20 per cent.

† Johnson employs the standard method of measuring income inequality; that is, ranking the population by income and measuring what percentage of total personal income accrues to the richest 10 per cent of the population, the second

> The disparity between rich and poor has increased enormously. For example, in 1946 the richest 10 per cent of the earners received about 20 times as much income as the poorest 10 per cent; whereas in 1971 they received 45 times as much. Similarly, in 1946, the income received by the richest decile equalled that received by the poorest 55 per cent of earners, whereas in 1971 their income equalled that of the poorest 64 per cent of earners.[4]

As Johnson remarks, the enormous increase in new wealth in Canada since 1946 has had little direct benefit for the poorer segment of the population but rather has gone into making the already wealthy wealthier. Whereas increases in income among the rich are measured in the thousands of dollars, among the lower income groups they are measured in the hundreds — crumbs from the table of the wealthy. In the case of the poorest deciles, there are no increases at all.

The average earner had an increase of purchasing power of $1,600 between 1946 and 1971, when measured in constant 1961 dollars. The richest 10 per cent had increases of $4,600, almost three times as much. The bottom 50 per cent had a total net increase of $360, while the poorest tenth lost an average of $125 per earner. Over the past 25 years, the richest 20 per cent of Canadian earners received half of all new income, while the poorest 50 per cent received only 20 per cent. The huge growth dividends since the war have been used to reinforce and increase inequality.

If the distribution of real gains in the period 1971-1974 is similar to the distribution in 1966-1971, then about 50 per cent of the increased GNP will have gone to the richest fifth of income receivers while the poorest fifth will have lost 1 per cent. But because of the uneven impact of the inflation, the loss among the poorest fifth is likely to be greater. It should also be noted that these figures, as gloomy as they are, understate the extent of inequality. Unrealized capital gains do not show up in the data, and income transformed into expense accounts does not appear as income. Tax "avoidance" (legal) and tax "evasion" (illegal) are a prerogative of the rich.

Nor, finally, does the much-vaunted welfare system or progressive taxation overcome these inequalities. So-called transfer payments from the rich to the poor have made no impact at all and the tax system, far from being progressive, on examination turns out to be regressive.

In theory, income taxes take a much higher proportion of

---

richest 10 per cent, and so forth. The more income going to the richest deciles and the less going to the poorest ones, the more unequal is the distribution of income.

income from the rich than from the poor. In practice, this tendency is vitiated by various deductions which reduce taxable income of the rich below their actual incomes. Thus the rich gain the political advantage of high nominal rates and the economic advantages of low effective rates. Even so, income taxes take a small step toward improving income distribution. But barely a third of all taxes are individual income taxes; an almost equal amount is collected in property and sales taxes which take a larger percentage of income from the poor than from the rich. There is an involved and still unsettled debate as to how completely corporations shift their taxes onto consumers by raising prices. To the extent that it is shifted, it has the same effect as a sales tax.

A study by Professor Thomas A. Wilson of the University of Toronto showed that when all taxes are taken into account, families whose total income from all sources was less than $2,000 per year paid more than 60 per cent of their gross incomes in taxes. For families at $10,000 per year, taxes took only 38 per cent of income, while above $10,000 little further progression occurred. A more recent study prepared by Allan Maslove for the Economic Council of Canada finds that, for families receiving less than $2,000 in income earned primarily from wages,* taxes from federal, provincial, and municipal sources took from 60 per cent to 150 per cent of that earned income in every province. Even when transfer payments of all kinds are included, Maslove found that the poorest income recipients still pay a much higher proportion of their income in taxes than by those who are better off (60 per cent for those receiving less than $2,000 a year; 35 per cent for those receiving more than $15,000 a year).

The Special Senate Committee on Poverty defined the poverty line for a family of four at $5,000 in 1969, or adjusted for inflation, $6,650 in 1974. In spite of the enormous increase in total wealth in the post-war period, fully 60 per cent of all earners still could not support a family of this size by 1974. Vast numbers of Canadians have substandard housing, poor health care, and nutritional deficiencies. This is a result of the structure of income and the failure of the market system to provide cheap basic necessities such as food and housing. Working people have adapted the family structure to compensate for this dismal situation. Over 40 per cent of families now have at least two persons in the labour force compared to less than 30 per cent in 1951. It is this doubling up of income earners that has allowed many families to escape impoverishment.

---

* Maslove calls this the effective tax rate on a "broad income base", which is simply income before taxes and before government income supplement programs. See his *The Pattern of Taxation in Canada*, Chart 5-1, p. 65.

In the 1950s and the 1960s, Canadian and American writers were singing the praises of the income revolution. It is likely true that income distribution improved somewhat from 1929 to 1945, mainly as a result of the devastating effect of the Depression on property values and incomes and the higher taxes and full employment of World War II. But the revolution was over by the time it was discovered, and a counter-revolution had set in.

Welfare rates across Canada fall well below the Senate Report's poverty line. In no province does it come higher than four-fifths of the poverty line. This should come as no surprise. If welfare rates were raised to meet basic family needs even at the poverty line level, hundreds of thousands of workers would be tempted to quit low-paying jobs in order to improve the living conditions of their families. Welfare rates have to be kept below decent levels in order to keep workers in the labour force. Were they to be raised even to the poverty line, the capitalistic labour market would be in danger of serious erosion.

In a society which depends on the wage incentive to force people to work, few would work for wages if an adequate income were available without work. One of the consequences of capitalism is that the motivation for work other than that based on wage incentives is effectively destroyed. In a society where individual material rewards are the main incentive to work, it follows that significant inequalities in labour earnings must exist in order to induce workers to work hard and to acquire new skills. The welfare system, in turn, must operate within the constraints imposed by the need to maintain this inequality.

Getting it Back

It seems reasonable to expect that the erosion of living standards after decades of relative prosperity would produce a degree of radicalization within the work force. The last few generations of workers have been sold on the idea that, whatever its faults, North American capitalism provides for the material needs of most people. We have all been raised on the idea that food, clothing, and shelter, at least, can be taken for granted. We were given every reason to believe that a new or fairly new home and a recent model automobile was part of the wages of labour. How will we adjust to the new situation, a life of hard times? The widespread anger and general distrust of the political and social structure raises serious questions about the political outcome of the economic crisis.

It is a matter of historical record that as living costs have increased so have work stoppages in the following year. In 1974, 9.3 million man-days were lost in Canada because of strikes and lock-outs, exceeding the previous annual record total in 1972. It is not a record that is likely to last long. The years 1974 and 1975 will go down as one of the most turbulent periods of modern labour history. The expectations of unions are clashing with a hold-the-line management policy, making confrontations inevitable. It is at times such as these that various spokesmen, purporting to speak for the "innocent victimized public," come forward with blatantly anti-labour measures such as compulsory arbitration, labour courts, and strike prohibitions. By the end of 1974, the B.C., Quebec, Saskatchewan, Ontario and federal governments had already forced striking workers back to their jobs.

One-third of the walk-outs in 1974 were illegal, occurring during the life of the collective agreement as workers sought interim pay raises and provisions that indexed their wages and salaries to the cost of living. In the month of September, 1974, 4,000 Quebec workers were conducting illegal strikes on top of 6,000 workers on legal strikes. Six months earlier, the Front Commun of Quebec unions, composed of the Quebec Federation of Labour (FTQ), the Confederation of National Trade Unions (CSN), and the Quebec Federation of Teachers (CEQ), held a special congress to formulate its demands that prices be frozen and that labour contracts be re-opened. The working document adopted by the Front Commun was titled "Rising Prices are Organized Theft." The unions pledged their support to locals that struck over the indexation demand even if it was in mid-contract and therefore illegal. Yvon Charbonneau, President of the CEQ, went so far as to declare: "It doesn't matter to us whether the means are legal or illegal. What matters is whether they are legitimate." In September, the Front sponsored a demonstration that rallied 8,000 people in support of the striking workers, though co-ordinated mobilization of the strike broke down with the reappearance of conflict among the three Quebec labour centres.

Workers in English Canada have not heard such a call to arms from their labour leaders, who have gone no further than to urge their affiliates to obtain cost-of-living clauses in their contracts. They have systematically backed away from all illegal strikes. The battles against inflation in English Canada remain a series of unconnected struggles conducted by isolated union locals, unsupported by their national or international offices or by their regional federations. Such has been the history of trade union struggles in English Canada ever since the days of the Winnipeg General Strike. Except for the co-ordinated effort to win the Rand formula and the 40-hour week after World War II, the only concerted actions in the last 30 years have been the campaign to purge the Communists from the labour movement in the late forties and early fifties, and the more recent drive to defeat the movement for independent Canadian unions.

It is the public sector that is producing the most explosive labour-management struggles. The old master-slave relationship in the public sector is coming to a swift end. The changes in this arena have serious political overtones. The three-week Toronto transit strike in the fall of 1974 gives a hint of things to come. Union members refused to obey special legislation that was passed to force them back to work. In the 1950s, when the railway unions were ordered back to work by Parliament, their leader Frank Hall said "We obey the law, even when the law is an ass." Robert Nielsen, an editorial writer for the *Toronto Star*, commented:

> The just ended Toronto transit strike is only one of several current proofs that respect for law . . . has sharply declined since Hall's day in the 1950's and '60's. . . . Defiance of back-to-work laws and injunctions by public service unions is commonplace, almost chronic in Canada today. . . . The law-abiding traditions of Canadians, a tradition based on understanding of the moral weight and political rationale behind the law, is being eroded.[5]

It seems unlikely that such blatant contempt for a law used to oppress working men and women is just a temporary phenomenon.

Governments at all levels have been spending disproportional amounts of tax dollars on services, subsidies, and concessions to business while services to people have also been growing rapidly.* Much public money is dissipated in incredible plunder and incompetence, top-heavy administration, and inordinately high salaries to senior administrators. The net effect has been to force lower-ranked public employees to subsidize services through substandard wages. What the governments have been saying to their employees is: "We'll never give you a fair deal voluntarily. You'll have to bludgeon it out of us." This is precisely what public employees have been in the process of doing. In his *Toronto Star* labour column in mid-October 1974, Ed Finn wrote:

> A few years ago, when the civil servants of Quebec staged their

---

* Expenditures at all levels of government on health, social welfare and education doubled from 6.5 per cent of Gross National Product in 1951 to 13.0 per cent by 1965. On this and other matters relating to government spending, see the exhaustive study of Richard M. Bird, *The Growth of Government Spending in Canada*. In a more critical vein see Richard Deaton, "The Fiscal Crisis and the Public Employees," *Our Generation*, Vol. 8, No. 14.

massive "common front" strike, it was considered one of those French-Canadian aberrations. Politicians in other provinces assured one another "it could never happen here." They should be jarred out of their complacency by now. They would have to be blind and dead not to be aware of the volcanoes of unrest rumbling in their once tranquil bureaucracies.

The federal government began its counter-attack in December 1974 by setting an unofficial 15 per cent per year ceiling on wage increases in the public sector. The new Liberal "hard-line" campaign picked up in the spring of 1975. It was pronounced in the June budget, which proclaimed the government's intention of setting an example for industry by bargaining tough with its employees. The government of Quebec was similarly provocative: after making offers that public employees could only refuse, it would enact emergency legislation empowering itself to decide the remaining issues. It is instructive to follow the developments as reported in the daily press:

March 12. The Liberal Cabinet prosecutes 1,700 General Labour and Trades workers for "illegal strike action" during the Public Service Alliance of Canada strike amidst the demands of the Canadian Manufacturers' Association to remove the right to strike from federal employees.

April 9. The Prime Minister warns labour to cut back strike activity. "Collective bargaining . . . will not remain free if it cannot be made less destructive than it is in Canada today."

April 10. John Turner announces the government's intention to propose a voluntary program of wage and price restraints. The same day a report on public sector strikes is presented by Jacob Finkelman, Chairman of the Public Service Staff Relations Board, proposing that his board have the power to order public employees back to work if Parliament is not sitting; to suspend designated employees who are legally forbidden to strike, should they participate in strikes; fire union officials who counsel such strikes; expand the number of workers forbidden to strike; prohibit strikes not authorized by bargaining agents.

April 11. Jean Chretien, president of the Treasury Board, charges 37 air traffic controllers for striking illegally during the PSAC strike.

April 12. Postmaster-General Mackasey suspends 308 postal workers in Montreal for one day and 15 indefinitely. Two days later he suspends 430 more postal workers, fires 9 others, most of whom are shop stewards.

April 23. Parliament orders Quebec longshoremen back to work.

May 8. John Turner releases details of initial federal restraint proposals. He hints that compulsory controls may be imposed in view of the fact that "Canadian wage settlements are running so far ahead of those in the U.S."

May 9. John Turner warns labour that if it is not prepared to accept voluntary wage restraint he will be forced to institute restrictive fiscal and monetary measures to push the economy deeper into recession, or to impose mandatory controls.

May 10. Prime Minister Trudeau issues a statement supporting the measures taken by Premier Bourassa of Quebec in placing four construction unions under trusteeship to bring "social order" to Quebec.

May 15. Postmaster-General Mackasey asserts that, increasingly, union members are voting no to tentative contract agreements for "the hell of it. Their rejection of the package is a rejection of all authority."

May 26. Mackasey insists that a "hoodlum element" has "infiltrated" the Quebec post office, causing all the trouble there. "Until they are weeded out," he says, "and the managerial rights are once more enforced, we will continue to have trouble in that area."

May 31. Louis Laberge, head of the Quebec Federation of Labour, is convicted by a Quebec Superior Court judge for allegedly encouraging industrial sabotage on the assembly lines at Hupp Canada Ltd., in Joliette. The Postmaster-General again goes after Quebec militants in the Canadian Union of Postal Workers, announcing his intention "to get these bandits out of the post office."

June 9. Four officers and a member of the International Longshoremen's Association are charged with organizing or taking part in an illegal strike. Fines are up to $10,000 for union officers and $1,000 for union members.

June 20. Louis Laberge is sentenced to three years in prison. Supreme Court Judge Marcel Nichols said he had decided on a prison term "to set an example in the light of the violence that has marked labour disputes in the province."

June 23. John Turner brings down his budget, in which he asserts that wage demands that have the effect of raising labour's share of the national income are "unrealistic" and will hurt Canadian trade. Turner promises that the federal government will hold the line in wage negotiations within the public sector, whatever the cost in terms of the strikes this policy would invoke.

The weakness of the trade union movement in Canada was no better revealed than in the silence emanating from trade union leaders during these crucial months. Without a concerted and coordinated counter-attack by organized labour, the state was well on its way to imposing the burden of a troubled economy on the shoulders of the working class.

The Limits of Unionism

There is no difficulty about defining the aim of trade unions. Trade unionism is collective action to protect and improve the living standards of people who sell their labour power against people who buy it. Unions remain the most important institutions of the working class. They were built by the blood, sweat, and tears of countless workers in the face of vehement opposition by capitalist owners and the state. It is necessary to acknowledge this, because what follows is a critique of trade unionism as it has developed in North America. Trade union leaders have a tendency to label all criticisms directed their way as anti-labour. Many have become painfully defensive and sensitive to criticisms of trade unions, particularly from the political left. In fairness, it is true that all too often the critics have accepted the media's image of organized labour as a composite of George Meaney, Dennis McDermott, and Archie Bunker, and Dede Desjardins. Besides being a gross oversimplification of what ails the labour movement, this popular image does a grave injustice to many dedicated and honest union leaders and activists, particularly at the local and shop floor level.

Trade unions are not essentially initiators. They respond to external forces over which they have little or no control — rising prices, unemployment, and acts of government. Changes in the demand for labour have a swift impact. Technological changes can also have an immediate impact, although their effect will usually be more enduring. Trade unions can only react to these forces. The price that they exact in terms of wages, job security, and fringe benefits is a production cost that can often be manipulated by employers. If the price seems excessive, it can often be minimized by replacing labour with more capital-intensive methods, by speeding-up production, or by passing higher wages on to consumers through higher prices. In these circumstances, the switch to more capital-intensive methods means that the higher wages paid to surviving workers is gained at the expense of those who are displaced. Even if no labour is displaced, higher prices rob them of part of their gains and take purchasing power away from the rest of the labour force. According to the late Walter Reuther, for every dollar of increased labour costs since 1947, General Motors by 1956 imposed about $3.75 in cumulative price increases on the North American car buyer. So in effect the United Auto Workers, taking a small share of the increased profits, became a kind of junior partner to General Motors.

Either way, the distribution system works to maintain the status quo. Only in circumstances where employers are unable to fully shift to more capital-intensive methods, and are unable to fully pass increased wages on to consumers, will there be a real change in the distribution of income. These circumstances usually arise during one course of the business cycle but they are typically reversed and profit shares recovered in other phases. It is for this reason that the share of wages in national income has remained remarkably stable over a long period of time. The normal collective bargaining process has thus failed to produce any fundamental alteration in the distribution of income.* Its more permanent effect has been a redistribution of income within the working class. Workers in industries that use a high proportion of capital to labour and that are basically monopolistic are able to win relatively high wages. Their favourable wages depend on these factors more than they do on the effectiveness of their trade unions. Moreover, they come at the expense of other workers in the service trades, agriculture, and light industry where productivity is low and monopoly conditions are absent. Fundamental alteration in the social division of income and wealth can come about only through a revolutionary change in the economic structure. A revolutionary structural change is one that transfers decision-making powers from a minority to the majority. As a first step it involves the transfer of ownership of the means of production from private to public hands. But trade unions have not been, nor are they today, revolutionary bodies — although they have been, and may again, serve as vehicles for radical change.

Historically, the capitalist system has suffered a deep economic crisis every ten or fifteen years. The advent of World War II and the Keynesian revolution made it possible for a majority of workers to earn rising incomes, with the result that there has been a relatively high degree of social stability over twenty-odd years. This period spawned a number of theories that went under the names of "the affluent society" or "the end of ideology."

---

* While this has been the pattern for over a hundred years there have been occasions where historical forces have caused a secular decline in the share of national income that is expropriated in the form of profits. Contemporary England is a case in point. A growing realization by the British working class of its own industrial strength has caused wages there to encroach upon profits. Money wage increases were able to threaten profitability because the competition forced on British capital from overseas prevents them from fully passing on the higher costs in the form of higher prices. Similar circumstances have prevailed in Italy since 1969.

All of us are now part of "the middle class," we were told. The fundamental economic problem has been solved. There are some residual problems like regional disparity and pockets of poverty, but these can be solved by "social engineering" within a pluralistic democracy and an economy capable of infinite growth. Growth puts an end to class war. There are no longer class divisions, only personal conflicts or small group frictions that can be dealt with by piecemeal action. There are no capitalists any longer, only managers whose responsibilities go beyond their shareholders. These theories seemed to be confirmed by the changing role of trade unions observed by many writers.

C. Wright Mills, in an early work, noticed the partial integration of union bureaucracy with that of the corporation. Stabilization requires that labour and business act to complement each other rather than oppose each other. The modern corporation must control labour costs as a stable factor of production in order to permit rational investment decisions. Its profit target programs a given percentage increase in labour costs. There is a variable of about 3 per cent. That 3 per cent is often what collective bargaining is all about. Businesses today don't mind if unions bargain collectively, as long as they do it within the system's rules, because these rules are set up to prevent unions from doing much harm. The long-term contract, moreover, assures that labour costs will be known, and, if properly policed, it guarantees labour peace for a specified period of time. Providing work stoppage occurs only when the contract expires, managers are free to operate at will within that time-frame, and can easily prepare themselves for a possible strike by stock-piling inventories.

"To ensure peaceful plants and profitable enterprise in a stable economy," Mills wrote, "the leaders of labour will deliver a responsible, which is to say, a well-disciplined union of contented workers in return for a junior partnership . . . , security for the union, and higher wages for the workers of the industry. The union takes over much of the company's personnel work, becoming the disciplinary agents for each other, and both discipline the malcontent elements among the unionized employees."[6] What Mills is speaking about is the institutionalization of class conflict, professionalizing it and rendering it more or less antiseptic.

This is a process that has been carried furthest in North America in the modern collective bargaining contract — complete with grievance procedures which remove the handling of grievances from the shop floor, and no-strike clauses between contracts. In the 1940s and earlier, union contracts were negotiated annually, giving the rank and file a chance to confront the boss once a year as an organized force. Today most contracts have been stretched for three and four years. Unions have become less and less active, with attendance at meetings dropping to 1 or 2 per cent of the membership because the local union is less and less engaged in the life of the worker. It centres on a staged exercise every few years, when top negotiators from the national or regional office meet with company officials behind closed doors. The illegalization of walk-outs between contract periods hampers union activism — the very issue over which the British trade union movement fought in the spring of 1973. In a few instances, unions have even bargained away "legal" strikes. The most recent example of this occurred in the United States when the Steel Workers of America agreed, without prior discussion by the membership and without ratification, to curtail strikes. As a sympathetic observer notes, "Little wonder that an increasing number of trade union members become anti-union, and even accept anti-labour, anti-strike attacks by the media and corporate spokesmen. Trade union leaders decry such sentiments among their members, but are unable to cope with them because their advocacy of business unionism is the real source of a drop in trade union militancy and support."[7]

A less sympathetic writer applauds these changes in collective bargaining which, in his words, have thawed "the frozen fronts of industrial conflict."[8] And the granddaddy of the apologists, Seymour Martin Lipsett, notes that "When the conflict of interest groups is legitimate, these 'conflict' organizations contribute to the integration and stability of the society. Trade unions should not be viewed primarily in their economic-cleavage function. They also serve to integrate their numbers in the large body politic and give them a basis of loyalty to the system."[9]

Which conflicts are "legitimate" and which "illegitimate" is of course the crux of the matter. Certainly, unionism typically emerged in the face of active and often brutal opposition of both business and the state. Presumably at that stage their actions were not "legitimate." But once the organization is established it seems to be the case that both parties seek a more amicable relationship, and as the organization enlarges, the emphasis shifts from organization to management, negotiation, and contract enforcement. Democratic checks weaken with centralization and the concentration of power in the hands of full-time functionaries. This is Michel's Iron Law of Oligarchy. According to Michel's Law, union leaders develop a "petty bourgeois" life-style. Social cleavage from the rank and file leads to ideological cleavage. The personal position of labour leaders tends to undermine whatever socialist commitment they might once have held: "What interest for them now has the dogma of social revolution? Their own social revolution has already been affected."[10]*

Trade unions in Canada have a permanent "civil service" of approximately 4,000 full-time staff. Their salaries and expense allowances give them a standard of living and a life-style that is far removed from the members they represent. Top officers in unions like the steel workers, the auto workers, and the machinists have salaries and allowances that are equivalent to about three times that of the highest-paid workers in the industries and five times that of the average workers.[11]

Desire for public approval is an additional inducement to moderation. An obsessive concern to be consulted in high places and a desire for the union's (i.e., union leader's) "place in society" to be given formal recognition lead union leaders to continue to express "reasonable opinions" and to restrict themselves to "legitimate" goals. Thus, few unions in North America have even begun to attack the ubiquitous management rights clause, found in so many collective agreements, which cedes to the employer "the operation of the employer's facilities and the direction of the working force, including the right to hire, suspend, or discharge for good cause and . . . to relieve employees from duties due to lack of work." The rapid changes in technology since the end of World War II with its related changes in work methods, job definitions and new skills have found the union bureaucracies unprepared.

"Corruption" of union leadership is far less important than the

---

* This point is made somewhat differently by the French Marxist André Gorz: "Historically, unions developed out of the workers' need for self-defense and self-organization. As long as they were genuine organs of self-organization, they tended to be quite radical. The turning point came when they were recognized as and considered themselves to be the sole lawful representatives of the working class within the capitalist system. As permanent institutions holding legal rights and responsibilities, labour unions developed into permanently structured—and therefore hierarchical and bureaucratic—organizations to administrate the 'interests' of the working class through juridically defined forms of bargaining and action. Such institutionalized organizations cannot, of course, be expected to jeopardize their self-interest (i.e., their institutional power and the position and status of their leaders within the capitalist state) by stimulating or defending aspirations and demands that run counter to the logic and power structure of the capitalist system. Thus demands that are not negotiable and have no chance of being accepted by capitalist managers, were eliminated from the outset. Labour unions saw it as their function to translate all demands that sprang up (or threatened to spring up) from the rank and file into propositions that would be acceptable to the representatives of capital. By repressing unnegotiable demands that did not fit within the system's logic and promoting demands that were or could become compatible with the functioning of capitalism, labour unions helped to integrate the working class into capitalist society." (*Socialism and Revolution*, p.p. 31-22.)

inherent limitations of the collective bargaining process as it has developed. The institutionalization and routinization of class conflict has removed the direction of struggle, and in large part the activity itself, out of the hands of rank-and-file workers and given it over to union-appointed professionals.

The present structure of the unions, of course, allows the rank and file veto power but no means of initiative in contract bargaining. Pressure is now being exerted to eliminate even this limited form of membership participation. Management spokesmen have consistently urged that union leaders be given final authority to conclude an agreement binding on their members. In some American unions this has already come to pass, in particular the notorious no-strike agreement negotiated by I. W. Abel of the United Steel Workers of America that I have already referred to. Canadian employers complain bitterly that, after signing a memorandum of agreement with union officials, they have it flung back in their faces by a majority vote of the employees. Now an influential Canadian government official, the assistant deputy minister of labour, William P. Kelly, has given his support to this management position. Kelly's trial balloon, floated at the 1974 annual meeting of the Canadian Chamber of Commerce, is based on the assumption that the managers of corporations can do business with their counterparts in the unions, providing the union managers are left alone to conclude an agreement. Most Canadian unionists insist on having a final say on the acceptability of proposed agreements, and this practice is so widely established that no union official would seriously propose that it be abandoned.

The acceptance of institutionalized collective bargaining has led to what British economist V. L. Allen calls "the myth of achievement . . . an illusion which magnifies fractional changes in wage rates or marginal improvements in employment conditions into resounding success."[12] In showing satisfaction with marginal improvements rather than being directly concerned about the distribution of income and devising a means of changing it, they accept the expectations that employers have deemed suitable for them, what Lipsett calls "legitimate demands."

To understand the obstacles to the radical transformation of the character of unions, one has to understand the role of the union official in the collective bargaining process. It is the collective bargaining process that defines the role of the union official. Within its terms, which are also enforced by law, his behaviour is set irrespective of his political philosophy. That is why there has been an essential continuity in the activities of trade unions despite marked changes in personnel and their political beliefs. Different behaviour is feasible only when the environment within which the union functions has changed.

It is C. W. Mills who again best articulates the ambivalence inherent in the trade union function. The union official, writes Mills, is "a manager of discontent." But he cannot suppress rebellion entirely and forever without rendering his organization and himself redundant. His task is to sustain a delicate balance between activism and passivism, a highly precarious exercise:

> During mass organization drives, the labour leader whips up the opinion and activity of the rank and file and focuses them against the business corporation as a pedestal of the system and against the state as the crown of the system. At such time, he is a man voicing loudly the discontent and the aspirations of the people next to the bottom, and he is seen and recognized as a rebel and an agitator. Yet, in fact, all the time that he is the leader of a live and ongoing union, the labor leader is in conflict with the powers of property: he is a rebel against the individual business units and their unmolested exercise of the powers which property conveys. In his timidity and fear and eagerness to stay alive in a hostile environment, he does not admit this, and he often believes that he is not a rebel in the senses named, but the fact remains that he is. He is serving the function of a modern rebel by virtue of what his organization must do to live; modern rebels need not be romantic figures. Yet even as the labor leader rebels, he holds back rebellion. He organizes discontent and then he sits on it, exploiting it in order to maintain a continuous organization; the labor leader is a manager of discontent. He makes regular what might otherwise be disruptive, both within the industrial routine and within the union which he seeks to establish and maintain.[13]

The Italian Marxist Antonio Gramsci once wrote that trade unions are "an integral part of capitalist society whose function is inherent in the regime of private property." In this sense trade unions are dialectically both in opposition to capitalism and a component of it. Marxists are right in insisting that as institutions trade unions do not challenge the existence of society based on a division of classes but merely express this division. The nature of the economy as a system is ultimately a political question. Since even the maximum weapon of trade unions, the strike, is simply absence, a withdrawal of labour, it follows that trade union action *by itself* cannot call into question the existence of capitalism as a social system. Even the occupation of factories is not a challenge to the system. The massed presence of the workers on the factory floor may be a symbolic demonstration that as producers the means of production belongs by right to them. But without taking hold of the levers of state power, such militant action can never give reality to this claim. Going a step further, all attempts at a general strike have failed to overthrow a social order — the revolutionary hurricane that swept Russia in 1905, no less than the May 1968 general strike in France and the general strike conducted by the Front Commun of Quebec in 1972. In combination with complementary forms of action trade unions can undoubtedly play an important role in a political crisis, but complete reliance even on the ultimate display of trade union strength, the general strike, is almost always doomed to failure. For a work stoppage, on however massive a scale, is still a stoppage, not the substitution of one social order for another. While such actions appear to be well beyond the realm of possibility in the near future in North America, it is instructive to so examine the limitations of trade unionism when taken to its most extreme form of collective action.

The Possibilities of Trade Unionism

In its origins and to this day unionism represents a reaction against economic exploitation. Since the capitalist's profit consists in the amount of social product withheld from the producers, there is bound to be conflict in a variety of forms between the two classes over the division of the product, as well as over the conditions of work. Workers remain workers no matter how much they are paid. They are exploited, "be their wages high or low," because only through this exploitation can the employer realize a profit. But under conditions of stable capitalism, the conflict seems fairly easily contained, as Eric Hobsbawm has put it, unless the "system fails to allow for the minimum trade unionist demand of 'a fair day's work for a fair day's pay'."[14]

This qualification deserves attention. The workers' concept of "a fair day's pay" is anything but fixed. Old standards seemed to have gone by the boards in recent years. "A fair day's pay" is the "good life" displayed in the TV commercials that most workers aspire to. There used to be a pecking-order that decided how each group in society fared, with doctors and lawyers at the top and service workers at the bottom, and with relative incomes between them fairly fixed and widely accepted. Now that pecking-order is being shattered, as traditionally passive labour organizations elbow their way to the forefront. A "fair day's pay" today is what you can get, and that depends on power rather than any fixed notion of one's place in the caste system. Inflation is the goad that has turned

formerly timid groups into roaring lions. The militancy is conta-
gious. It has touched off a scramble among all segments of the
labour force not just to re-establish their place in the line-up but to
catch up with other groups that have traditionally been far ahead in
the income hierarchy. This process of leapfrogging is only partly
related to inflation, and will likely continue regardless of the movement in price levels.

A second point is that the level of demand that can be easily
accommodated depends on the economic context. In some contexts
any demands for improvements are unacceptable, and in any situation there will be some level of demand that won't be tolerated.
Thus, while it is true that workers' economic demands can usually
be accommodated within the system, this is not universally the case.
It goes without saying that demands which restrict the rights of
management and which call for workers' control of the organization of production are 'illegitimate' demands that begin to question
the capitalist mode of production. But there are circumstances
where even wage demands can threaten the viability of the system.
To put the matter differently, trade union demands can be accommodated by capitalism providing the margin of profitability is sufficiently great to absorb them. This will depend on the extent of
their demands and the degree of flexibility that capitalism has
available to it.

In past periods of expansion, labour gains have usually been confined to a portion of the increase of production. And in past
declines, labour has usually accepted reductions. But it would be
wrong to regard this as an inevitable outcome, even acknowledging
the conservatism of the trade union movement. Workers come to
understand their collective power to determine their own destiny
from their direct experiences. Such experiences are to be had in
every strike and in every shop-floor struggle. But ordinarily they
are experiences of joint action among only the workers in one
department, one factory, one industry, against a particular capitalist. Only at moments of great social crisis do these experiences
develop the force to call into question the whole of the existing
society. "At such moments, the inability of the existing order to
satisfy even minimal needs forces people to go beyond the ordinary
boundaries of struggle to take class-wide action in organizing some
alternative forms of social life."[15]

It would be wrong to underestimate the obstacles in this path, as
a century of Marxists have been wont to do. "Growing up in a capitalist society, with the lessons of daily life methodically reinforced
by school and media, it is hard to take seriously (even) the possibility of some other way of living together, just as the idea of a

slave-free society occurred to no Greek. . . . We are more likely to submit to bearable evils than to try to tear everything apart, destroying all our daily routines and personal security, for something we can hardly believe in."[16]

The barriers to collective class action are numerous and formidable. Some of us live in metropolitan cities, others in small towns and hinterland regions; some work in huge factories, others in offices, schools, mines, restaurants, hospitals; some for private enterprise, others for the state; we are differentiated by skill, education, wage and status. These divisions, compounded by certain ideological precepts like racism and sexism, and all of which extend into life off the job, help to disguise the common position of wage workers. They are further reinforced by the structure of trade unions that segregates workers by industry and craft and sanctifies the hierarchy of wage and status.

All that can be said is that in periods of economic crisis the margin for reforms and improvement is minimized. Stagnation means that improved wages cannot be financed painlessly out of growth; so-called slumpflation means that great pressure will be exerted to increase profits to finance or re-finance investment; and fierce international competition means that there is less opportunity to finance increased wages out of price inflation. Such, roughly, is the current definition of reality. In the present context, even the traditional activities of trade unions can no longer be easily accommodated within the framework of contemporary capitalism. That is why trade union autonomy has come under attack in many Western nations. The attempt to manacle the unions is aimed at enforcing a net increase in the share of profits against wages in the national income. The working class will suffer a historic defeat if its weapon of economic struggle is confiscated from it. Its strength lies in its unity. It is precisely this unity and the organized discipline that is its expression that makes trade unions a necessary target for appropriation in times of instability.

Whatever the degree of collaboration of trade union leaders, the very existence of a trade union asserts the unbridgable conflict between capital and labour. To the extent that the economic function of trade unions is not performed by the official leadership it is assumed by rank-and-file organizations at the plant, office, and shop floor level. Bureaucratic repression of the struggle tends to lead to a revolt from below. During the McCarthy witch hunt era, under the behest of the Taft-Hartley laws of the U.S.A. and with the collaboration of liberal and social democratic union officers, radicals on both sides of the border were purged from positions of union leadership. As a consequence, political debate in North

American trade unions ceased for almost a quarter of a century. The mediocre and authoritarian leadership that consolidated its power during this period is now being challenged by a new generation of radicals. It is obvious that militancy is more effective in protecting workers' income than class collaboration. That is why the employers, including governments, are attempting systematically to isolate and discharge union militants. In this context the struggle to recover trade unions for their members takes on major priority.* It has become a necessary complement of the economic struggle. As one writer has said, "The fight for a more democratic and militant unionism is a fight against capitalist infiltration of and domination of the union movement."[17]

In Italy, France, and Great Britain, where the trade unions have not always been unable to constrain labour actions within the traditional boundaries, the survival of democratic capitalism as we know it is an open question. Even in North America and particularly in Quebec, many trade union leaders have been willing, or more likely have been forced, to articulate their members' heightened expectations. Hence the wage and strike explosions of the last few years. As one researcher put it: "The conjunction of chronic economic malaise with sustained or even heightened trade union pressure has inevitably created a situation of radical instability."[18]

As in the past, the struggles that necessarily arise in such circumstances — the Bolshevik Revolution, France's "May events" of 1968 and Italy's 'hot autumn' of 1969 — throw up new organizations at the point of production that bypass the trade union structure. But these can be sustained only by an aggressive strategy that extends beyond to political and economic power. Whether this process unravels or whether it is contained by the limited horizons of the trade unions and their political parties must remain an open question, which in the final analysis can be answered not by theoretical speculation but in the struggle itself.[19]†

---

* In Canada this struggle commonly takes the initial form of a fight for independent Canadian unions.

† Socialist theory has always insisted that the limitations of trade unionism must be transcended by the practice of a political party. Lenin expressed this view decisively when he wrote (1900): "For the socialist, the economic struggle serves as the basis for the organization of workers in a revolutionary party, for the reinforcement and development of the class struggle against the whole capitalist system. But if the economic struggle is regarded as something self-sufficient, then there is nothing socialist in it. In the experience of all European countries we have had many not only socialist but also anti-socialist Trade Unions. To assist in the economic struggle of the proletariat is the job of the bourgeois politician. The job of the socialist is to make the economic struggle of the workers assist the socialist movement and contribute to the success of the revolutionary socialist party."

The Front Commun

The most comprehensive challenge to the status quo in Canada is likely to come from Quebec. Discontent with the existing social arrangements has been shaped by French-Canadian nationalism, whose roots go back to the nineteenth century. Under the inspiration of the Catholic Church, concern for national identity and survival led to a retreat from modernizing forces and to a pattern of dependent capitalism in which Quebec offered cheap and quiescent labour for American and Anglophone hire. Nationalism became secularized in the 1960s, and the labour protest fused with it. The Church-dominated Syndicats Catholiques gave way to the Confederation des Syndicats Nationaux (CSN).* Through this evolution the CSN became more militant and radical than the "international"-union-dominated Quebec Federation of Labour (FTQ). A third major labour organization, also animated by radical goals, is the Quebec Federation of Teachers (CEQ). The FTQ was finally swung over to the radicalism of the other two federations, and in 1971 the three organizations formed a Front Commun, under the slogan *"briser le systeme."* This culminated in a massive confrontation with the provincial government in April 1972, when 200,000 teachers and civil servants went on strike. It was by far the largest walk-out in Canadian history.

In its Manifesto for a New Strategy, the FTQ says:

> We have tended in the past to deal with issues one at a time. . . . We thought it was better to defend the workers group by group, factory by factory, because in this way it was easier to look after their particular interests adequately. When we demanded political reforms, our objectives were very specific because we preferred making small gains to losing large battles.[20]

Noting the chronic problems faced by workers in 1971 — the oppressive working conditions in light industry, instability in formerly viable industries, a chronically high unemployment rate, two-thirds of the work force still unorganized, poor housing — the manifesto concluded that single-issue struggles could no longer be effective.

> Concentration of capital, the growth of monopolies and increasing state aid to capitalists have changed the ground rules. . . . Because of this, the balance of power which we tried to maintain has been greatly compromised.
> It is increasingly difficult to win decisive victories in isolation, tiny group by tiny group, or shop by shop. When we do win, the

---

* Confederation of National Trade Unions.

victories are here today and gone tomorrow and the whole process must be begun again a few months later. Anyway, the victories are only partial and don't deal with the other problems which beset workers: factory closures, unemployment, housing crises, etc. On this level, the partial reforms we manage to obtain through repeated protests are designed to pacify the masses and win elections rather than to find a definitive solution to the problems. Moreover, much of the seemingly progressive legislation merely permits better integration of the public and private systems so as to make possible the exploitation of the working class in a more "modern" way.

We must end our isolation and do battle on many fronts. This is a matter of legitimate self-defence. It is the nature of our economic and political system to crush us. We have no choice but to destroy it, so as not to be ourselves destroyed. Every demand we make which does not contest the very basis of this society can, at best, only result in minor improvement. This will not eliminate exploitation, but will just merely change its appearance.

We must aim at replacing the capitalist system and the liberal state which supports it by a social, political, and economic framework designed to satisfy the needs of the people, a government of the people which will turn the state apparatus and the products of the economy over to the people as a whole.

The new basis of unity among the three trade union centres surfaced during the *La Presse* demonstration of October 29, 1971, when over 10,000 workers took to the streets to oppose the Drapeau-Bourassa-Power-Corporation political axis. The workers marched behind the banner chanting the slogan "This is only the beginning." Four months later, the Front Commun called for a general strike in support of the contract negotiations with the Bourassa government. It asked for a minimum wage of $100 per week, job security for teachers and hospital workers, and a yearly 8 per cent wage increase. The Bourassa government went into action immediately, bringing down Bill 19 which imposed a collective agreement and setting heavy fines for any workers and union officials who did not comply immediately. The presidents of the three federations — Laberge, Pepin and Charbonneau, were sentenced to one-year prison terms. The three union leaders capitulated and advised their workers to return to work. With few exceptions they did so, but the actual jailing of the three leaders turned out to be the spark that set off a much more powerful explosion.

For a solid week, Quebec was paralyzed by a series of walk-outs and occupations that shook the very foundations of the system. Nearly every segment of the working class participated—steelworkers, teachers, journalists, textile workers, printers, hospital workers, construction workers, nurses, miners, store employees,

CEGEP students, maintenance employees in the schools, and municipal employees. As Bill 19 had temporarily immobilized the organization of the Common Front, the action represented the spontaneous outpouring of rank-and-file opposition to state repression.

The general strike began on May 9, the day Labèrge, Pepin and Charbonneau began serving their sentences. The pattern was set a day later in Sept-Iles, a mining town of 22,000, when the workers took over the town, closed down the mine and the port and all non-essential businesses, and occupied and controlled the local radio station. By May 12, nine towns were under workers' control, many schools were closed down, 80,000 construction workers were on strike, and 18 radio and TV stations were occupied, and all of Montreal's newspapers were forced to close down. The general strike ended on May 17, when the Front called for a truce period to study new government proposals.

A critique prepared by some workers at Saint-Jerome analyses the strengths and weaknesses that surfaced during the strike:

> This action, novel for Saint-Jerome, permitted scores of workers to begin discussing and recognizing the conditions of exploitation which bind them. Above all, it revealed the capacity of the Saint-Jerome working class to mobilize itself in precise actions when its rights are threatened.
>
> The 72-hour strike established for the working class the importance of ridding itself of those who preach a unionism of well-nursed gentility. The interventions at Rolland Paper and at Uniroyal demonstrated that most officials of the two unions involved there — who in the past had appealed for proletarian solidarity (in giving money, of course) have nothing in common with the struggle we have undertaken against the Government and its servants. When these officials break the picket line (at Uniroyal), or when they claim to have received their orders from their international's headquarters in Washington (at Rolland Paper), we ought to see in such official attitudes a sharp determination to stand apart and ignore the struggle conducted by the Saint-Jerome working class.

As regards weaknesses:

> The massive work stoppage, finally, poses in a pertinent and indeed crucial fashion the problem of political organization of the workers. The absence of organization, whether in a neighbourhood political action committee, in a workers' committee, or wherever, was painfully apparent. Our regional Common Front of the Laurentides, because it is based — by definition — on representation, created political limits which were finally recognized.

Throughout these days, there was a flagrant lack of co-ordination of the action, an absence which revealed the bewilderment of most people at the political tidal wave which had broken over Saint-Jerome. Despite certain efforts to pull together some organization in this quasi-general strike co-ordination did not begin until very late when many people were tired and strongly felt the need to return to work. Lack of co-ordination was reflected also in the marked absence of political content in the demands, or detailed explanations for the political education of the workers.[21]

The Front Commun was a long time in coming. It was during the height of Duplessis' power that the Quebec working class engaged in bitter and prolonged economic and political struggles, beginning with the two month long strike at the mining town of Asbestos in 1949, and continuing through the 1950s with the Dominion Textiles strike at Valleyfield (1952), Murdochville (1957), and CBC Montreal (1959). The trade union movement, together with the professional and educated sectors of the newly emerging middle class, was instrumental in defeating the conservative political order of Maurice Duplessis. But the Quiet Revolution that emerged from these struggles was a middle-class revolution. As sociologist Hubert Guindon has said, "the collective role of this new middle class is to be the impoverished agent of an 'administrative revolution' and this administrative revolution constitutes a new basis for the accrued power of the traditional elites."[22]

The manifestoes that emerged with the Common Front are remarkable documents. They contain an analysis of political economy and a collection of empirical data which in their clarity, scope and relevance, puts them leagues ahead of university textbooks in economics, political science, and sociology. In the best tradition of Marxism, they make the tools and concepts of political economy available to the working class in its day-to-day and long-term struggles. The authors of *It's Up To Us* clearly understand the limitations of the experiments in planning undertaken by the Lesage government:

It seems nobody noticed that you can only plan what you possess. How can the ordinary people impose their views on capitalist factory-owners and political bigshots and their parties? How are you going to tell businessmen that Quebec needs modestly priced houses and not luxury apartment towers? You can't plan if you don't possess the means of production. Since the state never had any intention of nationalizing the economy, the great planning drive had to fail. This failure made itself felt in many different ways, proving once again that property as a structure has permeated the tiniest details of economic and political life.

Not surprisingly, they argue for a worker-dominated socialist economy: social ownership of the means of production ("nationalization is the only possible way to reorient production so as to meet the needs of the people"); worker self-management; and state planning ("workers must control profit in order to invest it according to their own priorities").

The FTQ Manifesto cuts right through the liberal rhetoric of freedom, consumer sovereignty and the neutral role of the state. Its analysis deserves to be quoted at length:

> The capitalists believe that true freedom is that of the law of supply and demand, it is the freedom of advertising to exploit the consumer, the freedom of industrialists to suddenly fire thousands of bread-winners because profit margins in one sector or another of the economy have decreased.
>
> This beautiful vision of liberty is capitalism. In Quebec, this system bears the additional stamp of colonialism because most of our economy is controlled by American or Anglo-Canadian capital. Nevertheless, it's capitalism, equipped with everything it needs to operate.
>
> ... The control of political power by economic power is essential for the maintenance and development of this regime. Financiers must be assured that their liberty will not be threatened by political powers which might respond to the desires of the people. They, therefore, establish close relationships with political machines and support these governments which serve their interests. These are the bourgeois governments, generally referred to as liberal states.
>
> The liberal bourgeois state shows its true colours: it is the essential element which supports the capitalist economic system. Neither the Federal government, with its theoretical powers of economic control, nor the government of Quebec, that truncated political entity, is an impartial arbiter in conflicts between the working class and capitalists. Both Quebec and Ottawa are agents of economic power which is primarily American, English-Canadian to a lesser degree, and only minimally Quebecois. Thus, we must no longer regard the bourgeois state as the defender of the public interest.

A development of consequence that surfaced with the Front Commun is the radicalization of the teaching profession. According to the CEQ white paper, "The teacher is a producer of ideology. In the existing system, he's given the job of reinforcing the attitudes and behaviour of young people in accordance with the dominant ideology . . . So the teacher has a prominently political role." Teachers are "ideological workers" who must of necessity join rank and build solidarity with the working class "because the teachers share their condition."

Judged by the conventional standards of North American trade unionism, the labour movement in Quebec is a puzzle. The leadership seems to have embarked upon unwise adventures leading to serious setbacks. By these standards the Front Commun was a colossal error in tactics which ended up in total failure when a determined government broke the strike. But viewed from a perspective outside the North American norm, it cannot be looked upon as a total defeat. The Front Commun emerged as the vanguard of a social movement seeking both economic and political goals, using these events to sharpen the conflict between a power elite and the workers of Quebec.

The Front Commun was momentarily eclipsed after the general strike, but it re-emerged, somewhat weakened by jurisdictional disputes, with its March 1974 Congress on inflation. The dispute between the AFL-CIO-dominated FTQ and the Quebec-based CSN is a perennial one. "International" unionism has been a divisive force in Canada ever since it captured the labour movement back in 1902. Whether it will succeed in tearing apart the Front Commun remains a distinct possibility. Yet Quebec is a society in motion. The experience of the general strike and the massive education campaigns around the manifestoes will not likely be a forgotten moment in the struggles of Quebec's working-class population.*

"International" Unionism

It is the national and independent trade-union centre, the CSN, which forced the move to the left in Quebec labour. Its example is largely responsible for the radicalization in the American-affiliated FTQ. To remain credible, the FTQ had to keep in step. The absence of a similarly powerful independent trade-union centre in English-Canada goes a long way in explaining the inability of the labour movement in English Canada to challenge the status quo in a radical direction. Since its inception, the Canadian Labour Congress has been a puppet of its American-affiliated members, whose activities are ultimately governed by their conservative parent bodies. The combativity of English-Canadian workers as measured by the

---

* The General Strike of 1972 reveals both the limitations and the possibilities of this form of mass action. It gave expression to a heightened class consciousness, threw up new layers of local leadership and provided lessons to militants regarding the limitations of union mobilization in the absence of a political strategy and a political organization. A number of socialist groups formed over this period. Their experience and strategies are discussed in "Beginnings of a Socialist Movement," *Solidaire*, April 1975.

record number of wildcat strikes can hardly be doubted. That it remains fragmented, isolated, and devoid of political content is largely the responsibility of an inept and bureaucratized leadership that fears the radicalism of its own members as much as it does the power of the employers and the repression of the state.

The history of continental trade unionism coincides with the evolution of a continental economy. Just as a branch-plant economy produces a truncated, fragmented and inefficient industrial structure, branch-plant trade unionism produces a truncated, fragmented and weak labour movement.

There are 2½ million trade unionists in Canada, composing about one-third of the paid non-agricultural work force. About 60 per cent of them belong to "international," that is, American unions operating in Canada. They are grouped in over 10,000 locals with an average membership of only 240. This degree of fragmentation is particularly ludicrous in a country like Canada which has a higher degree of industrial concentration than the U.S.A.—with a few giant companies sharing monopoly control over major fields of manufacturing, resource industries, finance and other sectors. According to I. W. Abel, international president of the United Steel Workers, any union with fewer than 50,000 members is too small to cope with such concentration of business power. Yet in Canada all but nine unions are below the 50,000-member mark. Most of the tiny locals are branch unions of the "international" crafts. Their merger is prohibited by American constitutions which state that mergers in Canada can only occur after a merger has taken place in the United States.

As Melville Watkins has written:

> Americans unions in Canada necessarily inhibit the development of a Canadian labour movement. They do this by fragmenting the union structure. They do it by causing Canadian workers to relate in a limited economic way with U.S. workers in the same industry, rather than in a political way with Canadian workers in other industries. They do it by dampening national consciousness, since to raise the national question at any level is to risk having it spill over to the area of the labour movement itself.
>
> The issue is not only the fact of American unions in Canada, but the nature of American unions. Of all industrial capitalist countries, the American labour movement is the most committed to business unionism, and is also the most conservative if not the most reactionary. Hence, we are not surprised when John Crispo tells us that international unions have a moderating influence on Canadian labour. He cites that as a benefit—a plus

for the internationals—but others are allowed to disagree.[23]

The classic argument in defense of "international" unions is that multinational corporations are a fact of life and can only be fought effectively by multinational unions. Charles Levinson, secretary-general of the International Federation of Chemical and General Workers' Union, is the top labour expert on the subject of the multinational corporations. He has correctly pointed out that most global enterprises are centralizing their labour policies. This means that the vital decisions affecting workers in many lands are being made by the head offices rather than by management at the subsidiary level. It also means that unions are being forced to pit their economic strength against the total financial resources of the global corporations, not merely those of the subsidiaries with which they are negotiating. A production stoppage in any one plant need not disturb the over-all corporate operations if work can be easily transferred elsewhere.

The power of global corporations to neutralize the strike weapon is not merely theoretical. It is used. A 1970 strike at Ford's British operation provides an example. Henry Ford II coolly informed the British people that "we have got hundreds of millions of pounds invested in Great Britain and we can't recommend any new capital investment in a country constantly dogged with labour problems. There is nothing wrong with Ford of Britain but with the country." Shortly thereafter he shifted a proposed £30 million engine building operation back to Ohio. The following year he announced that Ford's next new major plant would be located in Spain, a country that offers "social peace."[24]

The management of America's global factories finds that its power to close an entire operation in one country and transfer everything but the workers to another produces a far more obliging labour force. Sensitive to the charge that they are resorting to "coolie labour," the global managers like to talk in terms of being better able to make use of "supply markets." Yet examples of "coolie labour" are plentiful. For example, Timex and Bulova make an increasing number of their watches in Taiwan, where they share a union-free labour pool with RCA, Admiral, and Zenith among others. Others have moved to Hong Kong to take advantage of a labour pool in which 60 per cent of the adults work a seven-day week and which includes 34,000 children, aged 14 or younger, half of whom work ten or more hours a day. Other multinationals are locating in Singapore because its government guarantees new industries freedom from "union trouble" for a given number of years in return for a minimum dollar investment. Altogether, the largest U.S.-based global firms such as Ford, Chrysler, Kodak, ITT and Procter and Gamble employ about one-third of their work force outside of the United States and Canada.

A study produced by the AFL-CIO contends that multinationals transferred 500,000 jobs from the U.S. to low-wage countries between 1966 and 1969. If anything, the trend since then has accelerated. Comparable figures on the effects of "run-away" shops in Canada are not available. However, from studies such as Shutdown, an Ontario Federation of Labour survey of layoffs in Ontario and research on "deindustrialization" done by the Ontario Waffle,[25] it is evident that the "runaway" plant is a cause of rising unemployment in this country.

Its threat to Canadian workers has not yet reached the proportions it has in the U.S., but it is only a matter of time before this problem, like so many others, spills across the border. Companies in the U.S. have used the "runaway" shop to undermine the strength of American unions which, unlike their Canadian counterparts have been unable to win settlements big enough to keep pace with rising prices. As Barnet and Muller, the authors of *Global Reach,* put it, the multinationals are increasingly pitting "the mobility of capital . . . against the immobility of labour." One factor that has kept the incidence of branch-plant shutdowns in Canada to modest proportions has been our lower labour costs. But this "advantage" is rapidly vanishing as the decline of union aggressiveness in the U.S. is counteracted by an upsurge of labour militancy in Canada. The net effect has been that unionized wages in this country are about at parity with those in the United States. Canadian unions can therefore expect a strong employer backlash, especially by branches of global corporations.

I cannot disagree with the proposition that in the age of the multinational corporation labour solidarity on a national basis is not sufficient. To combat the corporate colossi, unions will have to learn to operate on a global scale. But this does not necessitate organic unity. Indeed, Canadian workers know that international solidarity in the "internationals" is conspicuous mainly by its absence, a point graphically illustrated by the year-long strike of the Auto Workers at the United Aircraft plant in Longueuil, Quebec. With the approval of the government of Canada, which had given United a substantial grant, and with no apparent dissent from the headquarters of the "international" union, much of the work was shifted to the American plants of United. The internationals have consistently failed to adopt any practical measures in opposition to the recent round of branch plant closures. If plants are to be closed down it is best, from their point of view, that the closure take effect in the colony where the colonials and not themselves will suffer the consequences of mass unemployment.

This does not dispense with the question of multinational corporations. Capitalism has gone international, and if workers in Canada and elsewhere are to protect themselves they must act multinationally as well. But a truly international labour movement does not come by way of an imposed bureaucracy from the United States carried over by the labour lieutenants of American imperialism, but rather by the close co-operation of independent national labour movements.

The term "internationalism" is a potent force in the labour movement of all countries, including Canada. But when workers in other places speak of internationalism, they have in mind an assembly of workers representing many nations, meeting together as equals to discuss mutual problems and, where possible, deciding on co-ordinated solutions. The national sovereignty of each delegate is acknowledged and accepted. Matters internal to each nation remain the exclusive jurisdiction of each national centre. In Canada, the term "internationalism" has an altogether different meaning. At the 1902 Convention of the Trades and Labour Congress, where American unions first took over the Canadian Labour movement, a motion was passed amending the constitution of the TLC to the effect that "no national union be recognized where an international union exists." 23 unions, including one-fifth of the Trade Congress membership and a major portion of the Quebec trade unionists, were thereby expelled. By the end of the first decade of the century, 90 per cent of all unionists were part of American unions, but it was hardly a matter of their free choice.

Canadians appeared destined for "statehood" in the American labour system as early as 1900. In that year, a W. D. Mahon, who had represented the AFL at the Trades Congress convention, reported to the AFL convention that "The Congress compares more nearly to our State Federations than it does to the American Federation of Labour."[26] This was not the conception of the Congress held by its secretary, Patrick M. Draper. Draper wanted to see the Trades Congress become a full-fledged national labour centre that could charter unions who were not part of the "internationals." This is precisely what the AFL unions feared would occur as Canadian locals, instead of obeying AFL jurisdictional decisions, dues assessments and contract clauses, might be tempted to abandon the "internationals" and find easy refuge in the Trades and Labour Congress.

The AFL prepared itself well for the 1902 convention. Two delegates from Winnipeg reported back to the Winnipeg Trades Council that the Congress "was packed with delegates who through their respective internationals are affiliated with the A.F. of L. and further organizations and lobbying has been going on for months."[27] The triumph of the craft internationals was sealed by the election of John A. Flett, the AFL's salaried organizer, to the presidency of the Trades and Labour Congress. Flett took his orders from Gompers. If the "internationals" did not wish to organize a particular trade, industry, or area in Canada there was little the Congress could do about it. It lost all control over the expansion of trade unionism in the country and "became little more than a lobby charged with the defence of the international trade-union movement in the corridors of the Canadian parliament."[28]

The decision to subordinate Canadian trade unions to the AFL undoubtedly reflected a significant opinion within the Canadian labour movement leadership that regarded the continentalization of American organizations as inevitable and even desirable. For a promise of continued economic support by the "international" craft unions, labour unity in Canada was sacrificed. It never again achieved the unity forged before the 1902 convention. Moreover, it turned out to be a bad bargain. The much-heralded economic support was never really forthcoming. After the initial organizing drive in the early 1900s, the AFL spent most of its energy and funds in destroying rival industrial unions. In a recent work, *Gompers in Canada,* Robert Babcock shows that as early as 1908 the AFL was taking more money out of Canadian locals that it was putting in, and at no time did it allocate more than 2 per cent of total expenditures to its Canadian branches.[29] This entire pattern was to be repeated in the 1930s and forties when industrial unions were organized by Canadian workers and financed with Canadian funds, yet fell under the orbit of the CIO. Under the aegis of the CIO, after the initial organizing drive the union leadership ended up devoting most of its energies and funds to pushing the Communists out of the unions.

In the early 1900s, the crafts exported their jurisdictional wars to Canada and effectively sidetracked strong sentiment in favour of industrial unionism. In the opinion of labour historian H. C. Pentland, "the fanaticism . . . to hold back industrial unionism in Canada . . . delayed the effective unionization of large segments of the Canadian labour force by . . . at least twenty years."[30]

It wasn't only their jurisdictional wars that the crafts exported. It was also their ideological ones. Gompers in particular, blinded by a pathological anti-socialism, directed his Canadian lieutenant John Flett to work against the many prominent socialists in Canadian unions and prevent them from achieving positions within the Congress and local Councils. As a result of this mischief, both the Grits and the Tories were allowed to penetrate deeply into the working-class vote and labour radicals had difficulty in launching a political party that could give expression to the interests of labour. This pattern repeated itself 30 years later when, backed by the Central Intelligence Agency, the CIO exported its fanatical anti-communism to Canada. Lending financial and organizational assistance to David Lewis and the CCF, it succeeded in ridding the industrial unions of their Communist leaders.[31]

The degree of organizational autonomy of Canadian branches of "international" unions varies widely. At one extreme are the AFL-craft unions, particularly the building and printing trades in which the American headquarters exert tight control over the election and appointment of Canadian officers, collection and disbursement of dues, the content and procedures of collective bargaining and strikes, and the extent of co-operation with other unions and labour bodies. At the other extreme are a few CIO industrial unions that have reportedly achieved a high degree of autonomy. Even among these, however, there have been instances of flagrant intervention.

One such instance occurred in 1971, when the Douglas Aircraft workers, members of the UAW of Toronto, went out on strike. Nixon had put the wage freeze on American workers so Canadians were asked to carry the burden for the Douglas Aircraft workers of California. The Canadian members did not know about the understanding their union officers had reached with "international" headquarters that the strike would end as soon as the company offered a settlement similar to a recent auto agreement. The settlement was offered, but the workers turned it down. The strike now threatened production in the U.S. plants. The American union leaders tried several manoeuvres to cajole the Toronto workers back, including the appearance of 25 international representatives at a union meeting in Toronto. When this failed, President Woodcock ordered the local committee to appear at Solidarity House in Detroit. He ordered them back to work with the declaration that they were, as of then, cut off from strike pay, and that if they did not comply he would impose a trusteeship on the local. They complied.

Particularly since World War II, federal governments have on balance shown a preference to "international" unions as against independent Canadian organizations, especially those that have earned a reputation for militancy. Executives of American branch-plants have also favoured "international" unions. They find it more convenient to deal with branches of the same unions, negotiating and administering similar agreements on both sides of the border. In general, international unions have had a moderating influence on industrial conflicts in Canada.* On numerous occasions they have been accused by union locals of "selling-out" the members and signing "sweetheart deals" with the employers. Pressed by demands for greater autonomy, the Canadian Labour Congress at both its 1970 and 1974 conventions set forth guidelines which work towards this goal, but these efforts have brought forth little effect, and in fact are being openly defied by various "international" unions.

The Corporations and the Labour Unions Returns Act (CALURA) has required trade unions to make annual financial reports since 1962. Even its incomplete figures establish beyond much doubt that financial assistance from the U.S.A. is not essential to the viability of a Canadian labour movement. On the contrary, in every year since the CALURA Reports have been published, AFL-CIO unions have made a substantial profit from their Canadian membership. Over the period 1962-1972 the total profit has been $155 million. The annual breakdown is as follows:

1962	$ 9,511,000.00	1968	$11,970,000.00
1963	12,336,000.00	1969	9,863,000.00
1964	11,284,000.00	1970	13,743,000.00
1965	8,006,000.00	1971	24,970,000.00
1966	9,630,000.00	1972	26,425,000.00 [†]
1967	17,302,000.00		

There seems little doubt that if the $50 million plus that is collected each year from Canadian workers were retained in Canada, and if this nationalization of the labour movement were accompanied by a drastic streamlining of the structure of Canadian

---

* The best example of this favouritism is the SIU affair, in which the Liberal government, the RCMP, the shipowners, and the AFL joined hands to sink the Communist-led Canadian Seamen's Union. When the CSU embarked on a militant strike against the shipowners in the late 1940s and received worldwide support from other seamen's unions, the AFL came to the rescue of the shipowners. With the co-operation of the Liberal government, it illegally brought in a Chicago thug and criminal, Hal Banks, to head up the SIU and destroy the Canadian union. The TLC was forced to expel the CSU under threat from 14 international unions that they would withdraw their organizations from the TLC unless this was done.

[†] The breakdown for 1972 is as follows:

labour, then Canadian labour could easily finance its own operations and evolve into an effective movement.

In practice, the CLC has been largely ineffective as a trade union centre. When, for example, Canadian locals of the Teamsters Union were expelled from the CLC, they survived and flourished, continuing to raid locals of a Canadian union, the Canadian Brotherhood of Railway Transport and General Workers. They had the support of their own U.S. headquarters and the international building trade unions, whose Canadian locals were members of the CLC. The CLC has been more effective in deterring Canadian unions from raiding "internationals" because these lack outside, i.e., U.S., support. In consequence it has tended to reinforce the dominant positions of the "international" unions in Canada.

However, with domestic American economic expansion coming to an end, a growing cleavage is developing between American unions and Canadian workers. Because of the "runaway" shops and internal organizational and political weakness, American trade unions are stagnating. In 1945, 34.5 per cent of the work force was organized. Today it is less than 23 per cent and declining. During the 1960s the labour force expanded by 30 per cent while union membership grew by only 13 per cent. Apparently incapable of launching a serious organizational drive to get new members, American union leaders are becoming increasingly desperate to save the ones they have and support measures which transfer unionized jobs from the colonies to the U.S.

These strains will undoubtedly be causing many to question the benefit of "international" unions for Canadian workers. For as

---

Receipts from Canada	
Initiation fees	$ 1,095,000.00
Dues	33,359,000.00
Health & Welfare Assessments	5,563,000.00
Death Benefit Assessments	2,029,000.00
Strike Assessments	8,727,000.00
Fines	6,000.00
Work Permits	98,000.00
Other Assessments	1,788,000.00
Total	$52,665,000.00
Expenditures in Canada	
Gross Salaries, Wages, etc.	$14,321,000.00
Strike Benefits	7,758,000.00
Pension & Welfare Payments	4,161,000.00
Total Expenditures	$26,240,000.00
Profit for American Union Headquarters for 1972	$26,425,000.00

Canadian workers and Canadian unions perceive that the U.S. centre of union power is in opposition to their aims they will have no alternative but to politicize the issue and mobilize themselves and public opinion as they seek alternatives. As the contradictions surface we may expect to see the breakaway of whole Canadian sections. The growth of independent Canadian unions that results will do much to raise the consciousness of Canadian workers and thereby help to transform Canadian politics.

Labour and Politics: A Review

Canadian workers greeted the current economic crisis with a militancy that is unparalleled in the past quarter century. To the summer of 1975 at least, neither business nor the state was able to tame their aggressive mood and put a halt to the outbreak of illegal strikes that has spread throughout the land. In searching about for a new approach, Labour Minister John Munro dug up an old formula of William Lyon Mackenzie King — "a permanent tripartite council of labour, management and government. . .that would debate issues of national concern in the labour field and make recommendations for change." A series of meetings hosted by Finance Minister John Turner got underway in January 1975. Joseph Morris, head of the CLC, caught the mood of the government's initiative when he emerged from one of the meetings to say: "We are facing a threat to our entire social structure and we must accept the fact that it affects everyone . . . We are going to have to come to some general agreement about the economy as a whole; then each will have to operate within these agreements."[32]

At the national level, Canada's labour leaders have been in a state of confusion and paralysis through the length of the crisis, unable or unwilling to mobilize the rank and file in a co-ordinated fashion against the attack on trade unions. Above all, they have wished to avoid any form of political confrontation. In this they are joined by the New Democratic Party, "the official party of labour."

The present impotence of the NDP bears examination, for the attachment of the official trade union movement to that party and its predecessor, the Cooperative Commonwealth Federation (CCF), has had a continuing influence on the nature of working-class politics in English Canada.

The road that ultimately led to the founding of the CCF was a tortuous one with many and diverse detours. Other strategies and ideologies were tried by significant numbers of workers, farmers, and socialists before the CCF finally emerged in 1933.

"Labourism" — the election of independent labour candidates — was a practice that prevailed through the early years of the twentieth century. "Syndicalism" — the reliance on non-electoral techniques such as the single industrial union and the general strike, swept Western Canada after World War I. It died with the defeat of the Winnipeg General Strike and emerged only four decades later in the form of the Front Commun.

The Communist Party of Canada was born in 1922. Adopting as its basic program a policy advanced by the American Communists, Earl Browder and William Z. Foster, it called for the abandonment of attempts to create an independent industrial Canadian trade union movement and in its stead substituted a strategy of "boring from within" the AFL craft unions. However in the 1920s the U.S. unions carried out a purge of all known Communist supporters, forcing the Communist Party of Canada to seek alternative trade union formations. In the 1930s it began a highly successful campaign to mobilize the unemployed and the unorganized industrial workers into the Workers Unity League. With the rise of fascism in Europe, the Third International adopted a united front policy, causing the Canadian Communist Party to abandon the Workers Unity League and deliver the new unions it had organized to the AFL and ultimately the Congress of Industrial Organizations (CIO). For over a decade, the Communists were then locked in a battle against labour supporters of the CCF for control of the industrial unions. It lost that battle, in no small way due to its own decision to slavishly follow the line of the Third International despite its total inapplicability to conditions in North America. In the 1945 federal election, the party supported Mackenzie King and the Liberals against the CCF and the Tories in the ridiculous belief that King, like Franklin Roosevelt, was committed to a policy of continued friendship with the U.S.S.R. Following the Moscow Conference of Communist Parties in 1957, which determined that socialism could be won through the electoral process, the Communists have been attempting to forge "anti-monopoly" alliances with social democratic parties. While this strategy has had some limited success in Western Europe, where the Communist Party is strong, it has had no success whatever in Canada.

It is not surprising, then, that the only mass party of the left that has survived the Great Depression in Canada has been the CCF. What exactly was the CCF? The men who gathered together in Calgary in 1932 to discuss the formation of a new political party were a collection of Protestant clergymen, teachers, farmers, lawyers, small businessmen, professors, and a handful of trade unionists. They represented prairie farm organizations, various local independent labour parties, and the Marxist-oriented Socialist Party and Social Democratic Party. Prominent among them were two members of Parliament, James Woodsworth and William Irvine, and two university professors, Frank Scott and Frank Underhill. The consensus worked out at the Calgary meeting was finalized a year later at Regina when the Regina Manifesto was accepted as the philosophy and program of the new party.

To this day the Regina Manifesto remains a fascinating document, a curious mixture of Christian Socialism, Fabian Socialism, and Liberal reformism, with a twist of Marxism. It is critical to any understanding of the politics of the NDP. The Manifesto speaks of the "exploitation and domination of one class by another" but it rejects any notion of class struggle. The early CCF represented a moral revolt that rejected capitalist civilization but showed no understanding of the nature of the society which gave birth to this civilization. In the final analysis this is what accounts for its essentially utopian character. The Manifesto proposed revolutionary change by non-revolutionary means, a society given over to the principles of Christian love and socialist equality to be established through the parliamentary process. Having repudiated revolutionary means, it could only be a matter of time before it abandoned revolutionary ends.

The Manifesto condemns capitalism "with its inherent injustice and inhumanity", an economic system that necessarily fluctuates between "feverish periods of prosperity in which the main benefits go to speculators and profiteers, and catastrophic depression, in which the common man's normal state of insecurity and hardship is accentuated; [a system] which is marked by glaring inequalities of wealth and opportunity, by chaotic waste and instability and poverty. . . ." It insists that the supplying of human needs and not the making of profit "ought to be the principle regulating production, distribution and exchange." It says that "unregulated private enterprise and competition" has to be replaced by "economic planning," and it commits a CCF government to nationalize "the principal," though not all of, "the means of production and exchange." And it concludes in ringing phrases that "No CCF government will rest content until it had eradicated capitalism and put into operation the full programme of socialized planning which will lead to the establishment in Canada of the Cooperative Commonwealth."

The Manifesto insisted on the need for economic and social planning, but it would be planning by experts. There is no room for workers' control of industry and community control of social services in the early blueprints of the CCF. This strong tinge of technocracy would be one feature of the CCF that carried over to the NDP, particularly as it assumed provincial office in the sixties and seventies. The Manifesto included immediate measures to deal with unemployment and the crisis in agriculture, but these were explicitly regarded as short-term steps that would not, in themselves, achieve the ultimate objectives of the Party. Over the years this distribution between immediate and long-term objectives would be dropped as the short-term programs were pushed to the forefront. In fact, by the end of the 1940s, the short-term policies had become the sole preoccupation of the party. The ultimate objectives dropped out of sight.

The possibility that this would happen was openly discussed by the many Marxists who were actively involved in the CCF during its early days. An editorial appearing in the October 1934 issue of *CCF Research Review,* a monthly publication of the Saskatchewan CCF, warned:·

> The fact that the CCF is committed on paper to the establishment of socialism is of no consequence. The important thing is the activities of those who make up its membership. . . . It can, if it will, consolidate and educate the people of Canada to the idea of a new social order. . . . It is claimed by many on the other hand, that it has all the ear-marks of an impotent European social democracy, that it inevitably paves the way for a planned capitalism. . . . If this is so those of us who make up its membership must lack the backbone and energy to make it otherwise. . . . The CCF can be made into anything that those who have the will and energy decide to make it. If the forces of reaction within its ranks triumph we have ourselves to blame.[33]

A more pointed editorial in the August, 1934 issue, which has direct relevance for the NDP today, concluded that "to graft socialist legislation on the body of capitalism will undoubtedly give birth to a hybrid monster in which the cherries will continue to go to the ruling class. . . . Any legislation which may have a socialist flavour and would appear to be laying the foundation for socialism . . . will also lay the basis for a capitalism which is more solidly entrenched and much more difficult to remove."

The "sources of reaction within its ranks" did triumph. That was. already clear by the early 1940s as the membership allowed its organization to be taken over and controlled by a central and permanent bureaucracy of professionals — a development that was fought against by Woodsworth. Even in Saskatchewan, the membership agreed to modify the party program in order to appeal to a wider audience. The Saskatchewan CCF dropped its radicalism, most notably its policy of public ownership of land — a program that had long been urged by various farm organizations.* During its first two terms in office, the CCF government was able to accomplish much, but it grew increasingly distant from the grass roots movement of farmers, workers, and teachers, whose ideas, energy, and money had succeeded in electing and re-electing it. This spelled doom to a party that had to depend on the political activities of its membership to offset the economic power of its opponents and a hostile commercial press.

Saskatchewan is the best example of the evolution of social democratic political formations, because it was here that radicalism in the party was at its strongest. Lorne Brown, who has contributed much to an understanding of the history of prairie radicalism, lists three main causes for the drift to the Right.[34] The once vigorous constituency associations had become little more than organizations geared to fight elections. Political education virtually disappeared from the party. The party was swamped by new members, many of whom merely wanted honest government, others of whom had jumped on the bandwagon as a means of riding to power. Government policy was shaped more and more by the Cabinet and the civil service, with only indirect reference to the party rank and file. And the farm, labour, and teacher movements, instead of applying mass pressure on the governments, adjusted themselves to the politics of private lobbying. The chickens came home to roost in 1964 when the CCF was defeated, unable to rally its membership to conduct a vigorous campaign against the embattled doctors and the business establishment. It left office having created the most advanced welfare state in North America but without having moved the province any distance toward a socialist society.

It is commonly argued that the current-day NDP is a pale reflection of the socialism of the old CCF. While the NDP has strayed a good distance from the CCF, the socialism of the Regina Manifesto is easily exaggerated. It is useful to recall that the revolutionary socialists were always a small minority in the CCF. The CCF never strayed from its commitment to the parliamentary system. It had a profound belief in the wonders that could be performed if only the electorate could be educated to elect it to office. It never promoted the use of industrial action for political ends. As against class conflict, it fervently advocated the three P's — Peace, Persuasion and Parliament. While in its early days it advocated nationalizing the principal means of production, it always promised full compensation. And it soon shied away from nationalizing land. Collective

---

* This proved to be a disaster for the province, as private ownership of the land has led to the decimation of rural Saskatchewan.

farming was never part of its program. The CCF believed in hired experts to run industry and public services rather than elected councils of workers or community representatives. It never advocated any sweeping changes in the school curriculum, the legal system, the media, or the arts. These were all seen to lie outside of politics — better left to philosophers, professionals and businessmen. As regards the role of women in society, the family, child-rearing, native people, and life-styles, the CCF was basically traditional, even conservative in its outlook. CCFers believed strongly in the idea that economic growth makes for progress and that happiness lies in material abundance. Finally, the CCF view of the world economy never encompassed the idea of imperialism and Canada's role as a dependency of the U.S.A.

In short, the CCF was a thoroughly social democratic organization from its inception. Whatever deteriorations that would occur would start from this base point. And degeneration did set in. As early as 1942, the CCF had abandoned its goal of eradicating capitalism through nationalizing the principle means of production. The new objective was the establishment of the welfare state in Canada. By 1950, even the profit motive was riding high. CCF ideologue Frank Scott insisted that "We do not oppose the making of profit in all its forms; on the contrary, the profit motive, under proper control, is now and will be for a long time a most valuable stimulus to production."

By the early 1950s, the CCF was a pale reflection of its former self. Where the CCF of the thirties talked of eradicating capitalism, the CCF of the fifties talked of humanizing capitalism. Where the old CCF talked of a socialist economy, the new CCF talked of a mixed economy. Where the old CCF talked of removing the profit motive and competition and replacing it with social incentives and co-operation, the new CCF talked of controlling profits and removing excess profiteers. This drift towards liberal reformism was finally given full recognition in 1956, when the Regina Manifesto was replaced by the Winnipeg Declaration as the official statement of principles of the party.

It is not too difficult to reconstruct what was happening. While the CCF was beating a hasty retreat from the socialism of the Regina Manifesto, and drifting towards a liberal reformism, the Liberals and Conservatives were also drifting towards the same destination. The war taught everyone the value of government intervention. Liberal and Conservative governments would accept the responsibility for maintaining full employment and by now they also accepted the general idea of the welfare state. These new directions were in complete accord with the interests of the large corporations that these parties represented. As the 1950s wore on, there was little, in fact, to distinguish between the three parties. The CCF became identified in the public mind as the party that screamed "more" wherever pensions, hospitalization, and other such measures were announced. The other parties accepted the mixed economy. The CCF wanted it a little more mixed. It appeared to most people that the Liberals or Conservatives could do as much in the field of welfare and were better equipped to manage a mixed economy.

After its early electoral successes immediately following the war, the CCF was in clear danger of collapse. It needed some external help to survive. That help was to come from the Canadian Labour Congress. The AFL-CIO merger in the U.S. brought about in lock-step fashion the merger of the TLC with the Canadian Congress of Labour. It was the core of CCL unions that had, since the expulsion of the Communists, supported the CCF. For well over a decade, CCL politics had been dominated by the struggle between CCFers and Communists to control the industrial unions. Now it was the CCL unions in the new Canadian Labour Congress that were the driving force in the house of Labour for the new party.

The New Democratic Party was a creature of its times, of the Cold War and the "end of ideology" syndrome. "In the struggle between democracy and totalitarianism," code words of those days, the founding convention of the party decided that it would side with democracy. In brief, Communism, not capitalism, was named as the major enemy of the new party. Through the advent of Keynesian economics, capitalism was well on its way to solving the fundamental economic problems. What was left to do was to fill the gaps in the welfare state and redistribute income more equitably through a more rigorous application of the principle of progressive taxation and regional economic planning. A consensus developed around the notion of "nationalization where necessary but not necessarily nationalization." Only industry that displayed a consistent incapacity to operate efficiently was slated for public ownership. Keynesian controls and new techniques of economic planning to regulate the activities of giant corporations removed public ownership from the NDP's agenda. Serving the needs of people rather than the imperatives of profits would be accomplished not by nationalization but by occasional joint ventures with private industry and by establishing an investment board that would direct and control the expenditures of both government and giant corporations.

Old-time radicals felt that the principles of the CCF had been betrayed. The contrary view was unanimously expressed in the daily press; the new party was really the CCF in disguise. In fact, the NDP, like the CCF, is a party with a schizophrenic program that can never be implemented. As the authors of the Manifesto of the Front Commun point out: "You can only plan what you possess." Why would any company build up its reserves to expand its future operations, only to have our kindly social democractic government invest these reserves according to public priorities? Why, it may be asked, would these companies not ship their profits out of the country and expand elsewhere? Indeed, this is exactly what has happened most recently in the oil industry when provincial and federal governments tried to tax a larger share of its profits. Paralyzed by such threats of the private sector, an NDP government would have to abandon its system of controls or nationalize.

It seems that this is a choice that the recent crop of NDP leaders do not wish to face. Their bluff has been called in each of the three provinces ruled by NDP governments, and in most instances they have gracefully backed down.

More important is the utter bewilderment in party circles over how to respond to the current economic crisis. They have rejected a socialist reorganization of the economy as unpalatable to middle-class voters, and they have turned away from their old formula of economic planning which would force them into a corner they wish to avoid. What they are left with are the old trusty palliatives of boosting welfare rates and old age pensions to reduce the impact of inflation, injecting more public money into the economy to dampen the recession, and state ownership of a segment of the oil industry. These are the remedies of the fifties and sixties which offered some correctives in an expanding world economy. They do not touch the crisis of the 1970s. In their favour, there is at least something coherent about the Liberal budgets. They answer the corporations' demand that society put claims of profits ahead of those of wages on the grounds that profits are the source of new investment and therefore of new jobs. This argument makes a certain crazy sense as long as we accept the right of corporations to make basic investment decisions. It may appear incredible, and is in fact incredible, in a period when the anti-social character of corporate priorities is so clearly demonstrated. Yet it is logical within the framework of capitalist economics, and the well-tutored Liberal government bowed to its discipline.

There is nothing coherent or logical about the NDP response. A serious alternative to this course would envision a revolutionary change in the structure of the economy: socialization of the commanding heights of the corporate sector and central economic planning that would direct the economic surplus to the impoverished areas of society.

The Illusive Revolution

That the New Democratic Party has made its peace with capitalism is not surprising. There is hardly an instance of a mass party in western countries that has not deteriorated into a reform party safely integrated within the framework of parliamentary politics. This has been the historical experience of both social democratic and Communist parties. The reasons for this go deeper than mere betrayals by leaders. Selling out is usually more a symptom than a cause. Reformism arises under certain social conditions. "It is the political experience of that sector of the working class and the popular movement which is able to win substantial concessions within the framework of the existing capitalist order. . . . Such concessions can be made under the most adverse economic conditions, providing the social institutions and ideologies of capitalism remain intact."[36] Capitalism need not satisfy the demands of the entire population to remain viable, only those of the most organized and militant sectors of the population.

More particularly, leadership in social democratic parties has traditionally come from the upper echelons of the trade unions and from various segments of the "petty bourgeoisie" — most notably lawyers, teachers, clergymen, and professors. They see themselves as the representatives of the "people" and their task as wresting concessions from the traditional ruling class which will make life more generally tolerable. More recently, this leadership core has been joined by a group from the upper and middle echelons of management: professional administrators, engineers — Galbraith's technostructure, in short. It is not difficult to explain the attraction that a social democratic party has for this element: a branch-plant economy offers limited job opportunities for managerial personnel. It is in their self-interest to see an expansion of the state sector through a full-fledged development of welfare, health, education, etc., and a more vigorous development of state-owned enterprise. Economic nationalism and social democracy are its natural allies.

By this route this group, an ascending element within contemporary capitalism, has become a leading force behind state capitalism. It is important to add that the managerial group is essentially elitist and bureaucratic to the core. It has no interest in abolishing capitalist relations of production. Quite the contrary. It wishes to expand it through the state sector in which the dominant positions would be occupied by its members. Its function as administrators of capital and labour requires a hierarchical, that is, an authoritarian organization of work, as against a socialist, that is, a democratic organization of work. For this very reason, technocrats can coexist quite comfortably with union bureaucrats who are also managers of a sort.

When social democracy gets elected to office, the managerial element within it is bound to rise to prominence. It is the party's only source of administrative expertise. Judging from the experience of the New Democratic Party regimes in western Canada, social democracy "in power" produces three major results: (1) a proliferation of measures designed to protect "the people" against the abuses of the capitalist economy — consumer protection, legal aid, improved labour legislation, high minimum wage legislation, higher welfare rates, higher corporate taxes, elimination of premiums as the basis of financing health care; (2) a filling-in of the welfare state — expanding the scope of health care, provision of day care, more public housing, greater assistance to small businesses and co-operatives; (3) the expansion of state enterprise — a combination of take-overs of bankrupt or near bankrupt companies (e.g. Churchill Forest Industries, Morden Fine Foods and Saunders Aircraft in Manitoba, Canadian Cellulose in British Columbia); takeovers of inefficiently-run service industries (e.g. automobile insurance); joint ventures with private capital; resource-based marketing boards; expansion of existing utilities.

As regards protective measures and programs that extend the welfare state, social democracy is different only in degree from the capitalist parties. It moves sufficiently in advance of the other parties to retain the loyalty of its voting base. What distinguishes its advanced elements from other parties in power is its greater willingness to expand the scope and size of state ownership.* This secures the support of its managerial wing as well as incurring the wrath of the owners of capital and their political representatives. But while it removes a slice of the capital away from the private owners of business, it does nothing to break the business system. Rather it moves the business system into the public sector. One set of managers replaces another. As often as not they are the same personnel and what is more to the point, they function according to the same set of rules. The workers remain a dominated class, as removed as ever from the levers of power.

---

* Even here the differences can be easily exaggerated. Public ownership is a venerable institution in Canada, as Herschel Hardin has pointed out *(A Nation Unaware)*. In recent years, B.C.'s NDP government has set up the B.C. Petroleum Corporation, the Saskatchewan government has set up the Saskatchewan Oil and Gas Corporation, and the Manitoba Government has set up the Manitoba Mineral Resources Corporation. But Quebec has its Société Québecoise d'Initiatives Petrolières, Alberta has its Alberta Energy Corporation, and Ontario has its Ontario Energy Corporation.

I have claimed throughout this book that world capitalism is caught in a treadmill of generalized recession and generalized inflation and that conventional Keynesian remedies offer no solution but in fact are part of the problem. Since the end of World War II, most western economies have successfully prevented any sign of a workers' revolt against arduous and alienating labour by being able to provide steadily improving living standards for the majority of people. The current economic crisis has removed this margin of safety from the immediate range of most if not all the capitalist countries. Because of the international character of the crisis, they are not able, as in the past, to export their domestic recessions and inflations abroad. They have no alternative but to protect their capital by eroding living standards and debasing working conditions. Employers are already taking advantage of adverse economic conditions by demanding increased productivity through speed-ups and stretch-outs and impairing health and safety standards. Opposition to deteriorating working and living conditions is met by proposals to outlaw strikes under certain circumstances and to impose an incomes policy.

These are the "objective conditions" which, according to the mechanical Marxists, should spark a generalized workers' revolt. But these so-called "objective conditions" have come and gone for the better part of a century without producing a revolution in the developed capitalist societies. Even if an economic crash recurs, it cannot be seriously claimed that this would automatically catapult radical consciousness and social struggle against the system to new heights. We should have learned better from the experience of the 1930s. However, even today we can witness some self-proclaimed "vanguard" grouplets tying their hopes to a depression or some other catastrophe.

Economic breakdown by itself cannot produce a popular revolt. Indifference to oppression is not the source of apathy; neither is fear the sole or necessarily the main source. It also stems from a failure to identify the source of oppression and from the absence of a perceived alternative. Every instrument of civil society labours to cloud the issue, to misdirect the anger and to produce resignation. It is the totality of the bourgeois world view — the complex of prejudices, assumptions and rules of behaviour incorporated in all the institutions of civil society: family, school, media, work place — that infects its victims. Short of establishing a police state, a sign of profound weakness, the viability of any ruling class depends on its ability to persuade the lower classes that its interests are those of society at large, that through its instrumentalities their aspirations can one day be realized.

Lenin once said that "a revolution takes place when those above can no longer cope, and those below will no longer tolerate." This was undoubtedly the case for Russia, Cuba, and China when civil society had come apart and the struggle could therefore be opened and won on the political terrain. But instead of poring over the lessons of the great revolutions, socialists are better advised to learn some lessons from the defeated revolutions over the past half-century in the west.

The central fact of our own experience is the enormous strength and stability of civil society even when state power momentarily falters. In mature capitalist societies the state will not be toppled until the battle for civil society has been won. And civil society will be transformed not only when "those below will no longer tolerate," but also know, more or less, what it is they want and believe that there is a possibility of getting it. Without the totality of an alternative world view that challenges the totality of the bourgeois world view for the minds and imaginations of the people, any revolts produced by economic breakdowns are bound to end in defeat and demoralization.

As Antonio Gramsci, the great Italian Marxist, has said, capitalism has been "objectively" ready for burial since late in the nineteenth century. Notions of "constantly growing contradictions" or "ever more profound crisis" so popular among some of the "vanguard" sects have no scientific value. The crisis we are experiencing today is different from but no more "profound" than other crises in the past. And because crisis is endemic to capitalism, others will occur in the future. Social crises, of necessity, are of brief periods. Society cannot tolerate a vacuum for long. If society's victims do not intervene during the phase of dislocation to institute new forms of social organization, then the old ruling class, perhaps in new form, will revive and life will go on more or less on the old basis. The key question for today, just as it was in the past, is whether oppressed people and particularly the working class, find in themselves the necessary strength and consciousness to challenge the old rulers for supremacy. And that in turn depends on the extent to which revolutionary ideas and revolutionary visions have penetrated the contours of civil society.

If we do not have a revolutionary situation today, it is not for lack of a profound economic crisis, or because people still blindly identify with the values and assumptions of the prevailing order. An erosion of values has begun to set in. The United States lost the war in Vietnam because of the heroic struggle of the Vietnamese, but also because in the final analysis American youths could not be convinced that they should sacrifice their lives for the sake of upholding the American Empire. It is most unlikely that Canadians will agree to sacrifice some of their wages for the sake of Imperial Oil. Throughout the energy and food crises, few people were prepared to accept the official explanations for the shortages and the rising prices. Despite the best efforts of public relations experts, the oil companies failed to dampen popular suspicions that they were making a giant profit grab. A Gallup Poll conducted in December 1974 revealed that 50 per cent of all Canadians believe that rising food prices are due to "increased demand for profits by industry and business." The word "profit" has become synonymous in the minds of many with "rip-off," and corporation executives are busily speech-roaming the country trying to redeem their soiled reputation. Corporate capitalism is suffering a crisis of legitimacy. It extends beyond the economic realm to the political realm. But within the political realm it lies deeper than the cynicism produced by Watergate, the CIA, and other horror stories.

Political activity for the mass of people seems largely to have disappeared. Political life is almost exclusively limited to specialists. Most ordinary people are uninterested in it or frankly contemptuous of it. Politicians are generally considered as dishonest and, regardless of the party they represent, as part of "the same gang." So-called working-class political parties are organizations led by permanent party bureaucrats, professional politicians, trade union officials, middle-class reformers, small progressive businessmen, and a smattering of intellectuals. Politics is virtually a full-time occupation for these individuals. For the vast majority of the membership in these parties, political activity is confined to electioneering and fund-raising. For the population at large, politics at most means casting a ballot every few years. The political enterprise is managed in much the same bureaucratic way as the business enterprise and the trade union enterprise. And political managers are driven into the same kind of dilemma as business managers and trade union managers: how to achieve at one and the same time the participation and exclusion of those they represent. It is an insoluble dilemma, even more so in the political realm than in the economic realm. As somebody once said, in order to survive one has to eat but one need not take an interest in politics.

The entire population, particularly of North America, has drifted into a vast movement of private living. It attends to its own business while leaving to a few specialists the affairs of society over which it feels it can have no control. The young activists of the 1960s appear to be part of this drift. They are more conscious than ever of the reality of corporate power, but feel helpless in the face of it. Many have turned to marriage, the family, child-rearing, sexuality, and other interpersonal relations in the belief that something can be done in this sphere of personal politics. Others work in small groups engaged in research, educational and community projects. There is probably more of this kind of work being done than ever before, but it is isolated, unconnected, and essentially private.

Such total public apathy is of course a measure of silent contempt not only for the political machinery of contemporary capitalism but also for the values that it represents. It is a part of the social crisis that leads not to socialism, but to some form of fascism, not of the Hitlerian variety but a friendly fascism, an acceptance of strong government that promises to bring some order out of the economic chaos and the social disintegration.

The Revolutionary Project: A Sermon

For the first time in the living memory of most of us, it has become possible to begin to raise the question of an alternative ordering of society and to explain how a united movement of working people could actually build an alternative that would be in the best interest of almost everybody. This alternative cannot be simply negotiated through the parliamentary process, as the Chilean example has shown. It requires the mass mobilization of workers as a class that is ready and able to occupy and manage the instruments of production and distribution of both things and ideas. It is at least conceivable that this could be on the agenda of the working class of Quebec in the not too distant future. It remains wishful thinking to believe that it lies on the immediate agenda of the working class of English Canada.

Working people in all sectors of Canadian society are struggling furiously to protect their living standards despite the conservatism of their union leaders and the cajolings and warnings of politicians and governments. There is an undeniable willingness to confront private corportations and public bureaucracies—not just over wages but also the arbitrary rules and regulations that govern most work-places and the top-down system of authority. The working class is still divided in many harmful ways but there are signs of a deepening class consciousness and a growing class polarization.

Laws and governments that clearly defend the interests of private property are increasingly held in contempt.

The social consensus, defined in recent times as the liberal corporate welfare state, is breaking down. It is no accident that social democracy now finds itself in a state of paralysis, for the NDP is the progressive wing of that consensus.

But the socialist left outside the NDP is also in disarray—fragmented and isolated—either clustered in dogmatic, sectarian, feuding grouplets or free-floating in frustration and political impotence. There is no element here capable of giving a coherent socialist leadership to the on-going defensive struggles that define the existing reality. Calls for a new political party at this time are grossly premature. We must begin much more humbly.

To clear the way for putting forward an approach for action, it seems necessary to make a few key distinctions and draw out their implications.

The ultimate failure of social democracy is that by restricting its politics to the parliamentary forum, by marking off a special sphere that is political and confining its practice to full-time politicians, it must present itself as a respectable force that can manage society in an orderly way, that can control the masses rather than helping them to self-determination and self-rule. By conceding reforms from on high, it perpetuates the dependency of the working class, confirming the powerlessness of working people rather than liberating them from external controls. If freedom lies in the exercise of self-management of the institutions that shape our daily lives, social democratic reforms, rather than extending the sphere of freedom, substitute bureaucratic control for the controls of the market.

Herein lies the ultimate difference between reformism and socialism. To the moderates, reform means the bestowing of things—higher wages, pensions, social services—on the mass of people who are kept dispersed and impotent. What matters to socialists is not simply the extension of more and more of these "things," but the sovereign power of workers to determine for themselves the conditions of their social life.

A vital consequence of this distinction is that in the struggle to detach working people from the social democracy of the NDP, socialists will get nowhere by proclaiming their politics as simply being the politics of a more speedy implementation of government-imposed reform measures. People are not prepared to risk major confrontation with the dominant order for the sake of 300,000 new houses a year instead of 250,000, a publicly-owned oil company now rather than a promise of one a few years hence, a 5 per cent rise in real wages instead of a 3 per cent rise. The moderate position of the social democrats is entirely persuasive when it asks: "Why be in such a hurry? Why force things and provoke a head-on confrontation when, with a little patience, the same reforms can be won within a reasonable time and in a calm and orderly manner?" When the difference between social democracy and socialism is couched in terms that are quantitative rather than qualitative, a matter of degree and timing rather than kind, the moderates are bound to win. Ultimately such differences come down to the differences between right-wing and left-wing social democracy. This in fact was the character of the politics engaged in by the now-defunct Waffle group.

It is no doubt useful for socialists to point out that the social democrats, by restricting their politics to the parliamentary process, deny themselves the means of carrying out their own programs; that the dominant class meets partial infringements on their sanctuaries with over-all resistance; that they cannot win in circumstances where the opposition has everything to lose while the reformers are fighting for a specific program that does not warrant their total engagement. However pertinent, such arguments are not enough, for they encourage the idea that the difference between the socialists and the social democrats is simply one of degree and timing, a distinction that has little prospect of winning the support of the constituency of people that now follow the NDP.

The transformation of the human condition does not mean promising an immediate earthly paradise the day after the socialist democracy is proclaimed. It means that in the struggle to achieve every reform an internal dynamic is released that challenges the existing order and leads to further reform.

This strategy, best described by the French writer Andre Gorz,[37] is clearly distinguished from that of the "maximalists" who insist that all reforms are meaningless while the capitalist state continues to exist. The "maximalists" are no doubt right in pointing out that in a battle in which the enemy perceives that it has everything to lose, the strength that it will muster will far exceed that of the forces of reform who will not fully engage themselves in a struggle that does not pave the way for total victory. They are also right in pointing out that reforms gradually introduced are absorbed by the system and turned to the advantage of the capitalist class. This has indeed been the history of welfarism. The idea of "creeping socialism" corresponds to no kind of socialist reality, but instead to a galloping state capitalism.

Where the "maximalists" err, as Gorz explains, is in insisting that every engagement must be entered into by proclaiming its socialist intention. "This amounts to affirming that the revolutionary intention must *precede* the struggle and supply its impetus. This is a non-dialectical postion which evades the problem by treating it as though it were solved. For the fact is that the socialist resolve of the masses never springs out of nothing nor is it created by political programs ["correct line-ism"] nor on scientific demonstration. Socialist resolve is built in and by the struggle for feasible objectives corresponding to the experience, needs and aspirations of the worker." Elaborating, Gorz concedes that from a theoretical point of view there can be no liberation of the workers until the state in its present form, and the capitalist relations of production have been abolished. In *practice* their abolition will become a plausible goal if it comes alive as the meaning which daily actions and demands lead up to. To gather momentum, action cannot from the outset be directed against the total structure that is finally responsible for intolerable conditions; it must proceed from attacks on the "consequences" to reach back for ultimate "causes." "The workers are not *at first* interested in over-all political-economic changes. . . . It is by acting upon their present work situation that they will develop an interest in issues and struggles affecting society as a whole." And it is precisely the task of an initial leadership group to help to bring together those who might wish to engage in active struggle, co-ordinate and expand these actions and make the connections between consequences and causes. Only when active nuclei spring up in work-places and communities and become aware of the political roots of their discontent is it necessary for this much expanded group to acquire a political identity, a specific strategy and a concept of a future society that is integrally linked with day-to-day struggles.

An effective organization whose activities and political views are able to attract the majority of workers who are either unorganized or under the influence of different formations will never be launched by people who insist on speaking in the language of other cultures or other centuries or who blindly draw on the strategies of other revolutions. We certainly have much to learn from the writings of Marx, Lenin, Mao, Rosa Luxemburg and many others; but what is of primary value is the method of their analysis, not the conclusions they drew for their own situations. After all, as even a cursory reading of "the masters" shows, they fundamentally altered the strategies they prescribed as their own circumstances changed. There is no political "line" that will unlock the door to socialism in Canada. The superiority of one political formation over another does not simply stem from the "correctness" of its line.* In fact an effective movement or party does not claim to

---

* As Marx wrote in his introduction to *Critique of the Gotha Program*, "Every step

know in advance the answer to all of the questions it asks.

The imposition of "correct lines" from above may be necessary for the psychological security of certain individuals, but it is the surest path to isolation and sectarianism. The best way to induce participation, to promote an awareness and self-education, is to work out answers in the process of continuous debate, of testing in practice and constant reassessment — precisely what Mao means by "learning from the people."

At the most elemental level this might involve taping interviews with workers, conducting questionnaires that call for opinions as well as facts; preparing biographies, reports and video-tapes that show how the lives of people are shaped by the conditions of their work, by the workings of governments and the legal system, by the way news is filtered by the commercial media, and the values and images that the media projects; and by arranging meetings where the results of these efforts are fed back to workers and where they can be explored and discussed. At a higher level it could mean helping militants write and print pamphlets, find meeting places and regular opportunities for discussing and exchanging experiences. And at still higher levels help work out a synthesis that not only sums up immediate demands, needs, and aspirations but gives coherence to them in political and ideological terms — in short an alternative socialist vision of society against which a comprehensive strategy can be measured. I do not mean to impose any fixed agenda, but merely to outline some possible approaches. Whatever the forms that actions take, in the final analysis, these must depend on local circumstances. They must be rooted in a thorough examination of our political economy, Canada's role within world imperialism as a system, and an assessment of the relative strengths and weaknesses of anticapitalist forces within the community, workplace, trade unions, the women's movements, the native peoples' movement, and elsewhere.

What is missing from the revolutionary project is the revolutionary social movement. There is no revolutionary movement in Canada today. It is true that masses of people are increasingly fed up with, angry at, and suspicious of the profit system, free enterprise, growthmanship, "the affluent society," and other alleged verities of modern capitalism. But the hard reality is that most people are conditioned by a life and time of frustration and

---

of real movement is more important than a dozen programmes [i.e. "correct lines"] . . . By drawing up a programme of principles (instead of postponing this until it has been prepared by a considerable period of common activity) one sets up before the whole world landmarks by which it measures the level of Party movement."

defeat and are scarcely inclined to risk joining a group of visionaries who appear to them at best as hopeless dreamers, and at worst as country preachers telling people how they've sinned and imposing on them a predetermined blueprint for action.

The foundation of movement-building does not lie in producing media spectacles and media personalities, a strategy that increasingly shaped the actions of the student movement of the sixties and the Waffle movement. Nor does it lie in secret sects that send their cadres into organizations to find recruits or to work their way into leadership positions as "honest militants" without revealing their political views. It lies in the day-to-day process of organizing, in drawing lessons and showing connections, in sinking real roots in many situations, in engaging in concrete struggles on many fronts which win actual victories and thereby broadening people's sense of hope and possibility.

Within the labour movement, for example, radicals should be advocating the right of workers to strike at any time, and opposing contracts of more than a year's duration. They should also be advocating the self-management of strikes through debate in open assemblies, and the setting up of strike committees at the shop and factory level. They should oppose job classifications as a basis for wage payment, i.e. support the abolition of sharp pay distinctions between "skilled," "unskilled," and "professional" workers — the slogan used by the Fiat workers in Italy ("We are all equal on the production line") has application everywhere. They should promote worker control of health and safety, and veto-power over management prerogatives. While protection of living standards must be a priority, demands which stress material bonuses above all else only strengthen the hold of capitalist values. Economism must be pushed aside for socialist demands for worker control. Socialism can no more deliver an unending rise of private consumer possessions that can capitalism. It can produce an equalization of scarcity and a degree of democratization in day-to-day living that is unthinkable in capitalist societies. But these will not be achieved the day after the revolution is proclaimed. Responsible revolutionaries must begin to appeal to these values today.

A new political movement would educate and agitate for workers' self-management in factories, mines, offices, schools — wherever people work. Some capitalists may be able to raise wages by 5 or 10 per cent a year, but they cannot reduce alienation by even 1 per cent. There is nothing exceptional about alienated work. It is the way most jobs are organized and the way they are perceived by most workers. When tasks become so fragmented that there is no longer an object being worked upon but only endless motions being repeated upon minute matter, all the meaning is drained out of work. Even the people doing the work are scientifically dissected into their separate faculties. Neither the meaning of work nor the wholeness of being human are achieveable at the work-place. Yet the people do not forfeit their humanness. That is why, even as they tend to resign their politics to the specialist they continue to offer a permanent challenge to the power of management and foremen at the point of production. I am speaking here not only of official strikes or even of the many more unofficial ones, but also of the hidden, silent, informal day-to-day resistance that is part of the life of every office, every factory, every mine. But even when struggles in production reach some degree of intensity, it is difficult for workers to generalize their experience and move the global problems of society. This would be one of the tasks of a new movement.

Intellectuals have a place in such a movement, but they should not be regarded as some kind of elite that is destined to determine the actions of others. They have certain training, tools, and talents that others do not command. These must be put to work. Yet true intellectuals will not exchange one set of masters for another. The most creative and courageous intellectuals have withdrawn from orthodox parties in both East and West precisely because these parties have insisted on the subordination of their work to party doctrine. A new movement or party must create an atmosphere conducive to dissent and criticism.

The present lack of interest in politics raises a new requirement: that political activity should be about what really matters in life, that new methods of action be sought and that new relations between people should find expression in the movement. Traditional politics is dead, and for good reason. Few people can get excited about the machinations of a handful of professional politicians buzzing around the machinery of state with a view to taking it over. A revolutionary movement will activate people only as it concerns itself with their daily lives.

In drawing a distinction between what is a meaningful politics and what is a sterile politics, I have found this passage from the manifesto of the Solidarity group in England a useful guide:

> *Meaningful action* is whatever increases the confidence, the autonomy, the initiative, the participation, the solidarity, the equalitarian tendencies and the self-activity of the masses and whatever assists in their demystification.
> *Sterile and harmful action* is whatever reinforces the passivity of the masses, their apathy, their cynicism, their differentiation through hierarchy, their alienation, their reliance on others to do things for them and the degree to which they can therefore be manipulated by others — even by those allegedly acting on their behalf.

I believe that any new party must be pre-eminently an extra-parliamentary party committed to mass action around popular needs within all agencies of civil society. Under no circumstances would it rely primarily on a parliamentary road to social change. That does not preclude any electoral politics, but electoral activity must be viewed as secondary, to be engaged in only when the party has established its social base through mass action. Its identity as a socialist movement would then not be in doubt.

The sudden concern over material scarcity, the attack on living standards after years of relative prosperity, and the simultaneous appearance of mass unemployment have created a favourable climate for a growing awareness among working people. Questioning the authority of employers and the state is already on the agenda. But totalistic solutions imposed on an ill-prepared public by an elite vanguard are bound to be ignored. On the other hand, moderate reforms are easily co-opted and absorbed by the prevailing system. What is essential is the political party that actively intervenes in day-to-day struggles — in the work-place, in the schools, and in the neighbourhood — over wages, rents, food prices, speed-ups, lay-offs, plant closures, job allocations, safety, discrimination, day-care, health care, and environmental degradation; that provides immediate solutions and the possibility of short-term victories and that deepens these struggles and connects them, and develops an awareness of the need for a general struggle and a decisive show-down.*

There is no revolutionary party in Canada today. There are dozens of sects and groups, each with its own pet theories: which is the "primary contradiction" — capitalism or imperialism? or is it the oppression of the working class, or of women or of native people? which is the decisive sector that will make the revolution? of not heeding this distinction. The consequence of this distinction, *in practice,* is that party building is a process, not something that can be created by the pronouncements of a group of "founders." The history of the left is riddled with self-proclaimed vanguard groups who upon deciding the doctrine and program of "the new party," then proceed to look for people who agree with it. As Gorz has warned, "such organizations will never belong to the masses: they will belong to it. The cornerstone of future bureaucracy, dogmation and sectarianism will thereby have been laid." Gorz wisely counsels that an organization should not be larger than the actions that it can wage and the tasks that it can perform. When an organization becomes larger than what is required to effect the tasks that it can practically undertake, it is bound to become an end in itself, a bureaucracy that degenerates and exhausts its energy in self-preserving functions.

What segments of society would make up the party's constituency? Most of the producing elements of our society: industrial,
service, and clerical workers, women, native people, professionals,
students, and others. Most people, whether blue-collar or white-
collar, whether in the private sector or the public sector, work for a
living under conditions controlled by their employers. Housewives
do not work directly for capitalists, but their labour is essential for
the maintenance and reproduction of the labour power of the
working class. Most sectors of the working class experience similar
forms of oppression in factories, offices, schools, mines, hospitals,
railroads, etc. Their common conditions provide the material basis
for revolutionary consciousness and action. It is nonsense to speak
of "leading" sectors, though of course at any one time some groups
will be more advanced than others. Modern capitalism has succeeded in transforming class divisions into divisions between those
who give orders and those who take orders. Some are more autonomous than others but increasingly all perform a broken-up labour,
experiencing both alienation at work and the absurdity of life in
contemporary society. The decomposition of capitalist values
drives increasing numbers of professionals and youths towards a
radical re-evaluation of the system as a whole.

In Canada, as elsewhere around the globe, the struggle must be an
anti-imperialist one, for capitalism here is an extension of American capitalism as the Canadian economy is a northern extension of
the American economy. The struggle for an independant Canada is
no flight from the spirit of internationalism. It is the specific form
that internationalism takes in the age of the American global corporation. Wherever it reaches, the multinational corporation is
facing a similar kind of opposition, for it suffocates the will of
people everywhere to be free, to express themselves in their own
idiom, to develop their own culture and traditions and their own
economies. In joining this struggle, Canadians do not engage in an
empty chauvinism but in a worldwide campaign for an internationalism whose components are independent and sovereign peoples in all regions of the world.

A socialist movement would strive to make international solidarity in working-class struggles a living reality. Several decades
ago it was a real factor in working class life, but it has largely disappeared as most working-class organizations have lapsed into an
empty chauvinism. This is no endorsation of the phony "internationalism" of the AFL-CIO variety, which is labour imperialism in
the guise of internationalism, the other side of the coin to corporate
imperialism. A socialist party would work for an independent
Canadian labour movement that is capable of promoting a real solidarity with working people everywhere. In the age of the multina-

tional corporations, international linkages among workers of different lands is a matter of survival.

I have not intended here to propose an organizational model to create "the revolution." What I hope I have done is to direct attention to some of the self-destructive and crippling tendencies evident in the left and to call for a principled and non-dogmatic approach that calls upon reason rather than religion, study rather than sloganeering, co-operation rather than cultism. We must learn to avoid making a fetish of this element of the working class or that, of this "contradiction" or that. We must learn to take into account the wide diversity of needs and aspirations of all our working population — not just the blue collar proletariat; to recognize all strands of the web of contradictions that characterizes contemporary capitalist society; to join all struggles that are potentially anti-capitalist and anti-imperialist and to attempt to influence these movements by reason and example so that they may become a force for socialism. Indeed I can see no other way of attracting to socialism the numbers of people that will be required to realistically challenge the present order. The current crisis offers new opportunities but some form of modern-day barbarism is as easily on the agenda as socialism.

As Andre Gorz has written, the task of the revolutionary organization is defined by the vision of the socialist society and by the nature of the revolutionary process that will lead to socialism. Most of the world's population and a significant minority of North Americans still live in poverty. But much of our population lives at a level of at least modest physical comfort. They will not become revolutionaries solely to end material scarcity. The women's movement, the struggle for workers' control in industry, for community control, and elements of the environmental movement have begun to express visions of a qualitatively new society growing out of a rebellion against authority and coercion. The revolutionary process must synthesize the two strands which demand material security and democratic control. As Gorz says: "Revolutions are made not to get more . . . of what we already have, but to get something altogether different that will put an end of conditions that are felt to be unbearable."[38]

The essential aim of socialism is not to increase production and consumption, and it is not simply nationalization of the means of production plus planning. It is not, as someone once said, a backyard of leisure attached to the industrial prison. It is rather the destruction of the industrial prison itself, a project for the humanization of work and of society. Sooner or later the futility of chasing after more and newer things sends people to the real problems: what kind of production? which needs? what kind of work?

what type of relations between workers, neighbours, men and women, parents and children? what kind of direction for society as a whole?

People do not become revolutionaries to gain an extra 10 per cent wage increase, but to gain a new way of life. We must renew the long-abandoned project of setting forth our visions of a new society. It is not a matter of drawing up detailed blueprints in advance, but of establishing general principles.

Eliminating inequality would be a primary goal of a socialist society. The first step would be establishing immediate floors and ceilings on incomes to end the extreme of inequality at once. Gradually the society would move beyond that. Certain essentials like food could be made free; others, like housing, could be distributed according to need and rents set according to income. Ultimately the entire system of distribution through wage labour would be completely eliminated, with all necessities being distributed according to need. People with middle incomes are not part of the ruling class. To attack their living standards is to divide the working class. The primary purpose of the revolution is to unite all working people to expropriate the means of production, for it is private control of the means of production that is the most important source of inequality.

The socialist society would be thoroughly democratic and anti-hierarchical — based on work-place and neighbourhood councils merging into larger bodies for broader functions. Every effort would be made to break down the dichotomy of mental and physical labour and the separation of town and countryside. Just as workers should participate in management, so management should participate in work. The ultimate aim is to abolish all such distinction, and in the meantime concrete steps must be taken to move in that direction. The unlimited growth of the cities on the one hand, and the decimation of the countryside on the other, would be halted. To achieve as much direct democracy as possible, decision-making would be decentralized wherever feasible. Thus, for areas like housing, schools, and day-care there would be local planning; for others like transportation, energy production, and general investment and taxation, national and regional planning is essential.

Socialism is based on the belief in the worth and integrity of each individual. The socialist society would allow and encourage a great deal of social experimentation regarding communal living, child-rearing and work allocation, and it will struggle to eliminate sexism, racism and hierarchy. All individuals would share in necessary but unpleasant work. With the economy providing for essential and self-defined needs rather than wants that are created for them by industry and the media, the amount of necessary work would decline and scarce resources would be conserved.

It is of the utmost importance that all needs — for food, shelter, clothing, culture, education, leisure, recreation, etc. — be brought into balance with each other and with society's natural resources and environment. The absurd and ultimately disastrous notion of insatiable wants must be repudiated and defeated in theory and in practice.

It is vital to underline the essential totality of this vision. For example, worker control in enterprises that function in a world of competitive values, still dominated by material incentives and a culture of possessive individualism, simply transforms workers into capitalists, working against other workers rather than with them. A socialist society must be permeated with the idea and the practice of equality and co-operation and personal responsibility for the welfare of all.

There is nothing new about this vision. It brings together the socialist ideals that have attracted millions of people around the world. It is still a force of enormous potential power. To many it may seem as utopian as ever. And of course it is utopian. It is a society that must always be in the making. It is never fully realized; it must be perpetually struggled for. We are all utopians of a sort, those who sneer at the mere mention of revolutionizing social systems no less than myself. For they must believe that the existing social and economic order can be made to last forever by means of manipulation and superficial reforms that fail even to touch its increasing irrationality, destructiveness, and inhumanity. I prefer to be a utopian of the kind so beautifully described by Simone de Beauvoir: "Socialist Europe? there are moments when I ask myself whether it is not a utopia. But each idea not yet realized curiously resembles a utopia; one would never do anything if we thought that nothing is possible except that which already exists."

Notes

Notes to Part I

1. I am thinking here of the likes of Ralph Nader, Mel Hurtig, Robert Chodos, Phillip Mathias, Larry Pratt, Morton Schulman, the Latin American Working Group, *Last Post,* the North American Congress on Latin America, and the Pacific Studies Centre.

2. *Business Week,* June 29, 1974.

3. Lawrence F. Lifschultz, "Could Karl Marx Teach Economics in America?" *Ramparts,* April 1974.

4. P. Samuelson, A. Scott, *Economics, Third Canadian Edition,* p. 53.

5. *Ibid.,* pp. 412, 418.

6. See Stephen Marglin, "What Do Bosses Do?" and Katherine Stone, "The Origins of Job Structure in the Steel Industry," both published in *Review of Radical Political Economics,* Summer 1974; and H. Braverman, *Labour and Monopoly Capital.*

7. *Principles of Scientific Management,* quoted in Stone, "The Origins of Job Structure."

8. *Ibid.*

9. Victor Vroom, "An Industrial Social Psychology," in G. Lindsay and E. Aaronson (eds.), *The Handbook of Social Psychology.*

10. This and other examples of worker participation are discussed in Paul Blumberg, *Industrial Democracy,* J. A. C. Brown, *The Social Psychology of Industry,* and Judson Gooding, *The Job Revolution.*

11. See Charles Bettelheim, *Cultural Revolution and Industrial Organization in China;* Carl Riskin, "Maoism and Motivation," *Working Papers,* Winter 1974.

12. André Gorz, *Strategy for Labour,* p. 72.

13. Quoted in C. W. Gonick, "Socialism and the Economics of Growthmanship," in L. Lapierre, *et al.* (eds.), *Essays on the Left.* P. 141.

14. J. Gooding, *op. cit.*, pp. 67-90.

15. B. Commoner, *Closing of the Circle*, p. 143.

16. The argument here is drawn from M. Best, "Notes on Inflation," *Review of Radical Political Economics*, August 1972.

17. John M. Blair, *Economic Concentration: Structure, Behaviour and Public Policy*, P. 482.

18. Department of Consumer and Corporate Affairs, *Concentration in the Manufacturing Industries of Canada*, Appendix A.

19. *Ibid.*, p. 14.

20. This schema is fully developed in Robert T. Averitt, *The Dual Economy*.

21. Cited in Mark J. Green, "The High Cost of Monopoly," *The Progressive*, March 1972.

22. Quoted in C. W. Gonick, *op. cit.*, p. 140.

23. See K. William Kapp, *The Social Cost of Private Enterprise*.

24. F. M. Fisher, Z. Grilliches, and C. Klaysen, "The Cost of Automobile Changes since 1949," *Journal of Political Economy*, October 1962.

25. Mason, "The Apologetics of Managerialism," *Journal of Business*, January 1958.

26. Quoted in William Katz, "Responsibility and the Modern Corporation," *Journal of Law and Economy*, October 1960, p. 84.

27. "The New Place of Business" in E. Cheit (ed.), *The Business Establishment*, pp. 165, 172.

28. Quoted by Peter Newman, "The Bankers," *Maclean's*, February 1972.

29. Mason, *op. cit.*

30. N. Chamberlain, "The Life of the Mind of the Firm," *Daedalus*, Winter, 1969.

31. See, for example, the work of James Earley, "The Excellently Managed Corporation," *Papers and Proceedings of the American Economic Association*, 1956, May 1957.

32. See M. Zeitlin, "Corporate Ownership and Control: The Large Corporation and the Capitalist Class," *American Journal of Sociology*, March 1974; Don Villarijo, "Stock Ownership and the Control of Corporations," *New University Thought*, Autumn 1961 and Winter 1962.

33. Galbraith, *The New Industrial Estate*, Second Edition, p. xix.

34. Robert J. Larmer, in his recent book, *Management Control and the Large Corporation*, has conducted a number of statistical tests which found that the rate of profit earned by so-called "management" and "owner"-controlled firms was about the same.

35. John Porter, *The Vertical Mosaic*, Table 15, Appendix II.

36. *Ibid.*, P. 252.

37. *Ibid.*, p. 283.

38.   Larmer, *op. cit.*

39.   Robin Williams, Jr., *American Society*, p. 184.

40.   Quoted in Wallace Clement, *The Canadian Corporate Elite*, p. 157.

41.   See John Porter, *The Vertical Mosaic;* Frank and Libbie Park, *Anatomy of Big Business.* A historical analysis of Canadian banking may be found in Tom Naylor's work and in W. Clement, *The Canadian Corporate Elite.*

42.   *Globe and Mail,* May 31, 1972.

43.   Wallace Clement, *op. cit.,* pp. 263-5.

44.   See G. Myers, *A History of Canadian Wealth,* for an entertaining treatment of this subject.

45.   Quoted in R. Chodos, *The CPR, A Century of Corporate Welfare*, p. 19.

46.   *Ibid.,* p. 157.

47.   *Ibid.,* p. 118.

48.   W. Clement, *op. cit.*

49.   Daniel Bell, "The Break-Up of Family Capitalism," in *The End of Ideology,* p. 46.

50.   See W. Clement, *op. cit.,* pp. 185-7.

51.   *Toronto Star,* April 15, 1972, quoted in *ibid.,* p. 186.

52.   *Ibid.,* p. 243. Much of what follows leans on the material found in Clement's chapter.

53.   *Ibid.,* p. 244.

54.   *Financial Post,* June 9, 1973.

55.   *Globe and Mail,* August 31, 1971, quoted in Clement, p. 256.

56.   *Financial Post,* February 24, 1973.

57.   *Ottawa Journal,* March 5, 1973, quoted in Clement, p. 258.

58.   Porter, *op. cit.,* p. 305.

59.   C. B. Macpherson, *The Real World of Democracy,* p. 6.

60.   *Ibid.,* p. 11.

61.   Quoted in Ralph Miliband, *The State in Capitalist Society,* p. 79.

62.   *Ibid.,* p. 63.

63.   *Business Week,* January 27, 1975, p. 16.

64.   On this theme, see the work of Karl Polanyi, *The Great Transformation.*

65.   Samuelson and Scott, *op. cit.,* p. 749.

66.   M. Friedman, *Capitalism and Freedom,* pp. 161-2.

67.   For a more elaborate version of this argument, see M. Dobb, *Wages,* and T. Weisskopf, "Capitalism and Equality," in Weisskopf, Edwards, *et al* (eds.), *The Capitalist System.*

68.   *New Republic,* November 1974.

69.   *Ibid.*

Notes to Part II

1.   "The Rise and Fall of the Third Commercial Empire of the St. Lawrence" in G. Teeple (ed.), *Capitalism and the National Question*, p. 31.

2.   "The Efficiency (Contradictions) of Multinational Corporations," in G. Paquet (ed.), *The Multinational Firms and the Nation-state*, p. 52. Before his untimely death in 1973, Stephen Hymer, a brilliant Canadian economist, contributed some of the most insightful writing on the multinational corporation. All students of this subject owe a great debt to his work.

3.   Quoted in H. Magdoff and P. Sweezy, "Notes on the Multinational Corporation," *Monthly Review*, March 1966.

4.   The estimate is based on a projection by J. D. Behrman, cited in Kari Levitt, *Silent Surrender*, pp. 92-3.

5.   Quoted in Robert Scheer, *America After Nixon*, p. 93.

6.   "The Advantages of Being Multinational" in G. Paquet (ed.), *op. cit.*, pp. 103-8.

7.   United Nations, Department of Economic and Social Affairs, *Multinational Corporations in World Development*, p. 13.

8.   Henry Fowler, quoted in K. Levitt, *op. cit.* p. 110.

9.   *Ibid.*

10.   Scheer, *op. cit.*

11.   United Nations, *op. cit.*, p. 193.

12.   *Ibid.*, pp. 130-1.

13.   On this point, see Harry Magdoff, "The Logic of Imperialism," *Social Policy*, September-October 1970.

14.   *Business Week*, April 20, 1963.

15.   Quoted in C. W. Gonick, "Foreign Ownership and Political Decay," *Canadian Dimension Nationalism Kit*, p. 13. The above argument is drawn from this essay.

16.   Quoted in *ibid.*

17.   "The Coming Crisis of the Multinational Corporation," *ibid.*, p. 23.

18.   "Big Business and 'Dependencies'," *Foreign Affairs*, April 1972, pp. 527-8.

19.   United Nations, *op. cit.*, p. 20.

20.   Magdoff and Sweezy, *op. cit.*

21.   S. Hymer, "The Efficiency (Contradictions) of Multinational Corporations," pp. 62-3.

22.   Naylor, *op. cit.*, p. 2.

23.   See the author's article "Metropolis/Hinterland Themes," *Canadian Dimension*, March-April 1972; John Warnock, "Metropolis/Hinterland, the

Lost Theme in Canadian Letters," *Canadian Dimension*, June 1974; Melville Watkins, "A Staple Theory of Economic Growth," *Canadian Journal of Economic and Political Science*, May 1963.

24. Quoted in Henry Lafebre, *The New Empire*, pp. 25-6. Much of what follows is taken from this superb study. For the period of the eighteenth and early nineteenth centuries, see R. Van Alstyne, *The Rising American Empire*.

25. *Ibid.*, p. 28.

26. Naylor, *op. cit.*, p. 21.

27. T. W. Acheson, "The Social Origins of the Canadian Industrial Elite, 1880-1885" in D. S. MacMillan (ed.), *Canadian Business History*, pp. 164-6.

28. W. Kilbourn, *The Elements Combined: A History of the Steel Company of Canada*, pp. 20-1.

29. Naylor, *op. cit.* p. 24.

30. James Laxer, "The Political Economy of Canada," R. Laxer (ed.), *Canada Ltd.*, pp. 33-4.

31. W. T. Easterbrook and H. Aitken, *Canadian Economic History*, p. 520.

32. *Financial Post*, March 24, 1945.

33. C. W. Gonick, *op. cit.*, p. 17.

34. *Canada's First Century*, p. 294.

35. Quoted in J. W. Warnock, *Partner to Behemoth*, p. 119. This is a much neglected book that deserves to be better known.

36. *Ibid.*, p. 114.

37. Quoted in *ibid.*, p. 115.

38. B. W. Wilkinson, *International Trade: An Analysis of Recent Trends and Patterns*, p. 72.

39. Charles Taylor, *Snow Job: Canada, the United States, and Vietnam, 1954-1973*.

40. *The Canadian Economy and Disarmament*, p. 37.

41. "A Strange Kind of Neutrality," *Canadian Dimension*, September-October 1966, p. 5.

42. Both quoted in J. Warnock, *op. cit.*, pp. 141-2.

43. Quoted in J. L. Granatstein, "Revising Mike," *Globe and Mail*, May 3, 1975.

44. Naylor, *op. cit.*, p. 18. For different interpretations see Gad Horowitz, *Canadian Labour and Politics*, Chapter 1; H. G. J. Aitken, "Defensive Expansionism: The State and Economic Growth in Canada," in T. W. Easterbrook and M. H. Watkins (eds.), *Approaches to Canadian Economic History*; H. Hardin, *A Nation Unaware: The Canadian Economic Culture*.

45. Levitt, *op. cit.*, p. 63.

46. *Ibid.*, p. 139.

47. *Ibid.*, pp. 104-107.

48.   Samuelson and Scott, *op. cit.*, pp. 795-6.

49.   H. G. Aitken, *American Capital and Canadian Resources*, p. 60.

50.   *Ibid.*, pp. 66-7.

51.   See, for example, Harry Johnson, "Canadian-American Integration: A Time for Decision," in Finnigan and Gonick (eds.), *Making It: The Canadian Dream.*

52.   Quoted in C. W. Gonick, *op. cit.*, p. 18.

53.   *Lament for a Nation*, p. 47.

54.   G. Stevenson, "Political Disintegration of the Hinterland," unpublished manuscript.

55.   *Canada in Question: Federalism in the Seventies*, p. 111.

56.   Levitt, *op. cit.*, p. 145.

57.   Naylor, *op. cit.*, p. 32.

58.   *Foreign Ownership and the Structure of Canadian Industry*, p. 205.

59.   "The Coming Crisis of the Multinational Corporation," *op. cit.*, p. 24.

60.   Cited in R. Scheer, *op. cit.*, p. 288.

Notes to Part III

1.   Economic Council of Canada, *Third Annual Review*, p. 202.

2.   For a further explanation of "partial inflation" see *ibid.*, pp. 40-45.

3.   Quoted in Bank of Montreal, *Business Review*, September 1974.

4.   OECD, *Inflation, the Present Problem*, p. 35.

5.   See Jack Rasmus, "Wage and Price Freeze," *Canadian Dimension*, Vol. 9, Nos. 7, 8.

6.   Donald Smiley, *Canada in Question: Federalism in the Seventies*, p. 117.

7.   Quoted in Levitt, *op. cit.*, p. 10.

8.   Quoted in *ibid.*, p. 12.

9.   *Ibid.*, p. 13.

10.   *Journal of Canadian Studies*, February 1969.

11.   *Op. cit.*, p. 15.

12.   Sid Blumenthal, "CONTELPRO, How the FBI Tried to Destroy the Black Panthers," *Canadian Dimension*, Vol. 10, No. 6.

13.   "The Debt Economy," a special issue, October 12, 1974.

14.   These and other examples may be found in *Business Week*, October 12, 1974.

15.   *Business Week*, September 14, 1974.

16.   E. Rossi, "Nationalization in Italy," in M. Einaudo, M. Bye and E. Rossi, *Nationalization in France and Italy*, p. 200.

17.   *Business Week*, September 14, 1974.

18. *Ibid.*

19. "Workers and the Energy Crisis," *International Socialist Review,* June 1974.

20. Quoted in *Canadian Dimension,* Vol. 10, No. 2.

21. *Business Week,* March 3, 1975.

22. *Ibid.,* November 19, 1974.

23. *Ibid.,* October 12, 1974.

24. *Ibid.,* January 20, 1975.

25. *Ibid.,* February 3, 1975.

26. Quoted in *Labour Gazette,* June 1973.

27. D. Gordon, *Theories of Poverty and Underemployment,* p. 94.

28. *Financial Post,* December 21, 1974.

29. *Ontario Report,* Vol. I, No. 1.

30. *Newsweek,* September 30, 1974.

31. *New York Times,* December 29, 1974, Section 3.

32. *Ibid.,* September 15, 1974.

33. *Ibid.*

34. *Business Week,* October 12, 1974.

35. "A Planned U.S. Economy?" *New York Times,* May 18, 1975.

36. Felix G. Rohatyn, "A New RFC is Proposed for Business," *New York Times,* Financial Section, December 1, 1974.

37. What follows is largely drawn from André Gorz, *Socialism and Revolution,* and in particular his chapter, "A Socialist Strategy for Reforms."

Notes to Part IV

1. This chapter and the one following are basically elaborations of an article written for *Canadian Dimension* magazine, "The Current Crisis Marks the End of the Keynesian Era," Vol. 10, No. 5. As well, I have drawn upon Paul Mattick, *Marx and Keynes: The Limits of the Mixed Economy;* David Horowitz, *The Fate of Midas;* and various issues of *Monthly Review.*

2. J. M. Keynes, *The General Theory of Employment, Interest and Money,* p. 27.

3. Students of economics should consult with P. Sylos-Labini, *Oligopoly and Technological progress,* on this essential subject.

4. Keynes, *op. cit.,* p. 379, Paul Mattick, *Marx and Keynes: The Limits of the Mixed Economy,* provides an excellent discussion on this subject (pp. 109-118).

5. *Ibid.,* p. 322.

6. Quoted in R. Scheer, *America After Nixon,* p. 111.

7. Quoted in *ibid.,* p. 122.

8. D. Dillard, *The Economics of John Maynard Keynes,* p. 241.

9.   Keynes, *op. cit.*, p. 129.

10.   Quoted in D. Horowitz, *op. cit.*, p. 144.

11.   Ibid., p. 37. This thesis was brilliantly argued by Paul Baran, "National Economic Planning," in B. F. Haley (ed.), *A Survey of Contemporary Economics*, and more popularly in his *Political Economy of Growth.*

12.   *Monthly Review,* February, 1974.

13.   Quoted in P. Baran and P. Sweezy, *Monopoly Capital*, p. 212.

14.   This argument is drawn from H. Magdoff, *The Age of Imperialism*, pp. 186-191. The data, cited by Magdoff, are taken from "The Inter-Industry Structure of the United States," *Survey of Current Business,* November 1964.

15.   Seymour Melman, *The Permanent War Economy*, p. 237. See also James L. Clayton (ed.), *The Economic Impact of the Cold War.*

16.   Joan Robinson, "Marx, Marshall and Keynes," *Collective Economic Papers II.*

17.   Harry Magdoff, "The Economics of Imperialism," paper given at the annual meeting of the American Economics Association, December, 1969.

18.   Shoup, "The New American Militarism," *Atlantic*, April 1969.

19.   George Thayer, *The War Business: The International Trade in Armaments*, pp. 37-8.

20.   Magdoff, *The Age of Imperialism*, pp. 185-6.

21.   Quoted in *ibid.*, p. 176.

22.   *Monthly Review, loc. cit.*

23.   *Economics, Third Canadian Edition*, p. 1029.

24.   J. M. Keynes, "The General Theory of Employment," *Quarterly Journal of Economics*, February 1937.

25.   Dudley Dillard, "The Theory of a Monetary Economy" in K. Kurihara (ed.), *Post-Keynesian Economics*, cited in D. Horowitz, *op. cit.*, p. 23.

26.   *Ibid.*, p. 29.

27.   R. A. Gordon, "Investment Behaviour and Business Cycles," *Review of Economics and Statistics*, February 1955. Albert Safarian attempts to apply these concepts in his *The Canadian Economy in the Great Depression.*

28.   *Monthly Review*, September 1973.

29.   *Ibid.*

30.   *Business Week*, October 12, 1974.

31.   *Ibid.*

32.   David Deitch, "The Managed Depression," *The Nation*, August 31, 1974.

33.   *Business Week*, October 12, 1974.

34.   See his comments quoted in Part III, in the chapter "Why is This Crisis Different From the Others?"

35.   *Business Week*, October 12, 1974.

36. *Ibid.*

37. On the subject of the crisis in the banking system, I have drawn extensively from "Banks: Skating on Thin Ice," *Monthly Review,* February 1974.

38. Quoted in *ibid.*

39. *Ibid.*

40. All figures are derived from *Bank of Canada Review,* January 1975.

41. See OECD, *Inflation, the Present Problem,* pp. 19-23 and R. Boddy and J. Crotty, "Class Conflict and Macro Policy: The Political Business Cycle," *Review of Radical Political Economics,* Vol. 7, No. 1.

42. M. Kalecki, *Selected Essays in the Dynamics of the Capitalist Economy.*

43. *Ibid.,* pp. 138-141.

44. See Boddy and Crotty, *op. cit.* and the writings cited therein.

Notes to Part V

1. Melman, *The Permanent War Economy, American Capitalism in Decline,* p. 74.

2. *Ibid.*

3. *Ibid.,* pp. 85-86.

4. *Ibid.,* pp. 86-7.

5. *Ibid.,* pp. 87-88.

6. Cited in H. Magdoff, *The Age of Imperialism,* p. 43.

7. P. Baran and P. Sweezy, *Monopoly Capital,* p. 191.

8. Magdoff, *The Age of Imperialism,* pp. 20-21.

9. Cited in P. Sweezy and H. Magdoff, "Notes on Inflation and the Dollar," *Monthly Review,* March 1970.

10. V. Perlo, *The Unstable Economy.*

11. *Fortune,* May 1974.

12. The details of this campaign are taken from Richard DuBoff, "Trade War Exercises," *Canadian Dimension,* July 1973.

13. Quoted in D. F. Fleming, *The Cold War and its Origins,* p. 1096.

14. Kennan, "A Fresh Look at our Chinese Policy," *New York Times Magazine,* November 22, 1964.

15. John Gittings, "China and the Cold War," *Survey,* January 1966.

16. R. M. Nixon, "U.S. Foreign Policy for the 1970s: Building for Peace" (Report to Congress).

17. *Ibid.*

18. Quoted in I. Wallerstein, "Trends in World Capitalism," *Monthly Review,* May 1974.

19. Stanley Aronowitz, *Food, Shelter and the American Dream,* p. 46.

20. H. E. Meyer, "A Plant that Could Change the Shape of Soviet Industry," *Fortune*, November 1974.

21. *New York Times*, July 1, 1973.

22. G. Pollack, *Foreign Affairs*, April 1974.

Notes to Part VI

1. Lester Brown, *In the Human Interest*, pp. 71-2.

2. E. P. Reubens, *Challenge*, March-April 1974.

3. Brown, *op. cit.*, p. 53-59.

4. *Newsweek*, November 11, 1974.

5. Forbes, March 1974.

6. See C. Gonick and F. Gudmunson, "Food, Glorious Food," *Canadian Dimension*, Vol. 9, Nos. 1, 2.

7. James P. Grant, *New York Times*, August 28, 1974.

8. *Wall Street Journal*, November 12, 1974.

9. *Economist*, December 15, 1973.

10. E. Shaffer, *Canadian Dimension*, Vol. 1, No. 2.

11. *Business Week*, January 13, 1975.

12. See Peter R. Odell, *Oil and World Power*, for further details.

13. See Michael Tanzer, *The Energy Crisis, World Struggle for Power and Wealth*.

14. M. Bosquet, "The Energy Crisis Hoax," *Canadian Dimension*, Vol. 10, No. 1.

15. *Ibid.*

16. See James Laxer, *Canada's Energy Crisis*, pp. 45-6.

17. *Business Week*, January 13, 1975.

18. *New York Times*, November 27, 1974.

19. *Oil Week*, October 15, 1973.

20. *Toronto Star*, January 8, 1975.

21. Cited in Laxer, *op. cit.*, p. 107.

22. J. C. Russell, "Syncrude and Peter Lougheed: Giving It All Away," *Canadian Forum*, January 1974.

23. Laxer, *op. cit.*, p. 99.

24. Cited in "Banksland, Preview to a 50 Billion Dollar Eskploitation," *Canadian Dimension*, Vol. 8, No. 7.

25. *Oil Week*, April 9, 1973.

26. Joseph Yanchula, cited in *Toronto Star*, December 13, 1974.

27. EEC, *Eleventh Annual Report*, p. 150.

28. Cited in J. Laxer, "Canadian Manufacturing and U.S. Trade Policy," R. Laxer, (ed.) *Canada Ltd.*, p. 145.

29. "The Export Rip-off; The Civil Service Report," *Canadian Forum*, June-July 1973.

30. Laxer, op. cit., p. 145.

31. *Ibid.*, p. 146

32. P. Bourgault, *Innovation and the Structure of Canadian Industry*, p. 126.

33. Quoted in *Financial Post*, April 26, 1975.

34. Science Council of Canada, "The Multinational Firm, Foreign Direct Investment and Canadian Science Policy," p. 43.

35. *Ibid.*, p. 44.

36. Quoted in E. Shaffer, *op. cit.*

37. *Ibid.*

38. Samuelson and Scott, p. 416.

39. H. Miller, *Poverty, American Style*, p. 6.

40. E. J. Mishan, *The Cost of Economic Growth*, p. 20.

41. Hans-Magnus Enzenberger, "Critique of Political Economy," *New Left Review*, No. 84. This important article is the source of a number of ideas that appear in this and subsequent chapters.

42. L. Mumford, "The Highway and the City" in Garrett de Bell (ed.), *The Environmental Handbook*, pp. 192-3.

43. Quoted in B. Commoner, *The Closing Circle*, p. 253.

44. *Ibid.*, pp. 257-67.

45. Quoted in B. Weisberg, *Beyond Repair, the Ecology of Capitalism*, p. 50.

46. Gorz, *Strategy for Labour*, p. 71.

47. Quoted in C. W. Gonick, "Socialism and the Economics of Growthmanship" in L. Lapierre *et al.*, *Essays on the Left*, p. 137. This earlier essay contains a number of the ideas that I report in this chapter.

48. Ehrlich, *The Population Bomb*, pp. 161-2.

49. Stephen Rosenfeld, *Foreign Policy*, Spring 1974.

50. *Scientific American*, September 1974.

51. P. Ehrlich, *The End of Affluence*, p. 24.

52. Quoted in Hans-Magnus Enzenberger, *op. cit.*

53. P. Dooley, *Royal Commission on Consumer Problems and Inflation in the Prairies*, cited in Gonick and Gudmunson, *op. cit.*

54. B. Commoner, *op. cit.*, p. 237.

55. Lester Brown, *op. cit.*, p. 114-6.

56. *Ibid.*, p. 119.

57. Chi Feng, "Thirteen Consecutive Years of Rich Harvests," *Peking Review*, January 1975.

58. Brown, *op. cit.*, p. 96.

59. Orville Schell, "In China All Waste is Treasure," *Clear Creek*, February 1972.

60. Chi Feng, *op. cit.*

61. "Rational Distribution of Food Grain," *Peking Review*, January 3, 1975.

62. Shen Wen, "Going in for Farming in an Industrial City," *Peking Review*, March 5, 1971.

63. Tang Ke, "China's Stand on the Question of Human Environment," speech to the Stockholm Conference on the Human Environment, published in *Peking Review*, June 16, 1972.

64. *Peking Review*, December 7, 1973.

65. See his *The Great Ascent*.

66. This and early quotations may be found in R. Heilbroner, *An Enquiry into the Human Prospect*, pp. 37-9.

67. J. Gurley, "Capitalism and Maoist Economic Development," E. Friedman and M. Seldon (eds.), *America's Asia*.

68. Mao Tse Tung, "On Practice," quoted in Gurley, *ibid.*

69. *Peking Review*, February 24, 1967, quoted in Gurley, *ibid.*

70. *Peking Review*, March 10, 1967, quoted in Gurley, *ibid.*

71. *Ibid.*

Notes to Part VII

1. Quoted in R. Heilbroner, *The Future as History*, p. 22.

2. *Ibid.*, p. 46.

3. *New York Times*, October 30, 1974.

4. Hugo Helco, *The Nation*, August 31, 1974.

5. *New York Times*, September 1, 1974.

6. Raymond Williams, "Britain After the Election," *The Nation*, November 2, 1974.

7. "Factory Occupations," *Canadian Dimension*, Vol. 10, No. 1.

8. *New Statesman*, February 22, 1974.

9. Quoted in *Toronto Star*, August 24, 1974.

10. *New Left Review*, No. 76.

11. *Ibid.*

12. *Ibid.*

13. *Ibid.*

14. "Working Class Struggle in Italy," *Radical America*, Vol. 7, No. 2, p. 11.

15. Quoted in *Italy, New Tactics and Organization*.

16. "Italy, 1973: Workers' Struggle in the Capitalist Crisis," *Radical America*, Vo. 7, No. 2.

17. "Class Struggle and European Unity," *Lotta Continua*, November 7 and 8, 1972.

18. "The Elimination of Gaullism," *Canadian Dimension*, Vol. 10, No. 3.

19. *Ibid.*

20. Stephen Cohen, *Modern Capitalist Planning: The French Model*, p. 240-1.

21. *Ibid.*, p. 249.

22. *Ibid.*

23. Andrew Schonfeld, *Modern Capitalism*, p. 122.

24. Cohen, *op. cit.*, p. 33.

25. *Ibid.*, pp. 65-7.

26. Granick, *The European Executive*, p. 155.

27. Pierre Bauchet, *Economic Planning and the French Experience*, p. 36.

28. Quoted in Cohen, *op. cit.*, p. 203.

29. *Ibid.*

30. *Control Planning for the Market Economy*, pp. 184-5.

31. See G. Weisz, "France: Drift on the Right, Paralysis on the Left," *Canadian Dimension*, Vol. 10, No. 7.

32. *Time*, December 9, 1974.

33. *Imprecor*, June 20, 1974.

34. *Ibid.*

35. *Ibid.*

36. *The Nation*, November 23, 1974.

37. *Ibid.*

Notes to Part VIII

1. *New York Times*, January 1, 1974.

2. Jacob Morris, *Monthly Review*, Vol. 24, No. 4.

3. *Poverty in Wealth*.

4. *Ibid.*, p. 4.

5. *Toronto Star*, September 5, 1974.

6. C.W. Mills, *The New Men of Power*, p. 119, 224-5.

7. Melville Watkins, "The Trade Union Movement in Canada" in R. Laxer (ed.), *Canada Ltd.*, p. 184.

8.   R. Dahrendorf, *Class Conflict in Industrial Society*, p. 260.

9.   "Political Sociology" in R. K. Merton, L. Broom and L. S. Cottrel (eds.), *Sociology Today*, p. 113.

10.   *Political Parties*, p. 305.

11.   M. Watkins, *op. cit.*, p. 186.

12.   V.L. Allen. *Militant Trade Unionism*, p. 29.

13.   C.W. Mills, *op. cit.*, pp. 36-7.

14.   *Labouring Men*, pp. 334-5.

15.   Paul Mattick Jr., "Another View of the Working Class: Its Problems and Prospects," *New Politics*, Vol. 8, No. 3.

16.   *Ibid.*

17.   Perry Anderson, "The Limits and Possibilities of Trade Union Action" in Robin Blackburn and A. Cockburn (eds.), *The Incompatibles*, p. 278. This and other essays in this book have helped me to clarify my thinking on the historical role of trade unionism.

18.   Richard Hyman, *Marxism and the Sociology of Trade Unions*, p. 28.

19.   This is also the view of Richard Hyman, to whose work, cited above, I am much indebted.

20.   The quotations from the Manifestoes that follow are taken from D. Drache (ed.), *Quebec: Only the Beginning*, a work that translates in full the Manifestoes of the Front Commun.

21.   *Radical America*, September-October 1972 (Special Quebec issue), pp. 106-8.

22.   "The Social Evolution of Quebec Reconsidered," in M. Rioux and Y. Martin (eds.), *French Canadian Society*, p. 156.

23.   Watkins, *op. cit.*, p. 188.

24.   This example and the ones that follow are taken from Richard J. Barnet and Ronald Müller, *Global Research, the Power of the Multinational Corporations*.

25.   Published in R. Laxer (ed.), *Canada Ltd.*, pp. 147-52.

26.   Quoted in R.H. Babcock, *Gompers in Canada*, p. 74.

27.   *Ibid.*, p. 89.

28.   *Ibid.*, p. 101.

29.   *Ibid.* Appendix II, pp. 222-6. While Babcock admits that the figures he was able to obtain are incomplete, at the least what they demonstrate is that at no time in the early twentieth century was the Canadian labour movement the recipient of a great deal of financial aid from the "internationals."

30.   H.C. Pentland, *A Study of the Changing Social, Economic and Political Background of the Canadian System of Industrial Relations*, p. 121.

31.   See I. Abella, *Nationalism, Communism and Canadian Labour*.

32.   *Toronto Star*, January 9, 1975.

33. I am indebted to John Gallagher for bringing this document to my attention.

34. "A Hinterland Rebel," *Canadian Dimension*. Vol. 8, No. 8.

35. André Gorz, *Socialism and Revolution*, p. 158.

36. Stanley Aronowitz "On Organization: A Good Party is Hard to Find," *Liberation*, December 1973.

37. André Gorz, *Socialism and Revolution*, p. 65.

38. *Ibid.*, pp. 53, 69.

Notes for Further Reading

I

A plethora of books and tracts will undoubtedly be written on the economic crisis as it develops through the decade. Readers who wish to follow these developments closely should subscribe to some of the magazines and journals that regularly analyze the economy in a coherent fashion. In my work I have found *Monthly Review*, edited by Paul Sweezy and Harry Magdoff, to be my most useful single source. The address of *MR* is 116 West 14th St., New York, N.Y. 10011. A second, more academic source is the *Review of Radical Political Economics:* URPE, office of Organizational Services, Michigan University, Ann Arbor, Michigan 48104. *Business Week* magazine is by far the most reliable source from an intelligent business point of view. Canada has no business publication that displays the same degree of economic intelligence, but the *Financial Post* carries much information. A magazine I am associated with is *Canadian Dimension*, P.O. Box 1413, Winnipeg, Manitoba, R3C 2Z1.

II

The field of economics is so vast that it is genuinely hard to know where to begin recommending materials for further study. Readers that are just beginning to delve into economics may wish to consult Robert Heilbroner's *The Worldly Philosophers* (New York: Simon and Schuster, 1972) a highly readable account of the great economists and the development of their thought as it reflected the economic problems of the times. An elementary Marxist treatment that covers the same ground is E. K. Hunt's *Property and Prophets*

(New York: Harper and Row, 1972). Robert Heilbroner offers a critique of conventional economics in his essay "Is Economic Theory Possible?" in R. Heilbroner, *Between Capitalism and Socialism* (New York: Random House, 1970). A brief critique of conventional economics that also outlines a radical alternative is Herb Gintis, Ralph Pochada, "Economics in a Revolutionary Age," in James H. Weaver (ed.), *Modern Political Economy, Radical and Orthodox views on Crucial Issues* (Boston: Allyn & Bacon, 1973). In a similar but broader vein, students at all levels should read "The Commitment of the Intellectual," by Paul Baran, a powerful Marxist thinker. This essay and others appear in a volume of collected essays by Baran under the title *The Longer View, Essays Toward a Critique of Political Economy* (New York: Monthly Review Press, 1969).

More advanced students of economics will be interested in Ronald Meek's *Economics and Ideology* (London: Chapman and Hall, 1967) and Paul Sweezy's *Modern Capitalism and Other Essays* (New York: Monthly Review Press, 1974) and in particular his essays on "Modern Capitalism," "On the theme of monopoly Capitalism" "Toward a Critique of Economics" and "Themes of the New Capitalism." David Horowitz has collected an excellent series of essays by economists from various countries in *Marx and Modern Economics* (New York: Monthly Review Press, 1963). Also recommended is "Economists as Servants of Power" by Sam Bowles in *The American Economic Review*, 1972.

Three historical works that are required reading by all serious students of economics are Karl Polanyi: *The Great Transformation* (Boston: Beacon Press, 1957), Maurice Dobb, *Studies in the Development of Capitalism* (London: International Publishers, 1963) and Eric Hobsbawm, *Industry and Empire* (Penguin, 1969). Polanyi shows the difficulty of imposing the market idea on a non-market-oriented world, how the market system spread from the eighteenth century until it absorbed all aspects of life, the dislocations that it produced and the non-market protective responses that it generated. Dobb traces the historical development of capitalism, carefully locating its beginnings and distinguishing between the various phases of its development. Hobsbawm, a superb writer, focuses on the industrial revolution and the growth of empire. All three deal mainly with Britain. A more generalized history of capitalism is Oliver Cox's *Capitalism as a System* (New York: Monthly Review Press, 1964) which differs from the others in insisting that capitalism has its roots in commercial exploitation in international trade rather than production.

By far the best reader on the capitalist society is Richard

Edwards, Michael Reich, and Thomas Weisskopf (eds.), *The Capitalist System* (Englewood Cliffs: Prentice Hall, 1972). This carefully selected and edited collection ranges through "inequality", "alienation", "racism", "sexism", "irrationality", "imperialism", and "the capitalist mode of production." I will have reason to refer again to selections from this reader, but I wish particularly to single out Herb Gintis' "Alienation in Capitalist Society" and Tom Weisskopf's "Capitalism and Inequality." Although most of this book is of interest to a Canadian reader, the historical and institutional context is distinctly American. A Canadian version of *The Capitalist System* would be highly useful.

III

Among the vast number of books that have been churned out on the contemporary economic system, first on my list is *Monopoly Capital* by Paul Baran and Paul Sweezy (New York: Monthly Review Press, 1966) followed by Baran's earlier book, *The Political Economy of Growth* (New York: Monthly Review Press, 1957).

Robert T. Averitt, *The Dual Economy* (New York: W. W. Norton, 1968) makes a useful contribution to an understanding of the functioning of the modern corporation as does J. K. Galbraith, *The New Industrial State* (New York: New American Library, 1971) and chapters 2 and 3 of Baran and Sweezy's *Monopoly Capital*. Other useful books are Alfred D. Chandler, Jr., *Strategy and Structure: Chapters in the History of the Industrial Enterprises* (Boston: MIT Press, 1962); Robin Marris, *The Economic Theory of "Managerial" Capitalism* (New York: The Free Press of Glencoe, 1964), Edith Penrose, *The Theory of the Growth of the Firm* (Oxford: Basil Blackwell & Mott, 1959); John M. Blair, *Economic Concentration: Structure, Behaviour and Public Policy* (New York: Harcourt, Brace, Jovanovich, 1972); James S. Early, "Marginal Policies of 'Excellently Managed' Companies," *The American Review*, March 1956; R. J. Monser Jr. and A. Downs, "A Theory of Large Managerial Firms," *Journal of Political Economy*, June 1965; Robert J. Larner, *Management Control and the Large Corporation* (Cambridge, Mass.: Harvard University Press, 1970); Maurice Zeitlin, "Corporate Ownership and Control: The Large Corporation and the Capitalist Class," *American Journal of Sociology*, March 1974.

On the specific question of consumerism, J. K. Galbraith's *The Affluent Society*, Chapter 10 and 11 (New York: New American Library, 1963) remains an important contribution as does Thorstein Veblen's *The Theory of the Leisure Class* (New York: New American Library, 1953). André Gorz, "Private Priorities and Collective Needs" from his book *Strategy for Labour* is reprinted in

The Capitalist System. Paul Baran's "A Marxist View of Consumer Sovereignty," from his introduction to the second printing of the *Political Economy of Growth,* is reprinted in David Mermelstein (ed.), *Economics: Mainstream Readings and Radical Critiques,* (New York: Random House, 1973) a carefully selected collection of articles that covers a wide range of subjects and opinions. A technical discussion of the subject which I have always found to be among the best available is Maurice Dobbs, "A Review of the Discussion concerning Economic Calculation in a Socialist Economy" in his collection of essays, *On Economic Theory and Socialism* (London: Routledge and Kegan Paul, 1955). And, finally, Erich Fromm's "The Alienated Consumer," reprinted in *The Capitalist System* from his indispensable *The Sane Society.*

While studies in wage determination and the relationships between wages, prices, and employment abound, there have been few solid investigations of the labour process itself, the organization of work, the composition of the working class, and the hierarchical job structure. This has now been partly corrected by a major work by Harry Braverman, *Labour and Monopoly Capital* (New York: Monthly Review Press, 1975). Among other works that discuss some or all of these subjects I recommend Robert Blauner, *Alienation and Freedom: The Factory Worker and his Industry* (Chicago: University of Chicago Press, 1964); *Work in America,* Special Task Force to the Secretary of Health, Education and Welfare, (Cambridge, Mass.: MIT Press, 1973); Georges Friedmann, *The Anatomy of Work* and *The Industrial Society* (Glencoe: Free Press, 1961, 1955); Peter L. Berger (ed.), *The Human Shape of Work: Studies in the Sociology of Occupations* (New York: Macmillan, 1964); Richard Sennett and Jonathan Cobb, *The Hidden Injuries of Class* (New York: Knopf, 1972). The dual labour market is best explored in D. Gordon, *Theories of Poverty and Underemployment* (Lexington: D. C. Heath, 1972) and P. B. Doeringer and M. J. Piore, *Internal Labour Markets and Manpower Analysis* (Lexington: D. C. Heath, 1970).

On a broader plane, other institutions that both influence and reflect upon the organization of and attitudes toward work such as school, family, and the media are discussed in such works as *False Promises* (New York: McGraw-Hill, 1974) by Stanley Aronowitz, a wide-ranging and illuminating piece of writing by a former union organizer; Bruce Brown's *Marx, Freud and the Critique of Everyday Life* (New York: Monthly Review Press, 1973); Eli Zaretsky's *Capitalism, The Family and Personal Life* published in two parts in *Socialist Revolution* and reproduced in pamphlet form by *Canadian Dimension;* Erich Fromm's *Man For Himself* and *The Sane Society* (Fawcett) and *Beyond the Chains of Illusion* (New York: Simon &

Schuster, 1962); Sebastian de Grazia's *Of Time, Work, and Leisure* (Garden City: Doubleday, 1964); Mirra Komarovsky's *Blue-Collar Marriage* (New York: Random House, 1962); Simone de Beauvoir, *The Second Sex* (New York: Knopf, 1953); M. Benston and Pat Davitt, "Women Invent Society" and Marlene Dixon, "Women's Liberation, Chapter Two" both published in *Canadian Dimension's Special Issue on Women,* Vols. 10 and 8; R. Reiche, *Sexuality and Class Struggle* (London: New Left Books, 1970); various items in *Power, Politics and People, The Collected Essays of C. Wright Mills,* edited by I. L. Horowitz (London: Oxford University Press, 1963); B. Rosenberg, D. M. White (eds.), *Mass Culture, the Popular Arts In America* (Glencoe: Free Press, 1957); Satu Repo (ed.), *This Book is About Schools* (New York: Random House, 1970); Ivar Berg, *Education and Jobs: The Great Training Robbery* (Boston: 1971); George Martel (ed.), *The Politics of the Canadian Public School* (Toronto: James Lorimer, 1974); Samuel Bowles, "Unequal Education and the Reproduction of the Hierarchical Division of Labour" in the *Capitalist System;* P. Ariès, *Centuries of Childhood* (New York: Random House, 1970). *Work,* edited in two volumes by Ronald Fraser, (Penguin, 1968) and *Working People,* edited by Studs Terkel (Avon, 1975), present discourses about work and other subjects by people taped by the authors.

C. B. Macpherson's lectures in *The Real World of Democracy* (CBC Publications, 1965) provide an illuminating brief introduction to the rise and development of the liberal democratic state. Oliver Cox in his *The Foundations of Capitalism* (New York: The Philosophical Library, 1958) traces the role of the state in the economy beginning in the early mercantile period; the role of the state in the modern economy is best analysed in Ralph Miliband, *The State in Capitalist Society* (London: Weidenfeld, 1969). Brief treatments are provided in Paul Sweezy's "The Primary Function of the Capitalist State" and R. E. Edwards and Arthur MacEwan's "Ruling Class Power and the State" in *The Capitalist System.* C. W. Mills in *The Power Elite* (New York: Oxford University Press, 1959) attempts to explore the relationship between the state and other social orders in the American context. Readings on the state and imperialism are offered in a subsequent section of these notes.

IV

Since the time when Harold Innis dominated the field of Canadian political economy in the 1920s and 1930s, little of lasting value has been written until recent years. There are some notable exceptions. Donald Creighton, the great tory historian, built on the foundation of Innis's staple theory by shifting the focus from the production of staple commodities to the merchant capitalist class which financed the export-import trade and the communication links that carried the trade. His *Dominion of the North* (Toronto: Macmillan, 1957), a single-volume survey of Canadian history, and his earlier work *The Commercial Empire of the St. Lawrence, 1760-1850* (Toronto: Ryerson, 1937), written with magnificent historic sweep and clarity, remain landmarks in the literature. A recent essay by R. T. Naylor provides a brilliant overview on the nature of merchant capitalism, placing it in the context of a metropolis-hinterland framework and illustrating the far-reaching consequences of the domination of Canada's political economy by merchant capital as against industrial capital. His "The Rise and Fall of the Third Commercial Empire of the St. Lawrence" is the lead essay of a book of essays written from a Marxist perspective: Gary Teeple (ed.), *Capitalism and the National Question in Canada* (Toronto: University of Toronto Press, 1973).

An essay by Melville H. Watkins reinterprets the staple approach in the language of contemporary economic theory. This essay, first published in *The Canadian Journal of Economics and Political Science,* is reprinted in W. T. Easterbrook and M. H. Watkins (eds.), *Approaches to Canadian Economic History* (Toronto: McClelland and Stewart, 1967). The first half of Richard Caves and Richard Holton, *The Canadian Economy, Prospect and Retrospect* (Cambridge, Mass.: Harvard University Press, 1958) brilliantly relates Canadian business cycles from the turn of the century to the export of staple products. The staple theory, placed in a broader metropolis-linkland framework, is again discussed in a series of articles that appeared in *Canadian Dimension* magazine. Of particular interest are articles by Arthur K. Davis, Cy Gonick and Susan Altschul in Vol. 8, No. 6; by Peter Usher and Lorne Brown in Vol. 8, No. 8; and by John Warnock in Vol. 10, No. 2. Vernon Fowke has contributed a major study, from a western perspective, *The National Policy and the Wheat Economy* (Toronto: University of Toronto Press, 1957), which provides background to agrarian protest movements. In more recent times, Bruce Archibald has written a provocative essay on the under-development of the Atlantic Provinces, applying the economic theory of Andrew Gunder Frank, in "Atlantic Regional Underdevelopment and Socialism" in *Essays on the Left: Essays in Honour of T. C. Douglas,* ed. Laurier Lapierre *et al* (Toronto: McClelland and Stewart, 1971). Finally, David Caley has written an article called "Underdeveloping Prince Edward Island," produced as a pamphlet by the Development Education Centre, Toronto, 1973.

One of the few works of lasting value by liberal scholars is John

Bartlet Brebner's *North Atlantic Triangle,* first published in 1945 and reissued in paperback (Toronto: McClelland and Stewart, 1966), an attempt to assess the interplay of Britain, the United States, and Canada from the discovery of North America to the Second World War. Kari Levitt's *Silent Surrender* (Toronto: Macmillan, 1970), covers this ground in a more brief, analytical, and critical style, putting it in the context of the multinational corporation and demonstrating the erosion of Canadian economic sovereignty and the emasculation of the Canadian business class. The only comprehensive historical work on foreign ownership and control providing a wealth of information in a straightforward way remains Herbert Marshall, Frank A. Southard and Kenneth W. Taylor, *Canadian-American Industry: A Study in International Investment* (New Haven and Toronto: Yale University Press and Ryerson, 1936).

The impact of the United States in shaping Canada into a resources base is developed in a sound work by Hugh G. J. Aitken, *American Capital and Canadian Resources,* (Cambridge, Mass.: Harvard U. Press 1961). Resources is also the subject of James Laxer's works, *The Energy Poker Game: The Politics of the Continental Resources Deal* (Toronto: New Press, 1970) and *The Energy Crisis* (Toronto: James Lorimer, 1975). A *Resources Kit* produced by *Canadian Dimension* magazine (1975) includes a number of useful articles on the subject.

Contemporary concern over American domination of Canada has produced an outpouring of writing, some of it of continuing value. Phillip Sykes's *Sell-Out* (Edmonton: Hurtig, 1972) is a popular volume written by a professional journalist. A collection of semi-popular articles produced by the now defunct Ontario Waffle group, Robert M. Laxer (ed.), *Canada Ltd., The Political Economy of Dependency* (Toronto: McClelland and Stewart, 1973), attempts to discuss this question in a Marxist frame of reference. The contributions of R. T. Naylor, James Laxer and Melville Watkins are particularly recommended. An earlier collection, Ian Lumsden (ed.), *Close the 49th Parallel etc.,* (Toronto: University of Toronto Press, 1970) contains several valuable essays, particularly those by Michael Bliss on the tariff and foreign ownership, Mel Watkins on Canadian economic thought and Cy Gonick on foreign ownership and political dependency. Abraham Rotstein and Gary Lax (eds.), *Independence: The Canadian Challenge,* (Toronto: McClelland and Stewart, 1972) is a collection of articles that are meant to reflect the position of The Committee for an Independent Canada. It includes excerpts from the Wahn Report, the Gray Report and reports from the Science Council of Canada and articles by Rotstein, Walter Gordon and Eric Kierans. The Gray Report, whose proper title is

Foreign Direct Investment in Canada (Ottawa: Information Canada, 1972), contains much raw information on the subject processed in a highly sophisticated economic analysis. Finally *Canadian Dimension's Nationalism Kit* brings together articles by Gad Horowitz, Charles Taylor, Cy Gonick, Stephen Hymer, and Kari Levitt.

Not a great deal of lasting value has been written about the state in the Canadian economy. Hugh G. J. Aitken's "Defensive Expansionism: The State and Economic Growth in Canada," published in the Easterbrook-Watkins volume, is a useful contribution as well as the works by Naylor, Ryerson, Myers, Creighton, Porter and Clement.

Although much has been written about Canadian foreign policy, there are few memorable works. The best single volume by far is John W. Warnock's *Partner to Behemoth, the Military Policy of a Satellite Canada* (Toronto: New Press, 1970). Warnock is an advocate of the so-called "revisionist" school of cold war history. His study is thoroughly documented and represents a major contribution to the understanding of Canada in world affairs. Until the publication of Warnock's work, the best critical study was James M. Minifie's *Peacemaker or Powder-Monkey: Canada's Role in a Revolutionary World* (Toronto: McClelland and Stewart, 1960). Philip Resnick's essay "Canadian Defense Policy and the American Empire" in *Close the 49th Parallel etc.* also provides an excellent brief introduction to the subject. James Eayrs's two-volume work *In Defence of Canada* (Toronto: University of Toronto Press, 1964, 1967) provides a scholarly but readable account of Canadian defence policy from 1918 to 1945, written from a liberal perspective. *Last Post* and *This Magazine* have published a number of articles on Canadian policy in the Third World, and *Canadian Dimension's Canadian Foreign Policy Kit* features several articles by John Warnock and other contributors. Finally the Latin American Working Group publishes a regular newsletter on Canadian policy in Latin America.

V

The revival of Marxism has sparked a new interest in the question of class. Wallace Clement's *The Canadian Corporate Elite, An Analysis of Economic Power* (Toronto: McClelland and Stewart, 1975) provides a wealth of information and a careful analysis, unfortunately hobbled by an over-extended use of academic jargon. John Porter's earlier *The Vertical Mosaic* (Toronto: U. of Toronto Press, 1965), a theoretically looser but much more readable account, remains of value. A major contribution to the study of class in

Canada is the work of Leo Johnson. His "Development of Class in Canada in the Twentieth Century" in Gary Teeple's *Capitalism and the National Question in Canada* provides the most thorough statistical breakdown of class in Canada along with provocative thoughts on the historical consequence of a declining *petite bourgeoisie*. His Pamphlet *Poverty in Wealth* (Toronto: New Hogtown Press, 1974) examines the distribution of income in Canada in the post World-War-II era. An earlier work by Frank and Libbie Park recently republished, *Anatomy of Big Business* (Toronto: James Lewis and Samuel, 1973), disentangles the interlocking relationships between finance and industrial capital, emphasizing the growing control over both by U.S. interests. An essay by Daniel Drache on the ideology of the Canadian bourgeoisie in *Close the 49th Parallel, etc.* makes a useful contribution. *History of Canadian Wealth*, the entertaining 1914 account of corruption and rip-off in the eighteenth and nineteenth centuries by the famous American muckraker, Gustavus Myers, has been recently republished (Toronto: James Lewis and Samuel, 1972). On a more academic plane is David S. Macmillan (ed.), *Canadian Business History, selected studies, 1497-1971* (Toronto: McClelland and Stewart, 1972).

Little is available on the historical development of the working class in Canada. A remarkable annotated bibliography with a provocative introductory essay should prove of great assistance, R. G. Hann, G. J. Kealey, Linda Kealey, Peter Warrian, *Primary Sources in Canadian Working Class History,* (Kitchener: Dumont Press, 1973). Stanley Ryerson, *Unequal Union* (Toronto, Progress Books, 1968) is the only book that attempts to interpret Canadian history from Marxist class analysis. Besides providing some useful background to the early development of the working class, it also contributes to an understanding of the English-French relationship. A wealth of information is available in H. C. Pentland's, *A Study of the Changing Social, Economic and Political Background of the Canadian System of Industrial Relations,* done for the Task Force in Labour Relations (Ottawa, 1968). His article "The Development of Capitalistic Labour Market in Canada," *Canadian Journal of Economics and Political Science,* November, 1959, remains a classic in the field of labour history. Another study commissioned by the federal task force in labour relations is the best available history of Canadian labour: Stuart Jamieson, *Times of Trouble: Labour Unrest and Industrial Conflict in Canada, 1900-1966, (Ottawa: Task Force on Labour Relations, Study No. 22, 1968).* Jamieson's study is summarized and critically reviewed in a long article by Lorne Brown, "Myths of Peace and Harmony," *Canadian Dimension,*

Vol. 9, No. 5. *Canada Investigates Industrialism* (Toronto: University of Toronto Press, 1973) is a reprint of the famous Royal Commission on the Relations of Labour and Capital in 1889, a mine of information on working conditions in Ontario and Quebec towards the end of the nineteenth century. The editor of that book, Greg Kealey, has also prepared a pamphlet, *Working Class Toronto at the Turn of the Century* (Toronto: New Hogtown Press, 1973). Terry Copp's *The Anatomy of Poverty: The Condition of the Working Class in Montreal, 1897-1929* (Toronto: McClelland and Stewart, 1974) makes an important contribution. David J. Bercuson, *Confrontation at Winnipeg* (Montreal: McGill-Queens University Press 1974) provides useful background information to living conditions in Winnipeg from 1900 to 1919 as does Kenneth McNaught's biography of James Woodsworth, *A Prophet in Politics* (Toronto: University of Toronto Press, 1959). The popular works of James Gray, *Red Lights in the Prairies,* and the *Winter Years* (Toronto: Macmillan, 1966) also provide insight to conditions on the prairies. Living and working conditions in the 1930s are depicted in Michael Horn's *The Dirty Thirties* (Toronto: Copp Clark, 1972), a highly successful compilation of articles, documents, correspondence, reports, photographs, etc., covering all aspects of Canada in the Great Depression.

The People's History of Cape Breton is a popular pamphlet written in 1973. In a similar vein is The Corrective Collective's *She Named It Canada,* a cartoon history (Toronto: James Lewis and Samuel, 1973), and the same group's *Never Done: Three Centuries of Woman's Work in Canada* (Toronto: Canadian Women's Educational Press, 1974). On a more academic level is J. Acton, P. Goldsmith and B. Shepard, *Women at Work* (Toronto: Canadian Women's Educational Press, 1975). *Working People* by James Lorimer and Myfanwy Phillips (Toronto, James Lewis and Samuel, 1971) is an anthropological study of the daily life of four families living in downtown Toronto, the only work of its kind in Canada. Ian Adams's *The Poverty Wall* (Toronto: McClelland and Stewart, 1970) presents the many dimensions of poverty in moving portraits. Both these works can be supplemented by Don Shebib's fine film *Goin' Down the Road.* The much celebrated *Real Poverty Report* by Ian Adams, W. Cameron, B. Hill and P. Penz (Edmonton: Hurtig, 1971) is analytically weak, lacking in class analysis. Its strength lies in its description of the operation of the welfare system. *Canadian Dimension's* special issue, *"Why Canadian Workers are in Revolt"* (Vol. 8, No. 7) is also of interest, as well as the *Dimension Labour Kit.*

There are several adequate histories of Canadian trade unionism, each of which, however, suffers from the absence of any insight into or even any biographical documentation of the people who made up and led the labour struggles over the past century. Terribly congested and unanalytical, but the most comprehensive, is Harold Logan's *Trade Unions in Canada* (Toronto, Macmillan, 1943). A more readable and analytical account from a Marxist perspective is Charles Lipton's *The Trade Union Movement in Canada 1827-1959* (Toronto: New Canada Press, 1973). Two books that discuss the role of unions and political parties are Martin Robin's thorough *Radical Politics and Labour in Canada* (Kingston: Queen's University Press, 1963), covering the period from 1880 to 1930, and G. Horowitz's *Canadian Labour in Politics* (Toronto: University of Toronto Press, 1968), covering the period from the 1930s to 1966. They are both written from a social democratic perspective. Aside from Paul Phillips's excellent study *No Power Greater — A Century of Labour in B.C.* (Vancouver: B.C. Federation of Labour, 1967) there are no studies of the union movement in the various regions of Canada. Two more recent works deal with the historical development of "international" unionism in Canada. They are I. Abella, *Nationalism, Communism and Canadian Labour* (Toronto: University of Toronto Press, 1973) and R. H. Babcock, *Gompers in Canada* (Toronto: University of Toronto Press, 1975). Abella's book is of particular value in emphasizing the important role of the Communist Party in the formation of industrial unionism and in the left-right battles within the Canadian Congress of Labour. Both *This Magazine* and *Canadian Dimension* have published numerous articles on the question of "international unions" in Canada.

By far the best work on the Co-operative Commonwealth Federation, predecessor to the New Democratic Party is Walter Young's *Anatomy of a Party,* (Toronto: University of Toronto Press, 1969). Useful information is also to be found in Horowitz's *Labour and Politics* and for predecessors to the C. C. F. Robin's *Radical Politics and Labour in Canada.* All of these studies are written from a sympathetic point of view. No comprehensive work of value has yet been written on the New Democratic Party, although numerous articles have appeared in *Canadian Dimension, Next Year Country,* and *The Western Voice. Dimension's* special issue on the New Democratic Party (Vol. 7, No. 8) is of particular value, as is Lorne Brown's "Hinterland Rebels; The Story of the Saskatchewan Farmers' Movement," Vol. 8, No. 8, and Cy Gonick's "Schreyer's New Democrats," Vol. 9, No. 6.

Sheilagh and Henry Milner's *The Decolonization of Quebec* (Toronto: McClelland and Stewart, 1973) places the recent upheavals in Quebec in the context of Quebec's dependent relationship with English-Canada and the U.S.A. Marcel Rioux'

Quebec in Question (Toronto: James Lewis and Samuel, 1971) is perhaps the best introduction to modern Quebec nationalism written from separatist point of view. Pierre Vallières' *White Niggers of America* (Toronto: McClelland and Stewart, 1971) is both moving and revealing in describing the daily oppression and strains of growing up in a poor working-class Québecois family in a capitalist Anglo-dominated society. Léandre Bergeron's *The History of Quebec: A Patriote's Handbook* (Toronto: New Canada Press, 1971) has sold over 75,000 copies in Quebec. It is a simply written, often simplistic, and in places inaccurate history of Quebec, but written in a straightforward and popular manner that makes his class analysis lively and widely accessible. The manifestoes of the Common Front, models of popular Marxist exposition on the state of the Quebec economy and the tasks of the working class of Quebec, were prepared by the three trade union entres of that province and collected and edited by Daniel Drache in *Quebec — Only the Beginning: The Manifestoes of the Common Front* (Toronto: New Press, 1972). R. Chodos and Nick Auf der Maur in *Quebec: A Chronicle 1968-1972* (Toronto: James Lewis and Samuel, 1972) provide a journalistic account of events leading up to the October crisis and the events of the Common Front. A more analytical account of this period is to be found in *Canadian Dimension's* special issue (Vol. 7, Nos. 5 and 6), and *Dimension's Quebec Kit*, which includes important essays by Hubert Guinson, Charles Taylor, Jean-Guy Loranger and other writers. The *Last Post* and *Our Generation* report on Quebec politics regularly. *Solidaire*, an irregular publication, provides vital documents of various social movements. In an important article, "A Question of Strategy" *(Canadian Dimension,* Vol. 10, No. 73), Jean-Marc Piotte, a leading socialist intellectual, reconsiders and discards Quebec nationalism as an effective political vehicle of the working class.

Along with women, the Québecois, teenagers, and displaced farmers and Maritimers, the secondary labour market is composed of recent immigrants and native people. The most thorough study of immigration is Anthony H. Richmond's *Post-War Immigrants in Canada* (Toronto: University of Toronto Press, 1967). John Porter's *The Vertical Mosaic* also contains useful information.

A great deal has been written about native people in recent years. Among the better volumes are Maria Campbell, *Halfbreed* (Toronto: McClelland and Stewart, 1973); Hugh Brody, *Indians in Skid Row,* (Ottawa: Information Canada, 1971); Harold Cardinal, *The Unjust Society* (Edmonton: Hurtig, 1969); E. Palmer Patterson, *The Canadian Indian* (Toronto: Collier-MacMillan, 1971); Farley Mowat, *People of the Deer* (Toronto: McClelland and Stewart, 1952); T. C. McLuhan (ed.), *Touch the Earth* (Toronto: New Press,

1971); Heather Robertson, *Reservations are for Indians* (Toronto: James Lewis and Samuel, 1970); Waubageshig (ed.), *The Only Good Indian* (Toronto: New Press, 1970); H. B. Hawthorn (ed.), *A Survey of the Contemporary Indians of Canada* (2 volumes, Ottawa: Information Canada, 1966, 1967). Going back to the history of the fur trade viewed from the Indian perspective, Abraham Rotstein has written a fascinating essay titled "Trade and Politics: An Institutional Approach," *Western Canadian Journal of Anthropology*, 1971. This subject is explored more thoroughly in Arthur J. Ray, *Indians in the Fur Trade* (Toronto: University of Toronto Press, 1974). Events of the recent Indian uprisings are discussed in "The Occupation of Anicinable Park" by John Gallagher and Cy Gonick in *Canadian Dimension* (Vol. 10, No. 4), and "Welcome to Ottawa, the Native Peoples Caravan" by D. Ticoll and Stan Persky in *Canadian Dimension* (Vol. 10, No. 5). *Dimension's Native People Kit* is also a useful collection.

VI

Among the dozens of books that provide a popular exposition of Keynesian economics, the best to my mind are Dudley Dillard, *The Economics of John Maynard Keynes* (Englewood Cliffs: Prentice Hall, 1948); Lawrence Klein, *The Keynesian Revolution* (London: Macmillan, 1961); and Robert Lekachman, *The Age of Keynes* (New York: Random House, 1966). A good general introduction to modern macro-economics theory may be found in Howard Sherman, *Introduction to the Economics of Growth, Unemployment and Inflation* (New York: Appleton-Century-Crofts, 1964).

Paul Mattick's *Marx and Keynes, the Limits of the Mixed Economy* (Boston: P. Sargent, 1969) is a more advanced, highly provocative, and stimulating discussion. Other useful essays are contained in Horowitz (ed.), *Marx and Modern Economics;* Horowitz's essays "The Fate of Midas" and "Marx, Keynes and the Economics of Capitalism" in his *The Fate of Midas and Other Essays* (San Francisco: Ramparts Press, 1973); Paul Sweezy's "Keynesian Economics: The First Quarter Century" in his *Modern Capitalism and Other Essays*. The work of Michal Kalecki, the Polish economist whose writings predate and parallel Keynes, is now available as *Selected Essays on the Dynamics of the Capitalist Economy* (Cambridge: Cambridge University Press, 1971). A summary of Marx's cycle theory is provided in Paul Sweezy's classic, *The Theory of Capitalist Development*, Part 3 (New York: Monthly Review Press, 1956). Thomas Weisskopf's "The Problem of Surplus Absorption in a Capitalist Economy," published in *The Capitalist System*, is a useful brief treatment of the Keynesian dilemma translated to a Marxist framework. Paul Baran's essay "National Economic Planning" brilliantly demonstrates the obstacles to capitalist planning in the American context. This essay has been reprinted in the Baran collection, *The Longer View.* John G. Gurley, a long-time editor of the *American Economic Review,* demonstrates concisely in "Have Fiscal and Monetary Policies Failed?" *(American Economic Review,* May 1972, reprinted in Weaver [ed.], *Modern Political Economy)* that all government policy is ultimately related to protecting profit margins, and that in view of the erosion of U.S. economic power abroad and its disastrous effects on corporate profits, standard Keynesian measures have become increasingly ineffective.

If economic analysis is to be judged by its predictive ability, where conventional economists have failed miserably either to predict or to explain the present economic crisis, Marxist economists have scored brilliantly. The most consistently insightful economics is to be found not in the academic journals but in *Monthly Review,* the independent socialist magazine edited by Paul Sweezy and Harry Magdoff. A collection of their articles appearing between 1965 and 1972 has been brought together in a volume titled *The Dynamics of U.S. Capitalism, Corporate Structure, Inflation, Credit, Gold, and the Dollar* (New York: Monthly Review Press, 1972). Notable articles that have appeared in more recent years include R. Duboff, "Dollar Devaluation and Foreign Trade" (March 1972); Harry Magdoff, "A Note on Inflation" (December 1973); Jacob Morris, "Inflation" (September 1973); Paul Sweezy, "Keynesian Chickens Come Home to Roost" (April 1974); "Banks: Skating on Thin Ice" (February 1975); "The Economic Crisis" (March and April 1975). *The Review of Radical Political Economics* published a special issue in August 1972 titled *The New Economics and the Contradictions of Keynesianism.* Among its best articles are Frank Ackerman and Arthur MacEwen, "Inflation, Recession and Crisis, or, Would you Buy a New Car from this Man"; Walter Snyder, "Wage Controls, Monopoly Capitalism and the Contemporary Overproduction Crisis"; Richard DuBoff and Edward S. Herman, "The New Economics: Handmaiden of Inspired Truth"; Michael Best, "Notes on Inflation"; and E. K. Hunt, "The American Empire and the International Monetary Crisis." More recently, in Vol. 7, No. 1, 1975, this journal published an important article by R. Boddy and J. Crott, "Class Conflict and Macro-Policy: The Political Business Cycle."

Earlier studies that provide historical background to economic fluctuations are W. Arthur Lewis, *Economic Survey, 1919-1939* (New York: Harper and Row, 1969); Robert A. Gordon, *Business Fluctuations* (New York: Harper and Row, 1961, Chapters 14-16);

Alvin Hansen, *Business Cycles and National Income* (New York: W. Norton, 1951). Among the best Canadian studies are still W. A. Mackintosh, *The Economic Background of Dominion-Provincial Relations* (Toronto: McClelland and Stewart, 1964) and I. Brecher and S. S. Reisman, *Canada-United States Economic Relations,* Part 1 (Ottawa: Royal Commission on Canada's Economic Prospects, 1957).

VII

The most general study of the history of American expansionism is William A. William's *The Contours of American History* (New York: Quadrangle, 1966); his *The Tragedy of American Diplomacy* (New York: Delta, 1962), is a narrower but highly useful brief survey of the subject; R. S. Jones offers an admirably concise essay, "The History of U.S. Imperialism," in Robin Blackburn (ed.), Ideology in Social Science (London: Fontana, 1972). Richard Van Alstyne, *The Rising American Empire* (Oxford: Basil Blackwell, 1960) and Walter LaFeber, *The New Empire, An Interpretation of American Expansion 1860-1898* (Ithaca: Cornell University Press, 1963) cover the eighteenth and nineteenth centuries; the best of the revisionist histories of the cold war are David Horowitz, *From Yalta to Vietnam* (Penguin, 1967); Lloyd Gardner, *Architects of Illusion: Men and Ideas in American Foreign Policy, 1941-1949* (Chicago: Quadrangle, 1970); Walter LaFeber, *America, Russia and the Cold War, 1945-1966* (New York; Wiley, 1968); and the most exhaustive, Gabriel Kolko, *Politics of War: The World and United States Foreign Policy, 1943-45* (New York: Random House, 1960); Robert Scheer, *America After Nixon: The Age of the Multinationals* (New York: McGraw-Hill, 1974) carries the analysis to the present day, with the emphasis on the influence of the multinational corporation in shaping both domestic and foreign policy. A general reader that includes several important articles on the subject is Neal D. Houghton (ed.), *Struggle Against History: U.S. Foreign Policy in an Age of Revolution* (New York: Washington Square Press, 1968).

From an economic point of view the best analysis is to be found in Harry Magdoff, *The Age of Imperialism* (New York: Monthly Review, 1969). Magdoff has written a number of articles on the subject as well that are worth reading: "Militarism and Imperialism," "Economic Myths and Imperialism," and with Paul Sweezy, "Notes on the Multinational Corporation" *(Monthly Review,* February 1970, December 1971 and March 1966 respectively). All three are reprinted in *Modern Capitalism and Other Essays.* In a similar vein, *The Capitalist System* includes informed articles by Arthur MacEwan, "Capitalist Expansion, Ideology and

Intervention," M. Reich and D. Finkelhor, "The Military Industrial Complex: No Way Out," and two by Thomas Weisskopf, "United States Foreign Private Investment: An Empirical Survey" and "Capitalism and Underdevelopment in the Modern Economy." *The War Economy of the United States, Readings on Military Industry and Economy,* edited by Seymour Melman (New York: St. Martin's Press, 1971), contains an enormous amount of material on the military-industrial complex. Among the better general collections on U.S. imperialism is K. T. Fann and D. C. Hodges (eds.), *Readings in U.S. Imperialism* (Boston: P. Sargent, 1971). The *Dimension* kit, *American Empire, the Cold War and the Third World,* also provides a useful selection. The articles in Charles K. Wilber (ed.) *The Political Economy of Development and Underdevelopment* (New York; Random House, 1973) analyse foreign investment from the receiving end.

The rise of the multinational corporation has naturally spawned a great many studies that explore this phenomenon. Among the best is Richard Barret's and Ronald Muller's *Global Reach, The Power of the Multinational Corporation* (New York: Simon and Schuster, 1974). This is a mammoth work, thoroughly documented and eminently readable. An impeccable source is the United Nations Study, *Multinational Corporations in World Development,* 1973. A series of hearings called by various U.S. government agencies has presented a number of interesting reports: *Multinational Corporation* (U.S. Subcommittee on International Trade of the Committee on Finance, February 1973), containing among other items "U.S. Multinationals — The Dimming of America," a report prepared by the AFL-CIO; *The Multinational Corporation: Studies on U.S. Foreign Investment* (U.S. Department of Commerce, 1972); *The Multinational Corporation and the National Interest* (Report to the Senate Committee on Labour and Public Welfare, 1973). The writings of Stephen Hymer are particularly insightful. Two of his major essays are "The Multinational Corporation and the Law of Uneven Development" in J. N. Bhagwati, (ed.), *Economics and World Order from the 1970's to the 1990's* (New York: Macmillan, 1972) and "The Efficiency (Contradictions) of Multinational Corporations," in Gilles Paquet (ed.), *The Multinational Firm and the Nation State* (Toronto: Collier-Macmillan, 1972). Magdoff and Sweezy, *"Notes on the Multinational Corporation,"* cited earlier, is indispensable.

Among the many other works on this subject, I recommend the following: Michael Tanzer, *The Political Economy of International Oil and the Underdeveloped Countries* (Boston: Beacon, 1969); Edith Penrose, *The Large International Firm in Developing Countries: The International Petroleum Industry* (Cambridge, Mass.:

MIT Press, 1968), Mira Wilkins, *The Emergence of Multinational Enterprise: American Business Abroad from the Colonial Era to 1914,* (Cambridge, Mass.: Harvard University Press, 1970); Charles Levinson, *Capital and Inflation and the Multinationals,* (London: George Allen and Unwin, 1971); Hans Günter (ed.), *Transnational Industrial Relations,* (London: Macmillan, 1973); Robert Rowthorn, *International Big Business, 1957-1967* (Cambridge: Cambridge University Press, 1971). Among the more sympathetic works are Charles Kindleberger (ed.), *The International Corporation* (Cambridge, Mass.: MIT Press, 1970); George W. Ball (ed.), *Global Companies: The Political Economy of World Business* (Englewood Cliffs: Prentice-Hall, 1975).

VII

Barry Commoner's *The Closing Circle* (Bantam, 1972) is advertised on its cover as "the best book on ecology ever written." I have to agree. Commoner is lucid, sane and radical in the old sense of that term — getting at the root of the problem. In addition to Commoner, I have found Hans-Magnus Enzenberger, "Critique of Political Ecology" *(New Left Review,* No. 84) particularly useful in analysing the ecology movement and discussing ecology in class terms. Other works that I would recommend among the many that are available are Barry Weisberg's *Beyond Repair: The Ecology of Capitalism* (Boston: Beacon, 1971) and Lester Brown's *In the Human Interest* (New York: W. W. Norton, 1974), a balanced, non-hysterical treatment on the evidence of resource scarcity and population growth. E. J. Mishan's *The Costs of Economic Growth* (Penguin, 1969) is a highly provocative series of essays written from an individualistic point of view. The works of Lewis Mumford stand unrivalled as a definitive study of the origins and development of technological society. See for example his early work, *Technics and Civilization* (New York: Harcourt, 1934). A representative reader on the subject is Garrett de Bell (ed.), *The Environmental Handbook* (New York: Ballantine, 1970).

On the current food and energy crisis see Michael Tanzer, *The Energy Crisis: World Struggle for Power and Wealth* (New York: Monthly Review, 1974); James Laxer, *Canada's Energy Crisis* (Toronto: James Lorimer, 1975); Peter R. Odell, *Oil and World Power* (Penguin, 1973); E. P. Reubens, "The Food Shortage is Not Inevitable," *Challenge,* March-April 1974; Don Mitchell, *The Politics of Food* (Toronto: James Lorimer, 1975).

IX

A superb survey and balanced assessment of the literature on trade unionism and socialism is available in Richard Hyman's *Marxism and the Sociology of Trade Unionism* (London, Plutor Press, 1971). *The Incompatibles: Trade Union Militancy and the Consensus,* edited by Robin Blackburn and Alexander Cockburn (Penguin, 1967), offers some useful articles, particularly those by Perry Anderson and Victor Allen. The works of André Gorz, *Strategy for Labour* (Boston: Beacon Press, 1967) and *Socialism and Revolution* (Garden City: Doubleday, 1973), digest and synthesize the experiences of continental Europe and provide a challenging perspective. *Workers' Control: A Reader on Labor and Social Change,* edited by G. Hunnius, G. David Garson, and John Case (New York: Random House, 1973), contains an excellent selection of articles on the subject of workers' control, as does the *Dimension Kit on Workers' Control.*

I end these notes with a few suggestions about readings on socialism. An interesting critique of the Soviet Union is Charles Bettelheim's *Class Struggles in the USSR,* parts of which have been translated from the French by Paul Sweezy as "Nature of Soviet Society" in *Monthly Review,* (November 1974); also see their *On the Transition to Socialism* (New York: Monthly Review Press, 1971). Bettelheim's *Cultural Revolution and Industrial Organization in China* (New York: Monthly Review, 1974); John Gurley's "Marxist Economic Development" in the Mermelstein reader and C. Riskin's "Incentive System and Work Motivation: The Experience of China," (*Working Papers,* Winter 1974) are important sources on developments in modern China; and for Cuba, Maurice Zeitlin's *Revolutionary Politics and the Cuban Working Class* (New York: Harper and Row, 1970).

On a more general note, I would recommend Erich Fromm's *Marx's Concept of Man* (New York: Frederick Ungar, 1961); Harry Boyte and Frank Ackerman's "Revolution and Democracy," *Socialist Revolution* (July-August 1973), Isaac Deutscher's "On Socialist Man," *Canadian Dimension* (Vol. 4, No. 1); Paul Baran's "Socialism and Psychoanalysis," in Baran's *The Longer View;* Bruce Brown's *Freud, Marx, and the Politics of Everyday Life;* Martin Buber's *Paths of Utopia* (Boston: Beacon Press, 1966); André Gorz's *Strategy for Labour* and *Socialism and Revolution;* Gar Alperovitz, "Socialism as a Pluralist Commonwealth" in *The Capitalist System;* and from a libertarian perspective, Murray Bookchin's *Post-Scarcity Anarchism* (Berkeley: Ramparts Press, 1971). On a more critical note see George Lichteim, "What Socialism is Not," *New York Review of Books* (April 10, 1970) and R. Heilbroner "Reflections on the Future of Socialism" in his *Between Capitalism and Socialism.*

Index